PUBLIC SECTOR PERFORMANCE
a conceptual turning point

EDITED BY
Trudi C. Miller

THE JOHNS HOPKINS UNIVERSITY PRESS
Baltimore and London

The Johns Hopkins University Press, Baltimore, Maryland 21218
The Johns Hopkins Press Ltd., London

Library of Congress Cataloging in Publication Data
Main entry under title:

Public sector performance.
    Includes index.
    1. United States—Politics and government—Addresses,
essays, lectures.   2. State governments—Addresses,
essays, lectures.   3. Local government—United States—
Addresses, essays, lectures.   I. Miller, Trudi C.
JK21.P83   1984   350′.000973   83-23895
ISBN 0-8018-3146-6
ISBN 0-8018-3147-4 (pbk.)

Contents

FIGURES

TABLES

Preface

This volume evolved from reviews of the literature that were commissioned in 1979, when the editor was Program Manager in the Division of Applied Research at the National Science Foundation. The division was abolished in 1981. Since February 1982, the editor has directed the National Science Foundation's new Decision and Management Science Program. Despite the overlap of personnel and research interest, this volume has no official connection with the NSF; the opinions and findings expressed in this volume are those of the authors and do not represent the priorities or policies of the National Science Foundation.

The credibility of the strong conclusions about public sector performance and science contained in these chapters rests to a large degree upon the authors' credentials. Brief biographies appear at the end of the book.

Public Sector Performance

1

Overview: The Turning Point

Trudi C. Miller

W
e appear to be at a turning point in practice and thought about public sector performance. As a result of political activity, the rate of growth in public sector domestic expenditures has slowed, and there is ferment about scientific methods and theories in fields that address public sector performance. A new framework for comprehending modern government may be emerging.

This book assesses the literature in several relevant disciplines: political science, public administration, public policy, public finance, and management science. Most of the evaluations are critical, challenging many claims social scientists make to objectivity, rigor, accuracy, and knowledge. At the same time, the chapters reveal intense intellectual excitement and enthusiasm about some new and some old ideas. Together they suggest that social science may be "taking off" to new levels of methodological and theoretical maturity.

The authors present varied perspectives on research and practice. As editor, I have placed their evaluations between an introductory chapter, which focuses on criticisms of past research and management approaches, and a concluding chapter, which outlines what appears to be an emerging "design science" paradigm for political science, public policy, and administration. My overview and conclusion are tightly related because I describe the turning point as a change in underlying empirical assumptions about social structures and dynamics. I argue that the authors' criticisms reflect errors in the core assumptions that undergird the conventional "natural science" approach to social systems. The empirical assumptions that underlie my vision of the "design science" alternative are drawn from the research findings accumulated by the authors. These assumptions are, I hope, more accurate for political systems. Some readers may prefer other frameworks for comprehending the criticism and optimism voiced in these chapters. Ultimately, claims regarding

1

the existence or the nature of the "turning point" will be settled by future intellectual historians.

THE NATURAL SCIENCE PERSPECTIVE

The authors of this volume are critical of conventional research and management methods for the public sector. The problems include a lack of objectivity, inadequate theory-building, poor data, and failed predictions. Most of these criticisms reflect the damaging effects of inaccurate implicit empirical assumptions that undergird conventional definitions of social science. In the later sections of this introduction, I highlight the arguments in each chapter that bear on this assertion. In this first section I describe what I believe are the major assumptions.

The sophisticated mathematics and methods of conventional social science are governed by an image of "good science" which reflects inquiry in the biological and physical sciences around 100 years ago. This old-fashioned methodological paradigm requires simplifying assumptions about structures and dynamics that rarely apply to political systems. The major implicit, generally erroneous, assumptions are that (1) components of large-scale political systems (e.g., local governments, departments) are similar to one another in their parts and functions, and (2) regularities in behavior are immutable and unaffected by scientific inquiries.

In more colloquial imagery, social scientific inquiry is often assumed to be similar to the study of elephants. Disciplines explore different aspects in depth. Knowledge accumulates across disciplines and over time because the parts of the beast do fit together around a stable skeleton. Scientific investigation, even dissection of the subject, does not change the meaning of its parts or spoil the accumulated body of knowledge (though it may spoil a particular elephant). Once the elephant is thoroughly understood, the motion of various species in various environments can be explained and predicted from knowledge about characteristic bones and sinews. Thus, elephants can be studied using the assumptions of conventional social science. Essential parts and functions are similar over time and space, so generalization is possible, and the disposition of scientists toward the object does not change it.

Reflecting these images, the quantitative methods of conventional social science rest on implicit assumptions about the comparability, decomposability, autonomy, and stability of units of analysis. Regression, for example, works well if variables and their relationships are comparable across cases. If cases are not comparable, most variance is left in the error term, and different equations are needed for different samples.

Experimental methods are also designed for a static world composed of comparable cases. In the true laboratory experiment, the control and experimental cases are the same except for the intervention. Conducting a laboratory experiment also implies that the common or average case is similar enough to the researched pair over time to justify the study.

Quasi-experimental methods allegedly adapt pure experimental methods to social systems (Campbell and Stanley 1963); statistical methods adjust for differences among cases, interactions among variables, and changes over time. The idea is to isolate stable, persistent causes of behavior—the bones and sinews of cases. However, these adjustments produce definitive results only when the cases are sufficiently similar so that the number of adjustments can be limited, and the influence of a given adjustment is roughly the same across cases and over time.

Problems of adapting the classic methods of the "hard" sciences to social systems are well known. They stem from the differences between social systems and biological and physical systems. Cases, such as individuals and institutions, differ greatly, despite common labels such as "Irish," "legislature," or "local government." Isolating behavor (e.g., in the laboratory) produces different behavior, and observable regularities are likely to change qualitatively as a result of scientific (or journalistic) study (see Nagel 1961).

Social scientists know that social systems differ from the systems studied by the older sciences. They are taught that social behavior is dependent on context, culture, and history; that scientists' values and findings influence system behavior; and that social constructs (variables) have different meanings across individuals and organizations.

Although these differences between social systems and biological and physical systems are obvious, most conventional social science methods, such as those sketched out above, encourage investigators to deny the obvious. These conventional empirical methods focus on the repetitious aspects of social systems that often lack theoretical importance.

Thus, conventional social science fails to the extent that it encourages investigators to ignore the dynamics of social systems. To improve their science, social scientists must design methods that reflect the essential features of social systems the way the methods of the physical sciences reflect the essential features of physical systems. The physical sciences produce useful knowledge because their methods have external validity for physical systems; the social sciences will produce more useful knowledge when their methods have greater external validity.

CHAPTER 2: INTERGOVERNMENTAL CHANGE

Thomas Anton criticizes what he calls "global interpretations" of government change. Underlying each classification of global thinking—economic determinism, government accountability, balance of power, public sector legitimacy—are unstated images of how an effective, efficient political system works. These idealized images include the modernizing government that keeps pace with its modernizing economy, the competitive marketplace, and the American government that was created by the founding fathers. Analysis, for global thinkers, is to compare the way the world works to the way it ought to work according to unstated theories or images. Deviance of fact from theory indicates inefficiency, excessive government growth, institutional decay, and so on. What global thought lacks is articulation and tests of the theories about maximizing political performance that underlie conclusions.

Several of the global theories discussed by Anton reflect a model of superior government performance that is based on images of the physical and biological sciences. Labeled "scientific management," this model was especially important in political reform movements in the first half of the twentieth century. Its themes of hierarchy and autonomy remain significant today, as both empirical assumptions and prescriptions about government. To apply scientific management, government should be centralized, standardized, and, it follows, insulated from diverse local environments. As society develops, communications increase and problems become general in their territorial effects. Accordingly, policies are formulated at the national and, ultimately, the international levels. For top managers to identify and apply general laws across these vast areas, social organizations and subunits of government must be similar in structure and behavior. Therefore, insulating subunits (departments, job functions, people) from diverse environments and standardizing their parts and functions improves management.

As Anton's review indicates, the political reform movement spearheaded by this early twentieth-century vision of scientific management has largely run its course. Currently, normative theories based on ideal markets and the principles of the founding fathers are more fashionable. Ironically, however, assumptions about what ought to be (government ought to be centrally controlled, standardized, and insulated from local environments) have become assumptions about what is (according to critics, national government programs distort local government priorities). Thus, critics of centralized national government (current advocates of market mechanisms and old-time limited government) join advocates of scientific management in assuming that the national government controls the federal system.

Anton devotes the second half of his essay to the facts about the structures and dynamics of American government. In fact, the U.S. political system is not centralized or centralizable. Most activities at the state and local levels originate from those levels, and national policies are adapted over time to local conditions. From the vantage point of fifty years of theoretical and empirical literature, Anton also rejects a unidirectional view of political change.

My own assumptions are at once more traditional and more consistent with the available evidence about American federalism. I assume that change in social and governmental relations is both constant and unending as the "normal" state of all systems; that change is more likely to be cyclical than unidirectional; and that changes will proceed unevenly, with uneven and perhaps contradictory consequences that will themselves contribute to future cycles of change.

CHAPTER 3: WHY DOES GOVERNMENT GROW?

Patrick Larkey, Chandler Stolp, and Mark Winer go elephant hunting. Their criticism of the literature on government growth (decline) is that the empirical and theoretical schools do not meet: "In this literature, as in many social science literatures, the inductive work lacks theoretical rigor and the deductive work lacks empirical relevance." Assuming there is a phenomenon called "government growth" (elephant), inductive research should produce findings that have general application, and deductions from these findings should produce propositions that are proven through further testing.

As it stands now, research on government growth does not fit the conventional definition of good science. To start with, the empirical work is myopic. Data are selected by the criteria of availability, then relations are estimated to build general theory up from the data. One result of myopic empiricism is that findings do not accumulate. For example, measures of government size differ, so findings vary with the measures. Moreover, the measures are too narrow to be surrogates for the underlying variable of "government presence"; for example, most neglect the effects of court decisions. Similarly, myopic empiricism fails to produce generalizable functions—regression equations are fit in one country over time or across countries. Analysts try to construct general theories about causality from such findings, but because cases are diverse, there are almost as many so-called general theories as cases. Moreover, theories based on inductive studies treat government growth as inevitable and irreversible, because, for most of the twentieth century, this was the observed pattern.

Whereas the inductive work is myopically empirical, the deductive literature is hardly empirical at all. This literature employs sophisticated mathematics, but its simplifying assumptions are unrealistic. For example, most deductive theories attribute government growth to a single class of actor, such as bureaucrats, legislators, voters, interest groups, and government employees. But each of these theories is plausible, so their accumulation suggests that government growth is a product of many factors, each having only a marginal effect. Nevertheless, in this literature the impact of each central actor on government growth is modeled as if it were a powerful, underlying law (a bone or sinew).

Larkey, Stolp, and Winer close with the important observation that the requirements of the scientific method are better satisfied by quasi-experimental longitudinal case studies than by cross-sectional (one-time) comparative studies.

The advantage of comparisons, whether among governments or among time segments of the same government, is the advantage of experiments with control and treatment groups. If we can construct a situation in which governments are more alike than different, we may be able to understand differences causally. Unfortunately, governments differ in many dimensions, and the controls required overwhelm the data we have available or can gather. Governments are apt to resemble themselves through time more closely than they are to resemble other governments.

CHAPTER 4: INFORMATION SYSTEMS

Data are bedrock underlying science, management, and policy analysis. In their chapter, John King and Kenneth Kraemer explore prospects for enhancing government performance by strengthening information systems. Their conclusion is not sanguine:

> The studies cited here indicate that hopes for improving intergovernmental operation by improving information systems are largely misplaced. Even at the local government level, where one can easily find operational systems that work well, it is difficult to find advanced systems for planning and management that significantly affect how planning and management are done. There are continuing problems of shortages of accurate and appropriate data, technical staff for managing the technology, and analysts to interpret the data. Once the data have been interpreted, political problems may surface. These difficulties are exacerbated at the intergovernmental level because the data reported up from local governments are often not comparable, and their accuracy is difficult to assure. Attempts to impose standardization, management methods, reporting requirements, and other "systems" objectives from the top down have failed. Moreover, they probably will never succeed unless the autonomy that local and state governments now enjoy is diminished.

As the quote and prior chapters suggest, standardization and scientific management go hand in hand. Nonstandard data elements, which reflect real diversity among state and local governments, undercut scientific management.

The first half of chapter 4 describes attempts to improve management at the local level through introducing formal or scientific models for planning and management. These efforts have led to permanent changes, and presumably improvements, in the management of operations-oriented systems, such as billing, taxation, and accounting systems. However, attempts to design and implement models for planning, budgeting, and performance evaluation have been less successful. The more "political" the function, the less likely that a model will be permanently implemented.

Contrasts in the success of applying scientific management to operational, as opposed to political, functions reflect different degrees of standardization and consensus. Like elephants, operating systems are composed of relatively tangible, interchangeable parts. Volumes of water, property values, and obligations can be measured by independent systems. Between political challenges, anyway, these measurement systems are deemed to be objective. Similarly, fixed rates and procedures can be applied in a uniform manner to uniform measures; and a large number of standardized transactions, valued from a political perspective because they are uniform, can be executed. "Fair billing" and "honest" financial management mean treating like cases alike, and computerized, insulated systems contribute to the desired standardization.

Thus, standardization fosters scientific management and, in some applications, can be equated with "good government." Legal definitions of rates, measures, and procedures provide normative models that are agreed upon within political epochs, and government officials are held accountable for making reality conform to these ideals. Moreover, owing to widespread agreement on normative models for good government, financial and other operating systems can often be transferred across political jurisdictions.

By contrast, the components and processes of planning, budgeting, and evaluation activities are poorly defined and cannot be generalized across political interest groups, transactions, and time periods. Analysts have tried to standardize these functions by adopting common terms, such as objectives or goals, and common metrics, such as money. But the value and meaning of objectives (and money) are influenced by time horizon, argument, logic, language, life experience, and other factors. Even elaborate, rigorous methods to define, refine, and weigh agency goals produce results that are "partisan" to outsiders. Because it is nearly impossible to agree upon specific definitions of the goals of government or on the overriding importance of efficiency (saving money), it is rare that scientific management models influence political decisions.

Given their findings about the difficulty of applying scientific management methods within a single unit of local government, King and Kraemer are not surprised that these methods also contribute little to governing a nation composed of over 80,000 units of state, county, local, and special district government. Data definitions, even basic concepts for accounting, are established legally at the state level, and vary from state to state. As the heroic adjustments made by the staff of the U.S. Census of Governments suggest, functions, categories of personnel, and types of government are variously defined across states; even within states, definitions reflect local charters and traditions.

Data, even financial data, are not sufficiently uniform to support anything but aggregate national reports on the condition of local government, and even these aggregate findings are problematic across decades. Policy analyses produced with regressions and other forms of cross-sectional statistics, or through quasi-experimental analyses of "typical" cases, do not produce generalizations that are believed by analysts or practitioners who know that data definitions (and most operations) are not standardized across local governments.

CHAPTER 5: A DEMOGRAPHIC PERSPECTIVE

Thomas Muller attributes changes in the size of the U.S. public sector to demographic trends and their effects on government expenditures. His attribution is only partly successful, which raises important ontological and epistemological questions about the relative advantages of empirical (inductive) versus normative (deductive) theories.

Up to the mid-1970s, inductive empirical analyses (that take account of government diversity) are superior in explanatory power to normative theories, such as those advocated in chapters 6–8 and criticized in chapters 2 and 3. Theories that attribute government growth to national initiatives do not fit the data; empirical analyses that attribute growth to the consequences of local government diversity, independence, and responsiveness do.

Specifically, up until the mid-1970s demographic trends—primarily population migration—could explain most increases in public sector outlays, which occurred at the state and local, not the national levels. Population migration, in turn, is explained by differences among local governments. Middle-class families moved out of cities (mostly in the North and Midwest) that had well-established public services into suburbs and unincorporated areas (mostly in the South and West) that lacked public services. This has increased per capita expenditures for services in the cities, because existing facilities (for example, schools) served fewer clients, and because poorer families and elderly individuals, who require more services, remained. Simultaneously, government grew in smaller and unincorporated places, so aggregate public sector expenditures have increased.

Thus, government growth was faster than population growth or changes in the needs and preferences of the population as a whole; national figures indicating a decline in overall government efficiency during the 1960s are accurate and meaningful. But middle-class families acting on their own, not federal government officials, initiated and benefited from most of the governmental inefficiency that occurred. Efforts by federal officials and their big-city allies to better serve minorities and the poor may explain part of the initial middle-class migration out of the cities; these efforts did exaggerate initial differences in public sector expenditures between cities and other places. However, most of the contrasts in efficiency (cost per capita) between declining and growing places are a function of migration itself—of lags between population changes and expenditure changes. These lags reduce city efficiency and increase rural efficiency in the short run, which stimulates further migration.

After Muller takes account of the effects of population movement, there is very little variance in public sector expenditures to be explained by the actions of interest groups such as national level bureaucrats, politicians, self-serving "public" servants and the poor. This is just as well, because more immediate indicators of liberal or democratic interest group welfare do not vary much either. The growth of national government employment and expenditures has been far slower than the growth in state and local expenditures, which undercuts complaints about centralization. Also, the increase in the real wages of government bureaucrats (at all levels) has been small (the bulk of the increase has been in the number of bureaucrats, not their wages). Finally, net benefits to minorities, the poor, and the near-poor—the alleged targets of liberal reforms—have been marginal.

Since the mid-1970s, however, analyses have revealed a qualitative change in the determinants of government size (growth/decline). The effect on public expenditures of outmigration from cities has been more pronounced (costs are declining as a result of staff layoffs and facility closings), whereas the effect of inmigration to cities has been less pronounced (the growth of new services has slowed). In other words the constraint on governmental expenditures is evident in all types of governments throughout the nation. Even governments that have not experienced explicit referenda to control costs have curbed increases in taxes and expenditures.

The uniform downward shift in total governmental expenditures that occurred after the mid-1970s was not anticipated by demographic or other quantitative analyses of governmental expenditures; empiricists predicted continued growth. As Kirlin argues in the following chapter, predicting political change requires a theory that includes political movements. Kirlin goes on to provide a brief explanation of the mid-1970s shift. His analysis is similar to that employed by the global theorists, who are criticized in chapters 2 and 3, with the important difference that Kirlin explicitly identifies the source and content of his normative framework. Before the mid-1970s, there was a contrast between what the public wanted (less government, according to the polls) with what the public was getting (more interest-focused expenditures, tax laws, and regulation). Eventually, public discontent reached a critical point, and the tax limitation movement swept the country.

Combining Muller's figures with Kirlin's analysis, we find that before the mid-1970s, the political climate tolerated the growth of government involvement in social and economic marketplaces, though sentiment against it was growing. After the mid-1970s, government activities were curbed throughout the nation, and once-stable relationships between demographic trends and public sector expenditures (weak in declining cities and strong in growing places) changed to become stronger in declining cities and weaker in growing places. This case indicates that normative perspectives on political phenomena (accurate or not) can condition social behavior, sometimes by creating sudden alterations in what appear to be immutable empirical laws.

Together, the Muller and Kirlin chapters establish a turning point in the preferences of the authors for purely empirical, versus normative/empirical, analyses of government performance. The first three chapters discredit normative theories on at least two grounds: their value framework is often implicit, and their assumptions about national uniformity are often in error. Then Muller and Kirlin partially discredit the style of empirical analysis (aggregation of longitudinal case studies) that is preferred by the previous authors.

Chapters 6–9 explore composite normative/empirical approaches. These approaches are potentially compatible with empirical methods that assume governmental diversity and behavior changes over time. They address the likely effects of political efforts to alter observable behavior. To do this, they incorporate values and other humanistic factors in forecasts of social system behavior.

CHAPTER 6: A POLITICAL PERSPECTIVE

John Kirlin says the contemporary fields of political science, public administration, and public policy analysis employ a narrow and inadequate definition of "government"; they focus on its observable manifestation—service delivery.

> But service delivery is not the critical role of government. Government is the institution of society with singular obligations to facilitate societal choice-making and action. Its ability to make decisions and to act are the dominant dimensions by which governmental performance should be judged. Choices often revolve around service delivery, and so too does action, but capacity for choice making and action is not synonymous with service delivery. The capacity standard has deep roots in western political philosophy, was the overriding concern of the framers of the U.S. Constitution, and finds modern expression in several important critiques of the functioning of the U.S. political system.

As Kirlin defines it, government (and politics) is really about the formulation, diffusion, and implementation of political perspectives. It is a process during the course of which ideas become laws and institutions; and interests— sometimes narrow, sometimes popular—are served. Kirlin uses his definition of government to illuminate widely perceived failures of political science and policy studies. He also builds a broader framework for evaluating government performance on the basis of his broader definition of government.

Social science has been accused of fostering centralization, standardization, elitism, and the interests of social scientists at the expense of flexibility, pluralism, democracy, and objectivity. Kirlin highlights these problems and attributes them to the narrow definition of government and politics that has been adopted in the fields of political science, public administration, and policy analysis. The current focus on service delivery, observable institutions, and the values of policy makers and wealthy clients restricts rigorous intellectual activity to the status quo. This conservative bias is often at odds with the avowed values of the social scientists who conduct the research.

Kirlin's review also indicates that the political bias in social science is not confined to so-called applied research. The bias derives from the definition of science that undergirds the empirical revolution—logical positivism. This strictly empirical approach focuses analyses on the consequences of political choice—established, observable institutions. Since citizens may have political preferences that favor modification of established institutions, confining basic research to observable behavior has conservative implications.

The bulk of Kirlin's essay is devoted to the construction of a more realistic framework for evaluating public sector performance. Unlike that of scientific management, his framework is compatible with the diversity and flexibility that characterizes the U.S. political system. Standardization is applied sparingly only if there is general agreement that it should be. If consensus on goals and viable methods for implementation exists, standard, detailed, centralized controls and directives are warranted. If there is agreement on goals but not on a single implementation strategy, incentives (rewards and punishments for outcomes) are recommended. If both goals and mechanisms for implementation vary, interactive bargaining and learning strategies are recommended (see table 6.3).

Kirlin says that his framework for evaluating public sector performance is normative—he does not pretend to "scientific objectivity." But his framework for research and management is attractive from the perspective of science. It is more politically neutral than scientific management in the sense that it is not bound to a set of assumptions (about similarity and autonomy) that foster centralization (see table 6.2). Also its predictive power is greater than that of myopic empirical analyses, and it is in this sense better empirical theory.

CHAPTER 7: A PUBLIC FINANCE PERSPECTIVE

As Kirlin indicates, advocates of quantification in the field of political science were logical positivists who temporarily drove deductive, normative theorists out of the disciplinary establishment. Happily, economists in the subfield of public finance kept alive normative theoretical perspectives on key political questions, such as the structure of government. They also made good progress in quantifying these theories and using them in empirical research. Richard Aronson and Eli Schwartz review the public finance literature, which is mathematical, normative, and empirical. While problems remain, social scientists have made considerable progress in quantifying normative/empirical models of political choice.

Although the public finance literature is highly mathematical, the Aronson and Schwartz chapter, like the Johnson and Lewin review, is verbal. The objective is to provide an overview of the field as a resource for understanding and controlling public sector performance. Aspects of political theories (chapter 7) and of management structures (chapter 8) that have been and have not been successfully modeled are highlighted.

Public finance theories provide intellectual support for both the Democratic and the Republican programs. Theories of "public goods" justify expansion of national programs and involvement in state and local affairs that is associated with the Democrats. By and large the public goods literature favors centralization to realize equity objectives. In contrast, the "public choice" literature provides grist for the Republican mill with theories that apply the logic of efficient markets to policy making in the public sector. This literature focuses on efficiency and generally favors decentralization.

Both bodies of theory get into trouble when they are subjected to empirical tests in the real world, where connections between centralization and equity and decentralization and efficiency are mutable. The major weakness of the classic theories of public finance is that they are static. They model and predict the effects of a policy in only the first phase where the policy creates incentives to which actors (individuals, local officials, etc.) react. Factors that develop over time to change, and often reverse, initial responses are neglected.

The most serious of these time-related omissions is neglect of the new incentives that are created by initial reactions. Aronson and Schwartz illustrate this problem as it affects public choice theories.

> The findings of empirical tests of the Tiebout hypothesis and their possible implications are typical. The theory identifies rational behavior for a given set of actors under given conditions, and by and large people behave as predicted. However, their actions change conditions for others, who react in ways that alter the initial conditions and, therefore, the dictates of self-interest. This results in behavior that alternatively confirms and discredits theories that relate centralization and decentralization to equity and efficiency. Sometimes central action promotes efficiency; sometimes decentralization promotes equity.

Aronson and Schwartz are, however, heartened by research applications. They note that the training of public officials has improved to the point where many are quite capable of designing and applying mathematical policy models. These models are becoming sophisticated in anticipating feedback—reactions and counterreactions over time. Practitioners are rewarded for realism and punished for making poor predictions; they have to conceptualize the behavior of central actors in context and are accountable for failures. This fosters the development of implicit and explicit models that take account of factors such as changes in incentives over time.

CHAPTER 8: MANAGEMENT AND ACCOUNTABILITY MODELS

The normative/empirical models reviewed by Ronald Johnson and Arie Lewin focus on the performance of government entities, rather than on intergovernmental structures. Most of these methods are drawn from the fields of management science and accounting. The idealized model for the management science approach is the engineer's methodology for realizing the peak efficiency of a machine. There are serious problems in applying this model to social systems.

Measuring the efficiency of an organization is the critical focus of performance assessment. To accomplish this task it is necessary to relate the utilization of resources to the production of outputs. Ideally, efficiency measures utilize knowledge about both the production process and its performance potential. For example, the theoretical performance of an internal combustion engine is calculated from its engineering design data, and its actual efficiency is then related to its potential efficiency. In the case of public sector organizations, such efficiency calculations are not feasible at present because it is not possible to specify the organizational production system or to compute its theoretical output capacity. Furthermore, we lack single output measures that satisfactorily capture the full range of public sector goals. The basic problem of transforming multiple, noncommensurate output measures into a single aggregate performance indicator remains, though some methods hold promise of producing an assessment of overall productivity.

Not surprisingly, management science methods work best when they are applied to systems that have largely physical components. For example, they are regularly used in decisions about the allocation and maintenance of equipment. As we saw before, they also work for aspects of organizations (such as accounting systems) that have been standardized by professional and political agreements. However, most of the techniques discussed by Johnson and Lewin extend optimizing models to processes that have political elements, such as budgeting. As the quotation indicates, lack of agreement on the appropriate definition of government performance is a serious problem in these areas.

Some management science methods, discussed by Johnson and Lewin under the category of "goal models," are designed to deal with the problem of defining objectives. These methods often wrestle with several goals, which they reconcile and order, generally hierarchically. Performance measurement, described in the last section of the chapter, also deals with efforts to define goals in terms of measurable expectations for organizational behavior and policy impacts.

The field that has the longest history of defining measurable goals and standards, however, is the traditional field of accounting. Accounting research entails calling together leading practitioners, who represent affected entities, to state "accepted" and "preferred" practices for recording and reporting financial transactions. These statements are then circulated for review and comment. The resulting guidance is, presumably, close enough to existing practice to represent a feasible target for performance in the average case. Realization of this target is then monitored by accountants in the field, and violations of accounting standards may be punished through the political process.

As I argued before, the relative success of the accounting profession over the years in defining, monitoring, and enforcing standards for financial transactions lies behind relatively successful efforts to apply science in the public sector. As Johnson and Lewin point out, however, future progress requires more agreement on what is essential financial information and on standards for reporting this information. Indeed, more government compliance with accepted accounting standards would greatly improve prospects for applying scientific management to government. It would also increase citizen knowledge and political control.

Overall, Johnson and Lewin's analysis testifies to the importance of political and professional activities to define, monitor, and enforce performance standards. This reinforces Kirlin's point that political institutions are socially constructed.

CHAPTER 9: A DESIGN SCIENCE PERSPECTIVE

In the last chapter, I sketch out an intellectual framework for political science that is meant to be broad enough to embrace the content of the other chapters. I call this framework "design science." The design science concept is borrowed from Herbert A. Simon (1969), who uses it to describe the sciences of the artificial—sciences that deal rigorously with objects of inquiry that are constructed by design, usually by humans.

Political design science operationalizes Kirlin's definition of politics as that of choice making for society. Politics includes debates about values and the use of power to promote, monitor, and enforce the sway of some values over others. Political processes set, change, and overthrow the rules of the game that are addressed by other social sciences, such as economics and sociology.

Despite its breadth, political design science is quantitative. It includes rigorous normative methods for defining, refining, and institutionalizing values, such as those found in public finance and decision and management science. It also embraces rigorous empirical methods, including measuring the degree to which social processes are well ordered or subject to qualitative change. (These methods are sketched out in the last chapter.)

The political design science that I envision and attempt to describe in the last chapter does not exist yet. Looking across disciplines, we can find its components, but the assembly of these components into a coherent paradigm has yet to be accomplished.

REFERENCES

Campbell, Donald T., and Julian C. Stanley. 1963. *Experimental and Quasi-Experimental Designs for Research*. Chicago: Rand McNally.

Nagel, Ernest. 1961. *The Structure of Science: Problems in the Logic of Scientific Explanation*. New York: Harcourt Brace & World.

Simon, Herbert A. 1969. *The Sciences of the Artificial*. Cambridge, Mass.: MIT Press.

2

Intergovernmental Change in the United States: An Assessment of the Literature

Thomas J. Anton

THE PROBLEM

This paper offers a critical assessment of our current state of knowledge about intergovernmental change in the United States. Before attempting so ambitious a task, it is important to ask why it should be regarded as useful, or even desirable. All social inquiry begins from assumptions about what is, or is not, problematic; to attempt an assessment of our knowledge in this area, therefore, is to imply that intergovernmental change constitutes a "problem." What is the nature of that problem? What values appear to be threatened by what observed or asserted "changes" in American intergovernmental relations?

Few will be surprised to learn that answers to these questions are as varied as the writers who express their concerns. For some analysts, rapid growth in public expenditures is a major problem, either because such growth implies a reduction of personal freedom or because it is said to be accompanied by undesirable shifts in power relationships between levels of government. For others, the proliferation of new public programs at all levels of government has created a governmental system so complex that meaningful accountability of officials to citizens has been destroyed, leading to increased citizen apathy and decreased public trust in government. For still others, program proliferation accompanied by increasingly dense and frequent governmental interaction has created an "overload" problem, characterized by decreased governmental capacity to achieve stated objectives. When solutions to these "problems" are offered, more often than not they take the form of recommendations to simplify an otherwise overly complicated, chaotic, and inefficient governmental system.

Efficiency, accountability (through hierarchy), and clarity of purpose can hardly be said to be new values in the American polity, any more than proposals for more central coordination or greater efficiency can be regarded as innovative ideas for reform. Indeed, I shall argue that one of the more striking qualities of the recent literature on intergovernmental change is its general lack of changed thinking on what is said to be a problem of change. To the extent that recent authors have contributed anything innovative, it is a new mood of pessimism, derived from largely implicit images of despair. Serious writers now ask whether national governments can go bankrupt, or engage in intellectual hand-wringing over the "sobering" prospect that "excesses of pluralism" or "excesses of democracy" may cause the system to dissolve into mindless, purposeless disarray. For these new professionals of despair, the leading issue is no longer how intergovernmental relations work but why intergovernmental relations fail.

I mention this new pessimism primarily to reject it as a useful perspective on current developments in relations among American governments. It seems to me that judgments about whether the system is improving or decaying must follow, rather than precede, empirical analyses of intergovernmental behavior, observed for a long enough time period to sustain a judgment of "change." Remarkably enough, few of the writers who express global judgments of despair pay much attention to the large number of detailed, empirical investigations of governmental interactions, many of which investigations challenge their gloomy pessimism, nor do they pay much attention to events (or analyses of events) that took place prior to the past decade or so. On the other hand, few of the detailed empirical studies develop alternative analytic or normative frameworks that explicitly challenge theories of system failure. The global pessimists who suggest that the sky is falling are singularly unpersuasive, yet the scholars who produce convincing empirical work seldom offer conceptual frameworks that permit generalized conclusions to emerge from their "facts."

If there is a problem of intergovernmental change, then, it is primarily intellectual: we neither know enough about patterns of interaction over time to sustain empirical theories of change, nor do we possess conceptual frameworks adequate to the task of interpreting the data that we have. My assessment of the literature, therefore, will be intended to clarify this intellectual problem as much as to review what has been done. In doing so, I specifically reject the notion of "decay" or "crisis" as a starting point; I reject the implicit models of hierarchy and centralized rationality that characterize the perspectives of contemporary critics; and I reject the implication that a perfectible "end state" condition, beyond which no further change takes place, can or should be sought.

My own assumptions are at once more traditional and more consistent with the available evidence about American federalism. I assume that change in social and governmental relations is both constant and unending as the "normal" state of all systems; that change is more likely to be cyclical than unidirectional; and that changes will proceed unevenly, with uneven and perhaps contradictory consequences that will themselves contribute to further cycles of change. In applying these assumptions to intergovernmental relations in the American federal system, I do no more than affirm a perspective stated effectively some years ago by Carl J. Friedrich.

Federal relations are fluctuating relations in the very nature of things. Any federally organized community must therefore provide itself with instrumentalities for the recurrent revision of its pattern or design. For only thus can the shifting balance of common and disparate values, interests, and beliefs be effectively reflected in more differentiated or more integrated relations. In short, we have federalism only if a set of political communities coexist and interact as autonomous entities, united in a common order with an autonomy of its own. No sovereign can exist in a federal system; autonomy and sovereignty exclude each other in such a political order. To speak of the transfer of part of the sovereignty is to deny the idea of sovereignty which since Bodin has meant indivisibility. No one has the "last word." (1968, 7–8)

ASSESSMENTS OF CHANGE: GLOBAL INTERPRETATIONS

Discussions of governmental change are commonly afflicted by both conceptual and empirical problems. At the conceptual level, the question of what is changing can seldom be answered unambiguously, even for an issue as apparently clear-cut as growth in public sector expenditures. Where data are available, public expenditure growth or decline can be documented, but whether such trends constitute change depends on whether they are viewed independently or interpreted in relation to the economic system (i.e., relative to GNP), to other governments, or to individuals within society. It also depends on the time period for which such data are observed and the criteria used to determine how much growth or decline is enough to sustain a judgment of change. None of these matters is settled; such questions are decided by analysts working with some explicit or implicit criteria of relevance. For the more complicated issue of change in *patterns* of intergovernmental relations, analytical ambiguities seem far more serious. Conceptually, the "system" to be observed is often limited to the federal government, despite the existence of nearly 80,000 state and local governmental units. Including a larger number of units in an analytic system, however, presents formidable difficulties. Obtaining enough information to justify a claim of change is bound to be frustrated by the large number of units as well as the typical absence of baseline data sufficient to permit essential before-and-after comparisons. Change may be continuous and normal, but studying change is an abnormally difficult task.

These difficulties seem clearly evident in works I have chosen to refer to as "global" interpretations, which offer large (and often gloomy) conclusions about system change, derived from a perspective that focuses primarily on the Washington component of the federal government. The disjunction between conclusions offered and evidence adduced clearly reflects the enormous difficulty of gathering data for so large and complex a system and the equally apparent difficulty of conceptualizing such a system. These studies are nonetheless interesting, in part because they offer considerable insight into the values that often motivate studies of change. Four themes stand out among the global interpretations: socioeconomic determinism, governmental accountability, balance of power, and public sector legitimacy.

Socioeconomic Determinism

Perhaps the most enduring and comprehensive explanation for governmental change is the notion that such change is driven by changes in society and in relationships between groups or individuals in society. This conceptualization began to emerge forcefully in the early twentieth century, at a time when labor-management disputes associated with the emergence of the modern corporation were attracting attention, when evidence of widespread corruption in state and local governments was prominent, and when in consequence there was "an imperative social demand for extending the sphere of government and increasing its activities" (Ford 1909, 63). According to this view, long-term, irreversible changes in technology, modes of organizing production, and the scale of industrial and financial relationships create problems that require new governmental activities. Because these emergent problems typically are national in scope or consequence, pressure for national government action increases, leading to a long-term expansion of the number and size of national government programs, as well as an expansion of governmental activity at all levels. Both governmental growth and a gradual expansion of national government responsibility are thus "determined" by the problems associated with social change.

The basic ideas conveyed in this conceptualization have changed little over the past 70 years.[1] In 1908, at the annual meeting of the American Political Science Association, Leacock put forth the main elements of the argument. For him, "the progress of transportation, of intercommunication and the expansion of modern business enterprise has unified vast stretches of the United States, has rendered the whole country economically interdependent" (1909, 42). It was inevitable, he thought, that the largely artificial set of American governments (the states of Utah and South Dakota were referred to as "at best . . . astronomical expressions whose location can only be found by the aid of a solar observation") was "bound to give way. It is destined finally to be superseded by some form of really national and centralized government" (52). In 1922 Lowrie reaffirmed this view, noting how expansion of federal government power in war, Prohibition, and the regulation of interstate commerce generally confirmed the principle that "governmental power should be as broad as the problems with which it must deal" (382). The same principle supported Harold J. Laski's 1939 polemic on "The Obsolescence of Federalism." Writing in the midst of a severe economic depression for which neither state nor federal action had yet found a solution, Laski emphasized "that the unity which giant capitalism postulates in the economic sphere postulates a corresponding unity in the conference of political powers upon the federal government. There is no other way," he thought, to produce "a positive state" (369). If problems of industrialization, war, or welfare were to be met effectively, more government action in general, and more federal government action in particular, was essential. Noting that no political party really opposed these developments, Roscoe Drummond in 1949 concluded "that the trend to national government is overwhelming, inevitable, and irreversible" (4).

By the 1950s this deterministic model of governmental growth and national power augmentation had become conventional wisdom, but the desirability of continuing these trends came under question. At the request of former President Hoover, the Council of State Governments undertook a study of the federal grants-in-aid system for the first Hoover Commission, and called for a reassertion of the principle of dual federalism (Council of State Governments 1949). In 1953 Leonard D. White offered suggestions for countering "The March of Power to Washington" (White, 1953) that provided an intellectual foundation for the Commission on Intergovernmental Relations (the Kestnbaum Commission) (Commission on Intergovernmental Relations 1955) and the Joint Federal-State Action Committee, (Joint Federal-State Action Committee 1957, 1958, 1960) established at the suggestion of President Eisenhower to seek out activities that might appropriately be transferrred back to the states. Despite strong presidential support, the inclusion of nine state governors on this committee and "two years of effort in an atmosphere characterized by an absence of partisan disagreement or of conflict along governmental lines, there was," according to Graves, "still no significant accomplishment" (1964, 902).[2] The two programs recommended for transfer to the states amounted to less than $80 million in 1957, only 2 percent of federal grants in that year, but even this modest proposal was never implemented. Similar recommendations have occasionally been made since 1957,[3] but the fate of these proposals underlines the practical as well as intellectual power of the growth-nationalization theme. More recent writers, such as Kirlin (1979), have amended this theme largely by adding new social "problems'' (environmental protection or protection against income loss) that cause new federal programs through processes nicely described by Sundquist:

> As the problem begins to be recognized, it is seen as local in character, outside the national concern. Then, as it persists and as it becomes clear that the states and communities are unable to solve it unaided (partly because the same political groups that oppose federal action are wont to oppose state and local action too), the activists propose federal aid, but on the basis of helping the states and communities cope with what is still seen as *their* problem. Finally, the locus of basic responsibility shifts: the problem is recognized as in fact not local at all but as a *national* problem requiring a national solution that states and communities are mandated . . . to carry out—usually by inducements strong enough to produce a voluntary response but sometimes by more direct, coercive means. (1969, 11)

Although the socioeconomic explanation for governmental growth and nationalization has changed little in 70 years, evaluation of the consequences of these public sector changes has shifted a great deal. Until 1950, the dominant theme among serious writers had been the desirability, no less than the inevitability, of governmental growth and nationalization. International war, industrial and commercial integration on a national scale, or economic depression were hardly problems that could be handled without governmental intervention, nor could the poorly staffed and often corrupt state or local governments be expected to cope with problems of clearly national significance. Hence, national government expansion was as much a demand as an analytic conclusion. More federal government, in short, was good. Efforts of a Republican national administration through the 1950s to reverse these trends obviously reflected a different viewpoint, expressed by the National Association of Manufacturers in a December 1952 bulletin titled *Bring the Government Back Home:*

> The federal government is too big. It is so big and so complex that it cannot be efficiently managed by any man or group of men.
> The burden of its cost is now a greater load than the economy can carry and remain prosperous.
> The steady pressure for more power to regulate and control is a growing menace to individual and civil liberty.
> The increasing concentration of political power and economic control in the federal government is destroying the economic and governmental environment which is essential to the survival of the American system of free enterprise and to the preservation of the American constitutional system of a union of states.
> Unless the trend toward ever bigger government is halted, and until it is reversed, the states and private business alike face the prospect of ultimate, complete domination by the federal government. And complete federal domination IS totalitarianism.

These ideas have a familiar ring, but we have seen that they had little real impact in the 1950s. They were followed by another decade in which the federal government was again seen for the most part as a positive force in solving newly recognized social "problems," ranging from urban poverty and crime to environmental protection. Not until the 1970s did opposition to federal government size and complexity again emerge as a major theme of intellectual concern and national political debate.

Governmental Accountability

Critics of public sector growth express two main concerns: one is a fear that individual freedom is threatened by excessive governmental spending, the other is that governmental capacity to act is at some point threatened by such growth. With characteristic vigor, Milton Friedman has argued that public expenditure growth inevitably breeds financial crisis, and that financial crisis inevitably leads to loss of liberty and freedom (1976).[4] Observing New York City's fiscal problems against a background of visits to Chile and Great Britain (which he views as similar systems), Friedman says that "New York City has lost its liberty and freedom" because a state committee had been set up to deal with the financial crisis (10). Thus, the loss of individual freedom implied by higher government taxes is accompanied by crises that lead to loss of *local* self-government. Friedman appears to believe that political systems "tip" from freedom to nonfreedom at some point. Chile "tipped" when public expenditures consumed 40 percent of national income. Britain, with more wealth, "appears on the verge of tipping over at 60%" (14). Friedman's flop, accordingly, is set at 60 percent.[5] Governmental spending that reaches or exceeds 60 percent of national income will necessarily produce "a false road which leads to tyranny and misery, and not to freedom" (14). If Friedman is right, New Yorkers suffer under a tyranny, and Swedes, whose governments consumed 63 percent of Swedish GNP in 1977,[6] obviously suffer similar discomfort.

The stunning simplicity of these arguments is more than matched by writers who worry about the loss of governmental capacity or authority.[7] These writers suggest that governmental growth and diminished capacity are directly related: increases in public spending create inflationary pressures that are difficult to control, and the complexity created by large numbers of new programs renders solutions to *any* social problem—or achievement of any program purpose—less and less likely, especially without effective leadership. This, in essence, is the problem of "government overload" (Heclo 1977), attributed by Harvard scholars and others to "excesses of pluralism" (Beer 1977a), or to an "excess of democracy" (Huntington 1975a, 1975b), or to a "revolution of rising 'entitlements'" (Bell 1975, 1978). Although couched in general terms, the specific excesses referred to (when specific references are made at all) usually turn out to be the social programs adopted during the Great Society period of the 1960s or the more recent spate of programs designed to alleviate unemployment and poverty. Such programs are widely viewed to have failed, or at least to have not succeeded, but to have nevertheless proliferated so much that effective management or coordination has become impossible.[8]

These kinds of assertions, I should emphasize, are rarely addressed with evidence. Instead, the preferred vehicle is typically a set of imprecise images that dramatize the chaos, disorder, and lack of controlled purpose said to characterize the current system. Thus, a recent Advisory Commission on Intergovernmental Relations (ACIR) bulletin summarizes what is said to be a popular view as follows:

> growing numbers of people contend that government has become a monster of excessively pervasive and inordinately complex proportions. In this view, the proliferation of regulations and programs and the extreme *intergovernmentalization* of implementation have created a largely uncontrolled and unaccountable system—"Leviathan" run amuck. (Colella 1979, 6)

Another analysis in this same bulletin uses the Leviathan image to interpret sketchy data. The current system is said to be "in good part a mistake"; the "evidence of systemic overload is everywhere in Washington (and across the nation)," including "state houses, municipal buildings, and polling places throughout the land. . . . Local and state officials find it nearly impossible to exercise coherent policy or administrative control over the array of federal programs in which they participate." Overall, the oversized, disorganized, and careening federal government is seen to be "exporting" its own chaos down the line to state and local governments, undermining governmental accountability. Were it not for this federal monster, lower-level units presumably would be better able to manage their own affairs.[9]

Although dramatic, these images are derived from a conceptual foundation that is wholly inadequate to support the proposed conclusions. Words such as "monster" or "Leviathan" are value-loaded symbols that express negative, summary judgments rather than analytic assessments. Indeed, it is difficult to imagine a set of analytic concepts that could be clearly connected to such symbols. Phrases such as "inordinately complex," "extreme intergovernmentalization," and "coherent policy" come closer to analytic utility, since it is at least possible to imagine some empirical referents for the nouns. Use of modifiers, however, transforms these phrases into judgmental conclusions derived from unspecified political preferences rather than scientific analyses. The preferences are nonetheless apparent: simplicity, coherence, a single governmental hierarchy rather than multiple centers of influence. These are perfectly reasonable preferences for critics of federal expenditure growth to hold, but they are no more than preferences, subject to disagreement among those whose preferences or interpretations of reality differ.

Scientific or not, hostility to governmental growth and increased federal spending has become widespread during the past decade. The existence of national problems that require a national response continues to explain and justify national action, but the nature and form of that action now appears

Table 2.1.   Total Governmental Expenditures as a Percentage of GNP, for
Selected Nations, 1960 and 1973

Nation	1960	1973
Australia	23.1	27.3
Austria	30.3	36.6
Belgium	29.9	38.7
Canada	31.0	37.0
Denmark	25.0	40.7
France	32.5	37.5
Federal Republic of Germany	31.4	38.7
Italy	29.6	40.1
Japan	18.2	21.5
Luxembourg[a]	30.7	38.3
Netherlands	34.3	47.5
Norway	31.9	45.7
Sweden	31.5	45.7
Switzerland	20.6	25.2
United Kingdom	31.9	39.5
United States	28.1	32.4

Source: Nutter 1978, table B-1.

[a]Data for Luxembourg are for 1960 and 1972.

troublesome. We are not, to be sure, anywhere close to "Friedman's flop."
Indeed, the public sector consumes a smaller portion of GNP in the United
States than in most other advanced industrial nations (see table 2.1). Nevertheless, the size and disorganization of the federal government is believed
by many analysts to constitute a major crisis: the federal government now has
power but no purpose, no accountability, and no real control.[10] With these
issues we come to the third major theme in this literature: balance of power.

Balance-of-Power Interpretations

Whether conceived of as drift, flow, or march, the gradual augmentation of
national government power is the one trend that virtually all analysts accept as
true. Whether this trend is regarded as a change, however, depends very much
on the interpretation given to American federalism. For some years now, a
lively debate has been conducted between those who believe that the Constitution established a system of separate state and federal responsibilities and
those who believe that the Constitution created a system of shared federal-
state responsibilities. Writers such as Bryce (1895), Corwin (1950), and
Scheiber (1966, 1975), or, more recently, Lowi (1978, 1979), believe that the
Constitution created a system of "dual" federalism, characterized by coequal
federal-state sovereignty and strictly limited federal power. For these writers
the expansion of federal power into all areas of public responsibility is a major
change in the pattern of intergovernmental relations, and it is a change that is

viewed with considerable unhappiness. Other analysts, however, believe that no strict division between federal and state powers was ever intended or achieved by the Constitution. MacDonald (1928, 1923), Clark (1938), Anderson (1955, 1956, 1960), Grodzins (1960a, 1966), and Elazar (1962, 1972) all have contended that American federalism always has been "cooperative federalism," in which federal, state, and local officials share, rather than divide, power. Elazar's superb study of intergovernmental cooperation in the nineteenth century, *The American Partnership* (1962), makes clear that intergovernmental sharing of power and responsibility was typical from the very beginning of the republic; for him and other cooperative federalists, therefore, recent extensions of federal power represent no change in pattern, only a difference of condition. As Grodzins writes in his introduction to Elazar's book,

> One cannot hark back to the good old days of state and local independence because those days never existed. Government, to be sure, did far less in 1830 or 1890 than it does in 1962. (Federal expenditures in 1960 were three thousand times those in 1836.) Given the relative scale of public activities, it is probable that the extent of federal-state-local collaboration during the nineteenth century was equal to that which now exists. (ix)[11]

Grodzins offered this assessment in 1962, before most of the new programs associated with the Great Society had even been proposed, let alone implemented. Even cooperative federalists now admit that the surge of new federal program and funding activity that took place after 1960 represented a major new thrust—if not a new pattern—in the federal role. Dual federalists, of course, view expansion of federal activity since 1960 as a change so fundamental as to constitute a form of revolution. Lowi, who writes of a shift "from United States to United State," notes that programs such as General Revenue Sharing (GRS) have created a clientelistic relationship between all local governments and the national government, allowing the national government a far more decisive role in setting priorities and controlling events than ever before (1978, esp. 21–22). The system has become nationalized, the president is now the center of most important program activities, and both parties have agreed to support these developments. Vincent Ostrom, who like Lowi writes about the "Europeanization" of America, believes we have created something close to the French system of prefectural governments, in which state and local units act as little more than administrative extensions of the national government (1976). This shift of power to Washington has left state and local jurisdictions with little initiative, less independence, and virtually no control. In this new era of the "imperial presidency," power has become centralized as well as nationalized.[12]

Exactly when these revolutionary changes took place is a matter of some controversy. Elazar (1962, 1965), whose perspective emphasizes continuity rather than fundamental change, believes all elements of the present system were in place in 1913. Scheiber (1966, 1975) and Corwin (1950) trace the passing of dual federalism back to the 1930s, whereas Lowi (1978, 1979), Huntington (9175b) and Sundquist (1969) see the 1960s as the period when the new system was finally institutionalized. Nor is there consensus on the problem, if any, caused by this power shift. As we have seen, some writers see all power in Washington but little coordination of that power; for them the problem is a federal government so large and complicated that it is basically out of control. Others see all power in Washington and imagine that a single official, the president, has come to control that power. Hence, for them the problem is too much centralized control and an attendant danger of tyranny. A major source of these ambiguities, of course, is a general lack of precision in conceptualization and a quite noticeable disdain for developing evidence that might sustain conclusions about power. Analyses of the past decade, in particular, have focused attention almost exclusively on Washington, presumably on the assumption that any federal policy or activity will automatically be reflected in state or local action.[13]

To the extent that evidence of a power shift is offered, the evidence typically refers to the remarkable expansion of federal aid to state and local governments that has occurred in the past several years. One might argue, of course, that this recent expansion is not nearly as remarkable as many have suggested. In one of the very first studies of federal aid, for example, MacDonald noted that payments from the federal treasury to the states increased by a "phenomenal" rate of 1,700 percent between 1912 and 1925 (1928a, 5). Writing in 1928, MacDonald was referring to hardly more than a dozen programs, whose value to state governments was no more than $136.7 million in 1927.[14] Writing in 1974, Wright noted that some 40 grant programs had come into existence prior to 1958 and that

> by 1969 there were an estimated 160 major programs, 500 specific legislative authorizations, and 1,315 different federal assistance activities, for which money figures, application deadlines, agency contacts, and use restrictions could be identified. Federal grants jumped in dollar magnitude from $4.9 billion in 1958 to $23.9 billion in 1970. (10)

Program growth continued into the 1970s, producing some 450 major programs of categorical assistance by 1975, as well as roughly 100 grants for higher education, assorted block grants, and a variety of other assistance activities. From 1970 to 1975, federal grant expenditures more than doubled, and came close to doubling again by 1980. Since 1960, in fact, grants have been increasing at more than twice the rate of either GNP or total budget outlays (table 2.2). Although federal aid may well have increased as rapidly at some point in the past, it is surely not unreasonable to view the size and the rate of recent grant increases as quite remarkable indeed.[15]

For advocates of dual federalism and strictly limited federal government, federal aid expansion implies power centralization for several reasons, of

Table 2.2. Growth in Federal Grants-in-Aid and Nondefense Domestic Outlays, FY 1950–78 ($ billion)

Fiscal Year	GNP	Total Budget Outlays		Grants-in-Aid	Grants as % of Total Budget Outlays		Grants as % of State and Local Own Source General Revenue		
		Total	Nondefense		Total Outlays	Domestic Outlays	State and Local	State	Local
1950	264.9	42.6	30.2	2.3	5.4	7.6	13.6	26.1	2.1
1955	380.0	68.5	28.7	3.2	4.7	11.1	11.1	21.2	2.7
1960	497.3	92.2	47.1	7.0	7.6	14.9	16.1	31.1	2.6
1965	657.1	118.4	71.0	10.9	9.2	15.4	17.5	32.4	3.7
1970	959.0	196.6	118.0	24.0	12.2	20.3	20.1	33.6	5.1
1975	1,457.3	334.2	248.7	49.8	14.9	20.0	26.0	37.3	12.9
1978	2,060.4	461.2	356.0	77.9	16.9	21.9	28.2	37.0	17.5
1980	2,627.4	579.6	443.7	91.5	15.8	21.1	27.7	35.1	16.3

Sources: Office of Management and Budget 1980a, 1980b. U.S. Department of Commerce 1975, 1125–26, 1129, 1133; 1976, 46; 1978, 46.

Note: Figures on federal grants-in-aid to state and local governments systematically overstate federal aid to states, while understating federal aid to localities, because of the Census Bureau's practice of counting federal aid to localities passed through the states as federal aid to states (as in this table). Such federal aid later is classified in some Census Bureau tables as part of the category listing state aid to localities. Also, GNP figures are for fiscal year period. Budget figures are for total budget outlays.

which the most general is scale. Federal programs are now so numerous that no governmental activity, at any level, is untouched by the federal presence. Even fire protection, long thought to be the final bastion of purely local responsibility, is now covered by grant programs. As Sundquist writes, "There are no longer any constitutional barriers to the assertion of federal responsibility" (1969, 11).[16] Federal grants, furthermore, are now so large that they exceed property and sales taxes as the most important source of state-local revenue: an estimated $91 billion in grants were allocated in fiscal 1980. State and local governments have become more dependent on federal aid than ever before and, since it is widely believed that fiscal control implies policy control, it is also assumed that the federal government can exert far more influence now than ever before. According to critics, federal program priorities are substituted for state and local priorities; lower-level officials learn the habit of waiting for Washington to act on important matters; and the result is a general loss of capacity on the part of state or local officials. As program responsibility shifts to Washington, the national agenda becomes cluttered with local issues, while program administration becomes "super-marbleized" (Walker 1979), with all levels of government involved in all programs at all times. Whether viewed as "united state" or "nationalized government," it is clearly thought to be a mess.

Problems created by increased federal funding, moreover, appear to be exacerbated by the regulatory activity that has accompanied the explosion of federal grants. Through statute or administrative regulation a host of causes has come under some form of federal control: civil rights, consumer protection, environmental protection, minimum wage, sex and age discrimination, occupational safety, and many others. Federal regulations are often confusing and sometimes contradictory, but they are usually attached to grant programs and thus must be followed by the growing number of participants in the grant system. At the very least, lower-level units are forced to submit forms or reports indicating they have complied with stated requirements. Regulations may or may not be effective in achieving stated purposes, but they do generate large quantities of red tape and require a considerable investment of time. Unable to manage itself effectively, the federal government is accused of hindering the development of effective management among state and local jurisdictions.[17]

If there is something new in American intergovernmental relations, then, in this view it is the expansion in the number, scope, and size of federal programs designed to assist or regulate state and local governments. There is also a "new" explanation for this expansion. Whereas the older, deterministic view located the causes of governmental expansion in society, many writers today argue that government officials themselves have become the major source of new public activities. As government budgets have grown, resources available to bureaucrats have expanded, providing opportunities for active cultivation of legislative and constituency support. Program managers use public funds to stimulate constituency support for program expansion, creating irresistible pressures for public sector growth. The absence of political parties with clear and competing philosophies leaves the field open to single-issue groups, allied with and supported by public bureaucrats and legislators, to press for continuous program expansion.[18] A new "public sector politics" has arisen in which "producer interests" (to borrow a phrase from Tarschys) are now dominant.[19]

Public Sector Legitimacy

Perhaps the most sophisticated of the public sector legitimacy interpretations is Beer's widely acknowledged argument concerning the expanding political power of governmental interests (1973, 1976, 1977a, 1977b, 1978). According to Beer, the rise of professionalism in government, due to functional specialization, led to the development of a professional bureaucratic complex cutting across levels of government. During the 1960s, the professional bureaucratic complex promoted the expanded federal role through categorical programs, thereby stimulating the emergence of the intergovernmental lobby. As federal aid became an increasingly important revenue source for state and local governments, these "topocrats" paid more attention to the politics of federal aid in Washington, and coalesced into an intergovernmental lobby to insure the continued flow of federal assistance into their jurisdictions.[20] The rise of the professional bureaucratic complex and the intergovernmental lobby, in conjunction with the declining political power and initiative of the private sector, added a new dimension in the American national system of representation—new arenas of mutual influence among levels of government increasingly dominated by public sector interests.[21] A new danger also emerged: excessive pluralism, leading to ever-expanding federal expenditures and governmental overload.

Despite the initial appeal of this argument, neither a professional bureaucratic complex nor an intergovernmental lobby can fairly be regarded as new characteristics of American intergovernmental relations. Nor has the case been convincingly made that, relative to the private sector, public sector power has expanded, producing new arenas of mutual influence among levels of government.

Elements of the professional bureaucratic complex were already evident in the nineteenth century.[22] By the early twentieth century, what later became commonly known as the "iron triangle" was an established feature of our intergovernmental system, especially influential in the prereformed national budget process, when no executive budget existed and federal agencies dealt directly with Congress.[23] Functionally defined working relationships between federal and lower-level bureaucrats who administered federal grants were equally well established features of the early twentieth century.[24] These public sector officials were no less concerned with promoting the organizations they served and the programs they administered than their more numerous contemporary counterparts. It was the Department of Agriculture, after all, that stimulated the "farm bureau" movement that has become such an effective lobby[25] and, according to Key, one of the first grant programs in public health (the Sheppard-Towner Act of 1921) resulted from "a campaign led by various women's organizations in collaboration with the Children's Bureau" (1937, 15).[26]

Today's intergovernmental lobby similarly traces its lineage back to the early decades of this century: the National Governor's Conference was established in 1908; the International City Management Association in 1915; the American Municipal Association (later, the National League of Cities) in 1924; the Council of State Governments in 1933; the United States Conference of Mayors in 1933; the National Association of Counties in 1937; and the National Legislative Conference in 1948.[27] Repesentatives of these groups were no strangers to Washington prior to the mid-1960s.[28]

If there is some change in the activities of the professional bureaucratic complex and the intergovernmental lobby, therefore, it must lie in the increased volume and nature of interactions among these countervailing public sector forces relative to private sector interests. The "power to the producers" thesis, however, provides no clear conceptualization of this supposedly new representational system. A shift of power from the electoral to the administrative arena, accompanied by interlocking relationships between public bureaucrats and corporate clientele groups, suggests an American version of a new "corporatism," similar to conceptualizations currently being discussed by observers of European systems.[29] But no one has yet developed an effective image of a new American corporatism, perhaps because political and institutional conditions in the United States discourage the emergence of corporatist patterns of interaction (Salisbury 1977). Nor has there been a persuasive case made for the decline of private sector influence in American policy processes. If anything, private sector influence over governmental tax and expenditure policies appears to have increased considerably in recent months. Those who argue for the occurrence of some major "pattern change" must contend with major ambiguities of both substance and direction.

It is important to recognize that neither the professional bureaucratic complex nor the intergovernmental lobby constitutes a unified interest, advancing a common purpose, except in a trivial sense: all members want more money from the feds for their favorite programs. Divisions rooted in interorganizational and intraorganizational rivalries, in conflicting tendencies of areal versus functional responsibilities, in the duties of central versus line agency officials, and in ideology permeate the professional bureaucratic complex.[30] Similar divisions characterize the intergovernmental lobby.[31] Competition for program benefits behind a façade of unified support for "more" federal aid is a well-established pattern, noticeable even in the drive to pass GRS during the years preceding 1972.[32] Since then, the politics of federal assistance has been characterized by sharp disagreements among governmental lobby organizations over what programs to fund, what formulae to write, as well as which units should benefit. These are not accidental disagreements; they are rooted in the enormous diversity of the governmental system itself. And they are likely to become more pointed as the rate of increase in federal aid slows down.

In short, the appeal of the "new public sector politics" thesis evaporates when specific components of the argument are examined. Public bureaucrats are assuredly influential actors in program formulation, as are governmental lobby organizations, but these patterns can be traced for decades. New patterns of public sector–private sector interaction may have emerged, but if so, they are more likely to be found in the enormous expansion of federal loan, loan-guarantee, and tax expenditure programs of the past quarter century than in the comparatively modest activities said to be the focus of the intergovernmental topocrats. Relationships governing the expansion of federal government tax expenditures and loan- and interest-guarantee programs, however, have yet to be systematically examined.[33] Indeed, the lion's share of attention to recent intergovernmental trends has focused solely on grants-in-aid, especially GRS and direct federal-local programs.

Political and Analytical Values

What, then, is all the global shouting about? What might explain the recent outpouring of books and articles worrying about governmental growth and bankruptcy, particularly in a country whose governments consume a far smaller fraction of the national product than is consumed by governments in similarly advanced nations? Why the insistent focus on *federal* government spending and employment when, as we shall see, spending by state and local governments has been increasing at a much higher rate? And how do we account for the wildly different conclusions reached by observers of the same phenomena? Depending on which global interpretation is used, the president is either all-powerful or totally ineffective; Congress is either irrelevant or the source of most new policy initiatives; the people are either "excessively" democratic or increasingly apathetic. One clue to these puzzles is apparent in the form of the arguments offered: heavy utilization of symbols—that is, words that evoke larger meanings—but little empirical evidence. Another clue is suggested in the following excerpt from Austin MacDonald's 1928 study of *Federal Aid:*

> When men begin to talk about the danger of infringing the rights of self-government, they usually mean that they fear for the special interests of the sections they represent. They seldom go forth to do political battle for the sake of abstract political theories. The statesmen of the ante-bellum South talked much of states' rights; but they were trying to protect the special interests of the cotton-growing states. So when the statesmen of the new generation invoke the great god Demos to protect the people against the fearful consequences of a rising tide of nationalism, one may be pardoned a cynical glance to learn what section or sections they represent, and whether special interests may not be at stake. (1928a, 239)

The first of these clues suggests a conceptualization issue, and the second directs our attention to political values that may be at play. Other explanations are possible, but these two are worth at least a comment.

If we begin with political values, MacDonald's insight would suggest the utility of moving beyond the rhetoric of excessive federal spending to examine the beneficiaries of that spending.[34] In a rewarding analysis, Charles L. Schultze has demonstrated that nearly 90 percent of the growth in the ratio of domestic federal expenditures to GNP between 1955 and 1977 was accounted for by just three types of federal activity (Schultze 1976). More than half the growth, in fact, was traceable to a single set of federal programs, namely, social security, disability, and unemployment compensation payments to individuals. Schultze notes that these are programs to which the beneficiaries themselves have contributed, and thus (until recently) seldom subjected to public criticism.[35] Such criticism, he suggests, has been confined almost entirely to new programs of assistance to low-income families (which accounted for 14 percent of the growth) and the introduction of new social service and social investment programs between 1965 and 1970 (18 percent of the growth). By 1977, social investment grants-in-aid had risen to $21 billion and become, in Schultze's words, "the lightning rods for most of the criticism of domestic spending, especially, though not exclusively, from conservatives" (345). Had 1977 payments for low-income assistance and social investment programs remained at the same percentage of GNP they consumed in 1965, payments in 1977 would have been smaller by some $34 billion, or about 1.7 percent of GNP. As Schultze concludes, "One might say that the great political debate about federal spending for social welfare revolves around the propriety and effectiveness of the way 1.7 percent of the national income is being spent" (345).

Hostility to welfare expenditures from the public purse is, of course, an old story in American politics, as is the effort to mask that hostility behind a rhetoric of "principle." Gilbert Y. Steiner's work, however, has shown that opposition to welfare has far less to do with principle than with the organizational weakness of the poor, the visibility of welfare recipients, the discrepancy between taxpayers and beneficiaries, and other such "political" factors (1966, 1971, 1976). Harold L. Wilensky's interesting analysis in fact suggests the inevitability of a "tax-welfare backlash" in advanced industrial nations (1976). Wilensky also maintains that this backlash is difficult to contain under conditions of inflation, particularly in systems that lack a strong labor movement and strongly centralized political institutions. Under such conditions taxpayers become more sensitive to governmental costs and are more likely to express that sensitivity in hostility to welfare programs. A recent analysis of popular attitudes toward tax limitation measures in Michigan makes clear that many taxpayers do indeed support tax reduction (Courant, Gramlich, and Rubinfeld 1979a). This analysis also shows, however, that support for tax limitation is *not* associated with a desire to reduce public expenditures. "Fundamentally," the authors conclude, "the tax limitation movement does not appear to be an attempt to correct public sector-private sector spending imbalances" (34). Voters appear to think that taxes can be cut without reducing expenditures either because efficiency gains are possible or, the authors speculate, because of "the unending search for a free lunch" (35).[36] Not much principle here, but an interesting insight into the recent wave of tax limit proposals. The rash of such proposals appears to have created a context that has enabled the National Association of Manufacturers' rhetoric of a quarter century ago to become a mainstay of the academic "analysis" of 1980.

Although a resurgence of conservative values may well explain much of the recent furor over federal spending, the stereotypical forms in which diagnoses are usually made and solutions offered suggests a different kind of intellectual issue. Recall that the litany of complaints includes not just excessive growth but excessive complexity. There are so many different federal programs, controlled by so many different organizations, that neither control nor meaningful accountability is possible. To gain some measure of control over this "Leviathan run amuck," reformers typically argue that a stronger centralized authority is required to plan and coordinate federal activities according to a more coherent sense of federal purpose. A more centralized hierarchy could at once be more rational in terms of policy and more responsible politically, since there would be a single official—the president, obviously—to establish goals, coordinate subordinates, and assume responsibility for results. Both the diagnosis of fragmentation and the prescription of hierarchical integration have a long history in American politics, as Herbert

Kaufman's brilliant 1956 paper pointed out.[37] Precisely these ideas were applied to city governments at the turn of the century, to state governments in the 1920s, to presidential-congressional relations in the 1930s, to metropolitan areas in the 1950s and 1960s—and now to the organization of the federal government as a whole. Supporters of this quest for executive leadership were occasionally successful in achieving government reorganization, to a large extent because they were able to join with supporters of a second major value, neutral competence in the operation of government. Since both values were developed as sets of principles in the growing field of public administration, such political alliances could often be rationalized and promoted as "scientific" undertakings.

Kaufman saw clearly, however, that the alliance between "neutral competence" and "executive leadership" was bound to come unraveled, indeed, had already begun to disintegrate.

> The components of the "neutral" bureaucracy, by virtue of their expertness and information and alliances have become independent sources of decision-making power, and Presidents will probably find them no easier to direct—indeed, perhaps even more intractable than their partisan predecessors. (1956, 1070)

Accordingly, Kaufman judged that

> the language of public administration is likely to become increasingly strategic and tactical in tone rather than "scientific" . . . as the public administration groups aligned with the executive and with the bureaucracy, respectively, pull apart. The question that will be asked about suggested reorganizations is not, "What, according to the canons of management science, is the best organization?" but, "What will be the effect of this measure on the institution we support?" (1072–73)

Kaufman's 1956 insight seems to me to have been prophetically accurate. If scientific work is characterized by clear conceptualization, carefully drawn hypotheses, evidence to test the hypotheses, and precisely formulated conclusions, then very little of the recent global work on intergovernmental relations can be regarded as scientific. The disdain for data and use of politically loaded symbolism that characterizes much of this work becomes more understandable if we view it as strategic argumentation—a view that also helps to explain the quite divergent conclusions that can be found in this material. To gain some real understanding about patterns of intergovernmental change, therefore, we must turn away from these polemics to a quite different body of literature.

ASSESSMENTS OF CHANGE: EMPIRICAL ANALYSES

Inadequate as they are, the global interpretations have at least this virtue: they suggest what should *not* be done in assessing patterns of intergovernmental change. It makes little analytic sense, for example, to focus exclusively on the national government in Washington if the objective is to examine patterns of change among American governments in general. Washington is not only too narrow a definition of "system" for a nation of 80,000 governments, but excessive concentration on what goes on in the Capitol systematically prejudges the answer to one question while systematically obscuring other, more important, issues. Whether the federal government has more or less "power" has been the main question posed by globalists, but a focus on Washington permits nothing but a positive answer to be given: funds are always and programs are often being increased. Confusing growth with power is easy to do, particularly if no attention is paid to the implementation of federal programs by 50 states, 3,100 counties, 38,000 municipalities and townships, and 40,000 other units of local government. Paying attention to all these units is no small task, but census data and various other federal, state, and local data bases are available for exploitation. Other resources include a very large literature on local and urban governance, including the most sophisticated work available on the question of power; a smaller but nonetheless useful literature on state government; and even a tiny but fascinating literature on precisely the topic of *inter*governmental relations.

In what follows I draw upon these several bodies of literature, largely to 'clarify some of the issues raised by the globalists but also to underline the need for a conceptual framework more adequate to the task of understanding changing patterns of intergovernmental relations. The system examined includes all American governments. Because I begin with the assumption that relationships between these governments are always in flux, my initial question is, How can we observe and characterize these changing relationships? Note that I do not ask whether any one or any subset of these governments has more or less power. That question, in my view, is neither precise nor answerable, except in trivial ways. Nevertheless, I expect that this attempt to observe relationships rather than measure power should move us toward a better appreciation of the sources and consequences of intergovernmental change.

On Public Sector Size

Increases in governmental revenues and expenditures occur both because costs of existing activities increase over time and because governments undertake new programs. Whether or not such fiscal increments represent change depends on the criterion used to assess "change in relation to what?" In table 2.3, for example, we compare public sector revenues and expenditures, by level, to GNP for selected years since 1950. Within this period of close to three decades, the national product increased more than sixfold and total public sector activity increased from roughly a quarter of GNP in 1950 to well over a third of GNP in 1980. These increments, together with the associated increase in public sector payroll costs from 6.4 percent to 9.6 percent of GNP,

Table 2.3. Public Sector Growth Compared to GNP Growth, 1950–80 (%)

Year	GNP	Total Govt. Revenue	Total Govt. Expenditure	Total Govt. Payroll	% of GNP				
					Federal Revenue	Federal Expenditure	State & Local Revenue	State & Local Expenditure	
1950	286.2	23.3	24.6	6.4	15.2	15.7	9.0	9.8	
1960	506.0	30.3	29.9	7.9	19.7	19.2	11.9	12.1	
1970	982.4	34.0	33.9	10.2	20.9	21.2	15.3	15.1	
1980	2,626.0	35.5	36.5	9.6	21.5	23.5	20.3	19.7	

Source: Revenue and expenditure data from U.S. Department of Commerce 1975, 1119–34, various tables; *Government Finance* series, 1971, 1977. GNP figures from *Economic Report of the President, 1979*, 183, table B-1.

make clear that government at all levels is growing, relatively as well as absolutely. Note, however, that the really striking rates of increase since 1950 have occurred in the state and local sector, rather than in the federal government. Thus, to the extent that there has been a change from a previous pattern of cyclical increases and decreases in the public sector share of GNP (associated with war, depression, etc.), the pattern change appears to be led by state and local government activity.[38]

This conclusion is strongly reinforced when we examine the distribution of public sector employment and compare that distribution to either the national population or the civilian labor force. As seen in table 2.4, federal government employees as a percentage of total public sector employees declined from 33.1 percent in 1950 to only 17.9 percent in 1979. While the federal work force share was declining, state and local employment was increasing to 12.7 percent of the civilian labor force and 5.9 percent of the population as a whole by 1979. Between 1955 and 1979,[39] fewer than 500,000 employees were added by the federal government, but more than 8 million new employees went to work for state and local governments. Nearly 3.7 million people (up from 1.5 million in 1955) now work for state governments, while more than 9.4 million (up from 3.8 million in 1955) work for the cities, counties, townships, and school districts that comprise American local government. State and local governments were growth industries from 1957 to the end of the 1970s, with the federal government in a state of comparative decline in employment.

Although some analysts have suggested that increases in federal grants-in-aid have been more significant than federal employment in expanding federal control over state and local programs, that argument seems to me defective on several counts. One is that the most important increases in federal outlays have been for payments to individuals, particularly social security and other income security programs, rather than grants-in-aid to state and local governments: in fiscal 1979, estimated payments to individuals account for some 44.2 percent of budget outlays, compared to 16.3 percent for grants-in-aid.[40] Nor is it clear that grant programs are as coercive as they are sometimes said to be. Programs such as general-purpose fiscal assistance (GRS) attach no conditions on use. Much federal aid has been and will continue to be distributed in the form of block grants and no-match grants, both of which reduce federal coercive power. We shall see that even carefully defined federal "strings" are seldom as controlling in practice as they appear on paper. Most fundamentally, however, the coercive power of federal money depends to a very large extent on the organization and quality of the recipient units. To assume that federal funds coerce anyone is to assume that state and local units are little more than empty vessels, dependent on outside funds for both direction and energy. It is quite difficult to reconcile this view with the extraordinary recent growth of state-local taxes and employment. These units obviously have been active, but what have they been doing?

Table 2.4. Number of Public Sector Employees (Full and Part-time) by Level of Government, 1950–77

Year	Distribution %				% of Population					% of Civilian Labor Force				
	Fed.	State & Local			Total	Fed.	State & Local			Total	Fed.	State & Local		
		Total	State	Local			Total	State	Local			Total	State	Local
1950	33.1	66.9	16.5	50.4	4.2	1.4	2.8	.7	2.1	10.3	3.4	6.9	1.7	5.2
1960	27.5	72.5	17.3	55.2	4.9	1.3	3.5	.8	2.7	12.7	3.5	9.2	2.2	7.0
1970	22.1	77.9	21.1	56.7	6.4	1.4	5.0	1.4	3.6	15.8	3.5	12.3	3.3	8.9
1979	17.9	82.0	23.1	58.8	7.2	1.3	5.9	1.6	4.2	15.5	2.7	12.7	3.5	9.1

Source: Public employee data from U.S. Department of Commerce 1979a, 10. Civilian labor force data from Economic Report of the President, 1979. Resident population data from Bureau of the Census, various reports.

On Energy and Complexity in State and Local Government

Quite apart from the traditional state-local responsibilities of education, health, highways, and public safety, state political systems clearly have devoted a great deal of attention to the problem of intergovernmental relations during the past four decades. Although the results of these efforts seem largely unappreciated—indeed, they are nearly invisible!—they seem to me to be quite remarkable. Consider table 2.5, which lists the type and number of governments in the United States from 1942 through 1977.[41] In scarcely more than three decades, more than 93,000 school districts have been eliminated, some 2,000 townships have disappeared, while nearly 18,000 new special districts and 2,642 new municipalities have been created. On the average, therefore, over 3,300 government changes of some kind were made each year between 1942 and 1977 in the American states. This record of dynamic reformism seems all the more notable because the processes of change have been continuous. More than 41,000 school districts disappeared in the decade 1942–52, to be sure, but another 17,000 were eliminated between 1952 and 1957, 15,000 more were abandoned by 1962, and the next two census counts reveal further losses of 13,000 and 6,000, respectively. Similarly, special districts have increased steadily, as have municipalities, though in smaller numbers. Whatever else they have been doing these past four decades, state and local politicians obviously have been paying attention to the issue of governmental structure! It is clearly an issue that is *always* on the agenda.

No one who has ever spent time in a statehouse or city hall will find these trends surprising, although the magnitudes may seem unusual. State political systems vary a great deal, but the public sector groups established to articulate various governmental interests—e.g., the municipal leagues, township offi-

Table 2.5.   Types of Governments, 1942–77

Type of Government	Number of Governments							Change in Number 1942–77
	1977	1972	1967	1962	1957	1952	1942	
National	1	1	1	1	1	1	1	0
State	50	50	50	50	48	48	48	2
County	3,042	3,044	3,049	3,043	3,047	3,049	3,050	−8
Municipal	18,862	18,517	18,048	18,000	17,183	16,778	16,220	2,642
Township	16,822	16,991	17,105	17,142	17,198	17,202	18,919	−2,097
School District	15,174	15,781	21,782	34,678	50,446	67,346	108,579	−93,405
Special District	25,962	23,885	21,264	18,323	14,405	12,319	8,299	17,663
Total	79,913	78,269	81,299	91,237	102,328	116,743	155,116	−75,203

Sources: 1977 data from U.S. Department of Commerce 1979, 27. 1972 data from Department of Commerce 1973, 21, table 10. 1942–67 data from U.S. Department of Commerce 1975, 1086.

Note: Alaska and Hawaii are included from 1962 on.

cials' associations, associations of school boards—are an important presence in every state and an important source of initiatives for intergovernmental change. So are the real estate interests, industrial enterprises, and taxpayer groups, each of whom (among others) has a real stake in issues such as what responsibilities will be carried out by which governments on whose tax base. These issues are never finally settled because they cannot be finally settled; environmental or political change guarantees that one interest or another will press for some change every year, hence the continuous nature of organizational change. It is important to remember, nevertheless, that these continuous processes vary greatly from one state to another because of differences in traditions, institutional structures, and values. Illinois, the most "governed" state in the nation in 1942 (15,854 units), had eliminated 9,000 school districts by 1952, then reached a low of 6,453 units in 1962, and has since climbed back up to 6,621 units. Pennsylvania started out with 5,263 units in 1942 and claimed 5,247 in 1977, but along the way had as few as 4,936 units in 1972 and as many as 6,202 in 1962. Tennessee has climbed steadily from 328 units in 1942 to 906 units in 1977.[42] This state-by-state diversity is evident in table 2.6. Seen as a whole, the system is as diverse as it has been dynamic.

Given the comprehensiveness of these governmental changes, it is surprising that so little attention has been paid to their sources and their consequences. A major obstacle, presumably, is the necessity for individual state case studies, which are both expensive and time-consuming. Even a superficial review of these numbers, however, is enough to suggest interesting contrasts. Unlike Illinois, which eliminated most of its school districts by 1952, Michigan achieved the peak of its reorganizational activity from 1953 through 1958, when one school district was being lost every day.[43] This was a period of relative quiescence at the federal level, when the major federal interest was in transferring federal responsibilities to the states, yet some of the states were extremely active: nationwide, 12.3 percent of existing local governments were eliminated, but Nevada eliminated 54.7 percent, Minnesota eliminated 30.2 percent, Tennessee added 28.7 percent, and Michigan lost 23.7 percent. Close examination of trends in each of these states would be necessary to derive conclusions about sources and consequences, and comparison to other states with different dynamics at play would be essential to fill out a more comprehensive analysis.

It is instructive to contemplate the contrast between relative governmental quiescence at the federal level from 1953 through 1958 and the hyperactivity of state-local actions during the same period. Observing Washington only, we might conclude that a very low level of intergovernmental interaction was taking place; when state actions are taken into account, on the other hand, a much higher frequency of intergovernmental activity is revealed. If it were possible to imagine and measure something called "total" frequencies, we might even reach the conclusion that interactions between governments were

Table 2.6.   Changing Number of Governments, 1942–77

Area	Total	School Districts	Special Districts	Municipalities	Townships
Ala.	439	17	278	144	0
Alaska	−0	−0	−0	142	0
Arz.	−78	−167	52	37	0
Ark.	−2,358	−2,264	−187	93	0
Cal.	−342	−1,700	1,231	128	0
Col.	−898	−1,752	831	23	0
Conn.	86	2	101	−4	−5
Del.	141	11	126	4	0
D.C.	0	0	0	0	0
Fla.	409	28	260	122	0
Ga.	318	−34	293	60	0
Ha.	−0	−0	−0	1	0
Ida.	−693	−1,031	291	47	0
Ill.	−9,233	−11,075	1,703	137	1
Ind.	−188	−875	656	40	1
Iowa	−5,666	−4,397	316	22	−1,608
Kan.	−7,389	−8,305	955	36	−75
Ky.	413	−80	374	121	0
La.	−64	−1	−168	106	0
Maine	196	86	144	−27	−7
Md.	220	0	211	9	0
Mass.	358	75	284	0	0
Mi.	−5,472	−5,664	160	52	−20
Minn.	−6,960	−7,233	262	103	−91
Miss.	−956	−1,023	54	13	0
Mo.	−7,802	−8,117	58	183	−2
Mont.	−1,216	−1,467	240	11	0
Neb.	−4,821	−5,814	994	4	−5
Nev.	20	−98	114	5	0
N.H.	−39	−72	33	2	−2
N.J.	375	59	315	4	−3
N.M.	89	−17	76	30	0
N.Y.	−5,029	−5,324	289	8	−2
N.C.	272	0	231	41	0
N.D.	−1,358	−1,926	579	29	−38
Ohio	−735	−1,024	264	45	−18
Okla.	−3,424	−3,893	401	69	0
Ore.	−884	−1,469	539	46	0
Pa.	−16	−1,965	1,944	32	−28
R.I.	67	3	64	1	−1
S.C.	−1,471	−1,651	157	23	0
S.D.	−3,191	−3,229	146	10	−118
Tenn.	578	3	456	121	0
Tex.	−3,476	−5,021	1,116	431	0
Utah	190	0	175	16	0
Ver.	250	248	21	−17	−2
Va.	67	0	51	21	0
Wash.	−239	−846	631	44	−68
W. Va.	270	0	248	22	0
Wis.	−5,989	−6,159	109	61	−1
Wy.	−145	−322	170	7	0
Total	−75,203	−93,405	17,663	2,658	−2,092

Source: Bureau of the Census.

more frequent overall in the mid 1950s than they were during the 1970s. To suggest the idea is to reveal the significance of perspective in seeking to generate such conclusions. To suggest the idea is also to make clear how difficult it is to develop estimates about "more or less" without appropriate baseline measures to guide inference.

Even this brief review of admittedly gross indicators, however, suggests that much of the recent concern over excessive complexity, "hyperin-tergovernmentalization," and supermarbleization is overdrawn. Federal pro-grams and federal grants have increased, to be sure, and the *Catalog of Federal Domestic Assistance* did indeed list more than 1,000 programs, in-cluding 600 or so that provide financial assistance. The basic structure of the federal system of grants was nevertheless never as overwhelming as these numbers suggest. As revealed in figure 2.1, in 1979 only 100 of the grant programs provided fully 95 percent of total grant funds available, hardly an impossible number to comprehend.[44] At the state and local level, meanwhile, the intergovernmental system has become significantly *less* complicated over the last three decades. More than 93,000 school districts and over 2,000 townships have been eliminated, reducing the total number of governments by nearly half. Of the remaining 80,000 or so governments, moreover, some 12,000 of the special districts and 11,000 of the general purpose governments have no employees, and more than 12,000 of the special districts have no taxing power—these units can hardly be regarded as "active" governments. We are thus left with fewer than 60,000 active state and local governments, which have roughly 8 million more employees than in 1955, who are earning more money for an increasing level of skill. This is still a very large number of governments, but if there has been a change in the system over the past

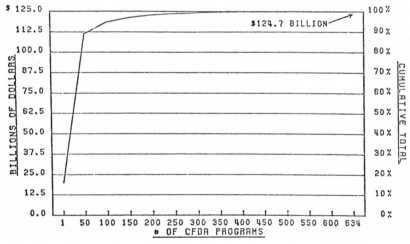

Figure 2.1   Concentration of Federal Assistance, State and Local Eligibility, 1979

several decades, it surely has been in the direction of less structural complexity and more governmental professionalization overall.

On the "Stimulating" Effect of Federal Aid

Most analysts agree that federal aid "stimulates" a higher level of state-local spending than would have occurred without federal funds, although the stimulation effect varies with the type of aid and with the passage of time.[45] To what extent, then, was the expansion of state and local government attributable to federal grants themselves? That federal aid has caused some new activities to be undertaken by states and cities seems undeniable. One way to see this relationship is to borrow a phrase from a study done by Robert Yin and his associates—"counterpart bureaucracy." Yin *et al.* argue that certain federal aid programs induce local governments to create new organizations "in direct response to the initiation (or cessation) of the relevant federal program" (1979, 6:26).[46] These counterpart bureaucracies maintain close relationships with appropriate federal agencies, are typically supported by "soft" (i.e., federal) money, and work to coordinate local participation in some federal program. Although Yin and his colleagues have in mind primarily more recent counterpart organizations such as CETA consortia or CSA agencies, they also recognize that the counterpart pattern has a much longer history. The establishment of local public housing authorities was required by the 1937 public housing legislation; local urban renewal authorities were stimulated by housing acts of 1949 and 1954; all but a handful of today's local and state planning agencies came into existence as a result of funds provided by Section 701 of the 1954 Housing Act; and local Model Cities and Community Action agencies were the result of legislation enacted in the 1960s. In addition, hundreds of regional and metropolitan agencies, from councils of governments to metropolitan transit authorities, have been stimulated by federal legislation in areas such as environmental protection, transportation, and health. It is therefore clear that federal programs have had a very important impact on state-local government structure, on the actors who become involved in the determination of program and budgetary priorities, and thus on the processes of state-local politics.

It is also clear that a variety of social and economic pressures caused state-local expansion independent of any federal action. Federal government civilian employment as a proportion of total government employment reached a post-1945 peak of 46 percent in 1951, after which the federal share steadily declined to its present 17.9 percent. State-local employment expansion thus began in the early 1950s and expanded by an annual average of more than 200,000 employees between 1951 and 1959. Most (80 percent) of this expansion was local, and much of that for schools, as school districts hired more teachers to keep up with expanding pupil enrollments. All this, I should emphasize, took place years before any significant expansion of the federal role in public education, years before the explosion of social programs in the 1960s, and a decade before the really large increment in federal aid during the 1970s. The metropolitan explosion around large cities also became a major social force in the 1950s, causing added pressure for more local engineers, planners, and other officials to handle problems associated with urban growth. If federal stimulus has been important, so too have the factors causing population growth and suburbanization, both of which elicited active responses from state and local governments across the nation.

On the Constraining Power of Federal Grants

Some analysts appear to believe that a state-local response to a federal grant program is less legitimate than a response to an economic or social problem arising from the immediate environment. Participation in a federal program is often said to "distort" local or state priorities, directing them away from local needs and toward nonlocal definitions of purpose. If a municipality creates a community development agency to run a housing program it otherwise would not operate, or if a state creates a criminal justice planning agency to distribute funds for crime prevention that might otherwise be used in the absence of federal money, one could argue that these are distortions. The fact that a number of local programs begun with federal "seed money" are later abandoned when federal funds are withdrawn suggests that such distortions do in fact take place. On the other hand, federal grants are often designed in ways that minimize their distorting effects, and there is considerable empirical evidence to show that such effects vary a good deal with the design characteristics of various federal programs. The important question is thus not so much whether federal programs distort local priorities in general, but rather, Under what conditions do federal grant programs result in changes in state or local behavior?

It is important to remember that some two-thirds of all federal grants historically have been distributed according to some formula, usually one that includes population among its terms. Many of these grants have gone to state governments, which in turn have distributed many of them to lower-level units. If there was distortion here at all, it could hardly have been attributed to federal programs. Moreover, during the early 1970s there was a noticeable expansion of block grants and formula-based grants (i.e., GRS) to local governments as well. Even grants aimed at some specific purpose have seldom stated purposes with enough clarity to be wholly restrictive, because support is far easier to build if goals remain vague.[47]

Quite apart from the diffuseness of federal program goals, however, the existing maze of state and local revenue and expenditure account structures, often pegged to fiscal years different from the federal fiscal year period, render it extraordinarily difficult for the federal government (or anybody else) to track federal program dollars as they "move" between governments and within governments across account entries.[48] The federal government never has had a comprehensive information system capable of monitoring how much money has been or is being spent in FY A, on program B, by agency C, within state D, in locality E, for purpose F. Nor has it employed a sufficiently large and well financed (let alone politically supported) core of program auditors to comprehensively enforce federal regulations on the uses of federal monies.[49] State and local governments have always been more free to decide how to spend federal funds than many recent critics of federal programs appear to believe.[50]

The uses of this freedom are documented for one of the largest categorical programs—public assistance—in a host of studies dating back at least to the early 1960s, virtually all of which either assume or document the enormous variety of welfare policies among the states. Explanations for this variety range from rather primitive statistical studies that relate welfare policy characteristics and socioeconomic conditions to the more sophisticated political explanations offered by Gilbert Y. Steiner. By examining cases of federal-state conflict over welfare policy and showing how such conflicts are resolved, Steiner provides persuasive insights into the development of "priorities" that are neither state nor federal, but state-federal (1966, 1971, 1976). A similarly fascinating insight is provided by Michael Preston in his study of California's federally assisted manpower program (1984). Tracing the development of that program for more than a decade, Preston describes the state's political victory over federal legislation and Department of Labor regulations, the transformation of state manpower programs that resulted, and the ultimate retreat to an earlier policy as the new initiative lost political support.

George Greenberg's 1979 study of the implementation of two federal programs (Partnership for Health and Early and Periodic Screening, Diagnosis, and Treatment) in three states (Michigan, Pennsylvania, and Alabama) provides a marvelously detailed recitation of very different political processes, a valuable insight into why federal agencies know so little about such differences (states report the disposition of federal funds for reasons of administrative convenience rather than to show actual uses), and this major conclusion:

> The principal finding for both 314(d) and EPSDT is that decisionmakers in the relevant state agencies acted "autonomously" without much direct influence from the legislature, the governor's office, medical providers, or outside interest groups. Nevertheless, the "autonomous" choices made by state officials were heavily constrained by pre-existing factors beyond their control. In the case of 314(d) such factors consisted of the accounting procedures of the state health department, the degree of detail with which the state legislature budgeted health department funds, the organizational placement of state health programs, the extent of county health department dependence on state health funds, and the uncertainty of continued federal funding. In the case of EPSDT, such factors consisted of the pre-existing

relationships established between the health and welfare departments, the staff capacity and professional competence of the agencies responsible for maternal and child health programs, the strength of the Medicaid program (level of fees, data capacities, provider participation), county health department autonomy, and others. A unique combination of constraints produced a different context of choice for each program in each state. (5–6)

Studies of this kind are valuable not simply because they portray interstate variety in the constraining effects of federal program requirements; they also make clear that the main sources of variation in the impact of federal strings are enormous differences in political-administrative processes from one state to another.

Municipal governments appear no less vital and no less able to bend federal program requirements to their own ends. Comprehensive studies of GRS by the University of Michigan, which surveyed 817 local units (Juster 1977)[51] and studied 5 cities in detail (Anton, Larkey, Linton, et al. 1975; Larkey 1975, 1979), and by the Brookings Institution, which conducted field studies in 57 local jurisdictions, as well as other research, has made clear that GRS uses were predominantly determined by local conditions and priorities.[52] While this conclusion might have been expected for GRS, which had no clear federal priorities attached, it has also been shown to be largely true for more constrained programs such as ESEA (Porter, Warner, and Porter 1973), CETA (Nathan et al. 1978; Cook 1979; Nathan et al. 1979), or CDBG (Nathan et al. 1977; Dommel et al. 1978, forthcoming; Dommel 1979). Indeed, the use of such programs to meet local rather than federal purposes has often been the major source of dissatisfaction with them. Studies in 12 cities led by the Brookings Institution show why local priorities can prevail:[53] local administrative and accounting procedures vary so much that knowledge of federal fund disposition is difficult to obtain, whereas federal "purposes" are typically flexible enough to accommodate a wide variety of local uses, providing plentiful opportunities to mix federal and local dollars. As a result, local officials are often able to "package" grants from a variety of programs to support a single local project. In the five-city study noted earlier, for example, Yin and his colleagues note that 13 of the 16 projects they examined had received federal assistance and that, of the 13 federally aided projects, 10 involved grants from more than one federal program.

The most prominent combinations were the different programs administered by EDA (e.g., Title I, 302, and local public works), different programs administered by HUD (e.g., urban renewal, historic preservation, disaster relief and CDBG), or a combination of EDA and HUD programs; this pattern may be increased in the next few years with the availability of funds under the UDAG program which, like CDBG monies, may be used in combination with existing federal programs. (1979, 7:7–8)

None of this should be taken to mean that federal programs are without constraining impact on state and local governments. Federal programs cause funds to be expended, agencies to be created, and policies to be pursued by lower-level governments that, without federal insistence, would not engage in such activities. But federal program influence is a variable, not a constant, and cannot be understood if the interactions between program managers and thousands of local or state implementing agencies are ignored. By treating federal programs as both pervasive and all-powerful, recent critics have turned attention away from a growing literature that has begun to give us some understanding of the conditions under which federal programs are more or less influential in local or state settings. Economists have shown that the type of grant instrument (i.e., formula vs. project grant, general purpose vs. categorical) makes a difference (Gramlich and Galper 1973) and political analysts have made clear that political structure (MacManus 1983; organization process (Greenberg 1979; Larkey 1979), and fiscal condition (Anton 1983) affect the uses and impact of federal grant programs by local and state governments. The challenge ahead is to move beyond polemics to a more systematic investigation of these, and perhaps other, conditions that determine the constraining power of federal programs.

On State-Local Management Capacity

The multiplication of grant programs, granting agencies, and local "counterpart" organizations has led some writers to wonder whether federal fragmentation has been exported to lower units, causing a loss in local management capacity. There can be little question, of course, that local government is a complicated undertaking, particularly in large cities, and that multiple federal programs can and do contribute to this complexity. Pressman and Wildavsky's (1974) celebrated case study portrays this set of problems with particular effectiveness. But the fragmentation of urban governance predates the upsurge of federal aid by a considerable period, as a study such as the one conducted by Sayre and Kaufman (1965) makes clear, and cases of management failure can be matched by cases of extraordinary success, as evident in works by Caro (1975) and Banfield (1965). There is some evidence, in fact, that recent increments of federal aid have *enhanced,* rather than detracted from local ability to coordinate and control resources. Studies in cities as different as St. Louis, Phoenix, Detroit, and Houston all suggest that the visibility of large federal program dollars has motivated increased attention by mayors and councils, leading often to an increased level of general coordination of otherwise fragmented programs.

A major difficulty, I suspect, is a naive presumption that the absence of visible efforts to coordinate implies an absence of coordination. An important work by Warren, Rose, and Bergunder (1974), later confirmed by Sonenblum, Kirlin, and Ries (1977), makes clear that conflict among the organizations of urban governance in some metropolitan areas is the exception rather than the rule, that each organizational unit has a "turf" that is well understood by other units, and that tacit coordination among units takes the form of refusal to invade another unit's turf except under extreme conditions. If these studies are right, visible horizontal coordination is seldom necessary—indeed, visible conflicts over jurisdictional space are a sign that existing coordination has broken down. Yin and his colleagues note that such visible coordination seldom occurs (i.e., is not visible), but they go on to make the very important point that coordination across time rather than across units is often visible and almost always a product of local rather than higher-level initiatives. In using federal funds, they write,

> the distinctive characteristic . . . at the local level has been *longitudinal rather than cross-sectional coordination*. A grant from one federal program, for instance, will be combined with monies from another federal program in the following year; similarly, funds from grant programs and bond issues may be used in a complementary manner over a period of time. . . . The problem of keeping a project in operation often translates into the ability to maintain project support over a period of time. (italics in original) (1979, 7:2)

Longitudinal coordination often takes place in imaginative ways. Milwaukee's inability to clear a site containing a registered landmark resulted in demolition of the site by the private owner, city purchase of the cleared site using CDBG funds, and use of LPW grant funds to construct new commercial facilities. The Detroit City Council approved an administration plan to use CDBG grants in 1980 and 1981 to secure a loan necessary to complete its new waterfront sports arena; inability to market a proposed bond issue was the immediate stimulus for this action. One may disagree with the substance of these kinds of actions without losing any appreciation for their imaginative approaches to problem solving.

On the "Success" of Federal Grants

Consideration of how federal grant dollars are actually used in local and state environments challenges the belief that most federal programs have been ineffective. Evidence of program ineffectiveness is not difficult to find but, as Yin and his associates point out, much of that evidence takes the form of contrasts between statements of program goals and reports of the use made of particular awards. The difficulty with such evidence is that local officials think in terms of projects, rather than individual awards, using multiple awards from any reasonable source to support an ongoing project to completion. To properly evaluate an individual award, therefore, an individual grant must be placed within a project context. "An award-oriented research design, which typifies most federal evaluation studies, is likely to produce misleading results because it will probably fail to capture the dynamics at the more aggregate project level" (1979, 7:12). If Yin et al. are correct, judgments about program inadequacy may reflect little more than conceptual inadequacy on the part of the evaluators.

Nowhere is this conceptual inadequacy more clear than in the treatment of time in program evaluation. Programs are often evaluated without any consideration of the time period within which one might expect an impact to be felt. Yet the passage of time is absolutely crucial to the formulation of judgment. In 1967 Martin Anderson published a blistering critique of federal urban renewal programs, then a decade old. The program was shown to have destroyed more housing units than it replaced, to have become a program of "black removal" in many places, to have distributed federal subsidies to persons and groups with absolutely no need for subsidy, and to have done little to check the continuing decay of central cities. It is fair to say, I think, that these intensely critical images have dominated public perceptions of the urban renewal program ever since.

A later paper by Haywood T. Sanders (1979), however, challenged each of these images. Observing urban renewal for its entire history, 1949–74, Sanders found the imbalance between housing units destroyed and units replaced to be far smaller than had been suggested, that 40.2 percent of the 98,000 acres of land acquired under the program were devoted to new housing as of December 1974, that though 57.9 percent of *families* displaced by urban renewal were black or other minority, 55.5 percent of the *individuals* displaced were white, and that "of the new housing units actually underway or completed from 1950 through June 1972, almost 55 percent are specifically designed for low- and moderate-income families, using both federal and state subsidy programs" (7). Sanders documented extraordinary variety in local renewal programs and showed that federal imposition of tighter constraints in 1967 actually increased local participation in the program (31). Land clearance and redevelopment take time, and some cities operated very poor and ineffective programs, but it would be quite difficult to conclude from Sanders's analysis that urban renewal as a whole was anything close to a "failure." The crucial and largely unanswered question remains, Under what conditions are various federal programs more or less successful?

The variable impact of time on evaluative judgment is also clearly revealed in Greenberg's analysis of health program implementation in three states. If the term *overload* has any meaning at all, surely it must refer to Pennsylvania's condition at the time it undertook to implement the Early and Periodic Screening, Diagnosis, and Treatment Program. Greenberg notes that welfare bureaucrats were already burdened by "crushing caseloads" but that "at the time EPSDT was implemented, the state was under a hiring freeze. Even without a freeze additional positions were not budgeted. At the time EPSDT was implemented, the Pennsylvania welfare department also had to implement SSI, nursing homes had to be reinspected and recertified as a result of local scandals, the state was attempting to separate the staffs of county boards of assistance into eligibility determination and social services workers, and the 1974–75 recession was increasing the number of applications for assistance" (1979, 211–12). Shortly after implementation, both the Pennsylvania Welfare Rights Organization and state physicians began legal proceedings to challenge state action. Not surprisingly, implementation did not go well. Years passed before the program began to function at all. Had "evaluation" been attempted within the first two years of the program it could only have been judged a failure. By the end of four years, however, the difficulties had been worked out, screening rates exceeded those in Michigan (which had implemented very smoothly), and Greenberg judges the Pennsylvania program to be one of the best in the country. Judgments depend on "when" no less than "what" in evaluating a program's success or failure.

On the Two Faces (at Least) of Dependency

It should now be apparent that much of the current concern about the state of intergovernmental relations in the United States is derived from stereotyped images of national centralization. A narrow focus on Washington encourages a belief that any program enacted in the Capitol is a program immediately implemented in 50 states and 80,000 local governments at the snap of a federal finger, as it were. Or, the common presumption that "he who pays the piper calls the tune" sustains a conviction that large increments in federal grant funds imply similar increments in federal control over local and state action. The federal government, according to these stereotypes, has become dominant, while state and local governments have become almost totally dependent and therefore incapable of effective action.

There is, of course, some merit to these beliefs. In table 2.7 it is clear that many of the largest and oldest American cities became fiscally dependent on federal dollars. When such dollars account for 40 to 50 percent or more of local budgets, it is difficult to imagine how federal funds could be withdrawn without doing serious damage to local operations. Even in these cities, however, the available evidence suggests that fiscal dependence does *not* imply program or political dependence. Whether federal dollars coerce local program activities or not depends on a variety of nonfinancial factors, including program character, local organizational structure, local values, political skill, implementation process, and others. In public education, long the most carefully regulated and professionalized public service, state funding dominance has little to do with the extent to which state rather than local control is exercised. Thus Wirt's careful and exhaustive analysis of this relationship finds "no support for the common belief that 'Control follows the dollar.' " Wirt continues

> This argument is *not* that the states fail to exercise control over their local schools; they do and extensively so. . . . But there is variation in this control, a considerable variation reflective of the heterogeneous history of our people. It is in explanation of why that variation exists that this paper differs from the folklore, for with cross-sectional data of considerable range and potential explanatory power, there is little support for that belief. . . . The linkage between . . . [authority and revenue] is today so tenuous as to be not characteristic of school policy in the American states. (1978, 23–24)

Table 2.7.   Federal Revenue as Percentage of Total General Revenue, Selected
Large Cities, FY 1964–65 and 1976–77

City	1976–77	1964–65
New York	6.54	1.25
Chicago	19.76	3.13
Los Angeles	17.74	1.26
Philadelphia	20.27	4.34
Detroit	23.74	4.67
Houston	12.23	2.29
Baltimore	15.93	2.96
Dallas	13.34	0
San Diego	20.22	1.71
San Antonio	32.81	2.36
Indianapolis	21.18	1.18
District of Columbia	44.90	26.29
Honolulu	32.38	4.12
Milwaukee	13.19	1.77
Phoenix	21.10	2.05
San Francisco	16.04	1.12
Memphis	19.38	.54
Cleveland	32.40	3.87
Boston	13.86	9.29
New Orleans	25.97	4.77
Columbus	19.79	4.00
St. Louis	19.51	.32
Seattle	21.28	.15
Denver	14.12	1.45
Kansas City	23.97	4.70
Pittsburgh	24.62	13.75
Atlanta	10.25	14.27
Cincinnati	17.95	9.69
Buffalo	28.36	1.61
Minneapolis	19.40	.54
Omaha	30.40	.37
Toledo	29.23	2.56
Oklahoma City	36.66	16.92
Fort Worth	29.24	4.25
Portland	25.35	.73
Newark	12.64	.09
Louisville	39.24	12.97
Long Beach	11.38	.08
Oakland	33.23	2.84

Source: U.S. Department of Commerce, Bureau of the Census, *City Government Finances,* for
FY 1976–77 and 1964–65.

These are similar to conclusions now beginning to emerge from studies of
European political systems, where central government grants and local expenditures have expanded together.[54] Although central government control is
sometimes decisive in shaping local priorities, as in the case of public housing
finance in Britain (McKay and Cox 1979), the larger and more professionalized local governments of Western Europe are equally able to impose
their own priorities in opposition to national plans. In Italy, where scholars

typically have assumed that local governments exercise little discretion, Sbragia has shown that the city of Milan's policy makers

> have been able to formulate and implement housing programmes which differed in important respects from national policies. They have provided a reliable source of funding for housing construction in contrast to the erratic funding provided by the national government. They have given higher priority than national policy makers to public housing; they have introduced a new construction technology: and they have geared housing programmes towards lower income groups rather than to the relatively more affluent groups favoured by the national governing coalition. (1979, 315)

In Sweden, national government grants now account for more than 25 percent of local income, but local policies in housing or social services vary enormously.[55] In France, which still retains some 36,000 local governments, big city mayors have become system regulators who, according to Crozier and Thoenig, "dictate their wishes to the local branches of state agencies. They act as regulators of neighboring communities, and the equal of the prefects— the prefects having lost their advantages as the natural spokesmen in Paris" (1976, 560–61). In West Germany a federal policy of regional revival, to be planned by *Länder* for local government (*Gemeinden*) implementation, was controlled and manipulated by local units, some of whom were prepared to reject *Land* grants rather than follow *Land* directives. Baestlein et al. (1978), who chronicle these events, point out that local reluctance to accept state grants posed a serious problem for the granting agency, whose main business was to dispose of the grant money. Grantors, in short, need grantees as much as grantees need funds for implementation. As Key noted in the 1930s, and as Pressman emphasized some years ago and Rhodes recently reaffirmed, dependence in multiorganizational systems is a two-way street.[56]

Mutual dependence implies not only that local actors can manipulate national initiatives but that local initiatives can become sources of national policies. Model cities and community action programs of the 1960s were largely products of local initiatives, and GRS was heavily supported and lobbied through Congress by local interests. Indeed, Martha Derthick's remarkable study, *Uncontrollable Spending for Social Services Grants* (1975) makes clear that the local initiative behind GRS was a dual thrust, only part of which was the visible lobby. The more fascinating source was the discovery, by a California state official, of a loophole in the 1962 welfare amendments that in effect permitted states to "milk" the federal treasury for unlimited sums for essentially general purpose support. As this discovery spread to other states, particularly Illinois, expenditures exploded, ultimately causing Congress to seek some mechanism for capping them. State-local agreement to a cap was part of the deal that produced GRS. From the federal point of view, the whole episode was a chaotic mess, but it is difficult not to be impressed by the imaginative—and profitable—initiatives of state officials.

CONCLUSION: TOWARD INNOVATION

Although American intergovernmental relations are always on the political agenda, rarely do they achieve the sustained interest of national, state, and local officials exhibited during the past several years. Even more rarely are proposals for comprehensive restructuring of federal-state relations offered by the nation's chief elected official. It is all the more disappointing, therefore, that the literature reviewed here has so little to contribute to this continuing debate. Global analyses focused on Washington repeatedly assert that some fundamental change, usually for the worse, has occurred or is occurring, without attempting to clarify the concept of change and without attempting to marshal the detailed evidence that would be required to sustain such judgments. On examination, most of these analyses reflect largely implicit preferences for a political system different from the evolving uncertainties of American federalism: hierarchy rather than polyarchy, clarity rather than ambiguity, simplicity rather than complexity, stability rather than uncertainty. In a real sense these preferences represent a protest against change more than an analysis of it.

A substantial number of available empirical studies challenge the hazy ambiguities of globalist thought. American governments have expanded significantly in size and cost, but the public sector continues to consume a smaller share of the national product in the United States than in most other advanced industrial nations. And, though federal government spending is considerably larger than state and local government spending, the real growth in public sector employment during the past three decades has occurred among state and local governments, which have become larger and more professionalized even as they have been reformed to eliminate thousands of unnecessary units. The federal government clearly has been a major influence in these developments through grants-in-aid, which have become a significant source of both state and local government revenue, and complaints about associated audit and reporting requirements. However, vaguely defined program goals, increased reliance on block grants rather than categorical grants, and federal reluctance to closely monitor federal fund use all have combined to give state and local governments considerable freedom in determining their uses of federal dollars. Public sector funding appears to have become more centralized, in other words, while decentralized control over program priorities has been largely retained.

These conclusions imply that the major change in intergovernmental relations has been expansion in the scope of governmental responsibility *in general*, rather than any significant alteration in traditional American patterns of multilevel program administration. Opposition to governmental growth appears to have placed the issue of federalism on the agenda once again. Now that we have entered a period of reduced growth, or even decline, it remains to be seen whether interest in the issue can be sustained. To sustain that interest, scholars will have to recognize that much of what is most significant about American federalism occurs outside of Washington, D.C., that there is pattern as well as variety in relations among governmental units, and that, more than anything else, we need to develop analytic concepts capable of organizing the wealth of available information into general statements regarding system structure and change. If we can do so, politics as well as scholarship may be enhanced.

NOTES

1. I focus here on the United States; more generally, however, the same set of ideas informs the early European writings on the determinants of public sector change (i.e., Wagner's Law) and has heavily influenced later studies. For a fruitful treatment of the evolution of these ideas, see Tarschys 1975. The same ideas also permeate the "modernization" literature; for an analysis of American federalism which draws on this set of ideas, see Beer (1973).

2. On the Kestnbaum Commission, see also Anderson (1955, 1956); on the Joint Federal-State Action Committee, see also Grodzins (1960a, 267–68).

3. As a political belief, the notion of sorting out "proper" functional assignments among levels of government may be more or less attractive, but this idea provides neither analytic nor practical help in determining the appropriate division of functions. As Austin MacDonald has convincingly argued for the American case: "The concept of a function as national or local varies with time and place. Highway construction may properly have been a local obligation only three decades ago; the advent of the automobile may have transformed it overnight into a matter of national concern. Public health may properly be a national function in the United States and a local function in another country, because of widely varying conditions" (1928a, 253–54). Such recurrent attention to what MacDonald referred to as "metaphysical distinctions concerning local and national functions" (254) consistently has been proven to be of little value in understanding, let alone engineering, intergovernmental change because it has been repeatedly demonstrated to be "a principle that is impossible of application" (254). For a similar assessment of the British case, see Webb (1920, 89–94).

4. See also Friedman's 1978 article and, more generally, the line of reasoning he presents in *Capitalism and Freedom* (1962). See also Meltzer and Richard (1978).

5. It is instructive to note, as Rose and Peters have (1978, 265), that disaster was once predicted if public sector expenditures were to consume more than 25 percent of the national product; see Clark (1945). Over the years, as governmental expenditures have increased, the threshold that *must* not be crossed lest liberty, freedom, and democracy be lost and political bankruptcy occur has commensurately been raised, with 60 percent being the current market ratio.

6. Lane and Lofgren (1979, 148). I call attention to the ratio of public expenditures to GNP in Sweden to underline our view that ratios of governmental financial activities to GNP provide nothing more than first approximations of the relative importance of public sector activities across time and space. They provide no meaningful yardsticks by which to measure the "desirability" or "dangerousness" of governmental activities; such judgments turn on the value placed on individual governmental expenditure program efforts. To further illustrate this point, consider the U.S. case for FY 1978: taken together, federal budget outlays ($461 billion), outstanding loans and loan guarantees ($440 billion), and tax expenditures ($124 billion) plus the $302 billion

raised and spent by state and local governments amounted to roughly 60 percent of the U.S. GNP ($2.1 trillion)—the threshold Friedman has argued represents a loss of liberty. Few would seriously argue, however, that liberty was lost in the United States in FY 1978.

7. For insightful critiques of this body of writing, see Etzioni (1977/78), McKay (1979), and Wirt (1979). More generally, see Steinfils (1979).

8. Contrast the differing assessments of the Great Society programs set forth in *Commentary* (1973), Ginzberg and Solow (1974), Glazer and Kristol (1976), and Levitan and Taggart (1976, 1976/77). For an insightful comparative assessment of the U.S. Welfare "crisis," see Rein and Heclo (1973).

9. See also Anderson (1980), and, more generally, Walker (1978). The Anderson, Beam, and Colella overviews of this theme are summary presentations of ACIR's recent five-year, ten-volume study of the changing role of the federal government. Although the ACIR study included case studies of program evolution in seven major functional areas, the systematic, empirical investigation of the range of possible effects of the evolving federal presence on state houses, municipal buildings, and polling places across the land was beyond the scope of ACIR's review.

10. Commenting on the events of the 1960s, for example, one writer (Drucker 1969) even claimed that the government seemed able only to make war and inflation—and the writer was not totally convinced about the government's ability to make war.

11. It should also be recalled that federal land grant policies in the nineteenth century played a large role in state and local politics through their influence on land use patterns; see, for example, Gates (1954).

12. The term *imperial presidency* is, of course, Schlesinger's (1974). It is worth noting that the same set of ideas and assumptions that permeates the intergovernmental literature informs the presidential literature; see Cronin (1970).

13. Even writers who dissent from the shift of power to Washington thesis frame their analyses as defenses of the role of the states; see Rockefeller (1962) and Sanford (1967).

14. During the period about which MacDonald was writing, the modern grant system was just being established and patterns of interaction among officials from all levels of government were just being institutionalized. These facts underline the political significance of the expanding levels of grant assistance MacDonald noted.

15. For analyses of the expansion and geographic distribution of federal aid, see Anton (1980a, 1980b); Anton, Cawley, and Kramer (1980).

16. See also Burdick (1923); Corwin (1923); esp. Charles A. Reich's excellent treatment of this theme in a series of articles (1964, 1965, 1966a, 1966b).

17. Stanfield (1980) presents a good, brief summary of this line of argument.

18. For discussions of the importance of single-issue interest groups, see, among others, Heclo (1979); and Wilson (1979). For intriguing treatments of the role of professional communities of policy experts in program advocacy, see Walker (1974, 1976, 1977); Heclo (1979).

19. Tarschys's argument is presented in his 1975 article in *Scandinavian Political Studies*. For a more detailed elaboration, see Daniel Tarschys and Maud Edwards, *Petita: Hur svenska myndigheter argumenterar for högre anslag* (Budget requests: How Swedish agencies argue for higher appropriations) (Stockholm: Liber Förlag, 1975).

20. Beer (1978) sees the professional bureaucratic complex and intergovernmental lobby as countervailing forces because they tend to seek different types of aid—i.e., categorical versus block grant. *Topocrat* is the word Beer and Macridis propose in order to avoid the mouth-filling phrase "state and local government official."

21. Beer (1976) defines private sector politics as "the behavior of individuals and groups trying to influence government in their private capacities" (127–28), and public sector politics as "the behavior of people and groups trying to influence government in their public capacities" (128).

22. It may be useful to recall that the original highway grant program emerged from a bill that had been drafted by the National Association of Highway Engineers following an extended period

of lobbying by public and private groups (MacDonald 1928a, 89–90; see also Dearing 1942 for a discussion of these lobbying efforts). More generally, see Elazar (1962) and Wilson (1976) for treatments of nineteenth-century bureaucratic politics. There is also a large body of research on various policy communities' activities in promoting social welfare legislation in the early twentieth century.

23. See the discussions of the national budgeting process prior to the Budget and Accounting Act of 1921 in Willoughby (1927), Marvick (1952), Smithies (1955).

24. See, for example, Key (1937). The New Deal programs sparked a vast literature on the administration of federal programs which sheds light on this theme.

25. See Baker (1939), Kile (1948), and Block (1960).

26. The role of the federal government's policies in stimulating policy innovation at state and local levels by altering the political resources (i.e., money, legal precedent, propaganda work) available to various actors in their attempts to define state and local politics in the early twentieth century merits mention in light of the recent debate over whether or not federal policies have fostered policy innovation at the state and local levels. See, for example, the debate between Walker (1969, 1971, 1973), who discounts the federal role, and Gray (1973a, 1973b), who suggests its importance. A large body of research done in the 1920s and 1930s attests to the innovative role of federal policies in the adoption and alteration of state and local policies over time (albeit the degree of federal influence was acknowledged to vary across space, time, and issue, and the question of whether the federal government was accruing too much power was a source of disagreement). For a small sampling of this literature, see Arneson (1922), MacDonald (1928a, 1928b, 1931, 1940), Graves (1934, 1936a, 1936b, 1938), Key (1937, 1940), and Clark (1938).

27. Jeremy F. Plant, National Associations of State, City, and County Officials, *University of Virginia Newsletter* 50 (6) (1974); 22, as cited by Beer 1976, 166, table 8.

28. See, for example, Martin (1965), Elazar (1967), Farkas (1971), and Caro (1975). More generally, on 1930s federal-local program arrangements, see also J. Williams (1936, 1939), E. Williams (1939), and Williams and Williams (1940).

29. For a flavor of this work, see Schmitter (1974, 1977).

30. Fesler (1949), and Kaufman (1967, 1973) present excellent analyses of the types of divisions that permeate the professional bureaucratic complex.

31. See, for instance, Farkas (1971).

32. Dommel (1974) convincingly documents these disagreements. On more recent disagreements, see Myers and Shannon (1979) and Stanfield (1979).

33. For a start, see Surrey (1957, 1970, 1973) (on tax expenditures), and Stern (1964, 1973); Lowi (1974, 1978, 1979), and Anton, Cawley, and Kramer (1980).

34. More generally, Henry Aaron (1978) provides an instructive assessment of the conservative force of scholarly research. See also Etzioni (1977/78, McKay (1979), and Wirt (1979).

35. On the recent politics of social security, see Derthick (1979).

36. Courant, Gramlich, and Rubinfeld (1979a, 35). See also Citrin's (1979) analysis of Proposition 13 in California.

37. Kaufman (1956).

38. A note on expenditure, revenue, and employment figures: There is no one "official" source of information reporting federal, state, and local government expenditure, revenue and employment patterns. Often there are two or more official sources yielding somewhat divergent images. The choice of which figures to use, thus, will affect resultant analyses, as will decisions about how to combine and present these figures (i.e., actual vs. per capita or ratio/percentage arrays of expenditure or revenue numbers), and how long a time period to cover. In interpreting the numbers we present below (as well as, more generally, the figures presented elsewhere in the literature), we urge the reader to keep these cautions in mind. For a detailed discussion of these issues with regard to federal expenditure patterns, see Anton, Cawley, and Kramer (1980).

39. The following calculations are based on public employee data from the 1957 and 1977 *Census of Governments*, and the 1980 *Statistical Abstract of the United States*.

40. Calculations are based on data in the Office of Management and Budget, *Federal Government Finances: January 1979 Edition* (Washington, D.C.: OMB, 1979, mimeographed).

41. A word of caution to the reader: the Census Bureau reports somewhat different units of government totals in its various reports. Following the bureau's definitions, in this paper *school districts* refers only to independent districts, not dependent school districts.

42. Calculations are based on Census Bureau governmental organization data, unless otherwise noted.

43. Calculations are based on data from the Department of Public Instruction (later Department of Education), State of Michigan, *An Analysis of the Receipts and Expenditures of the Michigan Public Schools,* Bulletin no. 1011 (Lansing: Michigan Department of Education, 1944/45–1977/78); and Michigan School Finance Study, a report by J. Alan Thomas, *School Finance And Educational Opportunity in Michigan* (Lansing; Michigan Department of Education, 1968), 298, 304.

44. It is also worth noting that of the 92 provisions in the tax laws, which are estimated to yield $206 billion tax expenditures in FY 1981, just 12 provisions will account for 69 percent of the $206 billion tax expenditures.

45. For useful reviews of the literature, see Gramlich (1970, 1977) and Gramlich and Galper (1973).

46. See also Yin (1980).

47. See Anton (1979b, 1980b) for elaborations of this argument.

48. See Anton (1964, 1966, 1979a). See Hale and Douglass (1977) and Larkey (1979) on the difficulty of tracking federal funds at state and local levels.

49. See, for instance, Congressional Budget Office (1976) and General Accounting Office (1979, 1980).

50. Since the 1920s there has been recurrent concern with what V. O. Key (1940) called (referring to Graves [1934, 1936a, 1936b, 1938]) "the fact of Federal influence—a matter of general significance in the evolution of federalism—rather than with the differentiation of situations in which that influence occurs" (7). Most of the recent expression of concern over the growth of federal program and cross-cutting regulations is of this genre. For illustrations, see Walker (1978), Heclo (1979), Anderson (1980), and Stanfield (1980). This type of study seldom responds to Key's call to probe deeply into the issue of whether, and under what conditions, certain federal regulations are enforced, by whom, and why. Significantly, however, a large body of studies has tackled these questions and yields substantively different images of the "constraining influence" of federal grants. See, for example, Arneson (1922), based on a survey of state officials; National Municipal League Committee on Federal Aid to the States (MacDonald 1928b), also based on a survey; MacDonald's own case studies (1928a); Key's intensive research (1937, 1940); and more recent works by Derthick (1970, 1972); Porter and Warner (1972); Porter, Warner, and Porter (1973); Murphy (1974); Greenberg (1979).

51. For a summary review of this report, see Juster and Anton (1977).

52. See also the Brookings Monitoring studies on GRS.: Nathan, Manvel, Calkins, *et al.* (1975), Nathan, Adams, et al. (1977), and Adams and Crippen (1978).

53. Reports are available on Houston (MacManus (1979), Phoenix (Hall 1979), and St. Louis (Schmandt, Wendel, and Tomey 1979). Forthcoming reports will focus on the following cities: Boston, Chicago, Cleveland, Detroit, Los Angeles, Rochester, and Tulsa. An analytic study of these reports, James W. Fossett's *Federal Grants in American Cities: The Politics of Dependence,* will also be published by the Brookings Institution.

54. For a review of this literature, see McKay (1980).

55. On the recent growth of national transfers in Sweden, see Anton (1977). For interesting evidence of local variation in social policy, independent of fund flows see Benny Hjern, *Statsbidrag som styrmetod: Problem vid implementeringen av en bostadssocial policy* (National grants as a steering method: Problems in the implementation of a social housing policy) (Gothenberg, Sive.: C. W. K. Gleerup, 1979).

56. Key (1937), Pressman (1975), and Rhodes (1979).

REFERENCES

Aaron, Henry J. 1978. *Politics and the Professors: The Great Society in Perspective.* Washington, D.C.: Brookings Institution.

Adams, Charles F. Jr., and Dan L. Crippen. 1978. The Fiscal Impact of General Revenue Sharing on Local Governments. Paper prepared for the U.S. Department of the Treasury in conjunction with the Brookings Institution's Monitoring Studies Group, August 15; rev. less technical version in *America's Changing Federalism* (tent.) ed. Richard P. Nathan and James W. Fossett. Forthcoming.

Anderson, Martin. 1967. *The Federal Bulldozer.* New York: McGraw-Hill; originally published by MIT Press, 1964.

Anderson, Wayne F. 1980. Intergovernmental Aid: Relief or Intrusion? *National Civic Review* 69(3): 127–32.

Anderson, William. 1955. *The Nation and the States: Rivals or Partners?* Minneapolis: University of Minnesota Press.

———. 1956. The Commission on Intergovernmental Relations and the United States Federal System. *Journal of Politics* 18(2): 211–31.

Anton, Thomas J. 1964. *Budgeting in Three Illinois Cities.* Urbana: Institute of Government and Public Affairs, University of Illinois.

———. 1966. *The Politics of State Expenditures in Illinois.* Urbana and London: University of Illinois Press.

———. 1977. Notes on Swedish National Government Grants to Local Governments. Unpublished paper, University of Michigan.

———. 1979a. Data Systems for Urban Fiscal Policy: Toward Reconstruction. Paper presented at the NSF. Conference on Comparative Urban Research, Chicago, April 26–27.

———. 1979b. Notes on Fungibility. Paper presented at the 40th National Conference on Public Administration, Baltimore, April 1–4.

———. 1980a. Outlays Data and the Analysis of Federal Policy Impact. In *The Urban Impacts of Federal Policies,* ed. Norman Glickman, 121–50. Baltimore: Johns Hopkins University Press.

———. 1980b. Federal Assistance Programs: The Politics of System Transformation. In *National Resources And Urban Policy,* ed. Douglas E. Ashford, 15–44. New York: Methuen.

———. 1983. *Federal Aid to Detroit.* Washington, D.C.: Brookings Institution.

Anton, Thomas J., Jerry P. Cawley, and Kevin L. Kramer. 1980. *Moving Money: An Empirical Analysis of Federal Expenditure Patterns.* Cambridge, Mass.: Oelgeschlager, Gunn & Hain, 1980.

Anton, Thomas J., Patrick D. Larkey, Toni R. Linton, et al. 1975. *Understanding the Fiscal Impact of General Revenue-Sharing.* Ann Arbor: Institute of Public Policy Studies, University of Michigan.

Arneson, Ben A. 1922. Federal Aid to the States. *American Political Science Review* 16(3): 443–54.

Baestlein, Angelika, Gerhard Hunnius, Werner Jann, Manfred Konukiewitz, and Hellmut Wollmann. 1978. State Grants and Local Development Planning in the Federal Republic of Germany. In *Interorganizational Policy Making: Limits to Coordination and General Control,* ed. Kenneth Hanf and Fritz W. Scharpf, 115–42. Beverly Hills: Sage.

Baker, Gladys. 1939. *The County Agent.* Chicago: University of Chicago Press.

Banfield, Edward C. 1965. *Political Influence.* New York: Free Press.

Beam, David R. 1979. The Accidental Leviathan: Was the Growth of Government a Mistake? *Intergovernmental Perspective* 5(4): 12–19.

Beer, Samuel H. 1973. The Modernization of American Federalism. *Publius* 3(2): 49–95.

———. 1974. Government and Politics: An Imbalance. *Center Magazine* 7(2): 10–22.

———. 1976. The Adoption of General Revenue-Sharing: A Case Study in Public Sector Politics. *Public Policy* 24(2): 127–95.

———. 1977a. Political Overload and Freedom. *Polity* 10(1): 5–17.

———. 1977b. A Political Scientist's View of Fiscal Federalism. In *The Political Economy of Fiscal Federalism*, ed. Wallace E. Oates, 21–46. Lexington, Mass. D. C. Heath.

———. 1978. Federalism, Nationalism, and Democracy in America. *American Political Science Review* 72(1): 9–21.

Bell, Daniel. 1975. The Revolution of Rising Entitlements. *Fortune* 91(44): 98–103.

———. 1978. *The Cultural Contradictions of Capitalism.* New York: Basic Books.

Block, William J. 1960. *The Separation of the Farm Bureau and the Extension Service: Political Issue in a Federal System.* Urbana: University of Illinois Press.

Bryce, James. 1895. *The American Commonwealth.* 3d ed. 2 Vols. New York: Macmillan.

Burdick, Charles K. 1923. Federal Aid Legislation. *Cornell Law Quarterly* 8(4): 324–37.

Caro, Robert A. 1975. *The Power Broker: Robert Moses and the Fall of New York.* New York: Vintage Books.

Citrin, Jack. 1979. Do People Want Something for Nothing?: Public Opinion on Taxes and Government Spending. *National Tax Journal* 32(2, supplement): 113–29.

Clark, Colin. 1945. Public Finance and Changes in the Value of Money. *Economic Journal* 55(229): 371–89.

Clark, Jane Perry. 1938. *The Rise of a New Federalism: Federal-State Cooperation in the United States.* New York: Columbia University Press.

Colella, Cynthia Cates. 1979. The Creation, Care, and Feeding of Leviathan: Who and What Makes Government Grow. *Intergovernmental Perspective* 5(4): 6–11.

Commentary. 1973. Nixon, the Great Society, and the Future of Social Policy: A Symposium. *Commentary* 55(5): 31–61.

Commission on Intergovernmental Relations (Kestnbaum Commission). 1955. *A Report to the President.* Washington, D.C.: U.S. Government Printing Office.

Congressional Budget Office, Comptroller General's Office. 1976. *The Number of Federal Employees Engaged in Regulatory Activities.* Staff paper prepared for Subcommittee on Oversight and Investigations, Committee on Interstate and Foreign Commerce, U.S. House of Representatives. Washington, D.C.: U.S. Government Printing Office.

Cook, Robert F. 1979. Fiscal Implications of CETA Public Service Employment. In *Fiscal Crisis in American Cities: The Federal Response,* ed. L. Kenneth Hubbell, 193–228. Cambridge, Mass.: Ballinger.

Corwin, Edward S. 1923. The Spending Power of Congress: Apropos the Maternity Act. *Harvard Law Review* 36(5): 548–82.

———. 1950. The Passing of Dual Federalism. *Virginia Law Review* 36 (February): 1–24.

Council of State Governments. 1949. *Federal Grants-in-Aid: Report of the Committee on Federal Grants-in-Aid.* n.p.: Council of State Governments.

Courant, Paul N., Edward M. Gramlich, and Daniel L. Rubinfeld. 1979a. *The Tax Limitation Movement: Conservative Drift or the Search for a Free Lunch?* Discussion Paper no. 141. Ann Arbor: University of Michigan, Institute of Public Policy Studies.

———. 1979b. Tax Limitation and the Demand for Public Services in Michigan. *National Tax Journal 32(2, supplement):* 147–57.

Cronin, Thomas E. 1970. The Textbook Presidency and Political Science. Paper presented at the annual meeting of the American Political Science Association.

Crozier, Michel, and Jean-Claude Thoenig. 1976. The Regulation of Complex Organized Systems. *Administrative Science Quarterly* 21(4): 547–70.

Dearing, Charles L. 1942. *American Highway Policy.* Washington, D.C.: Brookings Institution.

Derthick, Martha. 1970. *The Influence of Federal Grants: Public Assistance in Massachusetts.* Cambridge, Mass.: Harvard University Press.

————. 1972. *New Towns in Town: Why a Federal Program Failed.* Washington, D.C.: Urban Institute.

————. 1975. *Uncontrollable Spending for Social Services Grants.* Washington, D.C.: Brookings Institution.

————. 1979. How Easy Votes on Social Security Came to an End. *Public Interest, no. 54 (Winter): 94–105.*

Dommel, Paul R. 1974. *The Politics of Revenue Sharing.* Bloomington and London: Indiana University Press.

————. 1979. Block Grants for Community Development: Decentralized Decision-making. In *Fiscal Crisis in American Cities: The Federal Response,* L. Kenneth Hubbell, ed. 229–55. Cambridge, Mass.: Ballinger.

Dommel, Paul R., Richard P. Nathan, Sara Liebschutz, Margaret T. Wrightson, and Associates. 1978. *Decentralizing Community Development.* Washington, D.C.: U.S. Government Printing Office.

Dommel, Paul R., Victor Bach, Sara Liebschutz, Leonard Rubinowitz, and Associates. Forthcoming. *Targeting Community Development.* Project report to U.S. Department of Housing and Urban Development.

Drucker, Peter F. 1969. The Sickness of Government. *Public Interest,* no. 14 (Winter): 3–23.

Drummond, Roscoe. 1949. Are We Maintaining Our Federal System? *State Government* 22(2, supplement): 1–4.

Economic Report of the President, 1979. 1979. Washington, D.C.: U.S. Government Printing Office.

————. 1965. The Shaping of Intergovernmental Relations in the Twentieth Century. *Annals of the American Academy of Political and Social Science* 359 (May): 110–22.

————. 1967. Urban Problems and the Federal Government: A Historical Inquiry. *Political Science Quarterly* 84(4): 505–25.

————. 1972. *American Federalism: A View from the States.* 2d ed. New York: Harper & Row.

Etzioni, Amitai. 1977/78. Societal Overload: Sources, Components, and Corrections. *Political Science Quarterly* 92(4): 607–31.

Farkas, Suzanne. 1971. *Urban Lobbying: Mayors in the Federal Arena.* New York: New York University Press.

Fesler, James W. 1949. *Area and Administration.* University: University of Alabama Press.

Ford, Henry Jones. 1909. The Influence of State Politics in Expanding Federal Power. *Proceedings of the American Political Science Association at Its Fifth Annual Meeting, Washington, D.C., and Richmond, Virginia, December 28–31, 1908,* 53–63. Baltimore: Waverly Press.

Fossett, James W., and Richard P. Nathan. 1981. The Prospects for Urban Revival. In *Urban Government Finance: Emerging Trends,* edited by Roy A. Bahl. Beverly Hills: S. ge.

Friedman, Milton. 1962. *Capitalism and Freedom.* Chicago: University of Chicago Press.

————. 1976. The Line We Dare Not Cross: The Fragility of Freedom at 60 Percent. *Encounter* 47(5): 8–14.

————. 1978. From Galbraith to Economic Freedom. In *Tax Limitation, Inflation, and the Role of Government,* 52–81. Dallas: Fisher Institute.

Friedrich, Carl J. 1968. *Trends of Federalism in Theory and Practice.* New York: Praeger.

Gates, Paul Wallace 1954. *Fifty Million Acres: Conflicts over Kansas Land Policy, 1854–1890.* Ithaca: Cornell University Press.

General Accounting Office. 1979. *Grant Auditing: A Maze of Inconsistency, Gaps, and Duplication That Needs Overhauling.* Washington, D.C.: U.S. Government Printing Office.

General Accounting Office. 1980. *GAO Findings on Federal Internal Audit: A Summary.* Washington, D.C.: U.S. Government Printing Office.

Ginzberg, Eli, and Robert M. Solow, eds. 1974. *The Great Society: Lessons for the Future.* New York: Basic Books. Originally published as the no. 34 (Winter 1974) issue of *Public Interest.*

Glazer, Nathan, and Irving Kristol. 1976. *The American Commonwealth, 1976.* New York: Basic Books. Originally published as the no. 41 (Fall 1975) issue of *Public Interest.*

Gramlich, Edward M. 1970. The Effect of Federal Grants on State-Local Expenditures: A Review of the Econometric Literature. In *Proceedings of the 62d Annual Conference on Taxation, National Tax Association,* ed. Stanley J. Bowers, 569–93. Columbus, Ohio: National Tax Association.

————. 1977. Intergovernmental Grants: A Review of the Empirical Literature. In *The Political Economy of Fiscal Federalism,* ed. Wallace E. Oates, 219–39. Lexington, Mass.: D. C. Heath.

Gramlich, Edward M., and Harvey Galper. 1973. State and Local Fiscal Behavior and Federal Grant Policy. In Brookings Papers on Economic Activity, ed. Arthur M. Okun and George L. Perry. 1:15–58.

Graves, W. Brooke. 1934. Stroke Oar. *State Government* 7(12): 259–62.

————. 1936a. The Future of the American States. *American Political Science Review* 30(1): 24–50.

————. 1936b. Federal Leadership in State Legislation. *Temple Law Quarterly* 10(4): 385–405.

————. 1938. Influence of Congressional Legislation on Legislation in the States. *Iowa Law Review* 23(4): 519–38.

————. 1964. *American Intergovernmental Relations: Their Origins, Historical Development, and Current Status.* New York: Scribner's.

Gray, Virginia. 1973a. Innovation in the States: A Diffusion Study. *American Political Science Review* 67(4): 1174–85.

————. 1973b. Rejoinder to "Comment" by Jack L. Walker, *American Political Science Review* 67(4): 1192–93.

Greenberg, George D., with Robert C. Luskin. 1979. *Federal Program Implementation in Selected States: A Study of the Implementation of the Partnership for Health Act and of the Early and Periodic Screening, Diagnosis, and Treatment Program in Michigan, Pennsylvania, and Alabama.* Project Report to the National Center for Health Services Research, U.S. Public Health Service, U.S. Department of Health, Education, and Welfare, Washington, D.C., June.

Greenberg, George D., Jeffrey A. Miller, Lawrence B. Mohr, and Bruce C. Vladeck. 1977. Developing Public Policy Theory: Perspectives from Empirical Research. *American Political Science Review* 71(4): 1532–43.

Grodzins, Morton. 1960a. The Federal System. In Report of the President's Commission on National Goals. *Goals for Americans,* 265–82. Englewood Cliffs, N.J.: Prentice-Hall.

————. 1960b. American Political Parties and the American System. *Western Political Quarterly* 13(4): 978–98.

————. 1966. *The American System: A New View of Government in the United States.* Edited by Daniel J. Elazar. Chicago: Rand McNally.

Hale, George E., and Scott R. Douglass. 1977. The Politics of Budget Execution: Financial Manipulation in State and Local Government. *Administration and Society* 9(3): 367–79.

Hall, John Stuart. 1979. *The Impact of Federal Aid on the City of Phoenix.* A case study for the Brookings Institution "Federal Politics in Big Cities" Project, prepared under the direction of Richard P. Nathan and James W. Fossett and presented to the U.S. Department of Labor.

Heclo, Hugh. 1977. A Question of Priorities. *Humanist* 37(2): 21–24.

————. 1979. Issue Networks and the Executive Establishment. In *The New American Political System* ed. Anthony King, 87–124. Washington, D.C.: American Enterprise Institute for Public Policy Research.

Huntington, Samuel P. 1975a. The United States. In *The Crisis of Democracy,* edited by Michael Crozier, Samuel P. Huntington, and Joji Watanuk, 59–118. New York: New York University Press.
———. 1975b. The Democratic Distemper. *Public Interest,* no. 41 (Fall): 9–38.

Joint Federal-State Action Committee, 1957. *Report of the Joint Federal-State Action Committee to the President of the United States and to the Chairman of the Governor's Conference, Progress Report no. 1.* Washington, D.C.: U.S. Government Printing Office, December.
———. 1958. *Second Report of the Joint Federal-State Action Committee to the President of the United States and to the Chairman of the Governor's Conference, Progress Report no. 2.* Washington, D.C.: U.S. Government Printing Office, December.
———. 1960. *Final Report of the Joint Federal-State Action Committee to the President of the United States and to the Chairman of the Governor's Conference.* Washington, D.C.: U.S. Government Printing Office, February.
Juster, F. Thomas, ed. 1977. *The Economic and Political Impact of General Revenue-Sharing.* Ann Arbor, Mich.: Survey Research Center, Institute for Social Research, University of Michigan.
Juster, F. Thomas, and Thomas J. Anton. 1977. Introduction and Summary. In *The Economic And Political Impact Of General Revenue Sharing,* ed. F. Thomas Juster, 1–12. Ann Arbor: Survey Research Center, Institute for Social Research, University of Michigan.

Kaufman, Herbert. 1956. Emerging Conflicts in the Doctrines of Public Administration. *American Political Science Review* 50(4): 1057–73.
———. 1967. *The Forest Ranger: A Study in Administrative Behavior.* Baltimore: Johns Hopkins Press.
Kaufman, Herbert, with the collaboration of Michael Couzens. 1973. *Administrative Feedback: Monitoring Subordinates' Behavior.* Washington, D.C.: Brookings Institution.
Key, V. O., Jr. 1937. *The Administration of Federal Grants to States.* Chicago: Public Administration Service.
———. 1940. State Legislation Facilitative of Federal Action. *Annals of the American Academy of Political and Social Science* 207 (January): 7–13.
Kile, Orville Merton. 1948. *The Farm Bureau through Three Decades.* Baltimore; Waverly Press.
Kirlin, John J. 1979. Adapting the Intergovernmental Fiscal System to the Demands of an Advanced Economy. In *The Changing Structure of the City: What Happened to the Urban Crisis,* ed. Gary Tobin, 77–103. Beverly Hills: Sage.

Lane, Jan-Erik, and Curt Lofgren. 1979. Political Budgeting: A Framework for an Institutional Analysis of Swedish National Accounts. *Scandinavian Political Studies* n.s. 2(2): 141–60.
Larkey, Patrick Daniel. 1975. Process Models and Program Evaluation: The Impact of General Revenue-Sharing on Municipal Fiscal Behavior. Ph.D. Diss., University of Michigan.
———. 1979. *Evaluating Public Programs: The Impact of General Revenue-Sharing on Municipal Government.* Princeton, N.J.: Princeton University Press.
Laski, Harold J. 1939. The Obsolescence of Federalism. *New Republic* 98(1274): 367–69.
Leacock, Stephen. 1909. The Limitations of Federal Government. *Proceedings of the American Political Science Association at Its Fifth Annual Meeting, Washington, D.C., and Richmond, Virginia, December 28–31, 1908,* 37–52. Baltimore: Waverly Press.
Levitan, Sar A., and Robert Taggart. 1976. *The Promise of Greatness.* Cambridge, Mass.: Harvard University Press.
———. 1976/77. The Great Society Did Succeed. *Political Science Quarterly* 91(4): 601–8.
Lowi, Theodore J. 1974. Permanent Receivership: The New Governmental Pattern. *Center Magazine* 7(2): 33–42.

————. 1978. Europeanization of America? From United States to United State. In *Nationalizing Government: Public Policies in America,* ed. Theodore J. Lowi and Alan Stone, 15–29. Beverly Hills: Sage.

————. 1979. *The End of Liberalism: The Second Republic of the United States.* 2d ed. New York: Norton.

Lowrie, S. Gale. 1922. Centralization versus Decentralization. *American Political Science Review* 16(3): 379–86.

MacDonald, Austin F. 1923. *Federal Subsidies to the States: A Study in American Administration.* Philadelphia: University of Pennsylvania Press.

————. 1928a. *Federal Aid: A Study of the American Subsidy System.* New York: Crowell.

————. 1928b. Federal Aid to the States: Report of the Committee on Federal Aid to the States of the National Municipal League. *National Municipal Review* 17(10): 619–59.

————. 1931. Recent Trends in Federal Aid to the States. *American Political Science Review* 25(3): 628–34.

————. 1940. Federal Aid to the States: 1940 Model. *American Political Science Review* 34(3): 489–99.

McKay, David H. 1979. The United States in Crisis: A Review of the American Political Literature. *Government and Opposition* 14, no. 3 (Summer 1979): 373–85.

————. 1980. Intergovernmental Relations in the European Community Member States. C. E. S. Research Paper, Series 48. London: Centre for Environmental Studies.

McKay David, and Andrew Cox. 1979. *The Politics of Urban Change.* London: Croom Helm.

MacManus, Susan A. 1983. *Federal Aid to Houston.* Washington, D.C.: Brookings Institution.

Martin, Roscoe C. 1965. *The Cities and the Federal System.* New York: Atherton.

Marvick, L. Dwaine. 1952. Congressional Appropriation Politics: A Study of Institutional Conditions for Expressing Supply Intent. Ph. D. diss. Columbia University.

Meltzer, Allan H., and Scott F. Richard. 1978. "Why Government Grows (and Grows) in a Democracy." *Public Interest,* no. 52 (Summer): 111–18.

Murphy, Jerome T. 1974. *State Education Agencies and Discretionary Funds: Grease the Squeaky Wheel.* Lexington, Mass.: D. C. Heath.

Myers, Will, and John Shannon. 1979. Revenue Sharing for States: An Endangered Species. *Intergovernmental Perspective* 5(3): 10–18.

Nathan, Richard P., et al. 1977. *Block Grants for Community Development.* Washington, D.C.: Brookings Institution, contracted by the U.S. Department of Housing and Urban Development.

Nathan, Richard P., Charles F. Adams, Jr., et al. 1977. *Revenue Sharing: The Second Round.* Washington, D.C.: Brookings Institution.

Nathan, Richard P., Robert F. Cook, Janet Galchick, Richard Long, and Associates. 1978. Monitoring the Public Service Employment Program, Preliminary Report. In National Commission on Manpower Policy, *Job Creation through Public Service Employment: An Interim Report to the Congress,* vol. 2. Washington, D.C.: U.S. Government Printing Office, March.

Nathan, Richard P., Robert F. Cook, V. Lane Rawlins, Janet M. Galchich, et al. 1979. *Monitoring the Public Service Employment Program: The Second Round.* Washington, D.C.: Brookings Institution. Mimeographed.

Nathan, Richard P., Allen D. Manuel, Susannah E. Calkins, et al. 1975. *Monitoring Revenue Sharing.* Washington, D.C.: Brookings Institution.

National Association of Manufacturers. 1952. *Bring the Government Back Home* (December). In *The Nation and the States: Rivals or Partners?* ed. William Anderson, 5–6. Minneapolis: University of Minnesota Press.

Nutter, G. Warren. 1978. *Growth of Government in the West.* Washington, D.C.: American Enterprise Institute for Public Policy Research.

Oates, Wallace E. *Fiscal Federalism*. New York: Harcourt, Brace, Jovanovich.
Office of Management and Budget. Budget Review Division. Fiscal Analysis Branch. 1980a.
Federal Government Finances, January 1980 Edition. Washington, D.C.: OMB.
————. 1980b. Federal Grants-in-Aid to State and Local Governments, January 1980 Edition.
Washington, D.C.: U.S. Government Printing Office.
Ostrom, Vincent. 1976. The Contemporary Debate over Centralization and Decentralization.
Publius 6(4): 21–32.

Porter, David O., and David C. Warner. 1972. How Effective Are Grantor Controls?: The Case
of Federal Aid to Education. In *Transfers in an Urbanized Economy: Theories and Effects of
the Grants Economy*, ed. Kenneth E. Boulding, Martin Pfaff, and Anita Pfaff, 276–302.
Belmont, Calif.: Wadsworth.
Porter, David O., with David C. Warner and Teddie W. Porter. 1973. *The Politics of Budgeting
Federal Aid: Resource Mobilization by Local School Districts*. Beverly Hills: Sage.
Pressman, Jeffrey L. 1975. *Federal Programs and City Politics: The Dynamics of the Aid
Process in Oakland*. Berkeley and Los Angeles: University of California Press.
Pressman, Jeffrey L., and Aaron Wildavsky. 1974. *Implementation: How Great Expectations in
Washington are Dashed in Oakland; or, Why It's Amazing That Federal Programs Work at
All, This Being a Saga of the Economic Development Administration as Told by Two Sym-
pathetic Observers Who Seek to Build Morals on a Foundation of Ruined Hopes*. Berkeley and
Los Angeles: University of California Press.
Preston, Michael B. 1984. *The Politics of Bureaucratic Reform: Improving the Administration of
Minority Employment Programs*. Urbana: University of Illinois Press.

Reich, Charles A. 1964. The New Property. *Yale Law Journal* 73(5): 733–87.
————. 1965. Individual Rights and Social Welfare: The Emerging Legal Issues. *Yale Law
Journal* 74(7): 1245–57.
————. 1966a. The New Property. *Public Interest*, no. 3 (Spring): 57–89.
————. 1966b. The Law of the Planned Society. *Yale Law Journal* 75(8): 1227–70.
Rein, Martin, and Hugh Heclo. 1973. "What Welfare Crisis?: A Comparison among the United
States, Britain, and Sweden." *Public Interest*, no. 33 (Fall): 61–83.
Rhodes, Rod A. W. 1979. The Comparative Study of Local Government. unpublished paper,
University of Essex.
Rockefeller, Nelson A. 1962. *The Future of Federalism*. Cambridge, Mass.: Harvard University
Press.
Rose, Richard, and Guy Peters. 1978. *Can Government Go Bankrupt?* New York: Basic Books.

Salisbury, Robert H. 1977. Peak Associations and the Tensions of Interest Intermediation; or,
Why No Corporatism in America. Paper presented at the annual meeting of the American
Political Science Association, Washington, D.C., September 1–4.
Sanders, 1979. Heywood T. Sanders, Urban Renewal and the Revitalized City: A Reconsidera-
tion of Recent History. Unpublished paper, Institute of Governmental and Public Affairs,
University of Illinois, Urbana.
Sanford, Terry. 1967. *Storm over the States*. New York: McGraw-Hill.
Sayre, Wallace S., and Herbert Kaufman. 1965. *Governing New York City: Politics in the
Metropolis*. New York: Norton.
Sbragia, Alberta. 1979. Not All Roads Lead to Rome: Local Housing Policy in the Unitary Italian
State. *British Journal of Political Science* 9(3): 315–39.
Scheiber, Harry N. 1966. *The Condition of American Federalism: An Historian's View*. U.S.
Congress, Senate, Committee on Governmental Operations, Subcommittee on Intergovern-
mental Relations, 89th Cong., 2d sess., committee print, October 15: Washington, D.C.: U.S.
Government Printing Office.

————. 1975. Federalism and the American Economic Order, 1789–1910. *Law and Society Review* 10(1): 57–118.

Schlesinger, Arthur M., Jr. 1974. *The Imperial Presidency*. New York: Popular Library.

Schmandt, Henry J., George D. Wendel, and E. Allan Tomey. 1979. *The Impact of Federal Aid on the City of St. Louis*. A case study for the Brookings Institution. "Federal Politics in Big Cities" Project, prepared under the direction of Richard P. Nathan and James W. Fossett and presented to the U.S. Department of Labor.

Schmitter, Philippe C. 1974. Still the Century of Corporatism? *Review of Politics* 36(1): (January 1974): 85–131.

————. 1977. Modes of Interest Intermediation and Modes of Societal Change in Western Europe. *Comparative Politics* 10(1): 7–38.

Schultze, Charles L. 1976. Federal Spending: Past, Present, and Future. In *Setting National Priorities: The Next Ten Years*, ed. Henry Owen and Charles L. Schultze, 323–69. Washington, D.C.: Brookings Institution.

Smithies, Arthur. 1955. *The Budgetary Process in the United States*. New York: McGraw-Hill.

Soneblum, Sidney, John J. Kirlin, and John C. Ries. 1977. *How Cities Provide Services: An Evaluation of Alternative Delivery Structures*. Cambridge, Mass.: Ballinger.

Stanfield, Rochelle L. 1979. Fighting among Themselves. *National Journal* 11(16): 652.

————. 1980. If You Want the Federal Dollars, You Have to Accept Federal Controls. *National Journal* 12(3): 105–9.

Steiner, Gilbert Y. 1966. *Social Insecurity: The Politics of Welfare*. Chicago: Rand McNally.

————. Gilbert Y. 1971. *The State of Welfare*. Washington, D.C.: Brookings Institution.

————, with the assistance of Pauline H. Milius. 1976. *The Children's Cause*. Washington, D.C.: Brookings Institution.

Steinfels, Peter. 1979. *The Neoconservatives: The Men Who Are Changing America's Politics*. New York: Simon & Schuster.

Stern, Philip M. 1964. *The Great Treasury Raid*. New York: Random House.

————. 1973. *The Rape of the Taxpayer*. New York: Random House.

Sundquist, James L., with the collaboration of David W. Davis. 1969. *Making Federalism Work: A Study of Program Coordination at the Community Level*. Washington, D.C.: Brookings Institution.

Surrey, Stanley S. 1957. The Congress and the Tax Lobbyist: How Special Tax Provisions Get Enacted. *Harvard Law Review* 70(7): 1145–82.

————. 1970. Tax Incentives as a Device for Implementing Government Policy: A Comparison with Direct Government Expenditures. *Harvard Law Review* 83(4): 705–38.

————. 1973. *Pathways to Tax Reform: The Concept of Tax Expenditures*. Cambridge, Mass.: Harvard University Press.

Tarschys, Daniel. 1975. The Growth in Public Expenditures: Nine Modes of Explanation. *Scandinavian Political Studies* 10:9–31.

U.S. Department of Commerce. Bureau of the Census. 1973. *1972 Census of Governments*. Vol. 1, *Public Employment*, no. 2, *Compendium of Public Employment*. Washington, D.C.: U.S. Government Printing Office.

————. 1975. *Historical Statistics of the United States: Colonial Times to 1970, Part 2*. Washington, D.C.: U.S. Government Printing Office.

————. 1979a. *1977 Census of Governments*. Vol. 1, *Government Organization*, no. 2. Washington, D.C.: U.S. Government Printing Office.

————. 1979b. *1977 Census of Governments*. Vol. 3, *Public Employment*, no. 2, *Compendium of Public Employment*. Washington, D.C.: U.S. Government Printing Office.

————. Various years. *City Government Finances*. Washington, D.C.: U.S. Government Printing Office.

————. Various years: *Governmental Finances*. Washington, D.C.: U.S. Government Printing Office.

Walker, David B. 1978. A New Intergovernmental System in 1977. *Publius* 8(1): 101–16.
Walker, Jack L. 1969. The Diffusion of Innovations among the American States. *American Political Science Review* 63(3): 880–99.
_____. 1971. Innovation in State Politics. In *Politics in the American States: A Comparative Analysis,* 2d ed., ed. Herbert Jacob and Kenneth N. Vines, 354–87. Boston: Little, Brown.
_____. 1973. Comment: Problems in Research on the Diffusion of Policy Innovation. *American Political Science Review* 67(4): 1186–91.
_____. 1974. The Diffusion of Knowledge and Policy Change: Toward a Theory of Agenda Setting. Paper presented at the 1974 annual meeting of the American Political Science Association, Chicago, August 29–September 2.
_____. 1976. Setting the Agenda in the U.S. Senate: A Theory of Problem Selection. Paper presented at the 1976 annual meeting of the American Political Science Association, Chicago, September 2–5.
_____. 1977. Setting the Agenda in the U.S. Senate: A Theory of Problem Selection. *British Journal of Political Science* 7(4): 423–45.
Warren, Roland L., Stephen M. Rose, and Ann F. Bergunder. 1974. *The Structure of Urban Reform.* Lexington, Mass.: D. C. Heath.
Webb, Sidney. 1920. *Grants-in-Aid: A Criticism and a Proposal.* Rev. and enl. London: Longmans, Green.
Wilensky, Harold L. 1976. *The "New Corporatism," Centralization, and the Welfare State.* Beverly Hills: Sage.
Williams, Edward Ainsworth. 1939. *Federal Aid for Relief.* New York: Columbia University Press.
Williams, J. Kerwin. 1936. The Status of Cities under Recent Federal Legislation. *American Political Science Review* 30(6): 1107–14.
_____. 1939. *Grants-in-Aid under the Public Works Administration: A Study in Federal-State-Local Relations.* New York: Columbia University Press.
Williams J. Kerwin, and Edward A. Williams. 1940. New Techniques in Federal Aid. *American Political Science Review* 34(5): 947–54.
Willoughby, W. F. 1927. *The National Budget System, with Suggestions for its Improvement.* Baltimore: Johns Hopkins Press.
Wilson, James Q. 1976. The Rise of the Bureaucratic State. In *The American Commonwealth, 1976,* ed. Nathan Glazer and Irving Kristol, 77–103. New York: Basic Books.
_____. 1979. American Politics, Then and Now. *Commentary* 67(2): 39–46.
Wirt, Frederick M. 1978. Does Control Follow the Dollar? Value Analysis, School Policy, and State-Local Linkages. Paper presented at the 1978 annual meeting of the American Political Science Association, New York, August 31–September 3.
_____. 1979. Neoconservatism and National School Policy. Paper presented at the American Research Association Convention, April.
Wright, Deil S. 1974. Intergovernmental Relations: An Analytical Overview. *Annals of the American Academy of Political and Social Science* 416 (November): 1–16.

Yin, Robert K. 1980. Creeping Federalism: The Federal Impact on the Structure and Function of Local Government. In *The Urban Impact of Federal Policies,* ed. Norman J. Glickman, 595–618. Baltimore: Johns Hopkins University Press.
Yin, Robert K., et al. 1979. *Federal Aid and Urban Economic Development: A Local Perspective.* Santa Monica: RAND Corporation.

3

Why Does Government Grow?

Patrick D. Larkey
Chandler Stolp
Mark Winer

Nothing is easier than spending public money. It does not appear to belong to anybody. The temptation is overwhelming to bestow it on somebody.

—Calvin Coolidge

Perhaps the central normative question for political economy is, What role should governments play in social, political, and economic systems? This question has important positive companions: Why does government grow (or decline)? What are the consequences for social, political, and economic systems of a government of a given size and role? This chapter addresses primarily the easiest of the two positive questions, Why does government grow (or decline)?

The purpose of this chapter is threefold: (1) to provide an extensive, multidisciplinary bibliography of literature related to the question; (2) to summarize a few selected and very different theories of why government grows; and (3) to appraise these theories and indicate the most promising lines of future inquiry.

The literature on governmental growth is imposingly diverse. It ranges

Prepared with support from the Government Finance Research Center, the Municipal Finance Officers Association, and the National Science Foundation. A more extensive review of the same literature by the same authors can be found in the *Journal of Public Policy* 1, pt. 2, May 1981. We are indebted to a large number of people for substantive and editorial comments. The views expressed in this paper are the authors' and should not be attributed to other individuals or organizations.

from empirically stark, highly abstract formal models through heavily empirical, largely atheoretical treatments to the ideologically assertive, logically
loose verbal models of ideologues. The empirical work ranges from longitudinal studies of subnational governments to international cross-sections and
varies greatly in terms of how "government" is conceptualized and measured. Much of this diversity results from the different motivations for the
work. Some of the researchers attempt to measure and understand how government has changed, with no obvious theoretical or policy questions motivat-
ing the efforts. A step beyond this purely descriptive work is research that
searches for empirical regularities and associational relationships between the
size or composition of government and other variables. This work varies
greatly in the extent to which its authors endeavor to produce explanations of
why these empirical regularities and associational relationships exist.

CONCEPTUAL PROBLEMS

The literature on governmental growth suffers, as do many in the social
sciences, from measurement problems: it is not possible to measure desired
variables directly, and proxies must be used. There are many conceptions of
governmental "size" or "growth," which often employ any one of a number
of operational measures (e.g., governmental expenditures as a proportion of
GNP). It is helpful to have a clear conception of the phenomena to be explained before embarking on the explanation; this is, however, a surprisingly
uncommon practice in many areas of social science.

Unfortunately, it is difficult, if not impossible, to posit one or a few
measures of government that are common or adequate to the literature reviewed in this paper. A variety of measures have been used. Some of the
published data on ostensibly the same phenomena are inconsistent. Explaining the phenomenon of governmental growth theoretically depends directly on
what measures, what countries, and what time periods are selected for explanation. Thus, the discussion of measurement problems will be brief. For more
extensive treatment, readers should see Pryor (1968), Morss (1969), and
Aharoni (1977).

Public expenditure and tax collection are the most available, easily measured, and widely used indicators of the scope of public sector activity. Such
measures however, present many many conceptual problems. It is not obvious, for example, what should be counted as public and what as private, nor
is it obvious how the measures ought to be expressed (e.g., in per capita terms
or as a share of GNP, GDP, or NNP). These choices depend both on the
research purposes and on technical considerations (e.g., international or inter-
temporal comparability of data). Large differences among selected countries
in terms of tax revenues as a proportion of GNP appear in table 3.1. Most
notable is the fact that every country listed experienced growth in total taxes

Table 3.1. Tax Revenues Relative to GNP, Selected Countries

Selected Years 1966–1976[a]

| Country | Total Taxes[b] | | | | Percentage Distribution of Total Taxes, 1976 | | | | |
| | As Percent of Gross National Product | | | Per Capita[c] 1976 | Total | Taxes on Income and Profits[d] | Taxes on Goods and Services[e] | Social Security Contributions | Other Taxes[f] |
	1966	1971	1976						
Australia	24.12	26.45	29.98	$2,165	100.00	56.55	28.57	—	14.88
Austria	35.54	36.96	38.91	2,104	100.00	24.87	34.76	28.91	11.46
Belgium	32.85	36.14	41.87	2,876	100.00	38.28	27.45	31.61	2.66
Canada	27.56	31.16	32.88	2,859	100.00	46.72	31.91	10.52	10.85
Denmark	32.56	44.64	44.70	3,395	100.00	57.57	35.68	1.09	5.66
Finland	31.77	34.74	42.19	2,520	100.00	53.70	32.06	11.08	3.16
France	34.77	35.01	39.45	2,605	100.00	18.43	32.42	40.17	8.98
Germany, Federal Republic of	32.19	33.20	36.70	2,660	100.00	34.82	25.74	34.66	4.78
Greece	22.20	23.94	27.94	678	100.00	17.45	43.69	28.23	10.63
Ireland	27.96	32.24	36.81	924	100.00	30.18	47.78	13.25	8.97
Italy	28.98	31.14	35.82	1,089	100.00	22.74	28.10	45.84	3.32
Japan	17.63	19.41	20.91	1,059	100.00	41.15	19.01	25.53	14.31
Luxembourg	32.02	35.21	50.45	3,175	100.00	42.35	19.82	31.65	6.18
Netherlands	36.99	41.53	46.16	3,001	100.00	33.95	24.48	37.82	3.75
New Zealand	26.43	28.15	31.83	1,340	100.00	67.27	22.99	1.71	8.03
Norway	34.59	42.40	46.18	3,590	100.00	40.83	37.78	18.06	3.33
Portugal	19.12	22.92	26.51	430	100.00	20.15	39.42	29.82	10.61
Spain	14.96	17.48	20.27	585	100.00	23.76	24.92	45.44	5.88
Sweden	35.44	41.49	50.89	4,595	100.00	46.61	24.33	23.22	5.84
Switzerland	21.46	23.51	31.59	2,802	100.00	44.58	19.17	29.25	7.00
Turkey	16.97	20.85	24.87	249	100.00	36.78	36.76	19.92	6.54
United Kingdom	32.22	35.64	36.70	1,437	100.00	42.75	25.47	19.44	12.34
United States	26.85	28.76	29.29	2,199	100.00	43.34	18.08	24.62	13.96

[a]Primarily calendar years; however data for some countries are reported on a fiscal year basis.
[b]Tax revenues collected by all levels of government, recorded on a cash basis.
[c]In U.S. dollars.
[d]Includes taxes on capital gains.
[e]Taxes on the production, sale, transfer, leasing, and delivery of goods and rendering of services.
[f]Includes taxes on net wealth and immovable property; on gifts, inheritance, and financial transactions, employer payroll taxes other than social security contributions, and miscellaneous taxes.

Source: Tax Foundation, 1979.

as a percentage of GNP between 1966 and 1971 and between 1971 and 1976. It is also interesting that some of the countries, such as the United Kingdom and the United States where dissatisfaction with government is the strongest, rate relatively low on these measures.

There is an obvious downturn in total U.S. government spending as a percentage of GNP between 1970 and 1977 (see table 2.3). This downturn poses a problem for reviewing the U.S. literature because all of it deals with pre-1976 data; the theories in the literature are directed at explaining the long period of seemingly inexorable growth in governmental expenditures before 1976. Examining a richer set of financial measures, the phenomena become even cloudier. The U.S. federal debt as a percentage of GNP has been declining over a much longer period (from 74.5 percent in 1954 to 35.9 percent in 1980). Denominators other than GNP, such as the net national product (NNP) or net domestic product (NDP), show quite different trends. A variety of other measures shed light on the scope of governmental activity, such as the number of governmental units and public employment as a percentage of the total workforce. Researchers might also consider the number of regulatory agencies, the number of regulations, the number of pages of regulations, estimates of the privately borne costs of regulation, taxes as proportions of gross and disposable income, the composition of expenditures over time and the like.

All of the measures mentioned above are, individually and collectively, poor surrogates for the scope of public sector activity in any complete sense. Ideally, many researchers want to measure "public sector presence," the extent to which governmental activities change the behavior of individuals or organizations for better or worse. The problems in constructing such a measure are fairly obvious. Court decisions that cost the government a pittance out of pocket (e.g., forced bussing to achieve racial integration in schools) may have enormous efficiency and equity implications. Individuals will incur costs and benefits, both tangible and intangible, that will never appear in any social accounts.

Governmental growth, then, constitutes several phenomena. The most widely used measure is expenditures (or tax collections that correlate closely with expenditures) as a proportion of GNP. Most of the empirical literature deals with national aggregates. (Some of the more notable exceptions are Pryor 1968; Wilensky 1976; Furniss and Tilton 1977, all of whom disaggregate expenditures.) There is also a considerable body of formal literature that deals with metaphorical government in simplified, rational worlds.

EMPIRICAL APPROACHES

Heavily inductive approaches are common in the social sciences. Researchers represent data in various ways, observe patterns and regularities, and create verbal or mathematical models that "explain" these patterns and regularities. The next step, rarely justifiable, is to generalize these explanations across time and/or space. The two most prominent empirical generalizations on governmental growth are Wagner's Law and the displacement-effect hypothesis. Because governments grew inexorably over the periods upon which these generalizations were based, they are largely irrelevant to periods of relative or absolute decline in governmental size.

Wagner's Law

The earliest modern effort to explain the growth of public expenditures was by Adolph Wagner (1877, 1890). Wagner's Law of Increasing State Activity associates increases in real per capita income during industrialization with the growth of the public sector relative to the private sector. Observing a newly united, increasingly urbanized Wilhelmine, Germany, close at hand, Wagner broadly attributed growth in state activity to exigencies (an expanded need for law and order, education, socioeconomic regulation, etc.) arising from the increased complexity of industrialized society.

Although Wagner's qualitative, "causal-genetic" theorizing immediately inspired a few confirmatory empirical studies, it was soon consigned to an obscure corner of public finance thoery. With the exception of a cross-national study published by Brecht (1932), there is little evidence of studies of Wagner's Law between World War I and the early 1960s. The few related studies that were published in the 1950s focused not on Wagner's Law per se but rather on data and indicators of the size of the public sector (see Fabricant 1952; Musgrave and Culberton 1953; Kendrick 1955; Martin and Lewis 1956; Oshima 1957, and Ratchford 1959).

The mid-century revival of interest in Wagner's Law was centered, at least initially, in the welfare states of Scandinavia and in Great Britain, a country that was adjusting to welfare socialism and that had witnessed total government spending as a percentage of GNP rise from 25 percent (1940) to nearly 40 percent (1960) in two decades (Peacock and Wiseman 1967, tables A-6, A-12).

Neo-Wagnerian research of the 1960s and 1970[1] is characterized by single-equation cross-sectional and longitudinal analyses of governmental size (variously measured) as a function of a host of explanatory variables. It is difficult to separate those studies attempting to "test" Wagner's Law from those generally exploring various determinants of public sector size or growth. A persistent problem with the "law" is that it is not at all clear what is to be tested.

The majority of these generally descriptive studies of governmental growth lend weak statistical support to some operational version of Wagner's Law and focus on correlates of public sector expansion including inflation, wage rates, public sector employment practices, the redistribution of income, and various other microlevel and macrolevel socioeconomic indicators. The statistical results, however, are highly sensitive to samples and model specifications.

Schumpeter (1954) dismissed the work of Wagner, characterizing it as "atheoretical"; similarly, most contemporary economists show scant respect for modern causal-genetic economic theories such as those of Marxist and radical economists and modern institutionalists like Galbraith.

The Displacement-Effect Hypothesis

Concentrating on governmental growth in the United Kingdom, Peacock and Wiseman (1961) posited the displacement-effect hypothesis. Whereas Wagner's Law is a "demand-side" explanation (growth in the public sector as a response to the demands of industrialization), the Displacement-Effect Hypothesis considers the "supply side." The supply of public revenues in this view is constrained by the level of taxation that the public will tolerate. In times of social upheaval (e.g., wars, emergencies), the public acquiesces to methods of taxation and levels of revenue that would be considered too onerous under normal circumstances. Following these disturbances, revenues are "sticky downward" as expenditures for new public purposes quickly displace expenditures for emergency purposes. The displacement-effect hypothesis was induced from the discrete shifts observed in the level of governmental expenditure in twentieth-century Great Britain. It concomitantly explains why growth in public expenditures has tended to be relatively steady in "normal" periods until punctuated by a displacement.

In later research (Peacock and Wiseman 1967, 1972, 1979; Peacock 1979a, 1979b) Peacock and Wiseman have attempted to specify some of the mechanisms driving the displacement effect. Perhaps their greatest contribution, though, has been to establish a research agenda focusing attention on the revenue (or supply) side of the question of governmental growth as a complement to demand-side explanations typical of determinants studies (including those exploring Wagner's Law).[2]

Other Empirical Explanations

There are a number of other, less prominent empirical explanations for why government grows. Among the most plausible are "uncontrollable" programs and "open" economies.

Uncontrollable Programs and Bracket Creep.   Much has been made of the notion of the "uncontrollability" of governmental expenditures in recent years. In the last two decades the United States has experienced a proliferation of entitlement and other "formula" programs (e.g., medicare, old age and survivor's insurance, farm price supports, and interest on the public debt) that automatically receive appropriations to meet the demand of the entitled target population. The seeming inability of the political process to control (cut back) the short-term expenditures of these programs once they are established has given rise to great concern about uncontrollable expenditures as the source of governmental growth. (See Weidenbaum 1969 for one of the earliest discussions of uncontrollable programs and factors causing their growth in the United States.)

Concern with "uncontrollables" at the federal level in the United States, where they are estimated to constitute something over three-quarters of recent budget outlays, is reflected in the frequency with which federal expenditures are displayed in terms of controllability in public documents such as the *President's Budget Message to Congress,* the *Economic Report of the President,* and the *Budget Analyses of the Congressional Budget Office.* Derthick (1975) explores some problematic consequences of these programs and LeLoup (1978) examines their impact on budgetary allocation decisions.

Since in the long run everything is subject to executive and congressional review, arguments that governmental expenditures are "out of control" are, in essence, criticisms of political and bureaucratic processes that fail to exercise effective control. Although the notion of uncontrollables has great superficial plausibility, a closer statistical analysis of the vulnerability of programs to budget cuts reveals no significant difference between programs commonly characterized as uncontrollable and those viewed as controllable (Crecine et al. 1977).

The "bracket creep" explanation for government revenue growth is more insight than theory and has been common to journalistic discussions of governmental growth. With inflation, a progressive income tax with unindexed brackets will generate increasing revenues. As inflation moves taxpayers into higher marginal tax brackets, a real increase in public revenues results, and expenditures follow apace. Unless one believes the implausible—that policy makers are simply not aware of government-inflating mechanisms like entitlement program formulas or bracket creep—the mechanisms are not in themselves very satisfactory theoretical explanations of governmental growth. Rather, a theory must explicitly state why policy makers leave the mechanisms in place.

Open Economies and Big Government. David Cameron (1978) provides a provocative empirical study employing data for 18 capitalist nations from 1960 to 1975 that examines "five types of explanation . . . to account for the growth of the scope of governmental activity," drawn, to a large extent, from prior literature:

(1) The level and rate of growth in the economic product; (2) the degree to which the fiscal structure of a nation relies on indirect, or visible," taxes; (3) politics—in particular the partisan composition of government and the frequency of electoral competition; (4) the institutional structure of government; and (5) the degree of exposure of the economy to the international marketplace. (1243)

Cameron's empirical findings are worth noting as comments on earlier theoretical and empirical work.

(a) Contrary to Wagner's "Law", the rate of growth in the economic affluence of a nation does not contribute to the expansion of the public economy. . . . Instead, the analysis supports Wildavsky's argument that the public economy grows in relative terms, when economic growth is modest. . . .

(b) Contrary to Downs and to Buchanan and Wagner, budgets do not expand most easily when taxes are concealed in a "fiscal illusion". A high and increasing reliance on "hidden" taxes exerted a significant dampening effect of the degree of expansion of the public economy. . . .

(c) Contrary to the skeptics' view, politics is important in influencing the scope of the public economy. The partisanship of government is associated with the rate of expansion, and whether a nation's government was generally controlled by Social Democratic (and their Leftist allies), or by non-Leftist parties, provides a strong clue to the relative degree of change in the scope of the public economy[3]. . . .

(d) Contrary to our predictions, federalism tends to dampen the degree of expansion of the public economy and centralization tends to facilitate that expansion. . . .

(e) . . . A high degree of trade dependence is conducive to a relatively large expansion of the public economy. Nations with open economies were far more likely to experience an increase in the scope of public funding than were nations with relatively closed economies. (1253)

The empirical support for these conclusions with respect to the 18-nation sample is moderately persuasive. Cameron provides a plausible explanation for why the strong relationship exists between the openness of the economy and the size of the public economy, emphasizing industrial concentration and the role of organized labor. He concludes by noting two strong associations:

a strong positive correlation ($r = 0.83$) . . . between the size of the increase in the public economy and a measure of economic equality involving the difference in the proportion of all national income received, after taxes, by the top and bottom 20 percent of households . . . [and a] strong negative correlation between the size of the cumulative increase in the public economy and the changes in the proportion of GDP represented by private capital accumulation. (1258)

Cameron's work is extremely worthwhile in the midst of a largely unsatisfactory empirical literature on governmental growth. Yet it is perhaps more successful in posing interesting empirical phenomena than in explaining them theoretically.

Much empirical work in this area remains. Future empirical work will be most profitable if it posits and tests more complicated theories of governmental size. The theories must incorporate mechanisms that allow government to decline as well as grow. Also, there is a formidable amount of work conceptualizing measures and collecting data that must be done in conjunction with the theorizing if work in this area is to become more meaningful.

FORMAL MODELING APPROACHES

Few empirical phenomena are more central to the positive and normative theoretical concerns of political economists than the growth and size of governmental budgets and the revenue structures by which governments acquire the resources (revenues) to finance those budgets. The "size of government" phenomenon has spawned an enormous literature, much of which is directed at devising theoretical mechanisms that would explain why governmental budgets are larger than they ought to be or grow faster than they ought to grow. The "revenue structure" phenomenon has spawned a somewhat smaller literature, primarily directed at understanding the role of complex revenue structures in inducing "fiscal illusion" (i.e., taxpayer misperception of the cost of government) and hence a willingness on the part of the taxpayer-voter to pay more for government than the value of its goods and services warrants. (For recent work see Buchanan 1967; Tanzi 1973; Wagner 1976; Goetz 1977; Pommerehne and Schneider 1978; Hansen and Cooper 1979.)

Most theoretical explanations for the observed phenomena of budget size and revenue structure utilize rationality assumptions and some kind of market metaphor in which public goods and services are supplied or demanded. Proffered models are choice-theoretic in their assertions about decision behavior. The phenomena are explained as resulting from choice processes in which some set of actors—the "community," citizens, voters, taxpayers, interest groups, elected representatives, and bureaucrats—is endowed with well-defined preferences over relevant states of the world (e.g., budget size, revenue structures, public goods). Each actor chooses (and acts) self-interestedly to maximize expected utility subject to some constraints, which usually take the form of conflicting preferences of other actors, characteristics of a coalition formation process, or institutional norms (Noll and Fiorina 1978; Demsetz 1979).

Voter Models

The earliest formal political models of government activity are the median voter models developed by Downs (1957) and Black (1958) which assume that decisions are made directly by the voter. For example, voters might be deciding upon the size of the budget; each would have preferences over possible budget sizes and would vote in favor of the proposed alternative he or she would most prefer. In this case, the level most preferred by the median voter will defeat any other alternative. This level, then, is assumed to be the "optimal level," or the level desired by the population as a whole.

The conditions under which this median voter equilibrium exists are, however, very severe. They include:

- All voters have single-peaked preferences on the dimension (or issue) of concern. That is, each voter has a point of maximum utility (i.e., his or her ideal point on the issue) with utility decreasing or remaining constant as one moves away from that point.

- Decisions are made on a single dimension, which is independent of all other decisions being made.

- There is a binary-choice procedure. That is, paired comparisons are made between a proposed alternative and the current alternative with the winning alternative subject to new proposals in an endless sequential process. There are no costs associated with making proposals and every voter is free to do so.

- All voters vote for the alternative they prefer at every stage of the voting process. A voter never engages in a sophisticated gaming strategy.

- The decision is reached by majority rule.

If these conditions hold, the median voter's most preferred expenditure level, once it has been proposed, will defeat all others.

Figure 3.1 depicts an electorate of five voters, all of whom have single-peaked preferences over the level of public sector expenditures. The point of maximum utility for the median voter (voter 3's preferred level, "med") can defeat any other proposal. If a new proposal is to the left of the median, voters 3, 4, and 5 will defeat it by voting for "med." Similarly, a new proposal to the right of "med" will be defeated by voters 1, 2, and 3. It is crucial to this argument that all voters vote. Thus, even voter 5 will express a preference between "med" and some proposal further to the left. More recent voter models vary some of the initial assumptions and predict results differing from the median voter optimum. It is suggested that such a social outcome at variance with the median voter's ideal point is the cause of public discontent with the size of government. Three of the most interesting extensions of the median voter model are those of Meltzer and Richard (1978), Romer and Rosenthal (1978), and Courant, Gramlich and Rubinfeld (1979).

Another voter model framework for explaining governmental growth considers the role of public sector employees and is based on the observation that the voters who determine the level of governmental expenditure include the recipients of these governmental funds. Specifically, public sector employees participate in the decision that determines the funding (public expenditures)

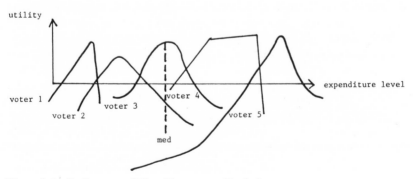

Figure 3.1 Preferences of Five Voters on a Single Issue

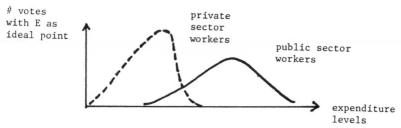

Figure 3.2   Preferences of Private and Public Sector Employees

available to them. Bush and Denzau (1977) and Courant, Gramlich and Rubinfeld (1979) have analyzed the impact of public sector employees on the level of spending adopted. These researchers argue that public and private sector employees have distinctly different sets of preferences on expenditure levels. In particular, the distribution of ideal points in the two sectors might look like those in Figure 3.2.

This leads to the basic conclusion of Bush and Denzau (1977). When private sector employees become public sector employees, their desired level of public expenditure increases. They now receive not only the benefits of the public goods but also the wages from these public expenditures. In a cyclic pattern, more and more public expenditures will be approved and increasingly more voters will become bureaucrats hired to help spend the increased expenditures. Eventually, an equilibrium will be achieved in which an increased budget no longer entails a larger number of employees but, rather, leads to greater wages for existing employees. Once stabilized, however, the resultant level of expenditures will be much greater than the original optimum preferred by the median voter.

If the condition of universal voter participation is weakened, the results are even more dramatic. One should expect public employees to vote more frequently than other potential voters, if only because they have a greater personal stake in the adopted budget level. Courant, Gramlich and Rubinfeld (1979) found greater public employee electoral participation in Michigan tax limitation proposals and argue that this leads to an expansion of the public sector. They show in the world of a formal model that "as long as the private sector retains its right to leave the community, and as long as all communities are not suffering high and rising tax rates, public sector monopolies ought to be kept in check by the simple optimizing behavior of those public employees." In the public sector, pressures that lead to increasing wages also lead to decreasing private sector employment levels. Obviously, in the limit there would be no private sector employees left to finance public sector wages. Thus, although the bureaucrat's voting behavior may lead to some increase in public expenditure levels, this increase is bounded.

All of the works discussed above show that even if voters are taken as the proximate decision makers on the level of public expenditures, there are numerous reasons why the actual level adopted could be unsatisfactorily high to a majority. That is, in many instances a majority would prefer that less be spent. It is also possible that the inefficiencies of the median expenditure level itself could be responsible for the discontent. Even when the median level of expenditure is adopted, it may not be Pareto-optimal; if some additional exchange of resources were allowed, all voters could be made better off (or at least as well off) as under the median allocation.

The actual processes for determining expenditure levels are much more complicated than the foregoing representations. At the federal level in the United States, a budget is developed by governmental agencies and the Office of Management and Budget. It is reviewed, altered, and approved by the president. The only real control voters have over this process is in the election of public officials. Three other types of models have been developed to deal with the expenditure decision at the institutional level. These are (1) models of legislative decision-making, which focus on legislators as utility-maximizing actors and examine the institutional rules under which they operate, (2) models of bureaucratic decision-making, and (3) models of interest-group behavior, which attribute disproportionate influence to particular organized demanders of governmental expenditures. These models do, of course, overlap considerably (e.g., bureaucracies can be considered a type of interest group), but it is useful to categorize the current arguments for the purpose of discussion.

Models of Legislative Decision-Making

The institutional procedures and legislative norms of the U.S. Congress and other legislatures all have a direct or indirect influence on the level of governmental expenditures. The principal works that make use of formal models to explore these relationships are those of Ferejohn (1974), Fiorina (1978), Weingast (1978), and Shepsle (1979). The specific focus of this research has been on the implications of "germaneness rules," "voting procedures," "universalism," and "reciprocity norms" on the structure of the legislation enacted.

Germaneness rules limit the scope and nature of amendments that can be considered by the legislature. As the term implies, voting procedures refer to rules governing the sequence with which legislation passes through subcommittees, committees, and the legislature as a whole. The principle of universalism describes the pressure exerted to have most legislation pass with large majorities, if not with universal approval. Rather than have minimal winning coalitions that exploit the losers, large coalitions form with favorable results to everyone. Finally, reciprocity is the norm that the concerned actors "should have their way." That is, when a committee reports a bill, other members should by default support it if it is not of particular significance to them.

> The odds are very high that majority rule as modified by universalism will depart from efficiency in the direction of over-production of public goods and services, or in short, economically excessive government activity. And, in fact, empirical studies suggest that various public sector activities associated with universalism are economically unjustified even in the very weak sense of unitary cost-benefit ratios. (Fiorina 1978)

Ferejohn argues that reciprocity across committees leads to expanded expenditures because of the nature of committee memberships. Legislators serve on committees that deal with programs for which they themselves are high demanders. Thus, each committee agrees upon a greater expenditure level than Congress as a whole would adopt by majority rule; the reciprocity norms guarantee that the committee's decision is approved by the committee of the whole. Germaneness rules help enforce these norms or agreements (e.g., induce reciprocity) by guaranteeing that massive revisions of legislation proposed by a committee are not possible. According to Fiorina, reciprocity and universalism are designed to enable legislators to maximize their individual goals and, specifically, their chances for reelection. If we assume a legislator's chance for reelection grows with increases in net benefits to his or her district, an individual legislator is made more secure by these norms.

In a simplified world in which each legislator favors one bill benefiting only his or her district, and in which the costs of any passed bill are allocated across all districts in some predetermined fashion, there is no guarantee of any equilibrium proposal to pass some (non-null) subset of bills that can defeat any other proposal. Each legislator has an incentive to seek out a winning coalition to pass his or her piece of legislation, yet once such a coalition is found which prefers the passage of some bills to the defeat of all, the eventual outcome is unpredictable.

Events may be more predictable if we impose legislative rules on the consideration of proposals. Let us assume that once a proposal to pass a set of programs is made, say, by a committee to the legislature, only three types of changes are possible: (1) a new program can be added, (2) an existing program can be deleted, or (3) a new program can be substituted for one in the proposal. It can be shown that either nothing will pass or the cheapest set of projects for a majority of new programs will be enacted.

Actual legislative procedures are still more complicated. There is not just one proposal from one committee but an entire set of proposals, one from each of several committees. In this situation stability disappears. M_c may not be able to make it through any committee. Although supporters of M_c are a majority in the legislature, they may not control relevant committees. The legislator has few clues as to which programs will eventually be passed. Yet if he simply agrees to pass all proposals, passage of his own program is guaranteed. The gain to his district is the benefit of passing his bill minus the district's share of the costs of passing all bills. The legislator will prefer this strategy in the long run as long as the net benefit to his district from approving all programs is greater than the district's expected gain from the passage of some randomly selected, majority-approved collection of programs. To enforce this preferred outcome, legislators adopt reciprocity and universalism norms.

This analysis ascribes government growth to uncertainties in legislative systems. To maximize chances for reelection, legislators must adopt norms and agreements that lead to the passage of large numbers of programs. This is true even though a majority would prefer to see some of these programs defeated. The only solutions to this dilemma appear to be (1) to change the institutional rules, (2) to increase public awareness of the costs of programs, or (3) to have fewer career legislators.

Some political economists, particularly Arnold (1978), have criticized this explanation for the growth of government. They feel that the conclusions summarized here are too dependent on the assumption that all the benefits of each program go to one district. Arnold argues that this type of ''pork-barrel politics'' makes up only a small percentage of governmental expenditures. He believes that legislative rules and norms may be useful to further explain the growth of government but that this will not have been adequately done until the actual characteristics of expenditure bills have been incorporated into these models.

Models of Bureaucratic Decision-Making

Niskanen (1971) has presented the best-known explanation of why government is larger than the optimal level implied by the median voter model. Niskanen's model focuses on the behavior of a budget-maximizing bureaucracy in which a bureau bargains with a legislative appropriations committee for funds. The committee, however, is a ''high demander'' of the bureau's goods and services, whereas the bureau is a monopolistic producer. As before, the committee members serve on a particular committee because they desire the goods and services it can allocate. Since the bureaucracy is the only supplier of the good, the committee appropriates the maximum amount for it. There is, then, no pressure to hold down the bureau's expenditures since all important groups of actors are committed to continual expansion.

Another view of bureaucratic decision-making comes from Noll and Fiorina (1978), who emphasize the distinction between growth of bureaucracy and growth of governmental services. They show that utility-maximizing legislators have an incentive to increase the size of the bureaucracy while decreasing the amount of services provided. Legislators, in this view, are again attempting to maximize their chances for reelection by providing facilitating services and public goods to their constituencies. Voters select the candidate promising the greatest individual welfare. This depends not only on what the candidate offers but also on how capable he or she is in delivering the promised services. Bureaus seek to maximize the number of bureaucrats employed. Noll and Fiorina argue that bureaucrats are not interested in maximizing the total budget. Items that may appeal to the individual voter, such as straight transfer payments, have little appeal to the bureaucrat. They argue instead that legislators want to increase the size of the bureaucracy.

In a system in which each individual's taxes are not directly related to the public goods an individual receives, legislators will gain the most by offering their constituents facilitating services. Legislators will attempt to maximize their chances of reelection by offering their constituencies services and allowing the bureaucracy to grow. Thus, Noll and Fiorina argue that the American political system, as currently structured, induces the expansion of the public sector work force without providing a countervailing force to the bureaucracy's desire to expand.

Margolis (1975) and Kamlet and Mowery (1980) criticize the Niskanen model of governmental growth on another plane. They fault Niskanen for focusing exclusively on the interactions among congressional committees while ignoring the impact of the executive branch. Kamlet and Mowery offer empirical evidence indicating a tendency for the Office of Management and Budget and the president to show leniency in cutting long-term budget authority as a side payment for accepting cuts in expenditure levels proposed to Congress. By "mortgaging the future" in this way, the executive branch reduces the margin for discretionary expenditures in subsequent years. Governmental growth is attributed, then, to growth in uncontrollable expenditures.

Models of Interest Group Behavior

One of the classical models of governmental decision-making described frequently is the "interest-group model." Interest groups lobby government for the provision or denial of certain benefits. These interest groups take opposing views on issues and must compete for governmental resources. It has often been hypothesized that this competition results in an efficient allocation of governmental resources.

Olson (1965) pointed out one of the major problems with this theory, the well-known "free-rider principle," whereby each individual in a large group has an incentive to let everyone else do the work. He or she can reap the benefits while paying none of the costs. Smaller groups will be more likely to go unopposed in their requests for governmental aid. Thus, government will fund more programs than actually desired. Salisbury (1978) discusses the role of interest groups in creating pressures for larger government. He argues that interest groups have had a minor impact on the creation of new programs, but that they are a major force in pressing for the enlargement of ongoing governmental activities.

Aranson and Ordeshook (1977) have extended and formalized models of interest groups demanding governmental growth. They start out with four basic assumptions.

1. Government provides both private and public goods. This can be viewed in two ways. In the traditional sense, government can provide private goods to groups and distribute the costs of the good to the population as a whole. In addition, every public good entails the provision of some private goods. The classic example of a public good, defense, also provides a private good to defense contractors. Thus some of the pressures government is responding to are the public provision of private goods.

2. Interest groups constitute the vehicle for putting pressure on government. These organized lobbying organizations include public employees, bureaus, and agencies within government as well as organizations more conventionally perceived as interest groups. They behave just like corporate, union, environmental, or consumer lobbying groups. They press their claims for the provision of desired goods.

3. It has been argued that people do not accurately perceive the costs or benefits of a program. The costs can be diffused and not directly related to a program, while benefits can be overestimated. Benefits are very visible and often exaggerated by politicians. Here it is assumed that people recognize the costs or benefits of a program only if they surpass some threshold level.

4. Finally, it is assumed governments act incrementally. They just pass or eliminate one program at a time.

Under these assumptions, an interest group can lobby government for the provision of a public or private good. Government, through legislators, decides which goods to provide. Aranson and Ordeshook find that under a wide variety of situations, it is possible that government will continue to provide private goods even when the costs of these goods exceed the benefits. The result can be modeled as an N-person prisoners' dilemma. All interest groups might prefer that no one get its private good provided by government. Still, each group would be motivated to lobby for the good it desires, which would then be provided.

Baumol's Disease

William Baumol, an economist, has joined medical scientists in having an ineradicable disease named after him. Baumol (1967) provided an explanation for governmental inefficiency and rising employment and other costs in the public sector, a disease of the body politic and the economy. The explanation is based on a formal two-sector model of unbalanced growth. Productivity in the service-intensive public sector is asserted to be lower than in the private sector. Yet the wage rate common to both sectors grows in accordance with the productivity in the private sector. Within this framework, Baumol demonstrated that technological progress in the private sector simply adds to the costs of the public sector. The core of the argument is very simple: With a common wage rate rising in accordance with efficiency gains in the private sector, costs will rise in the public (service) sector and will be unmatched by improvements in productivity. Furthermore, there is no incentive on the part of public employees to make such improvements.

Although Bradford, Malt, and Oates (1969) and Spann (1977) have derived some empirical support for Baumol's Disease, the highly stylized assumptions the model requires make it difficult to test. The declines since 1975 in U.S. public sector expenditures as a proportion of GNP and in public sector employment as a proportion of the total labor force pose interesting empirical puzzles for Baumol's theory. If the theory is correct, it implies that efficiency gains in the United States have become greater in the public sector than in the private sector. Has the disease been cured or, perhaps, contracted by the private sector?

As noted earlier, empirical generalizations about governmental growth were derived from data on periods of inexorable governmental growth and are therefore not very useful in thinking about governmental size in periods of relative or absolute decline. Much of the theoretical work in this section suffers from a normative bias: the presumption that government is too big or that it grows too fast. The most useful research will posit and test mechanisms of governmental growth and decline without tying those mechanisms to limited samples or normative presumptions.

RADICALS AND HERETICS

The Radical Disinterest

Governmental growth, from a radical perspective, may be a misplaced concern of ideological conservatives. It is certainly the case that the most strident antigovernmental growth research, misplaced or not, is from the Right, and that there is only a sparse literature on governmental growth on the Left (most examples of which treat the topic in passing rather than directly).

Not only does the Left generally feel less threatened by the growth in public expenditures (much of which is in transfer payments), but it has viewed the phenomenon of growing State intervention in the economy as predictable. For over a hundred years Marxists have, for example, linked the aggrandizement of State power with the "laws of motion of capitalism." Growth in government at this stage in the development of capitalism is simply accepted as a natural feature of the process of capital accumulation. Of course, given the loose verbal style of the theory, it would be difficult to make testable predictions or to find empirical phenomena inconsistent with the theory.

Despite the relative silence on the topic of governmental growth in Marxist research, it is possible to piece together a Marxist theory of public sector expansion, which, apart from vocabulary and rhetoric, provides insights that should be considered by non-Marxists. (For the most accessible and direct Marxist views on the capitalist States and its growth, see O'Connor 1973; Gough 1975; Foley 1978.) The capitalist State, Marxists typically argue, plays two fundamental and often contradictory roles.

- *Aiding in capital accumulation.* As the tool of the capitalist class (the owners of the means of production), the State must modulate economic crises, the most critical of which arise from "problems of underconsumption." "Crises of underconsumption" occur in the wake of the contradiction of holding down the wage income of the masses (and hence, consumption potential) while facing the need to sell an increasing amount of commodities to realize profits.

- *Legitimizing the soical order.* "Legitimation" refers to the process of defusing organized discontent by adopting reforms that provide concessions to various sectors of the working class. The classical Marxist example of legitimation is Bismarck's effective "buying off" of the entire German working class through the introduction of liberal social welfare legislation in the 1880s.

As economic crises become more severe (as they are expected to, according to Marxists), the need for State intervention in the capital accumulation process becomes ever greater. And the need to placate the working class (legitimation) grows perforce. Contradictory as these two interventions may be in terms of guaranteeing greater profits for the capitalist class, they lead unambiguously to a larger and more meddlesome (to capitalists competing against one another for shares of a smaller economic pie) State.

To give weight to these views perhaps requires faith in the structural inability of Western modes of production to sustain themselves—not a difficult leap in times of economic crisis. Nevertheless, these perspectives underscore the point that governmental growth may be an evil only in the eyes of privileged classes who must share ever-shrinking profits with a government that redistributes them to "others."

Blame It on John Maynard

Much has been made of the pernicious impact that gradual acceptance of Keynesian fiscal policy instruments has had on growth in the public sector. One of the most succinct statements of this view appears in *Democracy in Deficit: The Political Legacy of Lord Keynes,* by James Buchanan and Richard Wagner (1977). They do not, at least explicitly, condemn Keynesian macroeconomic theory as wrong-headed. Rather, their argument hinges on the proposition that the theory provides a "respectable" rationale for government to incur annual deficits that effectively reduce the perceived price of public services relative to private provision of services for the current generation of voter-taxpayers. As a consequence, they argue, the supply of governmental services (and federal spending) increases with the debt burden placed on disenfranchised future generations of taxpayers.

Keynesian economics is essentially devoid of descriptive and normative theories of public sector growth and, at least as originally developed, has less to say about the dynamics of adjustment processes than about their macrostatic relationships. In fact, many in the economics profession seem to view the question of governmental growth as a matter for political economy rather than for modern economic theory. Monetarists, for example, tend to fault Keynesian stabilization policy for its theoretically inimical impact on inflation and debt policy, for its insouciant assumptions, and for a host of other factors quite unrelated to governmental growth. To the extent that public sector growth is associated with increased government meddling with the equilibrating mechanisms of the free-market system, public sector growth is disruptive from a monetarist perspective. But here, at least in theory, the concern is with distortions caused by specific governmental intervention and not with the level of public sector expenditure per se.

What impact, then, has Keynesian economics had on governmental growth or theories of governmental growth? It clearly has served to focus attention on government as a nonpassive force on the economy. Empirically, though, it is often difficult to identify the precise nature of these governmental impacts. For example, it seems virtually impossible to distinguish empirically among at least three factors relating to the impact of fiscal policy. That is, growth in the public sector is attributable to:

1. growth in the public sector attributable to Keynesian theory.

2. growth attributable to poor implementation of discretionary fiscal policy (and whether or not implementation problems are structural or ameliorable).

3. growth attributable to policies simply masquerading as discretionary fiscal policy.

Nevertheless, this has not daunted efforts to understand the impact that deficit spending, abstracted from its immediate cause, has on governmental growth. Niskanen (1978), in an empirical study, argues that federal deficits have contributed to the increased level of federal spending. Part of the argument is tautological, since deficits are one means of financing expenditures. This line of empirical research would be much more interesting if it included the case of Japan, where deficits as a proportion of total governmental expenditures are twice those in the United States and governmental expenditures are lower by most measures.

The "Keynesian Revolution" may have changed people's views on the positive impact of government on the economy, but it has offered little in the way of a theory of government and, by extension, of governmental growth. Without a theory of government, it is difficult to "endogenize" the public sector in any model of the economic system. This difficulty explains the pointed lack of consideration of government in much of the work in economic growth theory. Since it is a branch of economics that explicitly focuses on the dynamic relationships among macroeconomic processes, one might expect it to have wrestled with governmental growth. And wrestled it has. Aggregate governmental expenditure is generally either included with consumption or investment expenditure, or is ignored altogether (Domar 1957, cited in Peacock and Wiseman 1961.

Short-sighted Officials and Cirrhosis of the Liver

Another explanation for growth in government is that it is an unintended consequence of government solving other problems. Kaufman and Larkey (1980), in a paper examining the budget growth in one city government over 55 years, argue that governments do not choose a particular budget size because the question How large should our budget be?, is essentially meaningless; there are no operational standards for knowing an optimal size or even whether one size is better than another. Rather, budget size evolves as a cumulative and largely unintended result of solving a succession of year-to-year budget problems. The city budget problem—balancing revenues against expenditures—is an operational, if not easy, problem.

A simple version of the whole argument is as follows. Politicians and bureaucrats are short-sighted, solving small, immediate problems rather than larger, long-term problems. Budget problems are temporally interdependent: the way in which this year's problem is solved materially affects what subsequent years' problems will be. Short-sighted, adaptive behavior in a domain that is temporally interdependent can lead to financial problems unsolvable by short-sighted, adaptive incremental solutions and to undesirable cumulative consequences (e.g., very large budgets or moderate-sized budgets and sharp reductions in services).

The level and composition of governmental revenues result, in the first instance, from decisions by government about what revenue sources to use (and to what extent) and from the decisions and actions of taxpaying entities. Any satisfactory explanation of the level and composition of governmental revenues must be based on satisfactory theories of how the relevant decisions are made. The level of expenditures is tied to the level of revenues (loosely in deficit-incurring national governments, and tightly in U.S. state and local governments with statutory balance requirements).

In financial decision-making, municipal managers and, to a lesser extent, legislatures are primarily concerned with solving the annual budget problem—approximately balancing revenues and expenditures each year. Legislatures, employees, revenue-yielding entities, and other environmental factors both partially determine the "budget problem" for management and constrain its behavior in solving these immediate, operational budget problems. There are no mechanisms for deciding holistically about optimal budget sizes or revenue structures. Search for changes in revenues and expenditures stops when a satisfactory solution to the annual balance problem is found.

Many important organizational decisions, particularly recurrent decisions such as those on budgets and personnel, are temporally interdependent. How the organization solves this period's decision problems partially determines both the problems and the set of solutions available in subsequent periods. The effects of seriatim decision processes are, to some extent, cumulative. Short-sighted, adaptive behavior in solving the individual decision problems in such a seriatim process can lead to cumulative consequences that were not intended in solving the problems piecemeal and that, when viewed historically with the benefit of hindsight, may be surprising and undesirable. If confronted with a clean slate and a holistic choice on the size and structure of municipal revenues for example, it is highly improbable that electorates, legislators, or bureaucrats would choose anything resembling what now exists.

The temporal interdependencies in decision making may be direct. Solutions to current problems may alter an organization's wealth position or its extant contractual obligations, making future problems more or less difficult. If a university spends part of its endowment for current operating expenses or if it tenures a large proportion of its faculty, its future budget and personnel problems become more difficult. A city government that relies on optimistic revenue forecasts to balance its budget, sells tax anticipation notes for cash in order to pay its bills, and agrees in labor negotiations to expensive, but deferred, fringe benefit packages and to provisions restricting managerial discretion on layoffs has dramatically altered its future budget and personnel decision problems.

The interdependencies may be less direct. The impact of current decisions on future outcomes can be mediated through the responses of individuals and organizations in the environment. Automobile manufacturers who control costs and price through such measures as reducing expenditures for rear shielding of gasoline tanks may face, in future periods, judgments to pay greater than the original cost saving, consumers' altered perceptions of product quality, increased direct regulation, and new, more punitive, product liability laws. Universities that balance budgets by raising tuition, increasing class size, and reducing student support services may face declining enrollments and reduced tuition revenues. City governments that raise visible tax rates (e.g., property tax rates) or fail to reduce rates rapidly to dampen the tax payment effects of inflation on property valuations may be inviting citizen-initiated limitations on revenues and/or expenditures.

In addition to varying in their directness, temporal interdependencies also vary in the immediacy and perceptibility of their consequences. Although the implications on the operating budget of a new indoor recreation facility may be obvious when the time arrives to staff, heat, and light it, the budget implications of changing the design of drainage for a road base to save a few thousand dollars in construction costs per mile may not be obvious even when the potholes appear in 10 to 20 years with greater frequency and severity than they would have with the original design. Learning is more likely in the first case than in the second because of differences in elapsed time and in the relative difficulty of understanding outcomes causally. By the time the potholes appear, the officials who changed the road design will probably no longer be in office. The new officials will be more interested in solving the pothole problem, perhaps using money generated from lowering design standards on current road construction, than in learning from the history of the current pothole problem to improve current decision-making.

Drinkers do not acquire cirrhosis of the liver through some holistic, prescient choice procedure; they acquire it a sip at a time over an extended period. The result reflects the cumulative effects of many prior decisions, each of which, when taken by itself, may have appeared unconnected to the cirrhotic condition and relatively unimportant. The terminal condition, however, is unintended and undesirable. From the vantage point of hindsight in a hospital bed, the patient's normative view of the many prior decisions (how they should have been made) may differ considerably from the descriptive view (how they were in fact made). Unfortunately, the physiological state of the liver has been altered in largely irreversible ways. It is too late for changed values or increased insight into the consequences of drinking to reflect in the decisions important to the patient. The learning process is faulty, in part, because the data that would permit adaptation—changing one's values or improving one's understanding of consequences for subsequent decisions— are disguised over much of the period during which the decisions (to sip or not) are made.

Even (or especially) for the well informed, the consequences of cirrhosis are unpleasant to attend to at the time of decision. There is utility in terms of immediate sensations in not attending to undesirable, imperceptible consequences of our every act, particularly when the act-consequence connections are stochastic and studied in a scientific field that we neither follow nor understand very well. For the moderately well informed, sometimes calculating individual there is always the hope that medical science will discover either a means of reversing the physiological processes or a foolproof liver transplant procedure or the hope that you are a physiological type not prone to cirrhosis. Or the reasoning may be that "something else will get me before cirrhosis, and I may as well as take my pleasures while I can."

Current municipal officials are, to a large extent, captives of decisions made by their predecessors. For example, if their counterparts 20 years earlier cut corners on road construction standards and sewer maintenance programs and acquired extensive park and recreation facilities (with their attendant operating costs) and chose not to fund the pension plan fully, it may be current officials who must either solve the problems (e.g., find the revenues to replace or maintain the facilities or abandon them) or devise a means of shifting the problems onto future officials. Like the drinker's liver, much of the context for municipal finance has a memory—its structure is gradually transformed both by the actions officials take and by forces beyond their control. Past decision behavior cannot be adequately summarized in theories of decision as "sunken costs" to be ignored in temporally interdependent processes with no beginning or end.

Voters, superior governments, and other elements of "institutional context" further constrain officials' behavior in solving the budget problem. They loosely specify infeasible solutions; voters with expectations about the level of taxes and services react when expectations are violated negatively. State governments constrain by statute what local officials can do financially.

Kaufman and Larkey's explanation for budget size and revenue structure is evolutionary; size and structure are the largely inadvertent results of city officials solving year-to-year budget problems in particular institutional contexts including constraints from voters and superior governments on the feasible solutions. The phenomena observed at any given point are better understood as accretions in a seriatim choice process than as the result of an implicit or explicit holistic choice. It is difficult to find anything normatively attractive about cirrhosis of the liver, but budget size and revenue structures are inherently neither good nor bad. Normative judgments must derive from either a feasible, prescriptive model or a positive model that has been altered slightly and manipulated to produce demonstrable "better" outcomes.

The notion that decisions on increments taken in sequence can lead to wholes of surprising magnitude is hardly new.

> In well-blended constitutions, . . . care must be taken to prevent men from committing any other breach of the law, most of all must a small breach be guarded against, for transgression of the law creeps in unnoticed, just as a small expenditure occurring often ruins men's estates. For the expense is not noticed because it does not come at all at once, for the mind is led astray by the repeated small outlays, just like the sophistic puzzle, "if each is little, then all are a little." This is true in one way, but in another it is not; for the whole total is not little, but made up of little parts. One thing therefore that we must guard against is this beginning; and the next point is that we must not put faith in the arguments strung together for the sake of tricking the multitude; for they are refuted by the facts. (Aristotle *Politics*, 421)

As Aristotle notes, "The mind is led astray"; the way in which decisions (and the information about decisions) are structured can lead to misperception and, from a rational view, suboptimal decisions.

PROBLEMS AND OPPORTUNITIES

The disparity between how much has been written and how little is known about governmental growth (and decline) is striking. None of the theoretical work is sufficiently developed and tested to be persuasive as a positive theory or useful as a prescriptive theory. Few empirical regularities have been discovered, and the conditions under which some of the seeming regularities might hold have not been explored. And yet, the topic of governmental size would seem to hold some real opportunities for academics to ply their theories. Moreover, the topic is enduringly important. The world needs theories that predict governmental size as a function of institutional arrangements and other controllable factors as well as immutable forces beyond mortal control. Also needed are theories about what differences the magnitude and composition of the public sector makes in terms of equity, efficiency, individual freedom, economic development, or anything that substantial numbers of people care about. Ideologies for or against more governmental activity are commonplace; persuasive theories that would support the ideological positions are not.

The entire body of research suffers from the sloppy empirical specification of "government" and "governmental growth." Conceptual and measurement problems are formidable, some arising from the difficulty of knowing what constitutes government and what does not.

> The impact of the public sector is not confined to the resources it owns or manages. Questions of public and private sectors' size are too often engulfed in emotional considerations of "too much government" or "government ownership as the only way to growth." However . . . government can control the private sector if it so desires and if it possesses the human capital or abilities to do so through a whole range of economic and political tools, regulations, and deeds. . . .
> The range of government help—or interference (depending on whether one enjoys the fruits of the act or suffers from it)—is quite wide. It can direct business behavior through inspection, licensing, sanctions, price control, foreign currency control, or moral suasion. Even in the very narrow field of creating new enterprises, government activities can range from initiation of new activities through the creation of economic conditions that will make such enterprises profitable, to financing of enterprises, to finally managing them through direct ownership. . . .
> In most countries today, there is a high degree of mutual dependence between the private and the public sector. Both sectors draw on the same resource pool of men and money. . . . The contributions of the public sector must be viewed not in terms of ownership but in terms of the direct and indirect impact of all its activities on the economy. (Aharoni 1977,78,286)

The difficulty in conceptualizing government also complicates the development of normative standards, as Aranson and Ordeshook note after reviewing some formal modeling literature.

All of these explanations for public sector size and growth share one important characteristic. No single explanation or set of explanations provides a measure of how large the public sector ought to be. Most of the explanations arise out of the belief that the public sector has grown too large. Indeed, in many instances that conclusion plainly motivated the original search for explanations for growth. But an explicit statement of how large the public sector ought to be is usually absent. (1980)

Much of the work on governmental growth, particularly the formal modeling work, suffers from the lack of an operational numeraire, an empirical equivalent to a model concept, particularly preferences. There is a great deal of political interest in the size of government, but this interest, manifested even in the processes for funding and publishing research, makes it difficult to do the "basic" research required on how the world works. Normative concerns are omnipresent. The chaos in conceptualizing government is reflected in the governmental growth literature, which proposes a number of alternative explanations for aspects of history but offers no answers about whether any particular government is too small or too large.

Tarschys (1975) in an extensive review of the literature on the growth of public expenditure, provided the taxonomy in table 3.2. This attempt to bring order to a chaotic collection of work is valiant, but only partially successful. As Tarschys himself noted in his original figure, much of the work belongs to more than one "mode." After a brisk review of 9 modes overlaid on 25 hypotheses (determinants), he concludes:

The above catalogue of potential determinants of rises in government spending is by no means an exhaustive list but merely a set of examples to illustrate the diverse

Table 3.2.   Nine Modes of Explaining Growth in Public Expenditures

Level	Perspective		
	Consumer	Finance	Producer
Socio-economic	Wagner Brecht Fabricant	Oshima	Baran & Sweezy Williamson Baumol & Oates Meidner
Ideological-Cognitive	Deutsch Easton Downs	Peacock & Wiseman Gupta	Niskanen Downs Parkinson Walker
Political-Institutional	Deutsch Sharkansky Timm Hjellum	Sharkansky Sachs & Harris Hinrichs	Niskanen Downs

Source: Tarschys (1975).

approaches that may be chosen in an effort to explain public growth. If the multitude appears staggering, it should be borne in mind that a truly thorough inventory of related factors would be far more extensive. Subdividing the nine fields in our diagram, we might easily arrive at fifty or seventy-five different processes or events that advance increase in public expenditures. A general theory of government growth does not seem to be around the corner. . . . It is doubtful that one could ever reach comprehension of the phenomenon by taking so many circumstances into consideration. Unless crucial variables are identified, the complexity of the process might even deter from further attempts to explain and predict trends in public policy and public spending. (37)

He further indicates that most of the work adopts a "consumer perspective" ("expenditures grow because there is a growing *demand* for public goods") and suggests turning research attention to "problems of financial structure and financial psychology," to "the problem of bureaucratic politics in its widest sense," and to "the routines of decision-making, the procedures of evaluation and review, and the very structure of the political decisions, which determine, among other things, the extent to which government activities are affected by changes in the environment." Regrettably, he provides no specific advice on how to transform mere attention to these topics into research.

Afxentiou (1979), like many others, deals critically with Wagner's Law and the many attempts to test it.

Despite its several methodological weaknesses, which erode its status to an almost empty proposition, or probably because of them, Wagner's "Law" has been tested extensively against the experience of various countries. Whether it is disproven or not seems to depend frequently on the selection of the periods covered or on the degree of aggregation of government expenditures or on the way the "Law" is being formulated. (20)

The author is similarly hard on Peacock and Wiseman's displacement-effect hypothesis.

The theoretical structure of the displacement effect is even weaker than that of Wagner's "Law." . . . Peacock and Wiseman simply plotted the growth of public expenditure in toto as well as adjusted for its war-related and defense components and GNP, all measured in constant prices, against time, and attributed the relative growth of public expenditure to an awakening of social awareness caused by war and its aftermath. The same method was applied to other countries [than Britain] and produced equally favorable results for the displacement hypothesis. But when tests more rigorous than crude geometrical graphs were employed most of the support provided to to the hypothesis had vanished. (21–2,25–6n)

The dissatisfaction of Afxentiou and other critics of the most prominent empirical approaches to the study of governmental growth arises from weak theory. In this literature, as in many social science literatures, the inductive work lacks theoretical rigor and the deductive work lacks empirical relevance.

Peacock distinguishes demand-side explanations for public expenditure growth from supply-side explanations, providing the following rationale for his emphasis on the supply side in his previous work (Peacock and Wiseman 1961, 1967):

> A major problem in attempting to apply dynamic consumer theory to explain the phenomenon of government expenditure growth lies in the fact that it is financed not by voluntary payments by consumers but by taxes. The political mechanism by which expenditure decisions come to be made modifies the process of choice as compared to the market, in two important ways. First of all the distribution of "purchasing power," as found, for example, in the voting system may differ markedly from the distribution of purchasing power as reflected in the prevailing (pre-tax) income distribution, either at the constituency or at the parliamentary level, and may vary markedly through time in a particular country. Secondly, the mode of decision making through voting must inevitably imply some degree of coercion, because the cost of obtaining unanimous decisions on all issues of public finance is clearly prohibitive save in the case of very small political units. The political facts of life are one of the major barriers to the deployment of econometric time series analysis in exploring the determinants of government expenditure growth using GDP or GDP per capita or some such variable, as the main explanatory factor. The empirical testing of this sort of hypothesis which postulates that per capita income is of strategic importance in explaining this growth rests on the assumption that all other variables, notably the political system, which may change markedly through time are so unimportant that they can simply be thrown into the error term. (1979a,106-7)

Serious theoreticians must confront data (and fewer "stylized" facts) if they are to contribute more than recreational mathematics. Empirical work must be directed by theoretical concerns if it is to become anything more than a groping exploration of an infinitely large, poorly recorded, and constantly changing panorama of human experience. Although not universally accepted, and even less frequently practiced, prediction is the "acid test" of theory, and being "demonstrably wrong" is an important, sometimes virtuous state. Theories in the social sciences are rarely "provable." Future research in this area should emphasize prediction and a variety of inductive and deductive procedures for exploring the limitations. There must be more publication of "beautiful hypotheses slain by ugly facts."

Research in the near future on the growth and decline of government should emphasize

- solving the many measurement and data problems.

- understanding the consequences of the size and composition of government.

- constructing positive theories—theories of "what is"—of the decision processes that proximately determine the size and composition of governmental expenditures.

The measurement and data problems are enormous in this area. There is very little reliable longitudinal data, and comparability problems for international cross-sections are staggering. Few incentives exist to encourage academics (an important class of prospective users possessing the conceptual frameworks essential to improving the data) to invest heavily in collecting data or in designing data collection systems. Such activities consume considerable time and lower publication rates. Good (comprehensible) data are not prerequisite to publishing "empirical" work; after all, as the excuse goes, "everyone knows the data are bad, but what can we do?"

There are no shortcuts to better data; improvement requires money and the time of talented people. Funding agencies, journal editors, publishers and others associated with academic promotion processes can contribute to the improvement of data collection by rewarding diligent efforts to understand the empirical bases of research. By the same token, diligent and ingenious theorizing about concepts that cannot be represented empirically and devising increasingly arcane methods for analyzing fundamentally bad data should not be rewarded so frequently.

A second area of recommended emphasis is on understanding the consequences of the size and composition of government. Unless we know something more about these consequences, the research on why and how governments become particular sizes and acquire particular compositions has interest only as an idle intellectual puzzle. The case, for example, of market forms of organization being superior to other forms is intuitively persuasive to many people. Unfortunately, the basic empirical research that would support such sweeping assertions about the superiority of market forms is scanty and inconsistent. In fact, the best empirical work on governmental growth, Pryor (1968) and Cameron (1978), is not comforting to market devotees. For the foreseeable future, researchers should focus on particular functional areas. With the "natural experiments" in deregulation (e.g., in the airline and trucking industries in the United States), scholars have an opportunity to address questions of alternative organizational forms with rigor.

There is a related "natural experimental" opportunity. Theoreticians who have been so diligent in constructing explanations of why government grows inexorably, particularly as a proportion of GNP, GDP, NNP, and the like, should take the decline of U.S. public sector spending (and the spending in other countries when the data are available) very seriously. The decline is a natural experiment, a turning point, that can provide a severe test for theories. A theory that cannot, in essentially the same form as it was used to explain inexorable growth, explain—or better yet, predict—the decline is a theory that probably has very little to say about the way the world works and should be modified or discarded altogether. Hopefully, the modifications will not simply make the theories more plastic to accommodate the phenomena. The inquiry should be directed at understanding the conditions under which the theories hold and fail, not to prove the theory by either finding an appropriate data set or a set of weakened assumptions to fit stylized facts. This natural experiment is an opportunity, somewhat rare in the social sciences, to winnow theories.

Another area of recommended emphasis is on constructing positive theories of the decision processes that proximately determine the size and composition of governments. Governments make decisions, usually on an annual basis, about what revenue sources (e.g., taxes) to utilize and the extent (e.g., tax rate) to which each source will be utilized. Governments also make decisions about how much to spend and about the form of expenditures. Taxpaying entities (individuals, households, and organizations) respond to government revenue and expenditure decisions in various ways; they may well adapt to alter incidence—to increase benefits from expenditures and to decrease the costs of payments to government. Theories of how governments and taxpaying entities make these decisions are ipso facto theories of the size, composition, and, to some degree, the consequences of government. Future research should more directly address these decision processes, individually and interactively, and multiple approaches to this research should be supported.

Some authors (e.g., Furniss 1979) strongly emphasize the need for comparative empirical research, specifically research that compares the experience of nation-states. Some comparative research should be done, but longitudinal work, comparisons of governments (or "public sectors") with themselves over time, is apt to be more profitable theoretically at present. The advantage of comparisons, whether among governments or among time segments of the same government, is the advantage of experiments with control and treatment groups. If we can construct a situation in which governments are more alike than different, we may be able to understand differences causally. Unfortunately, governments differ in many dimensions, and the controls required overwhelm the data we have available or can gather. Governments are apt to resemble themselves through time more closely than they are to resemble other governments. In general, the fewer the dimensions requiring control, the fewer degrees of freedom we require, and the more likely we are to be able to understand the processes causally.

The comparative approach may be most useful at microlevels. For example, in attempting to understand the consequences of alternative ways of organizing for policy performance, the international comparison may be the only analytically sound approach. Methodologically rigorous comparisons of the British, German, and U.S. railroad systems are potentially much richer and more profitable than a historical analysis of the U.S. system.

There is a need for a considerable amount of basic research in the substantive area of governmental growth, work with no obvious short-term "policy payoff." Some of this work must take place in peripherally related areas. Anthropologists observing tribes, sociologists analyzing small group behavior, and experimental game theorists studying university undergraduates may provide important insights into the human impulses to privatize some social functions and to consign others to the collective. There is a need to generate and discard metaphors and hypotheses more efficiently. "Any hypothesis, however absurd, *may* be useful in science, if it enables a discoverer to conceive things in a new way; but . . . when it has served this purpose by luck, it is likely to become an obstacle to further advance" (Russell 1963).

There are, then, at least two reasons for studying governmental growth: (1) to inform policy processes; and (2) to develop better theories of what most political economists would hold to be important phenomena. Without belaboring the philosophical issues (see Larkey 1979a, 1979b for more complete discussions), we believe that better theories, the product of basic research, are essential to better informed policy processes. The theory in this area is nascent, at best, and social scientists qua scientists have little to offer. Social scientists qua pundits, though, have offered a great deal of advice. Unfortunately, the theories that would enable social scientists to make better predictions than politicians, bureaucrats, or citizens of the consequences of alternative actions (e.g., the consequence of more or less government of certain kinds) do not exist.

The area does, however, present fertile ground for basic research. There are considerable data. There have been, and continue to be, significant natural experiments that are excellent grist for various theoretical mills. Finally, the area is intrinsically interesting to scholars from many disciplines, and in the event that useful predictive theories are developed, the potential policy benefits will be enormous. This is also the danger of constructing theory about any such highly politicized area. The temptation is always there to claim more than your "science" can justify.

NOTES

1. Studies of Wagner's Law and of determinants of public expenditures of this period include: Timm (1961); Höök (1962); Andic and Veverka (1964); Sacks and Harris (1964); Gupta (1967, 1969a, 1969b); Goffman (1968); Morss (1969); Bird (1970, 1971); Gandhi (1971); Goffman and Mahar (1971); Greytak, Gustely, and Dinkelmeyer (1974); Andre and Delorme (1975); Gørtz (1975); Michas (1975); Beck (1976); Buchanan and Tullock (1977); Wagner and Weber (1977); Ganti and Kolluri (1979); Glennerster (1979); Greene and Munley (1979); Mann (1980).

2. Research on government growth inspired by Peacock and Wiseman includes: Crowley (1971); Bird (1972); Rosenfeld (1973); Marr (1974); Oates (1975); and Diamond (1976). One scholar, Porter (1980), studying U.S. federal employment levels and acknowledging only the work of Parkinson (1957), has reinvented the Displacement Effect Hypothesis with a verbal model and weak descriptive statistics.

3. One skeptic was Pryor (1968), who found that politics was not important in a different sample.

REFERENCES

Afxentiou, P. C. 1979. *Patterns of Government Revenue and Expenditure in Developing Countries and Their Relevance to Policy.* Athens: Center of Planning and Economic Research.

Aharoni, Y. 1977. *Markets, Planning, and Development: The Private and Public Sectors in Economic Development.* Cambridge, Mass.: Ballinger.

Amacher, R. C., R. D. Tollison, and T. D. Willett. 1975. A Budget Size in a Democracy: A Review of the Arguments. *Public Finance Quarterly 3(2): 99–121.*

Andic, S., and J. Veverka. 1964. The Growth of Government Expenditure in Germany since the Unification. *Finanzarchiv 23 (January): 169–278.*

Andre, C., and R. J. Delorme. 1975. The Long-run Growth of Public Expenditures in France. *Public Finance 33(1/2): 42–67.*

Anton, T. J. Intergovernmental Change in the United States: Myth and Reality. Program in Urban and Regional Planning Working Paper, University of Michigan.

Aranson, P. H., and P. C. Ordeshook. 1977. Incrementalism, Fiscal Illusion, and the Growth of Government in Representative Democracies. Paper presented at the Fourth Interlaken Seminar on Analysis and Ideology, Interlaken, June.

————. 1977. A Prolegomenon to a Theory of the Failure of Representative Democracy. In *American Re-Evolution: Papers and Proceedings,* ed. R. D. Auster and B. Sears. Tucson: Department of Economics, University of Arizona.

————. 1980. The Political Bases of Public Sector Growth in a Representative Democracy. Paper presented at the annual meeting of the American Political Science Association, Washington, D.C.

————. 1980. Alternative Theories of the Growth of Government and Their Implications for Constitutional Tax and Spending Limits. Manuscript. March.

Aristotle. *Politics.* 1967. Cambridge, Mass.: Loeb Classical Library, Harvard University Press.

Arnold, R. D. 1978. Legislatures, Overspending, and Government Growth. Princeton University Working Paper; presented at the Conference on the Causes and Consequences of Public Sector Growth, Dorado Beach, Puerto Rico, November 1–5.

Baumol, W. J. 1967. Macroeconomics of Unbalanced Growth: The Anatomy of Urban Crisis. *American Economic Review 57(3): 415–26.*

Beck, M. 1976. The Expanding Public Sector: Some Contrary Evidence. *National Tax Journal 29(1): 15–21.*

————. 1979. Public Sector Growth: A Real Perspective. *Public Finance 34(3): 313–43.*

Bergstrom, T. C. 1979. Do Governments Spend Too Much? *National Tax Journal 32(2): 81–86.*

Bird, R. M. 1970. *The Growth of Government Spending in Canada.* Toronto: Canadian Tax Foundation.

————. 1971. Wagner's "Law" of Expanding State Activity. *Public Finance 26(3): 1–26.*

————. 1972. The "Displacement Effect": A Critical Note. *Finanzarchiv 30:454–63.*

Black, D. 1958. *The Theory of Committees and Elections.* Cambridge: Cambridge University Press.

Bonin, J. M., B. W. Finch, and J. B. Waters. 1969. Alternative Tests of the "Displacement Effect" Hypothesis. *Public Finance 24(4): 441–52.*

Bradford, D. F., R. A. Malt, and W. E. Oates. 1969. The Rising Cost of Local Public Services: Some Evidence and Reflections. *National Tax Journal 22(2): 185–202.*

Brecht, A. 1932. *Internationaler Vergleich der öffentlichen Ausgaben.* Leipzig and Berlin: B. G. Teubner.

Brennan, G. 1977. A Note on Progression and Public Sector Size. *Public Choice 32 (Winter): 123–29.*

Browning, E. K. 9175. Why the Social Insurance Budget is Too Large in a Democracy. *Economic Inquiry,* September 12(3): 378–88.

Brunner, K. 1978. Reflections on the Political Economy of Government: The Persistent Growth of Government. *Schweizerische Zeitung für Volkswirtschaft und Statistik* 114(3): 649–80.

Buchanan, J. M. 1967. *Public Finance in Democratic Process.* Chapel Hill: University of North Carolina Press.

———. 1977. Why Does Government Grow? In *Budgets and Bureaucrats: The Sources of Government Growth,* ed. T. E. Borcherding. Durham, N.C.: Duke University Press.

Buchanan, J. M., and G. Tullock. 1977. The Expanding Public Sector: Wagner Squared. *Public Choice* 31 (Fall): 147–50.

Buchanan, J. M., and R. E. Wagner. 1977. *Democracy in Deficit: The Political Legacy of Lord Keynes.* New York: Academic Press.

Bush, W. C., and A. T. Denzau. 1977. The Voting Behavior of Bureaucrats and Public Sector Growth. In *Budgets and Bureaucrats: The Sources of Government Growth,* ed. T. E. Borcherding. Durham, N.C.: Duke University Press.

Bush, W. C., and R. J. Mackay. 1977. Private versus Public Sector Growth: A Collective Choice Approach. In *Budgets and Bureaucrats: The Sources of Government Growth,* ed. T. E. Borcherding. Durham, N.C.: Duke University Press.

Cameron, D. R. 1978. The Expansion of the Public Economy: A Comparative Analysis. *American Political Science Review* 72(4): 1243–61.

Chaiken, J. M., and W. E. Walker. 1979. *Growth in Municipal Expenditures: A Case Study of Los Angeles.* RAND Report N-1200-RC. Santa Monica: RAND Corporation.

Citrin, J. 1979. Do People Want Something for Nothing?: Public Opinion on Taxes and Government Spending. *National Tax Journal* 32(2): 113–29.

Courant, P. N., E. M. Gramlich, and D. L. Rubinfeld. 1979. Public Employee Market Power and the Level of Government Spending. *American Economic Review* 69(5): 806–17.

Craswell, R. 1975. Self-Generating Growth in Public Programs. *Public Choice 21 (Spring): 91–97.*

Crecine, J. P., M. S. Kamlet, D. C. Mowery, C. Stolp, and M. Winer. 1977. The Controllability of "Uncontrollable" Federal Expenditures: Executive Branch Decision-Making. Paper presented to the Midwestern Political Science Association Meetings, October.

Crecine, J. P.; M. S. Kamlet; D. C. Mowery; and M. Winer. 1981. The Role of the U.S. Office of Management and Budget in Executive Branch Budgetary Decision-Making. In *Research in Public Policy Analysis and Management,* vol. 2, ed. J. P. Crecine, 327–57. Greenwich, Conn.: JAI Press.

Crowley, R. W. 1971. Long Swings in the Role of Government: An Analysis of Wars and Government Expenditures in Western Europe since the Eleventh Century. *Public Finance* 26 (1): 27–43.

Davidson, S., et al. 1977. *Does the Government Profit from Inflation? AEI Public Policy Forum, no. 7.* Washington, D.C.: American Enterprise Institute.

Davis, J. R., and C. W. Meyer. 1969. Budget Size in a Democracy. *Southern Economic Journal 36(1): 10–17.*

Demsetz, H. 1979. The Growth of Government. Paper presented at a conference on the Growth of Regulation, Hoover Institution, Palo Alto, Calif.

Denzau, A., R. J. Mackay, and C. L. Weaver. 1979. Spending Limitations, Agenda Control, and Voters' Expectations. *National Tax Journal 32(2): 189–200.*

Derthick, M. 1975. *Uncontrollable Spending for Social Service Grants.* Washington, D.C.: Brookings Institution.

Diamond, J. 1976. Econometric Testing of the "Displacement Effect": A Reconsideration. *Finanzarchiv 35:387–404.*

Domar, E. 1957. *Essays in the Theory of Economic Growth.* New York: Oxford University Press.

Downs, A. 1957. *An Economic Theory of Democracy.* New York: Harper & Row.

————. 1965. Why the Government Budget is Too Small in a Democracy. In *Private Wants and Public Needs,* ed. Edmund S. Phelps. New York: Norton.

Dubin, E. 1977. The Expanding Public Sector: Some Contrary Evidence—A Comment. *National Tax Journal 30(1): 95.*

Fabricant, S. 1952. *The Trend of Government Activity in the United States since 1900.* New York: National Bureau of Economic Research.

Ferejohn, J. 1974. *Pork-Barrel Politics.* Stanford: Stanford University Press.

Fesmire, J. M., and E. C. Beauvais. 1978. Budget Size in a Democarcy Revisited: The Public Supply of Private, Public, and Semipublic Goods. *Southern Economic Journal 45(2): 477–93.*

Fiorina, M. P., and R. G. Noll. 1978. Voters, Bureaucrats, and Legislators: A Rational Choice Perspective on the Growth of Bureaucracy. *Journal of Public Economics 9(2): 239–54.*

Flowers, M. R. 1977a. Multiple Tax Sources, Voting Equilibrium, and Budgetary Size. *Public Finance 32:210–24.*

————. 1977b. Revenue Structure, Fiscal Illusion, and Budgetary Choice: Comment. *Public Choice, 29* (Spring): 127–39.

Foley, D. K. 1978. State Expenditure from a Marxist Perspective. *Journal of Public Economics 9(2): 221–38.*

Forsman, A., et al. 1979. The Expansion of the Public Sector in Sweden in the Postwar Period. In *Postindustrial Society,* ed. B. Gustafsson. New York: St. Martin's.

Freeman, R. A. 1975. *The Growth of American Government.* Palo Alto, Calif.: Hoover Institute Press.

Friedman, M. 1978. From Galbraith to Economic Freedom. In *Tax Limitation, Inflation, and the Role of Government,* ed. M. Friedman. Dallas: Fisher Institute.

Frolich, N., J. A. Oppenheimer, and O. R. Young. 1971. *Political Leadership and Collective Goods.* Princeton, N.J.: Princeton University Press.

Furniss, N., and T. Tilton. 1977. *The Case for the Welfare State.* Bloomington: Indiana University Press.

Galbraith, J. K. 1971. *The New Industrial State.* Boston: Houghton Mifflin.

Gandhi, V. P. 1971. Wagner's Law of Public Expenditure: Do Recent Cross-Section Studies Confirm it? *Public Finance 26(1): 44–56.*

Ganti, S., and B. R. Kolluri. 1979. Wagner's Law of Public Expenditure: Some Efficient Results for the United States. *Public Finance 34(2): 225–33.*

Glennerster, H. 1979. The Determinants of Public Expenditure. In *Social Policy and the Expenditure Process,* ed. T. A. Booth. Oxford: Blackwell.

Goetz, C. J. 1977. Fiscal Illusion in State and Local Finance. In *Budgets and Bureaucrats: The Sources of Government Growth,* ed. T. E. Borcherding. Durham, N.C.: Duke University Press.

Goffman, I. J. 1968. On the Empirical Testing of Wagner's Law: A Technical Note. *Public Finance 13(3): 359–66.*

Goffman, I. J., and D. J. Mahar. 1971. The Growth of Public Expenditures in Selected Developing Nations: Six Caribbean Countries, 1940–65. *Public Finance 26(1): 57–74.*

Gordon, D. F. 1978. Debts, Keynes, and our Present Discontents. *Journal of Monetary Economics 4(3): 583–89.*

Gørtz, E. 1975. Den offentlige sektors relative størrelse og lønudviklingen for offentligt ansatte. [Public Sector Wage Increases and the Relative Size of the Public Sector. With English summary.] *Nationaløkonomisk Tidsskrift* 113(1): 115–21.

Gough, I. 1975. State Expenditures in Advanced Capitalism. *New Left Review (92):53–92.*

Gramlich, E. M. 1978. State and Local Budget Surpluses and Federal Grant Policies. In *Local Distress, State Surpluses, Proposition 13: Prelude to Fiscal Crisis or New Opportunities?,* Hearings before the Subcommittee on the City, Committee on Banking, Finance, and Urban

Affairs, House of Representatives, and the Joint Economic Committee, Washington D.C., July 25–26.

Greene, K. V., and V. G. Munley. 1979. Generating Growth in Public Expenditures: The Role of Employee and Constituent Demand. *Public Finance Quarterly 7(1): 92–109.*

Greenwood, R., et al. 1980. Incremental Budgeting and the Assumption of Growth: The Experience of Local Government. In *Public Spending Decisions: Growth and Restraint in the 1970s,* ed. M. Wright. London: Allen & Unwin.

Greytak, D., R. Gustely, and R. J. Dinkelmeyer. 1974. The Effects of Inflation on Local Goverment Expenditures. *National Tax Journal 27(4): 583–98.*

Gupta, S. P. 1967. Public Expenditure and Economic Growth: A Time-Series Analysis. *Public Finance 22(4): 423–61.*

————. 1969a. Public Expenditure and Economic Development: A Cross-Section Analysis. *Finanzarchiv 28(1): 26–41.*

————. 1969b. Using Various Statistical Measures to Analyze the Size of the Public Sector: Comment. In *Quantitative Analysis in Public Finance,* ed. A. T. Peacock. Praeger Special Studies in International Economics and Development. The Hague: Praeger.

Hansen, S. B., and P. Cooper. 1980. State Revenue Elasticity and Expenditure Growth. *Policy Studies Journal* (9(1): 26–33.

Höök, E. 1962. The Expansion of the Public Sector: Study of the Development of Public Sector: Study of the Development of Public Civilian Expenditures in Sweden during the Years 1913–1958. *Public Finance* 17(4): 289–312.

Jacobe, D. J. 1977. Federal Propensities to Spend and Tax. In *Budgets and Bureaucrats: The Sources of Government Growth,* ed. T. E. Borcherding. Durham, N.C.: Duke University Press.

Kamlet, M. S., and D. C. Mowery. 1980. Bureaucrats, the President, and the Growth of Government. Paper presented at the October meetings of the Association for Public Policy Analysis and Management, Boston.

Katz, H. 1980. *The Impact of Public Employee Unions in City Budgeting and Employee Remuneration: A Case Study of San Francisco.* San Francisco: Garland Press.

Kaufman, H. 1976. *Are Government Agencies Immortal?* Washington D.C.: Brookings Institution.

Kaufman, S., and P. D. Larkey. 1980. The Composition and Level of Municipal Revenues: An Adaptive, Problem-Solving Explanation. Social Science Working Paper, Carnegie-Mellon University, Pittsburgh. March.

Kelley, A. C. 1976. Demographic Change and the Size of the Government Sector, *Southern Economic Journal* 43(2): 1056–66.

Kendrick, M. S. 1955. *A Century and a Half of Federal Expenditures.* National Bureau of Economic Research Occasional Paper 48. New York: NBER.

Mackay, R. J., and C. L. Weaver. 1978. Monopoly Bureaus and Fiscal Outcomes: Deductive Models and Implications for Reform. In *Policy Analysis and Deductive Reasoning,* ed. G. Tullock and R. E. Wagner. Lexington, Mass: D. C. Heath.

————. 1979. On the Mutuality of Interests between Bureaus and High-Demand Review Committees: A Perverse Result. *Public Choice* 34(3/4): 481–91.

Mann, A. J. 1980. Wagner's Law: An Econometric Test for Mexico, 1925–1976. *National Tax Journal 33(2): 189–201.*

Margolis, J. 1975. Bureaucrats and Politicians: Comment. *Journal of Law and Economics* 18(3): 645–59.

Marr, W. L. 1974. The Expanding Role of Government and Wars: A Further Elaboration. *Public Finance* 29(3/4):416–21.

Martin, A. M., and W. A. Lewis. 1956. Patterns of Public Revenue and Expenditure. *Manchester School 24(3): 203–32.*

McMahon, W. W. 1971. Cyclical Growth of Public Expenditure. *Public Finance* 26(1): 75–105.

Meltzer, A., and S. F. Richard. 1978. Why Government Grows (and Grows) in a Democracy. *Public Interest* 52 (Summer): 111–18.

Michas, N. A. 1975. Wagner's Law of Public Expenditures: What is the Appropriate Measurement for a Valid Test? *Public Finance* 30(1): 77–85.

Morss, E. R. 1969. Using Various Statistical Measures to Analyze the Size of the Public Sector. In *Quantitative Analysis in Public Finance,* ed. A. T. Peacock. Praeger Special Studies in International Economics and Development. The Hague: Praeger.

Munley, V. G., and K. V. Greene. 1978. Fiscal Illusion, the Nature of Public Goods, and Equation Specification. *Public Choice* 33(1): 95–100.

Musgrave, R. A., and J. M. Culberton. 1953. The Growth of Public Expenditures in the United States, 1890–1948. *National Tax Journal 6(2): 97–115.*

Niskanen, W. A. 1968. Nonmarket Decision-Making: The Peculiar Economics of Bureaucracy. *American Economic Review* 58(2): 293–305.

———. 1971. *Bureaucracy and Representative Government.* Chicago: University of Chicago Press.

———. 1978. Deficits, Government Spending, and Inflation: What Is the Evidence? *Journal of Monetary Economics* 4(3): 591–602.

Noll, R., and M. Fiorina. 1978. Voters, Bureaucrats, and Legislators. *Journal of Public Economics* 7(2): 239–54.

Nutter, G. W. 1978. *Growth of Government in the West.* Washington D.C.: American Enterprise Institute.

Oates, W. E. 1975. ''Automatic'' Increases in Tax Revenues: The Effect on the Size of the Public Budget. In *Financing the New Federalism: Revenue Sharing, Conditional Grants, and Taxation,* ed. W. E. Oates. Baltimore: Johns Hopkins University Press, for Resources for the Future.

O'Connor, J. 1973. *The Fiscal Crisis of the State.* New York: St. Martin's.

Olson, M. 1965. *The Logic of Collective Action.* Cambridge, Mass. Harvard University Press.

Oshima, H. T. 1957. The Share of Government in Gross National Product for Various Countries. *American Economic Review* 47(3): 381–90.

Parkinson, C. N. 1957. *Parkinson's Law and Other Studies in Administration.* Boston: Houghton Mifflin.

Peacock, A. T. 1972. New Methods of Appraising Government Expenditure: An Economic Analysis. *Public Finance* 27(2): 85–91.

———. 1979a. *The Economic Analysis of Government and Related Theories.* New York: St. Martin's.

———. 1979b. Public Expenditure Growth in Postindustrial Society. In *Postindustrial Society,* ed. B. Gustafsson. New York: St. Martin's.

Peacock, A. T., and D. J. Robertson, eds. 1963. *Public Expenditures: Appraisal and Control.* Edinburgh: Oliver & Boyd.

Peacock, A. T., and J. Wiseman. 1961. *The Growth of Public Expenditure in the United Kingdom.* Princteon, N.J.: Princeton University Press.

———. 1967. *The Growth of Public Expenditure in the United Kindgom, 1890–1955.* London: Allen & Unwin.

———. 1972. Determinants of Government Expenditure. In *Public Expenditure Analysis; Selected Readings,* ed. B. S. Sahni. Rotterdam: Rotterdam University Press.

———. 1979. Approaches to the Analysis of Government Expenditure Growth. *Public Finance Quarterly 7(1): 3–23.*

Pluta, J. E. 1974. Growth and Patterns in U.S. Government Expenditures, 1956–1972. *National Tax Journal* 27(1): 71–92.

———. 1979. Wagner's Law, Public Sector Patterns, and Growth of Public Enterprises in Taiwan. *Public Finance Quarterly* 7(1): 25–46.

Pommerehne, W. W. 1978. Institutional Approaches to Public Expenditure: Empirical Evidence from Swiss Municipalities. *Journal of Public Economics* 9(2): 255–80.

Pommerehne, W. W., and F. Schneider. 1978. Fiscal Illusion, Political Institutions, and Local Public Spending. *Kyklos* 31(3): 381–408.

Porter, B. D. 1980. Parkinson's Law Revisited: War and the Growth of American Government. *Public Interest,* no. 60 (Summer): 50–68.

Pryor, F. L. 1968. *Public Expenditures in Communist and Capitalist Nations.* London: Allen & Unwin.

Ratchford, B. U. 1959. *Public Expenditure in Australia.* Durham, N.C.: Duke University Press.

Romer, T., and H. Rosenthal. 1978. Political Resource Allocation, Controlled Agendas, and the Status Quo. *Public Choice* 33:27–43.

Rosenfeld, B. D. 1973. The Displacement Effect in the Growth of Canadian Government Expenditures. *Public Finance* 28(3/4): 301–14.

Rostow, W. W. 1971. *Politics and the Stages of Growth.* Cambridge: Cambridge University Press.

Rupprecht, E. O. 1974. How Big Is Government? *Finance Development 11(1): 29–33.*

Russell, B. 1963. Plato's Theory of Ideas. In *Plato: Totalitarian or Democrat?,* ed. T. L. Thorson. New York: Prentice Hall.

Sacks, S., and R. Harris 1964. The Determinants of State and Local Government Expenditures and Intergovernmental Flows of Funds. *National Tax Journal* 1:75–85.

Salisbury, R. H. 1978. Interest Groups and Governmental Growth. Washington University Working Paper; presented at the Conference on the Causes and Consequences of Public Sector Growth, Dorado Beach, Puerto Rico, November 1–5.

Schumpeter, J. A. 1954. *History of Economic Analysis.* New York: Oxford University Press.

Shepsle, K. 1979. Institutional Arrangements and Equilibrium in Multidimensional Voting Models. *American Journal of Political Science* 23 (February): 23–57.

Skolka, J. V. 1977. Unbalanced Productivity Growth and the Growth of Public Services. *Journal of Public Economics* 7 (2): 271–80.

Spann, R. M. 1977. The Sources of Growth of Public Expenditures in the United States, 1902–1970. In *Budgets and Bureaucrats: The Sources of Government Growth,* ed. T. E. Borcherding. Durham N.C.: Duke University Press.

Stewart, J. D. 1980. From Growth to Standstill. In *Public Spending Decisions: Growth and Restraint in the 1970s.* ed. M. Wright. London: Allen & Unwin.

Tanzi, V. 1973. The Theory of Tax Structure Change during Economic Development: A Critical Survey. *Rivista di Diritto Finanziaro e Scienza delle Finanze,* 32(2): 199–208.

Tarschys, D. 1975. The Growth of Public Expenditures: Nine Models of Explanation. *Scandinavian Political Studies* 10:9–31.

Tax Foundation. 1967. *Growth Trends of New Federal Programs, 1955–1968.* New York: Tax Foundation.

———. 1979. *Facts and Figures on Government Finance, 20th Biennial Edition.* Washington, D.C.: Tax Foundation.

Timm, H. 1961. Das Gesetz der wachsenden Staatsausgaben. *Finanzarchiv* 21(January): 210–47.

de Tocqueville, A. 1835. *Democracy in America.* Oxford: Oxford World Classics 1965.

Trescott, P. B. 1955. Federal-State Financial Relations, 1790–1860. *Journal of Economic History* 15(3): 227–45.

Veverka, J. 1963. The Growth of Government Expenditure in the United Kingdom since 1790. In *Public Expenditures: Appraisal and Control,* ed. A. T. Peacock and D. J. Robertson. Edinburgh: Oliver & Boyd.

Wagner, A. 1877. *Finanzwissenschaft, Pt. I.* Leipzig: C. F. Winter.
————. 1890. *Finanzwissenschaft, Pt. II.* Leipzig: C. F. Winter.
————. 1893. *Grundlegung der politischen Okonomie.* Leipzig: C. F. Winter.
Wagner, R. E. 1976. Revenue Structure. Fiscal Illusion, and Budgetary Choice. *Public Choice* 25(Spring): 45–61.
————. 1977. Revenue Structure, Fiscal Illusion, and Budgetary Choice: Reply. *Public Choice* 29(Spring): 131–32.
Wagner, R. E., and W. E. Weber. 1977. Wagner's Law, Fiscal Institutions, and the Growth of Government. *National Tax Journal* 30(2): 59–68.
Watson, W. G. 1978. Bacon and Eltis on Growth, Government, and Welfare: Review Article. *Journal of Comparative Economics* 2(1): 43–56.
Weidenbaum, M. L. 1969. Budget "Uncontrollability" as an Obstacle to Improving the Allocation of Government Resources. In *The Analysis and Evaluation of Public Expenditures: The PPB System,* vol. I, a compendium of papers published by the Subcommittee on Economy in Government, Joint Economic Committee, Congress of the United States.
Weingast, B. 1978. A Rational Choice Perspective on Congressional Norms. *American Political Science Review* 72.
Weiss, S. J. 1969. Factors Affecting the Government Revenue Share in Less Developed Countries. *Social and Economic Studies* 18:348–64.
Wilensky, H. L. 1976. *The "New Corporatism," Centralization, and the Welfare State.* Beverly Hills: Sage.
Williamson, J. G. 1961. Public Expenditures and Revenue: An International Comparison. *Manchester School* 29(1): 43–56.
Wiseman, J., and J. Diamond. 1975. Comment: On "Long-Run Growth of Nondefense Government Expenditures in the United States." *Public Finance Quarterly 3(4): 411–14.*

4

Information Systems and Intergovernmental Relations

John Leslie King
Kenneth L. Kraemer

Other chapters in this book examine and evaluate approaches that can be used for describing the state of and directing improvements in the federal system of government in the United States. We take a slightly different approach to the issue by focusing on the critical component of information and the roles it plays both in the affairs of individual governmental units and in the interactions among governmental units at the same levels and at different levels. This focus on information, and more importantly on the systems by which information is developed, exchanged, and used within government, calls attention to the practical opportunities and constraints in improving the efficiency and effectiveness of intergovernmental action via information systems.

It has been suggested by some that we are approaching an "information society," in which the productive capacity of our society is invested more heavily in information-related activity than in other sectors, such as agriculture, industry, or services.[1] Although appealing, these visionary forecasts tend to be misleading. They promote the more grandiose expectations about the effects that new information technologies will have, while masking over fundamental properties of information, irrespective of the technologies used to manage it. Thus, though in this chapter we discuss information technology such as computerized information systems, our broader concern is with the formalized, established mechanisms and protocols for collecting, processing, manipulating, exchanging, and utilizing information within and among governmental units, regardless of whether or not such mechanisms and protocols use advanced technologies.

The importance of information management in government can be seen in the fact that nearly every governmental program, whether within a jurisdiction or across jurisdictions, begins and ends with the analysis of information. Moreover, the operation of programs takes place through the constant processing of information. Like many service industries, governments as enterprises are to a large extent involved in the information processing business. The effective management of information is necessitated by the very nature of government, and new technology to facilitate information management has often been funded and first used by government.[2] The ability of government to manage information in new and creative ways offers new opportunities for governmental action in carrying out its mandates. This is evidenced by the proliferation of information systems at all levels of government. Among the major institutional sectors of U.S. society, the federal government has long been by far the largest user of computer-based information systems (Mowshowitz 1976).

Curiously, however, it is only recently that serious attention has been directed toward the ways that inability to effectively manage information constrains developing effective governmental programs and operations. Although anyone connected with governmental decision-making is familiar with the expression "garbage in, garbage out," the truly critical ways in which data problems can constrain government's ability to respond to public needs is only now beginning to be addressed (Head 1982).[3]

In this chapter we address the question of how and where information systems fit in the general problem of improving public sector performance, specifically, improving intergovernmental performance. Many problems with governmental programs and policies can be traced back to problems in the information used to design and operate them. In addition, shortfalls in information fundamentally constrain future governmental options. Governmental programs are undergoing changes that reflect new political attitudes and fiscal constraints, and major intergovernmental shifts in responsibilities are occurring. How will information management issues affect the outcomes?

Uses of Information in Government

We make a distinction between two major kinds of information used in government.[4] *Operational information* refers to information collected in the process of carrying out routine operations of government, such as letting contracts, paying bills, issuing voter notices, keeping accounts, making up the payroll, and keeping track of taxes. This kind of information is generally of greatest importance to the jurisdiction where it is collected, since that is the jurisdiction whose operations it facilitates. Little operational information is shared intergovernmentally in its basic form. *Planning and management information* is used to monitor the operations of government and to assist in planning and decision making. Information for planning and management might be culled from operational information (usually in some reduced form such as summary statistics), but much is collected explicitly for planning and

management purposes. To the extent that information is shared intergovernmentally, it is often planning and management information.

Within the category of planning and management information we identify
three major kinds of uses to which such information is put. First, it is used for
status reporting, in order to determine the current state of some thing or things
within a given jurisdiction. Information used in status reporting is useful in
finding problems, in conducting very broad-brush performance assessment
(e.g., annual crime rates), in identifying trends, and in establishing base lines
against which other measures are compared (e.g., use of population as a
denominator in many comparison ratios). Status reporting information typically consists of measures of size (e.g., population, revenues), of events
(e.g., number of crimes committed, number of people unemployed, number
of marriages or divorces), or of outputs of organizations (e.g., number of
arrests, miles of road paved, number of welfare clients served). Such values
are often consolidated for comparison purposes into ratios, usually of outputs
as a function of size (e.g., arrests as a function of the size of the law enforcement agency). Status reports are important in determining need for structural
or management changes in operations or in programs as well as for planning
purposes.

Second, planning and management information can be used for *performance analysis,* usually a comparison across time or comparable units. Often
such analyses compare outputs to inputs (e.g., miles paved per dollar spent on
paving). Analyses often focus on short time-scales, such as month-to-month
trends or cross-sectional comparisons across departments or agencies. They
also tend to utilize narrowly defined measures, such as the gallons of water
pumped by a water utility or the number of trees trimmed by a park service.
The goal in performance analysis is usually to make "course corrections"
bring the operations of government in line with agreed-upon goals for performance—primarily to improve management of governmental operations.

Finally, planning and management information can be used for *compliance
analysis,* to determine whether an agency or a governmental jurisdiction is
complying with laws and regulations. Monitoring to ensure compliance tends
to be the key factor in such uses, the goal being to help maintain the integrity
of controls over governmental activity. Compliance analyses provide the evidence necessary to identify and collect failures of compliance on a reliable
and fair basis. Their primary purpose is to enhance enforcement of the directives of higher levels within the governmental hierarchy.

This factoring of information uses by government allows us to separate for
consideration information used solely for operations from that used in planning and management.

A Focus on Locally Generated Data

The objective of this paper is to examine experiences of efforts to manage
effectively information for use intragovernmentally and intergovernmentally.
However, we restrict our discussion primarily to examination of information

generated at the local government level and its use within local governments and intergovernmentally. This restriction derives from the rather specific focus of our own research on information systems in local government and from the fact that a considerable amount of research aimed at improving local government performance analysis and operations has been conducted over the last 15 years.[5] In contrast, relatively little research has been done on information management at the state and federal levels that is useful in examining intergovernmental issues. Thus, the focus on locally generated information is practical and necessary. We believe that this focus does not constrain the analysis significantly, given the broad base of experiences at the local level and the local origin of most intergovernmentally shared information.

Using the distinctions between operational information and planning and management information, we can factor information generated by local governments according to the diagram in figure 4.1. Most locally generated

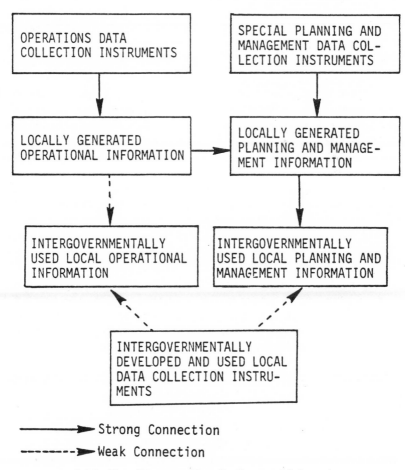

Figure 4.1   Flow Diagram of Locally Generated Information

information is used for local operations support. Some of this operational information is also used in summary form for planning and management at the local level. Information collected specifically for planning and management is a less significant aspect of local government information management, but it is considerable nonetheless. Most locally generated information that is reported upward into the intergovernmental system is planning and management information, often drawn from operational information systems. Very little information developed strictly for operational uses at the local level finds its way into the intergovernmental system. This characterization of the use and flow of locally generated information provides a context for the analyses presented here.

INFORMATION SYSTEMS FOR LOCAL GOVERNMENT USE

The vast majority of information systems in local governments are targeted for operational uses, which benefit the most from automated information systems (King and Kraemer 1983). There are several reasons for this. Operational uses of automation usually revolve around record keeping and processing of financial information, both of which are major components of most local government administrative activity. These kinds of applications readily lend themselves to computerization, since they involve tasks that computers do well: calculating, printing, and record keeping (Danziger 1977, 1978). Nevertheless, there have been major efforts over the past two decades to apply automation more extensively to processing of data for management and planning needs in local governments. These efforts have been made primarily at the local level, with local funds, and in pursuit of local objectives (Kraemer and King 1978). In some cases, however, state and federal monies have been distributed to improve local computer capabilities for management and planning, and in a very few cases large development projects have served as prototypes (Kraemer and King 1979).

The net effect of these efforts is difficult to assess in terms of whether it is "disappointing" or "encouraging." It depends on what one is looking for. A profile of experiences with the development of such systems can be generated, however, and we have compiled a summary of findings that provides an overview of experience.

To begin, the research shows that there have been major strides forward in use of locally developed information for management and planning purposes. Operational systems generate a great deal of information that might be used for planning and management in local governments, and efforts have been made to tap into this information in both general and specific ways. At the general level, the Urban Information Systems Inter-Agency Committee (USAC) project did a complete inventory of separate information systems in two USAC cities (Charlotte, N.C., and Wichita Falls, Tex.) as a prelude to development of comprehensive integrated municipal information systems. These inventories revealed over 300 distinct operational information systems, each dealing with data of potential value for planning and management (Kraemer and King 1979).

More specifically, many local governments routinely collect information that provides basic indications of status and performance (Kraemer, Dutton, and Northrop 1981; ICMA 1979; Balk 1975a, 1975b, 1975c, 1976, 1978; Brosz and Morgan 1977; National Commission on Productivity 1973; King and Kraemer 1983). This includes budgetary information, information on hours worked by different personnel on various tasks, "outcome" information (such as crime incidence statistics and fire reports), and trend information created by analyzing these measures over time. Additionally, development projects have been aimed at creating continuously updated data banks for management and planning from the operational systems of local governments. Such data banks have been built in Washington D.C., Los Angeles, Milwaukee, and several other large cities. Although data bank efforts have not been rigorously evaluated, their continued survival alone is modest testimony to their viability. Several introspective case studies by participants in the data bank efforts provide convincing evidence that they are successful in organizing municipal data, making it easily accessible, and applying it to specific information and decision situations faced by elected officials, top managers, and planners (Chamberlain 1980; Mindlin and Levy 1980).

Beyond efforts to develop pilot systems using operational information for planning and management, many systems use data collected especially for planning and management purposes (Kraemer, Dutton, and Northrop 1981). These systems utilize data collected from surveys and other analyses as well as operational data, and usually incorporate advanced analytical techniques, such as modeling, to present likely "outcomes" of various policies from which decision makers must choose (Burt et al. 1972). Good examples of such systems are Fiscal Impact Budgeting Systems (Dutton and Hollis 1980; Dutton and Kraemer 1980), land use and transportation analysis systems (Chamberlain 1980; Steger and Laidlaw 1980a, 1980b), urban development models (Pack 1975; Pack and Pack 1977a, 1977b; Bamberger 1980; Steger and Laidlaw 1980a, 1980b), revenue and expenditure forecasting systems (Bahl 1978), integrated financial management systems (Kraemer and King 1980a, 1980b; Stallings 1980), and systems to improve delivery of various urban services (Yin et al. 1976; Chaiken et al. 1975; Chaiken 1978; Feller and Menzel 1978; Kraemer, Dutton, and Northrop 1981). Such systems have sparked considerable interest in using computing and other information technology to process locally generated data for local planning and management. Despite notable problems with the implementation of existing systems, there continues to be sizable investment in the development of new systems.

The presence of such systems generates hope that advanced technologies and techniques can improve both the operational and the planning/managerial performance of local governments. However, closer examination of the experiences with these systems reveals the second major finding of our review: they often meet with outright failure in implementation, and even in "successful cases" results often differ from expectations. Indeed, many of the most acclaimed efforts to build innovative information systems for local government planning and management have ended up as practical failures. These include the efforts to build large integrated urban information systems (Kraemer and King 1979), attempts to develop large-scale urban planning models (Lee 1973; Pack and Pack 1977a, 1977b), experiments in implementation of fiscal impact budgeting systems (Dutton 1981; Kraemer 1981), and myriad programs to transfer systems based on management science/operations research techniques into local governments to improve local service delivery (Urban Institute 1971; Bingham 1976; Baer, Johnson and Merrow 1977; Lambright 1977; Lambright and Flynn 1977; Chaiken 1978; Savas 1978; Wright, Hall and Hatry 1978; Yin 1979). It is unfair to say that these systems have been complete failures; in nearly all cases post-project study has revealed important new knowledge about what can and cannot be done with such systems. However, since such development and demonstration projects are usually intended to produce improvements in performance rather than new knowledge in the broad sense of the term, we call these efforts practical failures.

Why have so many advanced projects for applying information technology to management and planning tasks of local government met with disappointment? The studies reviewed indicate several major areas of mismatch between the technological "package" proposed as a solution and the problem it is supposed to help solve. None of these technologies or techniques can be seen simply as a discrete tool, to be taken and implemented as one might wield a hammer. Rather, they come in packages that include many important human, political, and organizational assumptions.[6] Three inaccurate assumptions that account for much of the shortfall between a package of expectations and reality involve data availability, technical knowledge, and political organization behavior.

Lack of Appropriate Data

Curiously, most local government officials feel that there is an abundance of data collected in normal operations that could be useful for planning and management but that these data are not organized in a manner that makes them useful. In the 1976 URBIS study of information systems in 700 local governments, over 90 percent of the chief executives surveyed felt that they could have made managerial and planning use of the data collected by their governments for operations purposes if only the data were better managed

(Dutton and Pearson 1975; Kraemer, Dutton, and Northrop 1981; King 1982).

More substantial evidence of the problem of matching data to needs can be found in evaluations of systems to improve performance assessment and modeling capabilities. The data needed for rigorous performance assessment are generally lacking in local governments (Balk 1975a, 1975b; Keller 1975; MacGillivray 1979; Baron 1980). The shortfalls in data availability take several forms. Most local governments tend to keep detailed records only of inputs to service generation. At best, these include the budgetary allocations to different programs and line items, records of person-hours devoted to certain tasks, and, occasionally, expenditure data for line items and programs. And, even these few records usually are not maintained in a manner that facilitates performance assessment. Data on actual outputs are not usually kept routinely, and if they are kept, they tend to be very gross indicators. Crime statistics, for example, fluctuate for many reasons, and it is very risky to attribute changes in such figures to changes in law enforcement performance. Finally, output data that local governments do keep often provide only a crude indication of quantity of service delivered—for example, gallons of water pumped or tons of garbage collected. These measures can be useful for evaluation of straightforward service components such as water utility output, but they do not inform evaluators of the qualitative aspects of service output. Qualitative assessment techniques have been proposed and used (Hatry and Blair 1976), but they tend to be ad hoc measures that are not incorporated into routine data collection tasks in most local governments.

Similarly, case accounts of model development and implementation efforts indicate that the difficulty of getting data is the major constraint on use of advanced modeling techniques and technologies (Pack 1975; Chaiken 1978; Kraemer, Dutton, and Northrop 1981). Bahl's review of expenditure forecasting in state and local governments notes that lack of proper data results in the most appropriate techniques for forecasting being too difficult, forcing forecasters to use less reliable techniques on their data. This is especially true in revenue forecasting, where personal income is commonly used to reflect local economic growth, despite serious flaws with the indicator (1978). Lack of data for analysis plagues other areas of local government analysis; for example, Jennings and Hester comment on the serious lack of good historical data for local government socioeconomic indicators analysis (1977). Even fairly routine planning such as capital budgeting can be constrained by such problems (Gordon, Larcker, and Tuggle 1969).

Thus, there seems to be an appearance of riches in data for planning and management purposes but a genuine drought of truly useful data. This realization is not new. Problems of developing and maintaining good data bases for analysis have been evident since the earliest efforts to develop automated models. This does not hinder efforts to develop new systems, however, and it appears that a recursive cycle has led simultaneously to increased sensitivity to the difficulties of getting the right data for new systems and to improved means of acquiring the data needed.

Lack of Technical and Analytical Capability

U.S. local governments, taken collectively, are by far the most advanced in the world in their uses of automated information systems for planning and management purposes. When the data are closely examined, however, it can be seen that the most advanced forms of computer applications are spread thinly across the population of local governments (King and Kraemer 1983). A strong bias toward use of computing whenever appropriate seems to prompt local decision-makers to adopt advanced systems (Dutton and Kraemer 1978), but the lack of skilled technicians to develop and implement such systems hampers growth. Generally speaking, local governments have difficulty competing with industry for the top computing systems personnel. Civil service requirements and other constraints make it hard to offer the salaries that would draw the best people away from industry, and the continued shortage of qualified systems analysts and programmers aggravates the problem.

Similarly, sophisticated analytical tools such as models are not widely deployed among U.S. local governments. Little direct research has been conducted on the extent of use of such techniques, but work has been done on use of modeling systems for special analytical purposes which provides an overview of the issues. This research has shown that a relatively small percentage—between 6 and 11 percent—of the larger local governments (i.e., those over 20,000 in population) utilize models such as Fire Station Locator marketed by PTI (King and Kraemer 1979). It is true that a larger proportion of local governments acquire the models, either in the form of the directions to carry out the modeling or in the form of a computer program that does the modeling, but actual implementation and routinized use of a model are much less likely to occur than simple acquisition. Many of these modeling systems are in the public domain, and therefore are available for little or no cost. Also, some are marketed by agencies with an active interest in seeing the models adopted, so local government exposure to their availability is high. Thus, it is not surprising that models do find their way into governments. The implementation and routinization of modeling is a much more difficult undertaking than acquisition, however, because it requires the presence of skilled staff, adequate data, and data processing resources not available in many local governments.

Even if the technical expertise to select, build, and implement advanced planning and management systems were readily available in local governments, most lack skilled analytical resources to deal with the outputs of the systems (Hatry 1978; King and Kraemer 1983). Analytical capability is obviously a critical component in the successful use of such systems, yet its role and importance often are underestimated. Analyses of performance or planning must inform the design of the systems themselves and the data collection instruments and techniques they utilize. In other words, systems and data collection plans must be built around the expected analyses, in order to ensure that critical data needed for complete analysis are collected and the means to process them are available. The lack of qualified analytical capability precludes not only effective use of these systems but usually the appropriate design of the systems and the collection of necessary data to support the analyses.

These findings suggest that there are few shortages of technical components such as computer systems in the quest to apply information technology to local government planning and management. Rather, the shortcomings are in ensuring the continued availability of the data necessary to do the analyses desired and in the shortage of technical people to build the systems, operate them, analyze the data, and introduce findings into the policy-making and analytical processes that local governments actually follow.

Behavioral and Political Aspects

Finally, the shortfall in delivery of automated systems for planning and management can be traced in part to unrealistic expectations about such systems. Strictly operational information systems prompt relatively few controversies. The objective is usually to build a system that quickly and efficiently does a discrete task, such as print the tax bills or voting lists. However, when the objective of an information system is to assist in management, policy making, or planning, behavioral and political factors become much more critical.

Political and behavioral factors can have a pervasive impact on all aspects of system development and use. For example, the possible political and control-oriented uses of systems affect the ways in which data can be collected (Kling 1980; Kraemer, Dutton, and Northrop 1981; Markus 1981; Danziger et al. 1982; King 1983). This can be seen clearly in the case of systems designed to assist in performance assessment (Keller 1975). Data collection systems that depend on employee self-reporting often result in underreporting, since employees find it inconvenient to keep track of what they do. Also, self-reporting can yield distorted data, as employees might find it easier to make up their entries than actually to check or keep track. The political character of performance measurement stems from the fact that such measurement can sometimes be used for political purposes and certainly can be used to reward or punish. Organized labor has always been concerned with performance measurement plans for the simple reason that there is a substantial history of management using data from these measurements to force "speed-ups" or other demands on workers. Unions can be very resistant to any efforts at performance data collection. Thus, the ways in which employees perceive how the systems are going to be used affects their behavior in providing data to the systems. This, in turn, can dramatically distort the actual use of performance measures.

Beyond the data serving as input to systems for planning and management are political issues in the assumptions that underlie the systems and the ways in which they are purported to be useful. This is particularly true in the case of model-based systems employed for planning purposes. In the process of building and using such models myriad decisions are required for development of estimates for the parameters of the models. These decisions are frequently made by people who have no understanding of how the quality of the estimates they use will affect the output of the model (Dutton and Kraemer 1980; Dutton and Hollis 1980; Dutton 1981; Kraemer 1981). Thus, the generally rational concepts and algorithms that go into the building of a model do not ensure rational and reliable model outputs, since these depend on the character of the data, judgments about parameters, and the model itself. Nevertheless, model output is frequently assumed to be a scientific estimate of what is real, rather than simply a representation of a possible reality built around the data input to the particular model.[7]

Moreover, models are more often used to rationalize decisions already made for political or other reasons than to assist in the process of decision making. A typical rule of thumb for use of model output is, If it conforms to what those in power say, it is "proof" they are right; if it does not conform, the model is "unreliable." Models, it seems, typically serve one of three political roles: to compare the probable outcomes of a narrow range of politically determined alternatives (Pack and Pack 1977a; Dutton and Kraemer 1980); to advocate a particular politically determined choice (Pack and Pack 1977b; Chaiken 1978; Dutton and Kraemer 1980); or to illustrate why an alternative undesirable to those in control is "unacceptable" on more rational grounds than politics alone (King and Kraemer 1979). This phenomenon is not limited to local government use of models. Several studies have shown that models serve political roles in most situations where controversial issues are being debated (Greenberger, Crenson, and Crissey 1976; Fallows 1982; King 1982). The effect of the politicization of modeling varies from situation to situation. In some cases the models simply become weapons used by all sides in the debate, and thus have relatively little impact on the final political outcome. In other cases models are the unique province of one faction and are used to that faction's benefit. In still other cases the fact that models produce "firm" estimates of impacts causes retrenchment and hardening of positions, thus making final political resolution more difficult.

These observations are not intended to suggest that model use in local governments has predominantly negative or even inconsequential impacts. Indeed, it appears that the single most important contribution of models to decision making and planning is to encourage and reinforce improved discipline and attention to detail on the part of analysts and politicians alike. Nevertheless, the fact that models and other systems intended for planning and management exist within a specifically political environment ensures that the outcome of their use will be political. Such systems cannot have a uniform and predictable impact, positive or negative. When systems provide results that reinforce the power of reigning coalitions, they tend to be adopted and used. When they produce results that reflect unfavorably on ruling coalitions, they lose support, at least from the ruling coalition. As long as these systems are parts of larger political battles they will be political in their own right (Danziger et al. 1982).

Thus, the ways in which systems for planning and management are used for political purposes have a major impact on how well such systems fare. In many cases, models and other advanced systems have "failed" because of behavioral and political, not technical, factors. Some researchers characterize these failures simply as problems of "implementation" or "communication," but this helps to perpetuate an artificial distinction between such systems as technical and political artifacts. The moment that technical systems are applied to such politically rich domains as management and planning they become ipso facto political instruments.

Summary

The foregoing findings from the literature and from our own research suggest that considerable progress has been made in applying information technology to the needs of local governments. The most striking and lasting contributions of such technology have been in the area of improving the efficiency and effectiveness of operational systems, such as billing, taxation, and accounting. This coincides with the fact that these are the most widely and extensively developed kinds of applications now used by local governments. There also have been major efforts to apply computing technology to development of improved information and analysis capability for planning and management. Some of these systems have proven successful, but they have tended to be the relatively simple systems that produce reports based on data from operational systems or that focus on very discrete management and planning problems with adequate data models for analysis. Larger, more ambitious efforts to create planning and management information systems have frequently failed, due to lack of appropriate data for analysis, lack of technical and analytical expertise to build and run the systems and analyze the results, and political and behavioral factors that inevitably arise when efforts are made to move information technology into politically charged decision-making situations.

It is both difficult and, we believe, fruitless to try to ascertain whether applications of information systems technology to local government operations and planning and management have been "satisfactory." Clearly, the answer to such a question depends heavily on what one believes to be the primary goals of local government and the appropriate means for achieving those goals. We do feel, however, that the experience thus far in development and use of information systems by local governments is reassuring. Experience has shown that the technology does offer promise for improving the routine housekeeping and record management tasks of government. These tasks might not be as exciting as those in the more politically sensitive areas of local government policy-making, but they are nonetheless essential to effective governmental function. The fact that local governments spend heavily and readily for such systems is a vote of confidence in their utility.

By the same token, local governments have been comparatively reluctant to invest heavily in more "innovative" applications of information technology to planning and management tasks. This seems sensible given the serious problems facing successful development and use of such tools. Moreover, it reflects something that is often overlooked in assessments of the success of new innovations: they are expensive. Many of the most ambitious efforts to create information systems useful in local government planning and management have been heavily subsidized by federal agencies, so the true local costs of such efforts have been distorted (King and Schrems 1978; Kraemer and King 1978). When a local government itself faces the prospect of a multi-million-dollar investment in creation of an information system with no sure guarantee of success, it will tend to decline the offer. Some might argue that this conservatism restrains the effective development and use of such systems, but we disagree. Since local governments do not have sufficient market power to lead the computing and information technology industries, they must be prudent followers. Unlike the Department of Defense, individual local governments cannot afford to invest millions of dollars per year in developing advanced computerized planning and management (i.e., command, control, and logistics) systems.

Overall, U.S. local governments have tended to quickly and successfully exploit proven capabilities of information technology, while steering clear of the most experimental applications. There are three exceptions to this pattern: some local governments have successfully pioneered use of certain experimental technologies; other local governments have participated in efforts (usually subsidized by federal funds) to create innovative "demonstration systems" that can be transferred to other local governments at relatively low cost; and many local governments have elected to participate in very narrowly targeted, intergovernmental, operations-oriented systems such as the National Crime Information Center. These three exceptions, together with the general observations on local government experience with information systems presented above, form the basis of the next section.

INTERGOVERNMENTAL USE OF LOCAL
GOVERNMENT INFORMATION

Most local government information systems serve operational needs of local administration. In contrast, most intergovernmental systems have been designed to help with planning and management aspects of intergovernmental programs. Given the difficulties local governments face in developing and using systems for planning and management at the local level, one would expect serious problems in creating such systems for use intergovernmentally. Indeed, this is the case. With a few notable exceptions, the systems built to expedite planning and management on an intergovernmental basis have proven not to work too well (King 1982).

Problems in Intergovernmental Information
Systems for Planning and Management

To understand how and why this is so it is useful to look first at how locally generated information is used on an intergovernmental level. Of the three general kinds of planning and management uses of information (status reporting, performance analysis, and compliance analysis), the most widespread at the intergovernmental level is compliance analysis. This has traditionally been true at the state levels as well, where local governments have been required to demonstrate compliance with fiscal and programmatic directives issued by their state governments. In recent years, as the direct federal-to-local programs have proliferated, upward reporting of data for compliance analysis from local-to-federal government has increased as well. The second most widespread use of local data by state and federal government agencies has been status reporting, usually in the process of determining whether and to what extent a local government deserves state or federal financial support for programs. Again, as the number of intergovernmental programs, especially grant programs, has expanded, the requirement for upward reporting of status data has increased. Finally, as the grant programs have expanded, concern at the state and federal levels has grown over how well local governments are using the funds they receive. This concern is manifested in efforts to develop upward-reporting requirements of information that can be used for performance analysis. This area of local data use by state and federal governments is still the least developed.

Experiences with intergovernmental reporting of financial information for compliance analysis illustrate the basic difficulties with creating intergovernmental information systems for planning and management. Such a focus is useful because these compliance analysis (or "accountability") reporting systems are among the longest-standing systems and because difficulties with them are amplified in systems for status and performance analysis. Accounting and reporting rules for how local governments must manage their fiscal affairs at least provide standards against which to compare the behavior of any given local government. More complicated and "fuzzy" questions about what a local government's "status" regarding a particular problem might be, or what a government's "performance" in carrying out a mandate has been, are exceedingly more difficult to answer because the basic criteria of evaluation are so poorly defined and inherently relative. This analysis, therefore, focuses on experiences with local government data and reporting on fiscal and financial matters. Such systems are usually used to ensure "compliance" with accepted accounting principles or rules mandated by higher levels of government and often to document local claims on other levels of government (e.g., receiving "bailout" funds to compensate for fiscal problems or to cover for revenue losses due to Proposition 13 kinds of legislation).

The first major conclusion we can draw about upward-reporting systems for local financial information is that the resultant centrally maintained data sets are plagued by inadequacies in accuracy and comparability of the data (CSC/GAO/OMB 1972; Coopers & Lybrand 1976, 1978; Anton 1978, 1979), and by differences in data needs and perceptions of data meaning among relevant officials who review such data (Balk 1975a; Quinn 1975, 1976). Accuracy and comparability deficiencies are due in many cases to the fact that data collection practices for performance assessment are not standardized, or when they are, the standards are inadequate, infrequently updated, and insufficiently monitored and enforced (Balk 1975a). Standardization is sometimes hampered by the fact that people in different roles need different kinds of data—that is, both data on different variables and data on the same variables but from different perspectives. The same data can reveal different things to different actors, making consensus difficult to reach.

The situation on the state level becomes even more critical in the national context, due to the high degree of variation in reporting requirements among the states.[8] Local governments are creatures of the states and are subject to the reporting standards imposed by state constitutions and directives. State-by-state differences in reporting requirements were relatively invisible prior to increased federal-local cooperation, but recently these differences have emerged as a national issue. For example, defaults of local governments occurred numerous times prior to the near collapse of New York City in the late 1970s, and such defaults were generally perceived as local problems or, at most, state issues to be resolved between the state and local levels (ACIR 1973). But the advent of high levels of direct federal-to-local funding (with its attendant need for local-to-federal reporting) coupled with the prospect of municipal defaults of national significance has increased concern that more standard local government reporting across the states is necessary (ACIR 1976, 1977a, 1977b).

A particularly compelling example of need for better information for analysis of financial condition of local governments can be found in the area of pension obligations that governments carry (Jump 1976a, 1976b, 1978; Kohlmeier 1976; Tilove 1976). This became a major issue in the case of New York's near default and remains so. Yet, there is little good information about whether such widespread concern about pension obligations is warranted (Jump 1976a, 1978). Financial reports seldom contain the most basic and useful indicators of pension obligation (e.g., plan termination liability), and the information they do carry lends itself to misinterpretation by nonspecialists.

The fact that local governments vary widely in their financial behavior (e.g., debt to wealth ratios maintained, fund surpluses maintained, propensity of levying of new taxes) undoubtedly also creates problems of comparability. However, since it is precisely local government financial behavior that either causes or enables default situations to emerge, it is necessary to have clear-cut standards of behavior to use as norms in identifying developing problems.

Such standards have been proposed, but they illustrate a basic problem noted earlier about planning and management information systems: that a precise definition of the questions to be answered in analysis must guide data collection. As an example of the kinds of questions one might ask about financial condition of a local government, ACIR (1973) proposed six "early warning signs" of fiscal trouble:

- An operating fund revenue-expenditure imbalance in which current expenditures significantly exceed current revenues in one fiscal period.

- A consistent pattern of current expenditures exceeding current revenues by small amounts for several years.

- An excess of current operating liabilities over current assets (i.e., a fund deficit).

- Short-term operating loans outstanding at the conclusion of a fiscal year (or, in some instances, the borrowing of cash from restricted funds or an increase in unpaid bills in lieu of short-term operating loans).

- A high and rising rate of property tax delinquency.

- An unexplained sudden substantial decrease in assessed values.

ACIR complained that the data were not available to do such analyses, but the problem goes deeper. Each of these early warning signs contains adjectives that can derive their value only from comparison to baseline data or standards—"significantly in excess of" in the first; "small amounts" in the second; "an excess of current operating liabilities" in the third; and so forth. The simple fact that a city runs a small fund deficit or encounters a rising rate of property tax delinquency might not necessarily be a true sign of trouble; it might just reflect cyclical behavior in the government's revenue stream or the condition of the economy. Only by having baseline data can small and probably insignificant anomalies be distinguished from major warning signs early on. Yet, the incomparability of local government data within states and especially across local governments in different states makes establishment of such base lines difficult. Also, serious questions can be raised about whether meaningful base lines can be created at all, which in turn challenges the sensibleness of having systems to compile and analyze these kinds of data on a widespread intergovernmental basis.

The second general finding is that the current standards for reporting, meager as they are, are not widely or adequately implemented. There seems to be a consensus that local government practices for keeping and reporting financial information are not as well developed or closely followed as they should be (Comptroller General 1977a, 1977b; Jump 1978; Lehan 1978; White 1978; Williams 1978; Patitucci 1980). Most local governments maintain only systems that meet rudimentary needs for local and state oversight, and in many cases the information kept and reported does not even adequately meet these needs. It was concluded in the case of the near default of New York City, for example, that confused financial accounting and reporting obscured many questionable financial management practices and that this kept many of the city's severe problems from view long enough for the crisis to reach a serious point (Comptroller General 1977a, 1977b, 1978; Jump 1978).

The generally accepted accounting principles (GAAP) model, on which most accounting and reporting at the local government level is based, can adequately guide systems that are applied primarily to checking legal compliance and stewardship. However, because these systems tend to focus on fund flows (i.e., expenditures) to the exclusion of cost-of-services (i.e., expenses), they tend not to provide data for assessing efficiency, economy, or performance (Bahl 1978; Holder 1978; Williams 1978; Patitucci 1980). Capability is also lacking in many cases for adequately tracking expenditures related to specific federal grants, although efforts are underway to try to develop practices that will better document the degree to which the intentions of the grantors are reflected in grantee behavior. Finally, the actual operating needs and constraints of local governments often conflict with even the relatively simple accounting structures now employed. Perhaps the best example is what happens under governmental accounting structures in which the absence of appropriation prohibits recording of expenses. In order to maintain continuity, expenses still are incurred, even when appropriation approval is late. This results in misrecording of expenses to ''comply'' with the letter of the law.

Thus, many current accounting and reporting standards are well intentioned but difficult to apply in a manner that meets local, state, and federal needs. The GAAP approach is sensible as a suggested guideline, but it is not *required;* nor is it likely that the full set could be required given the autonomy that states, and many local governments, now enjoy in the matter of how they keep their records.

A third general conclusion again relates to existing standards and their shortcomings. In addition to the GAAP there are myriad specific reporting requirements surrounding particular intergovernmental fund-flow mechanisms (e.g., categorical grants, revenue sharing, welfare reimbursements). The methods used to develop federal standards for local reporting (committees representing various interests) often produce mandates that are overly complex, fragmented, and unresponsive to user and local needs (Holder 1978). Because the varied interests involved in the procedures have somewhat different objectives, the standards adopted tend to be a mixture that tries to please everyone but in fact satisfies no one. The variance in expected uses of data makes standards fragmented and difficult to shape into a cohesive, integrated program that local governments can implement. Difficulties of implementation make it hard for local governments to do more than meet the minimum requirements, resulting in less than adequate servicing of local needs as well as needs of state and federal agencies. Also, the reporting requirements developed to manage particular grants programs are often complicated and burdensome to local governments. An ACIR (1977a) survey of city and county officials regarding the most serious problems local governments face in dealing with federal categorical grants administration lists the fourth most serious problem out of 25 as "the complexity of auditing, accounting, and reporting requirements" for federal categorical grants. The dependence of local governments on federal support through various grant programs makes this a serious issue. Many local governments desperately need the money the grants provide, yet the reporting regulations consume much local staff time. Among the specific complaints are:

- Regulations for programs are often published only after the programs go into effect.

- Regulations and rules can and do change without notice.

- There is no similarity between the federal and state accounting procedures, which often requires keeping separate sets of books for grant accounting.

- Grant management circulars suggest guidelines that the funding agencies themselves frequently do not follow.

Since grant programs are essentially transfers of money to local governments, the only effective control the federal agency can hope to maintain over compliance with the intent of the grant programs must come through financially based regulations (Break 1978; Hovey 1978). The complicated and burdensome nature of this web of reporting requirements reflects the fact that an increasing number of relatively independent federal agencies and offices established grant programs for local governments. Thus, the pressure to establish standardized accounting and reporting requirements for all federal grants has come mainly from the local governments, which are in a weak position since they are receiving and not giving the money. Complaints about require-ments have sparked federal initiatives to ameliorate the problem (Freeman and Nuttal 1980) but with little genuine relief as yet.

Finally, based on the fact that intergovernmental programs and relations are usually in a state of flux, it can be expected that local government infor-mation reporting standards will continue to change. The information demands of various states and federal agencies will be fragmented due to the different needs for data by these entities, yet the need for more coherence in reporting practices will tend to force periodic efforts to standardize reporting, at least among the higher-level government agencies most frequently in need of local data. Most important, however, is that operational activities of local govern-ments become more complicated as the intergovernmental linkages grow. This increasing complexity virtually ensures that existing reporting standards, and even those now under development, will be insufficient to meet the endemic demands for "good" information. Thus, there will be continued efforts to improve reporting through incremental, and occasionally wholesale, changes in standards.

A Special Case: Intergovernmental Operational Systems

In contrast to the intergovernmental systems for planning and manage-ment, the limited experiences with systems for intergovernmental transfer of operational data seem to be working reasonably well. The only large-scale intergovernmental operational system operating to date is the FBI-admin-istered National Crime Information Center (NCIC). The NCIC system is a nationwide network of computers and telecommunications technology that is used to collect and share information on stolen property, wanted or missing persons, and criminal histories. It shares such information among federal, state, and local government law enforcement officials. The system began in 1967 with files on stolen autos, firearms, and license plates as well as on wanted persons, and has since expanded to include stolen securities, stolen boats, missing persons, and criminal histories (including identification infor-mation, arrest records, judicial dispositions, and custody records) (Marchand 1980a, 1980b).

NCIC has had its share of troubles. Chief among them has been the difficulty of obtaining accurate and timely data for its files. For this reason many local governments prefer to use state-run systems connected to the NCIC network. The state-level data seem to be more accurate, and the chances are greater that a local agency will get the information it needs from its state's own system (Marchand 1980a). Despite these data problems, NCIC and its associated systems have survived and grown in use since they were first instituted. We believe that operational systems like NCIC are more promising examples of how intergovernmental systems might be built, because they illustrate the key difference between systems for discrete operations in which the "facts" are relatively easy to determine (e.g., a person is either wanted or not), as opposed to systems for planning and management, where there can be difficulty in determining what the data really mean (e.g., what does a 4 percent increase in violent crime mean even if the number is accurate?).

Such systems are very expensive to build and maintain, and thus far most of the costs of NCIC have been borne by the federal government. Whether such an investment will continue is unclear, but we think it is likely that even if the federal government's role diminishes in this area, the states will pick up the difference. Most states with a need for centralized criminal records and information systems now have them, and they will maintain them with or without NCIC. Moreover, they will probably continue to link to other state systems if the NCIC network loses funding. The reason the systems enjoy popularity is that when they do work (i.e., someone gets a "hit"), the utility of the system is clearly demonstrated.

Similar operational systems might be developed in cases where local governments are engaged in administering funds distributed nationally, such as in welfare and health payments systems. As with NCIC, a number of major problems accompany the basic idea of national systems containing personal data, and such systems will not be built without controversy. Nevertheless, we expect that there will be more development of operational intergovernmental information systems, especially between local and state governments, if the federal government decentralizes some national programs and passes them to the state level and local governments continue to feel financially squeezed.

Summary

It is not surprising to find that the development and implementation of satisfactory intergovernmental information reporting systems for planning and management is a difficult task. The very fact that local governments themselves have trouble dealing with such systems, even within their relatively well understood local circumstances, suggests that these problems are amplified at the intergovernmental level. As a general rule we believe that serious problems with understanding and interpreting the meaning of data increase the farther the analyst is from the source of the data and the more disparate the sources from which the data come. Thus, although there might be a need for extensive local government data for status reporting, performance analysis, and compliance analysis at higher levels of government, there is no guarantee that such data can be easily provided, at least within the means and budgets now available for the task.

On the other hand, as information systems technology continues to offer greater price/performance attractiveness, it seems likely that systems to facilitate intergovernmental operations will grow. These systems are useful mainly in functions where federal, state, and local desires intersect. One such function has been law enforcement. Others might include administration of justice, welfare, and health care programs. Eventually, taxation systems and educational records systems might seem appropriate for intergovernmental information systems.

IMPLICATIONS FOR INTERGOVERNMENTAL RELATIONS

The studies cited here indicate that hopes for improving intergovernmental operation by improving information systems are largely misplaced. Even at the local government level, where one can easily find operational systems that work well, it is difficult to find advanced systems for planning and management that significantly affect how planning and management are done. There are continuing problems of shortages of accurate and appropriate data, technical staff for managing the technology, and analysts to interpret the data. Once the data have been interpreted, political problems may surface. These difficulties are exacerbated at the intergovernmental level because the data reported up from local governments are often not comparable, and their accuracy is difficult to assure. Attempts to impose standardization, management methods, reporting requirements, and other "systems" objectives from the top down have failed. Moreover, they probably will never succeed unless the autonomy that local and state governments now enjoy is diminished.

This conclusion suggests that, contrary to some expectations, information technology will not prove able to resolve the difficult problem of balancing the advantages and disadvantages of centralized versus decentralized arrangements for government responsibility. The goals of uniformity in operations and attention to national objectives require centralization of plans and action; the goals of local efficiency and flexibility to meet local objectives cannot tolerate centralization of plans and action and must be decentralized. There has been hope that the use of information systems would help ensure compliance and encourage congruity with federal objectives among local and state governments. Generally speaking, this has not happened. Simply asking local governments to report numbers does not give state and federal agencies much control over how local governments behave. Those local governments that avoid compliance with regulations can simply obfuscate the ways in which they are doing so. The myriad technical and operational problems that beset information systems provide a great many ways in which reports can be adjusted to give a certain impression. And even when the inaccuracies in data that are reported upward are not intentional but result from problems in the system or mistakes, inaccuracies hamper effective use of the data at the higher level.

The question remains, How best can information systems assist in the functioning of the intergovernmental system? The first suggestion is to support and encourage the use of such systems where they seem to work best—for operational tasks at the local level. Presumably, more efficient and effective functioning of local governments as independent units helps the performance of the intergovernmental system. Second, the experiences in building and using information systems for planning and management at the local level should be examined more closely to provide direction on where to go (and not to go) in future development efforts. Third, it should be recognized that instabilities in the basic structures and protocols under which programs are administered tend to destroy the utility of many systems designed to assist the programs.

The latter point is especially important given the suggestions for changing the nature of the intergovernmental system in significant ways through the "new federalism." A likely scenario for the new federalism would have operational responsibilities for major programs devolve to state and local governments, with oversight to ensure that national goals are met (e.g., minimum benefits, equal treatment, accountability of operations) continuing to reside within the federal government. If so, the new federalism should *not* rely on the building of comprehensive, detailed information systems to provide compliance information as its primary control mechanism. The tremendous flux generated by the change to such a new arrangement precludes for years the appropriate design of the upward-reporting systems that would be necessary to monitor compliance in a useful manner. Detailed local information systems may serve a role in assisting local federal investigators who are dedicated to on-site monitoring of compliance, but they would not work well for assisting in compliance monitoring at a national level.

NOTES

1. These predictions are particularly prevalent in works by Bell (1973, 1981), Hiltz and Turoff (1978), Porat (1978), Carne (1979), Engleberg (1979), and Martin (1979).

2. The development of computing and information processing owes much to the support of the U.S. government, especially the Bureau of the Census (for supporting the work of Herman Hollerith), the military (for supporting the development of the first electronic computer, as well as computer graphics, time sharing, and most high-level languages), and the space program (for supporting development of a wide array of digital control and communications applications).

3. Most of the federal concern about information has concentrated on problems with information systems. This concern is evident in the listings in the *Monthly List of GAO Reports* issued by the General Accounting Office. At least one study reporting on problems of information systems or systems management in a federal agency can be found in each issue. This has been the case for at least the past ten years.

4. This distinction is not new to this chapter. It was developed and articulated in a very detailed way in the formation of the USAC project to build operations-based integrated municipal information systems in the early 1970s (Kraemer et al. 1974), and the general concept of this distinction can be found much earlier in management literature. See also Kraemer and King (1979).

5. We and others at the Public Policy Research Organization have been conducting research on the use of information technology in local governments since the early 1970s. See Danziger (1977), Kraemer and King (1977, 1978), Kraemer, Dutton, and Northrop (1981), Danziger et al. (1982), and King and Kraemer (1983). Other major streams of research concerning local government financial management are reviewed in Petersen et al. (1978), and research related to performance and productivity analysis in local government can be found reviewed in Hatry and Fisk (1971), Urban Institute (1975), Hayward (1978), and Washnis (1980).

6. The package metaphor is derived from several sources. Ivan Illich described the transfer of educational programs as conveying a package of components including educational philosophy, technology, and administrative mechanisms (1971). Stewart expanded on this concept in his analysis of the transfer of physical technology to underdeveloped countries (1977). The metaphor has become an important concept for focusing the research carried on by the Public Policy Research Organization, especially that related to the "infrastructure" necessary to support computing activity (King and Kraemer 1978; Kling and Scacchi 1979, 1982; Kraemer, Dutton and Northrop 1981; Scacchi 1981; and King and Kraemer 1983).

7. Beyond the research on use of models in local government our own recent research into uses of computerized modeling systems in U.S. federal government agencies confirms these general findings about problems with model use (Fallows 1982; King 1982; Kraemer and Campbell-Klein 1982).

8. The problems in accuracy of data regarding local government at the federal level go beyond the mismatches due to aggregation error in upward reporting, as noted in Cawley and Kramer (1979).

REFERENCES

ACIR. 1973. City Financial Emergencies: The Intergovernmental Dimension. No. A-42. Washington, D.C.: Advisory Commission on Intergovernmental Relations.

ACIR. 1976. Federal-State-Local Finances: Significant Features of Fiscal Federalism. No. A-63. Washington, D.C.: Advisory Commission on Intergovernmental Relations.

ACIR. 1977a. Measuring the Fiscal "Blood Pressure" of the States, 1964–1975. Washington, D.C.: U.S. Government Printing Office.

ACIR. 1977b. Significant Features of Fiscal Federalism, 1976–77. 3 vols. Washington, D.C.: U.S. Government Printing Office.

Anton, Thomas J. 1978. Creating a Data Base for Intergovernmental Fiscal Analysis. Intergovernmental Fiscal Analysis Project Paper No. 1. Ann Arbor: University of Michigan Program in Urban and Regional Planning.

————. 1979. Data Systems for Urban Fiscal Policy: Toward Reconstruction. Ann Arbor: University of Michigan Program in Urban and Regional Planning.

Baer, Walter S., Leland L. Johnson, and Edward W. Merrow. 1977. Government-Sponsored Demonstrations of New Technologies. Science 196:950.

Bahl, Roy. 1978. Revenue and Expenditure Forecasting by State and Local Governments. Paper presented at the AAAS Intergovernmental Research and Development Symposium on Management, Finance, and Personnel, Reston, Va., June.

Balk, Walter, ed. 1975a. *Administering State Government Productivity Improvement Programs.* PG-245859. Springfield, Va.: National Technical Information Service.

————. 1975b. *Improving Government Productivity: Some Policy Perspectives.* Beverly Hills: Sage.

————. 1975c. Technological Trends in Productivity Measurement. *Public Administration Review* 5(2): 128.

————. 1976. Decision Constructs and the Politics of Productivity. In *Productivity in Public Organizations,* ed. Marc Holzer, 173–95. Port Washington, N.Y.: Kennikat/Dunellen Press.

————, ed. 1978. Symposium on Productivity in Government. *Public Administration Review* 38(1): 1–50.

Bamberger, William. 1980. Urban Development Modeling. In *Computers in Local Government: Urban and Regional Planning,* ed. K. L. Kraemer and J. L. King, no. 2.8.2. Pennsauken, N.J.: Auerbach.

Baron, C. David. 1980. Obtaining Information for Government Program Evaluation. In *Accounting in the Public Sector: Some Urgent Problems,* ed. R. Ingram, 299–308. Salt Lake City: Brighton.

Bell, Daniel. 1973. *The Coming of the Post-Industrial Society.* New York: Basic Books.

————. 1981. The Social Framework of the Information Society. In *The Microelectronic Revolution: The Complete Guide to the New Technology and Its Impact on Society,* ed. Tom Forester, 500–49. Cambridge, Mass.: MIT Press.

Bingham, Richard D. 1976. *The Adoption of Innovation by Local Government.* Lexington, Mass.: Lexington Books.

Break, George. 1978. Intergovernmental Finance. In *State and Local Government Finance and Financial Management: A Compendium of Research,* ed. J. Petersen, C. Spain, and M. Laffey, 95–104. Washington, D.C.: Government Finance Research Center.

Brosz, Allyn, and David Morgan. 1977. *Improving Municipal Productivity.* Norman: Bureau for Government Research, University of Oklahoma.

Burt, Marvin R., Donald M. Fisk, and Harry P. Hatry. 1972. Factors Affecting the Impacts of Urban Policy Analysis: Ten Case Histories. Working Paper 201-3. Washington, D.C.: Urban Institute.

Carne, E. B. 1979. The Wired Household. *IEEE Spectrum* 16(10): 61–62.

Cawley, Jerry, and Kevin Kramer. 1979. Reconciling Treasury's "Federal Aid to States" Report with Community Services Administration's "Geographic Distribution of Federal Funds" Report. Ann Arbor: University of Michigan Program in Urban and Regional Planning.

Chaiken, Jan. 1978. Transfer of Emergency Service Deployment Models to Operating Agencies. *Management Science* 24(7): 719–31.

Chaiken, Jan, T. Crabill, L. Holliday, D. Jaquette, M. Lawless, and E. Quade. 1975. *Criminal Justice Models: An Overview.* R-1859-DOJ. Santa Monica: RAND Corporation.

Chamberlain, Simon. 1980. Land Use Planning; Toronto Case Study. In *Computers in Local Government Urban and Regional Planning,* ed. K. L. Kraemer and J. L. King, no. 2.3.4. Pennsauken, N.J.: Auerbach.

Coe, Charles. 1980. Financial Reporting Requirements and Their Impact on Financial Management Systems. In *Computers in Local Government Finance and Administration,* ed. K. L. Kraemer and J. L. King, no. 2.2.1. Pennsauken, N.J.: Auerbach.

Comptroller General of the United States. 1977a. Long-Term Fiscal Outlook for New York City. PAD-77-1. Washington, D.C.: General Accounting Office.

————. 1977b. New York City's Efforts to Improve Its Accounting Systems. FGMSD-77-15. Washington, D.C.: General Accounting Office.

————. 1978. Improving Federal Agency Efficiency through the Use of Productivity Data in the Budget Process. FGMSD 78-33. Washington, D.C.: General Accounting Office.

Coopers & Lybrand and the University of Michigan. 1976. *Financial Disclosure Practices of the American Cities: A Public Report.* New York: Coopers & Lybrand.

————. 1978. *Financial Disclosure Practices of the American Cities: Closing the Communications Gap II.* New York: Coopers & Lybrand.

CSC/GAO/OMB (Civil Service Commission, General Accounting Office, and Office of Management and Budget). 1972. *Measuring and Enhancing Productivity in the Federal Sector.* Washington, D.C.: U.S. Government Printing Office.

Danziger, James. 1977. Computers, Local Governments, and the Litany to EDP. *Public Administration Review* 37(1): 28–37.

————. 1978. Computer Technology and the Urban Fiscal Crisis. *Urban Systems* 2(3): 105–19.

Danziger, James, William Dutton, Rob Kling, and Kenneth L. Kraemer. 1982. *Computers and Politics: High Technology in American Local Governments.* New York: Columbia University Press.

Dueker, Kenneth L. 1981. An Approach to Integrated Information Systems for Planning. In *Computers in Local Government Urban and Regional Planning,* ed. K. L. Kraemer and J. L. King, no. 2.1.2. Pennsauken, N.J.: Auerbach.

Dutton, William. 1981. The Rejection of an Innovation: The Political Environment of a Computer-Based Model. *Systems, Objectives, Solutions* 1(4): 179–201.

Dutton, William, and Martha Hollis. 1980. Fiscal Impact Budgeting Systems. In *Computers in Local Government Urban and Regional Planning,* ed. K. L. Kraemer and J. L. King, no. 2.9.1. Pennsauken, N.J.: Auerbach.

Dutton, William, and Kenneth L. Kraemer. 1978. Determinants of Support for Computerized Information Systems: The Attitudes of Local Government Chief Executives. *Midwest Review of Public Administration* 12(1): 19–40.

————. 1980. Automating Bias. *Society* 17(2): 31–64.

Dutton, William, and Sigfried Pearson. 1975. Executives Cite Common Data Systems Problems. *Nation's Cities* 13(10): 28–30.

Enbleberg, O. 1979. The Way to the Information Society. *Information Privacy* 1(3): 282–90.

Fallows, Susan. 1982. *The TRIM/MATH Models Case Study.* Irvine: Public Policy Research Organization, University of California.

Feller, Irwin, and David Menzel. 1978. The Adoption of Technological Innovations by Municipal Governments. *Urban Affairs Quarterly* 13:469–90.

Freeman, Robert, and Donald Nuttal. 1980. The GAAFR Restatement Principles: An Executive Summary. In *Accounting in the Public Sector: Some Urgent Problems,* ed. R. Ingram, 69–72. Salt Lake City: Brighton.

Gordon, L. A., D. F. Larcker, and F. D. Tuggle. 1969. Informational Impediments to the Use of Capital Budgeting Models. *Omega* 7(1): 67–74.

Greenberger, Martin, Matthew A. Crenson, and Brian L. Crissey. 1976. *Models in the Policy Process: Public Decision-Making in the Computer Era.* New York: Russell Sage Foundation.

Hatry, Harry P. 1978. The Status of Productivity Measurement in the Public Sector. *Public Administration Review* 38(1): 28–34.

Hatry, Harry P., and Louis Blair. 1976. *Program Analysis for State and Local Governments.* Washington, D.C.: Urban Institute.

Hatry, Harry P., and D. M. Fisk. 1971. *Improving Productivity and Productivity Measurement in Local Governments.* Washington, D.C.: Urban Institute.

Hayward, Nancy S. 1978. Productivity Improvement in the Public Sector. In *State and Local Government Finance and Financial Management: A Compendium of Current Research*, ed. J. Petersen, C. Spain, and M. Laffey, 86–94. Washington, D.C.: Government Finance Research Center.

Head, Robert V. 1982. *Federal Information Systems Management: Issues and New Directions*. Washington, D.C.: Brookings Institution.

Hiltz, Starr, and Murray Turoff. 1978. *The Network Nation*. Reading, Mass.: Addison-Wesley.

Holder, William. 1978. Financial Accounting and Reporting by Governmental Units. Paper presented at the AAAS Intergovernmental Research and Development Project on Management, Finance, and Personnel, Reston, Va.

Horwood, Edgar. 1981. Planning Information Systems: Functional Approaches, Evolution, and Pitfalls. In *Computers in Local Government Urban and Regional Planning*, ed. K. L. Kraemer and J. L. King, no. 2.1.1. Pennsauken, N.J.: Auerbach.

Hovey, Harold. 1978. State-Local Intergovernmental Finance. In *State and Local Government Finance and Financial Management: A Compendium of Research*, ed. J. Petersen, C. Spain, and M. Laffey, 105–12. Washington, D.C.: Government Finance Research Center.

ICMA (International City Management Association). 1979. *Using Productivity Measurement: A Manager's Guide to More Effective Services*. Washington, D.C.: ICMA.

Illich, Ivan. 1971. *Deschooling Society*. New York: Harper & Row.

Jennings, Hal, and John Hester. 1977. *A Handbook for Implementing a Fiscal Impact Analysis System for North-Central Texas*. Dallas: Department of Research and Planning Coordination, North-Central Texas Council of Governments.

Jump, Bernard, Jr. 1976a. Compensating City Government Employees: Pension Benefit Objectives, Cost Measurement, and Financing. *National Tax Journal* 29:240–42.

————. 1976b. *Financing Public Employee Retirement Programs in New York City: Trends since 1965 and Projections to 1980*. Occasional Paper no. 16. Syracuse, N.Y.: Metropolitan Studies Program, Syracuse University.

————. 1978. Public Employment, Collective Bargaining, and Employee Wages and Pensions. In *State and Local Government Finance and Financial Management: A Compendium of Research*, ed. J. Petersen, C. Spain, and M. Laffey, 74–85. Washington, D.C.: Government Finance Research Center.

Keller, L. E. 1975. Performance Measures System and Local Government. *Public Productivity Review* 1(2): 30–46.

King, John L. 1982a. The Data Resources, Incorporated Model Case Study. Irvine: Public Policy Research Organization, University of California.

————. 1982b. Local Government Use of Information Technology: The Next Decade. *Public Administration Review* 42(1): 25–36.

————. 1983. Centralized versus Decentralized Computing: Organizational Considerations and Management Options. Irvine: Information and Computer Science Department, University of California.

King, John L., and Kenneth L. Kraemer. 1978. Electronic Funds Transfer as a Subject of Study in Technology, Society, and Public Policy. *Telecommunications Policy* 2(1): 13–21.

————. 1979. Operations Research Technology Transfer in the Urban Sector. Irvine: Public Policy Research Organization, University of California.

————. 1983. *The Dynamics of Computing*. Irvine: Public Policy Research Organization, University of California.

King, John L., and Edward Schrems. 1978. Cost-benefit Analysis in Information Systems Development and Operation. *Computing Surveys* 10(1): 34.

Kling, Rob. 1980. Social Analyses of Computing: Theoretical Perspectives in Recent Empirical Research. *Computing Surveys* 12(1): 62–110.

Kling, Rob, and Walter Scacchi. 1979. Recurrent Dilemmas of Computer Use in Complex Organizations. *Proceedings of the 1979 National Computer Conference* 48:107–16. New York: AFIPS Press.

———. 1982. The Web of Computing. In *Advances in Computers,* ed. M. Yovits, vol. 21. New York: Academic Press.

Kohlmeier, Louis. 1976. *Conflicts of Interest: State and Local Pension Fund Asset Management.* New York: Twentieth-Century Fund.

Kraemer, Kenneth L. 1981. The Politics of Model Implementation. *Systems, Objectives, Solutions* 1(4): 161–78.

Kraemer, Kenneth L., and Cecelia Campbell-Klein. 1982. A Reanalysis of Data on Federal Agency Use of Computerized Planning Models. Irvine: Public Policy Research Organization, University of California.

Kraemer, Kenneth L., William Dutton, and Alana Northrop. 1981. *The Management of Information Systems.* New York: Columbia University Press.

Kraemer, Kenneth L., and John L. King. 1977. *Computers and Local Government,* 2 vols. New York: Praeger.

———. 1978. Development of Urban Information Systems: Status and International Relevance of United States Experience. *International Review of Administrative Sciences* 44(3): 221–33.

———. 1979. A Requiem for USAC. *Policy Analysis* 5:313–49.

———. 1980a. Integrated Financial Management Systems: Dayton Case Study. In *Computers in Local Government Finance and Administration,* ed. K. L. Kraemer and J. L. King, no. 2.3.3. Pennsauken, N.J.: Auerbach.

———. 1980b. Integrated Financial Management Systems: Integrated and Independent Designs. In *Computers in Local Government Finance and Administration,* ed. K. L. Kraemer and J. L. King, no. 2.3.1. Pennsauken, N.J.: Auerbach.

Kraemer, Kenneth L., William Mitchel, Myron Weiner, and O. E. Dial. 1974. *Integrated Municipal Information Systems: The Use of the Computer by Local Government.* New York: Praeger.

Lambright, W. Harry. 1977. *Adoption and Utilization of Urban Technology: A Decision-Making Study.* Syracuse, N.Y.: Syracuse Research Corporation.

Lambright, W. Harry, and P. Flynn. 1977. Bureaucratic Politics and Technological Change in Local Government. *Urban Analysis* 4:93–118.

Lee, Douglas B., Jr. 1973. Requiem for Large-Scale Models. *Journal of the American Institute of Planners* 39(2): 136–78.

Lehan, Edward. 1978. Public Budgeting. In *State and Local Government Finance and Financial Management: A Compendium of Research,* J. Petersen, C. Spain, and M. Laffey, 34–41. Washington, D.C.: Government Finance Research Center.

Lodal, Jan. 1976. Improving Local Government Financial Information Systems. *Duke Law Journal* (6): 1113–55.

———. 1979. Financial Information Systems Should Serve Managers. *Public Management* 61(6): 2–5.

MacGillivray, Lois. 1979. *A Report on Fire Research.* Research Triangle Park, N.C.: Research Triangle Institute.

Marchand, Donald. 1980a. National Information Systems. In *Computers in Local Government Police and Fire,* ed. K. L. Kraemer and J. L. King, no. 2.6.3. Pennsauken, N.J.: Auerbach.

———. 1980b. *The Politics of Privacy: Computers and Criminal Justice Records.* Arlington, Va.: Information Resources Press.

Markus, M. Lynne. 1981. Implementation Politics: Top Management Support and User Involvement. *Systems, Objectives, Solutions* 1(4): 203–28.

Martin, James. 1979. *The Wired Society.* Englewood Cliffs, N.J.: Prentice-Hall.

Miller, Trudi. 1980. Management Science: A Post–Proposition 13 Alternative. Paper presented at the annual meeting of the American Society for Public Administration, Honolulu.

Mindlin, Albert, and Nathan Levy. 1980. A Local Government Computerized Statistical Information System. In *Computers in Local Government Urban and Regional Planning,* ed. K. L. Kraemer and J. L. King. Pennsauken, N.J.: Auerbach.

Mowshowitz, Abbe. 1976. *The Conquest of Will: Information Processing in Human Affairs.* Reading, Mass.: Addison-Wesley.

National Commission on Productivity. 1973. Opportunities for Improving Productivity in Solid Waste Collection. Washington, D.C.: National Commission on Productivity.

Pack, Howard, and Janet R. Pack. 1977a. The Resurrection of the Urban Development Model. *Policy Analysis* 3(3): 407–27.

————. 1977b. Urban Land-Use Models: The Determinants of Adoption and Use. *Policy Sciences* 8:79–101.

Pack, Janet R. 1975. The Use of Urban Models: Report on a Survey of Planning Organizations. *AIP Journal,* 191–99.

Patitucci, Frank. 1980. Government Accounting and Financial Reporting: Some Urgent Problems. In *Accounting in the Public Sector: Some Urgent Problems,* ed. R. Ingram, 4–16. Salt Lake City: Brighton.

Petersen, John E., Catherine L. Spain, and Martharose Laffey, eds. 1978. *State and Local Government Financial Management: A Compendium of Current Research.* Washington, D.C.: Government Finance Research Center.

Porat, Mark U. 1978. Global Implications of the Information Society. *Journal of Communication* 28(1): 70–80.

Quinn, Robert E. 1975. Management Information Systems, Task Structure, and Organizational Effectiveness. In *Administering State Government Productivity Improvement Programs,* ed. W. Balk. PB-245859. Springfield, Va.: National Technical Information Service.

————. 1976. Productivity, Management Information Systems, and Resistance: Toward a Better Understanding. *Public Productivity Review* 2(1): 5–20.

Savas, E. S. 1978. Problems in Applying Urban O.R. *Handbook of Operations Research* 2:415–20. New York: Van Nostrand Reinhold.

Scacchi, Walter. 1981. The Process of Innovation in Computing. Ph.D. diss. Department of Information and Computer Science, University of California, Irvine.

Stallings, Wayne. 1980. Integrated Financial Management Systems: Key Features and Implementation Considerations. In *Computers in Local Government Finance and Administration,* ed. K. L. Kraemer and J. L. King, no. 2.3.2. Pennsauken, N.J.: Auerbach.

Steger, Wilbur, and Charles Laidlaw. 1980a. Land Use and Transportation Models: A Structural Comparison. In *Computers in Local Government Urban and Regional Planning,* ed. K. L. Kraemer and J. L. King, no. 2.3.2. Pennsauken, N.J.: Auerbach.

————. 1980b. Land Use and Transportation Models: An Overview. In *Computers in Local Government Urban and Regional Planning,* ed. K. L. Kraemer and J. L. King, no. 2.3.1. Pennsauken, N.J.: Auerbach.

Stewart, F. 1977. *Technology and Underdevelopment.* New York: Macmillan.

Tilove, Robert. 1976. *Public Employee Pension Funds.* New York: Columbia University Press.

Urban Institute. 1971. *The Struggle to Bring Technology to the Cities*. Washington, D.C.: Urban Institute.

————. 1975. *The Status of Productivity Measurement in State Government*. Washington, D.C.: Urban Institute.

Washnis, George, ed. 1980. *Productivity Improvement Handbook for State and Local Government*. New York: Wiley-Interscience.

White, Michael. 1978. Capital Budgeting. In *State and Local Government Finance and Financial Management: A Compendium of Research*, ed. J. Petersen, C. Spain, and M. Laffey, 86–94. Washington, D.C.: Government Finance Research Center.

Williams, James M. 1978. Accounting, Auditing and Financial Reporting. In *State and Local Government Finance and Financial Management: A Compendium of Current Research*, ed. J. Petersen, C. Spain, and M. Laffey, 86–94. Washington, D.C.: Government Finance Research Center.

Wright, Virginia, J. L. Hall, and Harry Hatry. 1978. *An Examination of Productivity-Related Findings from the Four-City Projects and the RAND and PTI Fire Deployment Analysis Approaches*. Washington, D.C.: Urban Institute.

Yin, Robert. 1978. Production Efficiency versus Bureaucratic Self-Interest: Two Innovative Processes? *Policy Sciences* 8:381–99.

Yin, Robert, K. Heald, M. Vogel, P. Fleischauer, and B. Vladeck. 1976. *A Review of Case Studies of Technological Innovations in State and Local Services*. R-1870/NSF. Santa Monica: RAND Corporation.

5

A Demographic Perspective

Thomas Muller

The last decade ended a half century of uninterrupted growth of the public sector, federal, state, and local. Since the end of World War II, government has grown more rapidly than the private sector, inevitably increasing its share of the GNP. Many observers believed, and some continue to maintain, that this growth would continue through the 1980s and beyond. I shall focus on demographic causes of governmental growth in the 1970s and 1980s.

Examining the effect of demographic changes on local and state finances appears, at first, to be a rather easy task. Most of the persons who will demand government services during the 1980s were counted in the 1980 census; only a small percentage of service demand will come from those yet to be born. Thus, basic service demand can be estimated from existing national population data. However, national data alone do not tell us *where* the demand will take place. It may occur in cities that have established school, sewer, public safety, and other basic government services. Or, as a result of population migration, it may occur in suburban and unincorporated areas that do not have established services. In the 1970s, population redistribution was the major source of upward pressure on governmental expenditures, particularly on expenditures for services delivered by state and local government. Population movement from core cities to unincorporated areas and from densely populated northern industrial areas to the South and West is expected to continue through the 1980s, though at a slower pace.

A second difficulty in demographic analyses is that changes in apparent needs for service may not be translated into increases and decreases in governmental expenditures. At least two factors complicate the relationship between service demands and expenditures. First, expenditures are less responsive to population decreases than they are to population increases, so per capita expenditures tend to rise in areas that are experiencing a loss of population (e.g., core cities). Second, there is a marked decline in governmental expenditures after 1977 that is not explained by changes in national statistics or population movements. As a result of the tax limitation movement, a decline in population is more likely to produce a decline in governmental expenditures, and a population increase is less likely to produce a comparable rise in expenditures. The rapid growth of government at the state and local level which characterized the 1960s and 1970s has been halted, despite the persistence of some demographic trends that have in the past been associated with growth.

Contributing to the halt in state and local outlays has been the reduced federal level of direct federal funding to states and localities. This assistance peaked in 1978 and declined in constant dollars in the subsequent three years. Sharp reductions are projected for 1982–86, and the apparent reluctance of states to substitute their own funds to replace federal funds suggests a "no-growth" period during the 1980s.

DEMOGRAPHIC CHANGES AT THE NATIONAL LEVEL

Changes in the demand for state and local services can be attributed to two major demographic factors: the age structure of the population and the number of new households. For some services, such as education and police protection, the age structure is the most crucial factor, whereas for others, such as fire protection, the number of new housing units is the important demographic variable.

Population Growth and Age Structure

Although the population of the nation will continue to grow, its rate of growth is anticipated to decline, continuing a long-term trend. Birth rates have declined steadily since the beginning of the twentieth century, with the exception of the late 1940s and the 1950s. In the peak year, 1955, there were 25 births per 1,000 population; two decades later, the birth rate declined to 14 per 1,000. Fertility rates per woman declined drastically in the 1970s, from 2.43 births in 1970 to 1.77, or below replacement rate, in 1976.[1] The decline has been about equal for both whites and blacks. However, in view of higher initial fertility rates, the rate for blacks remained considerably above the replacement level in the late 1970s.

Mortality rates continue to decrease, but only slowly. In 1976, the average white person could expect to live to age 74, whereas nonwhites had a life expectancy of 68. Although the gap among races is being reduced, the gap in life expectancy between men and women is likely to continue.

Combining these trends in mortality and birth rates, the total U.S. population is projected to increase from 222 million to 244 million between 1980 and 1990. This is a rise of 22 million, or close to 10 percent. Moreover, the age distribution of the population will change considerably. The number of children under the age of 10, which declined sharply in the 1970s, will rise again, by close to 20 percent, during the 1980s. This rise is primarily attributed to the greater number of women in the 15–40 age group rather than to a substantial increase in the birth rate. The number of persons 14 to 24 will decline, with sharp rises in the number of persons in their 30s and 40s (see table 5.1). About 4 million more persons will be over 65 in 1990, compared to the beginning of the 1980s. The aging of the overall population is reflected in the median age of all individuals, which increased from 27.9 in 1970 to 30.2 in 1980 and should increase to 32.8 in 1990.

Household Formation

To estimate future household formation, it is necessary to examine several variables: the number of young adults added to the population, marriage and divorce rates, changes in life style, and the financial ability of potential households to own or rent housing.

Marriage and divorce rates are important insofar as they affect both the number of households and their size. Following a decade or more of year-to-year fluctuation, such rates are likely to stabilize during the 1980s. The marriage rate in recent years peaked in 1972, when there were 11 marriages per 1,000 persons and then declined moderately to 10 by 1976. It is projected that marriage rates will remain at current levels or rise during the next decade, assuming that there will be marriages among those who had previously postponed this commitment for various, primarily noneconomic, reasons. Although births by nonmarried women continue to rise, these births, particularly among white women, remain only a small percentage of all births. Thus,

Table 5.1.   City-Suburban Population, by Age (%)

Age Group	1970			1974			1977			1990
	City	Suburb	U.S.	City	Suburb	U.S.	City	Suburb	U.S.	U.S.
5–13	16.9	19.7	18.6	15.2	17.2	16.4	13.9	15.7	15.2	14.5
14–17	7.2	8.2	7.9	7.4	8.2	8.0	7.1	8.1	7.8	6.0
18–24	12.4	10.3	11.1	13.1	12.2	12.3	13.8	12.7	12.9	11.2
25–34	12.5	12.8	12.3	14.3	14.6	13.9	15.6	15.8	15.2	18.3
35–44	10.8	12.5	11.4	10.1	11.6	10.9	9.9	11.8	10.9	16.3
45–64	21.3	20.1	20.6	21.0	20.3	20.6	20.9	20.4	20.4	20.6
65+	10.6	7.7	9.6	10.8	8.0	9.9	11.4	8.4	10.4	13.3
Total	100.0	100.0	100.0	100.0	100.0	100.0	100.0	100.0	100.0	100.0
Median Age	29.2	27.4	28.2	29.4	28.1	28.8	30.0	29.1	29.5	32.8

Source: U.S. Department of Commerce 1975, 1977, 1978.

increases in nonmarriage household formations are unlikely to result in a corresponding increase in births.

The divorce rate also affects household formation, since permanent divorces (those without remarriage) increase the number of households and reduce their size. In 1960, the divorce rate reached its lowest point since World War II, 2.2 per 1,000, whereas both 1977 and 1978 show the divorce rate at its historic high of 5.1 per 1,000. Although many factors influence divorce rates, the social climate—emphasis on women's rights, reduced social cohesion, and lower birth rates—is now more conducive to divorce. Contributing to this pattern are expanding employment opportunities, since in their absence, most divorced women without an independent income would have difficulty maintaining a reasonable standard of living.

These factors, however, seem to have already been taken into account as new marriages are contemplated. There is less social pressure for women to be married, but an awareness appears to be growing that such an arrangement can be mutually beneficial. The recent slight increase in the birth rate (from 15.0 per 1,000 women in 1978 to 15.8 per 1,000 in 1980) suggests that most women prefer to have children, which remains economically and socially very difficult outside marriage.[2] There are also indications among the very young of a more conservative attitude toward established institutions, an attitude that would be reflected in both marriage and fertility rates.

Reflecting these changes, the number of households, based on "average" (U.S. Bureau of the Census 1979b) estimates, is projected to increase from 78.2 million in 1979 to 88.6 million in 1985 and to 96.7 million in 1990. Given the assumption that trends in the 1970s will continue, projections by the Bureau of the Census indicate that the percentage of husband-wife households of all households would drop from 42.0 percent in 1980 to 35.8 percent at the end of the decade, while the number of female householders with no husband present would increase from 14.9 percent to 17.1. Regardless of the assumptions associated with various projections, all estimates indicate a continuing drop in household size.

The size of the average family has fallen steadily from 3.74 persons in 1940 to 3.58 in 1970. During the 1970s, the decline was more severe, and current projections are that the average family will have only 3 persons by the end of the 1980s. The number of persons per family under the age of 18 was only slightly above 1 in 1980 and is expected to decrease to 0.94 by 1995. These numbers represent the Bureau of the Census middle-range estimate. A more conservative estimate, based on higher marriage and fertility rates, would result in larger families and households, with their average size remaining closer to the 1980 level. The most reasonable, if subjective, estimate is that household size will be somewhere between the Census Series II projections and estimates based on rising marriage and fertility rates. Thus, though family size will continue to decrease during the 1980s, the declines should be smaller in comparison to the previous decade.

The number of new households depends not only on demographic and social conditions but on the general economy. Most projections for the 1980s are that growth in household personal income will be very slow, with an average of 1 to 2 percent annually (Muller, Soble, and Dujack 1980). Indeed, such income actually fell between 1974 and 1981. Low rates of economic growth should tend to discourage the formation of more single-person households, and house sharing by unrelated individuals should become more common. (Exceptionally low household construction in the early 1980s makes this outcome almost inevitable.) Also, while economic growth rates are projected to be low, the cost of housing, due to high interest rates, is anticipated to rise somewhat more quickly than all goods and services, although the differential should narrow substantially. Rising real costs of housing and low production of residential units in the early 1980s will further discourage the demand for new housing units and thus reduce household formation rates.

POPULATION DISTRIBUTION

Most changes in the demand for public services in the 1960s and 1970s resulted from population redistribution caused by the migration of households to areas receiving few public services, such as unincorporated areas on the periphery of standard metropolitan statistical areas (SMSAs). This movement appears to have peaked in the 1970s. Net migration to nonmetropolitan areas from SMSAs was only 350,000 between 1965 and 1970, but in the following five years it rose to 1.6 million. Then, despite high energy prices and premature discussion of a "back to the city" movement, close to 1.4 million more persons migrated to nonmetropolitan areas between 1975 and 1980. Although energy costs and other factors are expected to slow the movement to the country in the 1980s, the trend will continue. In the past, population movement to places with no established services resulted in a rapid growth of government.

Concurrently, the urban core loses population as people move from older, more densely populated areas to nonmetropolitan areas. This implies a reduction of demand in the cities. At least in the short run, however, the demand for and cost of many services has not declined proportionately to population loss. Thus, services are maintained in urban areas, and per capita costs increase (Muller 1977).

As we will see shortly, population movement from urban areas caused a marked increase in total expenditures for public services in the 1970s, especially at the state and local levels. Expenditures grew as a result of population increases but did not decline as a result of population decreases. In the 1980s migration is abating somewhat, and, for a number of reasons, service costs in the "sunbelt" and the "frostbelt," as well as in urban and rural areas, will tend to equalize. Therefore, demographic factors, including the long-observed decline in the birth rate as well as a decrease in migration, will reduce pressures for governmental growth. In addition, the effects of economic stagnation and the tax limitation movement are likely to alter the degree to which demand for service is filled.

Metropolitan Change

In discussing demographic changes in central cities, it is important to distinguish those growing spatially because of annexation and those maintaining stable political boundaries. Most older northern cities, as a result of both legislative constraints and the existence of incorporated communities on their boundaries, have not grown spatially. Most of these cities did not fare well economically, while those with annexation tended to have strong economies.

Between 1970 and 1980, populations of large central cities (those with 200,000 or more residents) in northern states declined by several million persons, although the rate of decline seems to have been curtailed somewhat in the second half of the decade in comparison to the previous five years. Most large cities in the South and West are showing smaller increases than in earlier years, whereas those without annexation, including San Francisco and Atlanta, continue to lose population. Indeed, cities with growing populations, with practically no exceptions, had substantial annexation during the 1970s. For example, cities that incorporated the largest areas through the annexation process were, in ascending order, Houston, San Antonio, Dallas, Memphis, and El Paso; all gained population (see table 5.2). The six states that account for most annexation nationally are, in descending order, Texas, California, Arizona, Oklahoma, Illinois, and Tennessee (see table 5.3). Despite annexations, however, both large (200,000 and over) and smaller central cities

Table 5.2.   Annexation by Large Cities, 1979

City	Land Area, 1970 (sq. mi.)	Area Added by Annexation, 1970–79 (sq. mi.)	% Land Area Added by Annexation, 1970–79	% Pop. Change, 1970–80
Houston	434	123	28.3	29.2
San Antonio	184	80	43.5	20.1
Dallas	266	81	30.5	7.1
Memphis	217	65	30.0	3.6
El Paso	118	121	102.0	32.0
Kansas City	57	54	94.7	−4.2
Austin	72	44	61.1	36.3
Columbus	135	46	34.1	4.6
Phoenix	248	74	29.7	35.2
Birmingham	80	19	37.5	−5.5
Fort Worth	205	38	18.5	−2.1
Tulsa	172	58	33.7	9.3

Source: U.S. Department of Commerce 1980.

Table 5.3.   Annexation by State, 1970–79

State	Sq. Mi. Annexed	Est. Pop., Annexed Areas
Texas	1,472	456,000
California	716	221,000
Arizona	480	123,000
Oklahoma	361	38,000
Florida	319	151,000
Illinois	376	210,000
North Carolina	248	233,000
Tennessee	340	220,000
Minnesota	425	37,000
Colorado	251	103,000

Source: See table 5.2.

Note: Includes states with largest annexed areas, except Alaska.

collectively lost about 4 percent of their total population in 1970–77. In fact, several cities with considerable annexation, such as Fort Worth, lost residents. City gains in the sunbelt were more than offset by losses in northern states, where all large cities lost population.

The extent to which population losses in large central cities in the late 1970s compared to earlier years represents a trend is difficult to determine. For example, based on annual estimates, population loss rates in St. Louis, Seattle, Chicago, and New Orleans were lower in the second half of the 1970s compared to the earlier years in the decade. However, New York City, which attracted several hundred thousand legal and illegal immigrants, and Baltimore show accelerated losses. Thus, what appears to be emerging is population stability in perhaps two-thirds of the large cities, with others continuing to lose population at the same rate as, or more rapidly than, in the early 1970s.[3] Los Angeles, supposedly losing population in the early 1970s, actually showed a 5 percent gain for the decade as a result of massive immigration rather than a slowing of outmigration. These data do not support the hypothesis that there has been a general "return to the city" movement. At best, they suggest a slowing down of population losses, with immigrants frequently replacing the mostly white outmigrants.

Outmigration from cities has been substantially higher than population loss, as natural increase adds about 375,000 persons annually to cities. As shown in table 5.4, the difference between estimated outmigration and population change was about 1.1 million in 1970–78. Annual net outmigration from cities between 1970 and 1978 averaged about 1,450,000 per year, though total population was reduced by only 265,000. With increases attributed to births over deaths estimated at 0.6 percent, this would mean that about 750,000 immigrants came to cities annually, a number too high to be reasonable. The total number of immigrants entering the country legally dur-

Table 5.4.   Annual Population Change, Central Cities (in thousands)

Factor	1970–73	1973–78
Population Change	−363	−259
Net Outmigration	−1480	−1430
Difference	−1117	−1171
Natural Increase[a]	383	375
Other[b]	734	796

[a]Based on natural increase in central cities of 0.6% annually.
[b]E.g., immigration.

Source: Population change data from U.S. Bureau of the Census, *Population Estimates and Projections,* various issues. Net outmigration data from U.S. Bureau of the Census, *Mobility of the Population of the United States,* various issues.

ing the 1970s averaged about 400,000. Since aliens are concentrated in highly urban states (almost half reside in California, New Jersey, and New York), it is reasonable to assume that one half, or 200,000, annually settle in central cities. In addition, illegal immigrants contributed perhaps another 150,000. Thus, we can explain three quarters of the differences between population drop and outmigration.[4]

Migration from cities is selective in terms of the characteristics of households that move compared to those that remained. During the 1970s, about one third of net movement was among those 25 to 34 years old, with very few in the 20 to 24 or over 65 years of age categories moving from central cities. The age group that accounts for one quarter of net movement from cities is 5 to 14 years old. It is therefore evident that young households with young children are the most likely to move out of cities.

This statistic is borne out by migration data showing that the dominant share of population losses in central cities was among white families with one or more children under the age of 18 residing at home. In addition to race and family status, the other important variable affecting the probability of migration from central cities is income. Except for the elderly population, the likelihood of a household leaving the city rises as income increases, peaking at the $15,000-income category. This selective migration process helps to explain why mean income among central city residents declined by 5.4 percent between 1970 and 1977 while income among suburban residents declined by less than 2 percent. One of the observed changes during the later part of the 1970s was a slowdown among persons over 65 moving out of cities, which implies a more rapid aging of the city population than was the case in the late 1960s and early 1970s.

Migration from central cities is no longer limited to the white population. Blacks are leaving cities in increasing numbers, as illustrated by the fact that between 1975 and 1980, an average of 133,000 blacks annually left central cities. As a result of this trend, the black population, which increased by 6 percent in central cities between 1970 and 1974, appears to have stabilized in subsequent years.

As a share of the white population, however, the black population has continued to rise. In addition, the Hispanic population of the cities is growing at a rate of over 3 percent annually, owing to high birth rates and immigration. These trends suggest that more than half of the population of the majority of our central cities will be nonwhite or of Spanish origin in 10 to 15 years. While some may dispute this projection, it should be noted that at least 20 large cities (populations of 100,000 or more) in 1980 were in this category. Among these cities are the second and third largest in the nation, Chicago and Los Angeles, followed by Detroit (6th), Baltimore (10th), San Antonio (11th), Memphis (14th), Washington D.C. (15th), Cleveland (18th), New Orleans (21st), and St. Louis (26th).

Regional Patterns

The 1970s was a period of accelerated population movement from northern states to the South and West. As can be seen in table 5.5, inmigration to the "sunbelt" region remained stable during the 1970s, and migration to the West accelerated in the late 1970s. As is the case among movers within metropolitan areas, persons crossing regional boundaries also tend to be young, with above-average income and educational levels. This explains, in part, why there were no gains in personal income in northern states in 1970–77.

Interregional migration projected for the 1970s as well as the current demographic profile will affect not only total population growth but its distribution in the 1980s. Several states, such as Arizona, Colorado, and Florida, are projected to have large population increases, but the most rapid growth in these states will be among the population under age 5 and over age 65. For example, the proportion of those over 65 is expected to increase by 47 percent in Arizona during the decade. However, states with outmigration in the 1970s, including New York and Illinois, are projected to have the number of elderly increase by less than 10 percent. The overall pattern suggests that service demand for the very young and old will increase during the decade.

During the 1980s, migration to western states is likely to be as rapid as it

Table 5.5.   Net Internal Migration, 1965–80 (in thousands)

Region	1965–70	1970–75	1975–80
Northeast	−715	−1342	−1486
North central	−637	−1195	−1173
South	656	1829	1764
West	696	708	893

Source: U.S. Department of Commerce 1981c.

was in the earlier decade, but net migration to the South should be somewhat slower. In part, massive investment in western energy resources, though slowing down during the mid-1980s, should encourage further inmigration, while high energy costs should increase the comparative advantage sunbelt states in the Southwest and West have over northern regions.

Metropolitan / Nonmetropolitan Migration

The 1970s, in contrast to previous decades, showed a reversal of the rural-to-urban migration pattern. This reversal can have significant implications on the type of service outlays, since the cost of many public services rises with population size and density.

The movement of households can best be illustrated by changes in the housing stock. Between 1970 and 1977, the number of dwelling units in urban areas increased by 14 percent, in nonurban areas by 33 percent. In urbanized states, such as New York, New Jersey, Pennsylvania, and Missouri, there was substantial outmigration from metropolitan areas during the 1970s and substantial inmigration to nonmetropolitan cities and counties. In fact, the only significant exception to this pattern can be found among rural states in the South and Midwest, such as Mississippi and North Dakota, where the patterns of the 1950s and 1960s remain.

Nationally, annual population growth in metropolitan areas averaged 0.6 percent, and in nonmetropolitan areas 1.3 percent in 1970–78. This movement is expected to continue. In the absence of high energy prices, the movement would probably accelerate during the 1980s. Although energy prices may reduce the rate of rural movement in the short run, the flow is not expected to change in intensity over a longer time period. It is important to note, however, that immigration to the nation, both legal and illegal, is highly concentrated in larger cities and metropolitan areas. This pattern tends to mask the rate of movement from urban to nonurban areas among the base population.

IMPACT OF DEMOGRAPHIC CHANGES ON
DEMAND FOR PUBLIC SERVICES

Although all demographic changes have some impact on the demand for public services, there are substantial differences among major local and state services. As shown in table 5.6, the demand for two services are linked directly to the number of births: public schools and higher education. By contrast, added demand for fire protection and several other services depends to a considerable extent on the number of new housing units, about two-thirds of which are built in response to new household formation. Among the remaining services, the number of persons reaching specific age categories is

Table 5.6.   Impact of Demography on Public Service Demand

Function/ Primary Demographic Characteristic	Primary Nondemographic Factor
Birth Rate	
Public school	Private school enrollment
	Federal-state mandates
Higher education	Private school enrollment
Household Formation	
Fire protection	Nonresidential construction
Sanitation	Federal funding
Recreation	Personal income
Financial administration and general control	—
Age Distribution	
Health/hospital—No. persons 65+	Federal funding
Highways/mass transit—No. persons 16–25	Federal funding
Police protection—No. persons 14–35	General crime rate
Household Composition	
Welfare / AFDC	Public funding

the most important demand variable. Although service demand depends on several demographic and nondemographic characteristics, typically one demographic factor explains a considerable proportion of changes in demand.

Between 1970 and 1977, outlays for the two services most closely linked to birth rates, public schools and higher education, increased less rapidly than those for any of the other major service categories shown in table 5.7. Among services linked to household formation, sanitation increased more rapidly than average, whereas added outlays for fire protection were close to the mean. Among age-related expenditures, police protection and health and hospital expenditures increased rapidly, but highway outlays show an absolute reduction in constant dollars.

By far the most striking feature of table 5.7, however, is the reduction in outlays (in constant dollars) between 1977 and 1980, when inflation reduced each $1.00 to less than $0.74. Outlays in general declined by almost 6 percent in real terms, and outlays for schools declined by over 9 percent in the three-year period. Economic and political factors are the crucial forces that explain this reversal from real growth to real decline. Personal income did not increase in the late 1970s, and governments were discouraged from raising taxes. (An analysis of these economic and political factors is provided by John Kirlin in the next chapter.)

Jurisdiction Size

Jurisdiction size influences costs, making services in the city more expensive than services in the country. Resulting differences in tax levels is one factor that has stimulated population movement.

Table 5.7.   Changes in per Capita State and Local Outlays, FY 1970–80 ($ 1977)

Service	1970 ($)	1977 ($)	1980 ($)	% Change, 1970–77	% Change, 1977–80
Public Schools	287	330	301	15.3	−9.1
Higher & Other Education	117	145	131	23.0	−9.0
Highways	126	107	108	−15.0	0.9
Public Welfare	112	160	148	42.8	−7.5
Health and Hospitals	75	104	104	32.7	0
Police Protection	34	48	44	41.8	−8.3
Fire Protection	16	20	18	25.0	−10.0
Sanitation (incl. sewerage)	27	41	n/a	62.9	—
Parks & Recreation	9	14	18	64.2	28.6
Interest on Debt	34	53	48	52.9	−7.7
Other General Outlays	171	239	272[a]	39.8	13.8
Total Outlay	1008	1261	1192	25.1	−5.8
Federal Funds	287	330	301	15.0	−8.8
Per Capita Personal Income	6076	6979	6998	15.5	0.3
Percent Outlays of Personal Income	16.6	18.1	17.0	9.0	−5.0

Source: U.S. Department of Commerce 1972, 1979a, 1982.

[a]Including sanitation.

One of the fiscal patterns observed during the 1970s was the continuing and, in fact, increasing difference in outlays and the number of municipal employees per capita in jurisdictions grouped by population size.[5] As shown in table 5.8, workers per capita in police, fire, parks and recreation, and sanitation (other than sewerage) increases steadily as population rises, suggesting scale diseconomies. Sewerage treatment, highways, and government administration appear to have no economies or diseconomies associated with size. Although sewerage treatment employs very few people in small communities, this represents the absence of central treatment plants rather than operational efficiency. In jurisdictions under 10,000 persons, some services, such as parks maintenance or street cleaning or trash hauling, are not provided at all by the public sector, explaining low employment levels (see Manson and Muller 1981).

Lower outlays in smaller communities represent not only fewer employees but lower wages per employee. As shown in table 5.8, average wages in communities with fewer than 5,000 residents were about $800 per month, whereas cities with more than a million inhabitants paid their employees close to $1,400 per month. Differences in wages between small and large communities were large in New York and Minnesota, small in Ohio and Georgia. Nevertheless, the relationship between size and wages was observed in every state and region.

Overall, the positive relationship between population size, per capita out-

Table 5.8. Municipal Personnel per 10,000 Residents, by City Size, 1977 (population in thousands)

Service	1,000 and Over	500–999	300–499	200–299	100–199	50–99	25–49	10–24	5–9	Under 5
Police	42.7	45.0	29.7	27.0	25.0	22.0	21.1	21.4	22.9	17.7
Fire	15.4	15.6	19.4	19.2	18.6	15.6	14.9	11.7	7.2	2.2
Sewerage	2.8	4.4	6.0	4.3	4.5	3.6	4.1	4.4	4.3	2.5
Highways	8.2	9.6	9.2	9.9	8.9	8.3	9.2	10.2	11.9	10.3
Parks & Recreation	8.6	13.1	13.9	13.6	10.5	9.1	7.4	5.9	4.4	0.3
Sanitation (not incl. Sewerage)	12.3	9.8	8.3	11.9	8.1	6.0	6.3	6.9	7.8	4.3
Govt. Administration	11.8	17.4	14.3	14.1	11.9	10.9	10.6	10.8	11.7	12.8
Earnings, October 1977 ($)	1,384	1,171	1,145	1,061	1,080	1,095	1,012	942	859	803
Payroll per Capita[a] ($)	371	283	214	214	196	150	130	103	91	63

Source: U.S. Department of Commerce 1979c.

[a]All services.

lays, and municipal wage at the metropolitan level has been established, according to Peterson and Muller (1979). This study indicated that population size explains about 25 percent of the variation in expenditures at the SMSA level. The same positive relationship is found in nonmetropolitan jurisdictions as these increase in size above 2,500. Thus, it is expected that as communities increase in size as a result of natural increase and net migration, outlays for services will also rise.

During the 1980s, one can expect most population growth to be taking place in jurisdictions with fewer than 100,000 residents, as most larger cities continue to lose population. This shift in population from larger to smaller jurisdictions will result in lower outlays and fewer employees per capita. Almost all older large cities, including Philadelphia, Detroit, Cleveland, and Pittsburgh, have reduced the number of municipal employees, since their tax base eroded with the loss of economic activity and population. Although service demand was not reduced in proportion to their population loss, one can expect fewer municipal employees as population declines further. Employment gains in smaller communities will not fully offset, at least on a per capita basis, losses in large cities.

Similarly, wage differentials between larger and smaller cities, particularly in northern regions, will be reduced as fiscal pressures in large urban centers temper wage increases, whereas wages in smaller southern and western communities should rise more rapidly than in other areas of the nation.

Police Services

Almost all crimes in the 1980s will be committed by persons born before 1979. Therefore, neither birth nor mortality rates will directly affect crime rates in the 1980s. However, crime rates are very sensitive to age distribution, because crime, particularly violent crime, is concentrated among persons between the ages of 14 and 24. As shown in table 5.9, 54 percent of all crimes (based on arrest rates) are committed by this age group, although it represented, in 1978, only 21 percent of the population. Persons over 45, who constitute almost one-third of the population, commit only 7 percent of all violent crimes.

Crime rates increased sharply during the early and mid 1970s, stabilized in the 1976–78 period, and increased again in 1979. Based on national changes in the age distribution, the outlook for the 1980s should be continued stability if crimes per capita by each age group remain constant. Factors other than age influence crime, but it is probably the most important factor affecting violent crime.

Population movement also has a significant influence on crime rates. Historically, the correlation between outlays for police services and population growth has been high, and cities have had more crime than rural areas (Muller 1977). Thus, one can anticipate that growing areas will have more rapid crime

Table 5.9. Age Distribution and Crime Rates, 1978–90

Age Group	% of All Violent Crimes, by Age Group, 1978	% of Pop., by Age Group, 1978	Ratio of Crimes/Pop., 1978	Pop. Distribution, 1978 (in millions)	Crime Distribution (CP ratio × pop.)	Pop. Distribution, 1990 (series 11)	Crime Distribution (ratio × pop.)	% Difference, 1978–90
1–13	3.5	21.5	0.16	44.7	57.2	51.9	8.3	15.3
14–17	17.9	7.6	2.36	16.7	39.4	12.8	30.2	−23.9
18–21	22.6	7.8	2.90	17.1	49.6	14.5	42.0	−15.3
22–24	13.4	5.4	2.48	11.9	29.5	10.6	26.3	−10.8
25–34	25.3	15.5	1.63	34.0	55.4	41.1	67.0	20.9
35–44	10.0	11.1	0.90	27.2	24.5	36.6	32.9	34.4
45–54	4.7	10.6	0.44	23.2	10.2	25.3	11.1	9.1
55–64	1.9	9.5	0.20	20.2	4.0	20.8	4.1	4.0
65+	0.7	11.0	0.06	23.9	1.4	29.8	1.8	2.8
Total				218.9	221.2	243.4	224.7	1.1
Per Capita				—	1.01	—	0.92	−8.9

Source: U.S. Federal Bureau of Investigation 1980.

Table 5.10.   Violent Crimes per 100,000 Residents, by Region, 1972–79

Region	1972	1978	1979	% Change 1972–79
Northeast	450	529	590	31.1
North central	335	378	409	22.1
South	391	479	529	35.3
West	438	608	661	50.9
Total	398	487	536	34.7

Source: U.S. Federal Bureau of Investigation 1972, 1978, 1979.

rate increases and higher demands for police and correctional services than areas with stable populations. This is illustrated by changes in crime by region between 1972 and 1978. As shown in table 5.10, crime in the South and West increased more rapidly than in northern and north central states. Indeed, by 1978, crime rates in the West were exceeding those of any other region.

Crime and arrest rates also vary by other demographic characteristics, including race and sex. For example, 32 percent of all arrests in cities during 1978 were of nonwhites, a higher percentage than their share of the population. Thus, if minority populations rise in cities, projected crimes (or arrests) would be expected to rise, *holding other variables constant.*

In addition to activities related to crime, traffic control is a major police function. There is strong correlation between the number of persons with driver licenses and the number of private vehicles. Since most young persons obtain such licenses between the ages of 14 and 21, changes in this age group should affect future traffic levels. Indeed, the number of persons in this group will fall off sharply during the 1980s (from 40 million to 27 million), which should stabilize the number of automobiles on the road as well as road accidents. This, in turn, would reduce the demand for those police services associated with vehicular traffic.

Transportation

Most local and state outlays for transportation are directed at the construction and maintenance of highways. Unlike other expenditures, outlays for highways declined nationally during the 1970s. This is attributable, in part, to the slow increase in total miles of road, less than 0.6 percent annually between 1970 and 1976. In a number of states, mileage actually declined. The slow growth in highways has taken place during a period of rapid increase in the number of cars, buses, and trucks, from 108 million in 1970 to 128 million in 1977, or an increase of 19 percent in a seven-year period. Total miles traveled between 1970 and 1976 increased from 1.12 trillion in 1970 to 1.41 trillion in 1976, or by 26 percent, roughly equal on an annual basis to increases in motor vehicle registration. In the years of 1974 and 1979, however, actual motor vehicle miles traveled decreased, whereas the number of cars and trucks in use increased only *1 percent* annually between 1977 and 1980 (Motor Vehicle Manufacturers Association 1981). It is difficult to project changes in the 1980s, given current uncertainties over supply and price. Overall, demand linked to national demographic characteristics has already peaked and will decline in the early 1980s as a result of fewer persons entering age groups in which driver licenses are typically obtained, and lower household formation rates in the late 1980s. For example, the number of cars in use climbed by 30.2 percent between 1970 and 1979, but by only 1.0 percent between 1979 and 1981.

Once again, however, population movement contributes to demand for public services. The number of vehicles registered between 1970 and 1977 increased the most rapidly in Florida (48 percent), New Hampshire (52 percent), Wyoming (52 percent) and Nevada (55 percent). Lowest increases were in New York (15 percent), New Jersey (23 percent), and Iowa and Kansas (24 percent). Not surprisingly, outlays for highways increased in southern and western states compared to those located in the northern regions. Per capita outlays in growing states increased by 16 percent between 1957 and 1977, but they declined by 22 percent in states with outmigration (1977 Census of Government, 1979).

Health Care

The demand for publicly funded health care is a function of several variables, but age distribution appears to be the most important. Per capita public health outlays for persons 65 and over are 15 times greater than such outlays for persons under the age of 19. Indeed, 67 percent of all outlays for persons over the age of 65 are public, compared to less than 30 percent for those younger. In 1977, $28 billion in public funds was spent on the elderly, or one-half of total public funds for health care, although this age group represents only 10.8 percent of the population (see table 5.11).

Projections for the 1980s, based on current demographic trends and changes in per capital outlays during the 1970s, indicate that public outlays (in constant dollars) will increase by 118 percent. Based on population changes alone, health care costs would increase by 15 percent during the 1980s. However, if both population and per capita trends in outlays are considered, public sector outlays, assuming no increase in the public sector share, would rise to $124 billion by 1990. The local and state sector share would be $37 billion of the total (Muller, Soble, and Dujack 1980).

Outlays for health care tend to be higher in northern states and metropolitan areas compared to the South and nonmetropolitan areas. This pattern reflects differences in the cost of medical care and state-local actions. During the 1980s, the cost of medical care among regions should stabilize, although urban-rural differences are likely to remain. Rapidly growing states, such as

Table 5.11. Per Capita Outlays for Health Care ($ 1977)

	1971			1977			% Change 1971–77		
	1–19	19–64	65+	1–19	19–64	65+	1–19	19–64	65+
Total	212	487	1280	253	661	1745	19	36	36
Private	158	368	456	175	471	476	11	28	26
Public	54	119	825	78	190	1169	44	60	42
Percent Public of Total	25.5	24.4	64.5	30.8	28.7	67.0	—	—	—

Source: U.S. Department of Health, Education, and Welfare 1979.

Arizona, Colorado, and Florida, can expect the largest increase in public health outlays, since their adult population is projected to increase by over 20 percent during the 1980s.

Household Growth

Based on recent trends and projected population migration, most new housing will be built on the periphery of urbanized areas—in the outer suburbs of metropolitan areas, on the periphery of smaller cities, and, in unincorporated areas, both near and at some distance from established urban centers. Most new housing built in older central cities will replace existing housing stock.

Fire Services

The expansion of housing on the urban periphery will obviously increase the demand for fire services. Concurrently, the demand for this service in high density cities with population losses will not slacken. However, cost of fire protection depends not only on demand loads but on the number of voluntary fire personnel. The number of paid personnel is only 0.4 per 10,000 population in communities with fewer than 1,000 residents, the highest per capita in the 100,000–500,000 population range. The low number public employees in small communities reflects the almost exclusive use of volunteers in places with fewer than 10,000 residents (Manson and Muller 1981). A considerable proportion of the housing constructed during the 1980s can be expected to be protected by such personnel. However, other households will locate in larger southern and western urban communities, which will require an expansion of paid fire department personnel, and thus outlays. This pattern has been evident in recent years, during sustained growth in these regions.

Between 1957 and 1977, outlays per capita for fire protection in states with rapidly growing population, such as Florida and Arizona, increased by 133 percent, compared to half the increase in states with stable population. Most of the difference in the rates of increase between the two categories of states occurred during the 1970s. These data indicate a convergence in outlays among growing states and those with essentially stable population during the 1970s. With continued growth projected in such states as Arizona, Florida, and New Mexico, future real growth in fire protection outlays can be expected to be concentrated in these states and in the urban periphery of metropolitan areas in northern regions. By contrast, central cities in northern states should have practically no increases in demand during the 1980s for fire services. However, demand cannot be expected to drop despite projected decreases in population, since areas with abandoned buildings, for example, have a higher frequency of fire than those with fully occupied buildings.

Sanitation

Outlays for sewerage treatment facilities and collection systems are linked to the following demographic characteristics: total population change, number of new households, location of new housing units, and housing density. Holding other variables constant, outlays for sewerage treatment facilities would increase as population grows, since there is a strong linkage between population and use of water, including waste water. In reality, however, the location of new population is more important than a change in population. In some older urban areas, existing facilities are underutilized; thus, an increase in the number of households would result in some increase in operating outlays, but there would be no need to construct new facilities. By contrast, even small additional growth in areas close to utilizing their existing capacity can trigger the need for substantial capital investment. Housing density is another variable, since in very low density areas it is not economically feasible to provide centralized facilities. Septic tanks are therefore utilized, which involve a totally private capital outlay.

It is often argued that sewerage treatment costs are lower in areas of high population concentration and density. There is certainly some validity to this position, since collection system costs per user are indeed lower in areas of high density. Large sewerage treatment plants also tend to show scale economies, except for very large facilities. Thus, one could anticipate that greater population density would result in relatively lower per capita outlays, although operating outlays are less sensitive to density.

Given the economies associated with urban sewer systems, the population distribution pattern of the 1970s, expected to continue into the 1980s, will exert upward pressures on governmental expenditures. Because of continued movement from the urban core outward at both the regional and interregional levels, most net new housing units will be built in areas where the per capita cost of providing centralized sewer systems will be high. The actual level of outlays, however, will depend on political and economic factors—the willingness of state and federal agencies to provide funds for the construction of new, or upgrading of existing, facilities. If the trends of the 1970s were to continue, outlays for sewerage treatment facilities would continue to climb as a result of both the location of new housing units and pressure to meet EPA standards. However, federal assistance during the early 1980s has diminished, and EPA standards are being modified. Thus, while the demand for sewerage treatment facilities is continuing as the population decentralizes, federal funding has been curtailed. Fiscal difficulties at the state level have limited new construction.

As expected, increases in sanitation outlays were more rapid in southern and western states compared to those in the North. The differential rate increase is attributable to the 1972–77 time period, when outlays in rapidly growing states more than doubled. However, on the average, per capita outlays in growing states remain below those in states with more stable populations. The lowest outlays occur in low density—rural states such as Mississippi and Montana—and the highest outlays are in higher density, highly urban states—Florida, New York, and New Jersey, for example. This reflects the use of noncentralized sewerage treatment (or the absence of any treatment) in rural areas. Manson and Muller (1981) substantiate this claim with data from the Appalachian region, showing outlays in communities with fewer than 1,000 residents about $1 per capita, rising to $17 per capita in 1977 for cities with over 100,000 residents.

Public Schools

Public schools accounted for 28 percent of all state-local outlays in 1970 and 26 percent of the outlays in 1977, with expenditures concentrated at the local level. In fact, 53 percent of the total local government payroll is allocated for instructional and other school personnel.

No public service demand is as directly linked to a demographic characteristic as are public schools, since all children able to do so are required by law to attend school. As private enrollment has remained stable at about 11 percent of total enrollment, it is reasonable to assume that close to 90 percent of all children born in the late 1970s and early 1980s will attend public schools during the decade.

The National Center for Educational Statistics (1978) projects enrollment in elementary and secondary schools to decline until the mid 1980s. Enrollment may increase marginally after the mid 1980s in lower grades, but will continue to decline in secondary schools (see table 5.12). These projections are consistent with Bureau of the Census population projections, which show that the number of persons age five to nine will decrease from 14.5 million in 1977 to 13.4 million in 1985, but will rise to 15.8 million by 1990. Despite the stability of the enrollment projections, the center projects a 22 percent real rise in public school operating outlays in the 1977–87 period and a 31 percent rise in per pupil outlays during the 10-year interval, based on recent trends (see table 5.13). However, school expenditure data as of 1982 show no increase in outlays when adjusted for inflation.

Table 5.12.   Enrollment in Public School Systems, 1963–86 (in millions)

School Year	Elementary K–8	Secondary 9–12	Higher Education (Public)
1964	29.3	10.9	3.1
1970	32.6[a]	13.0	5.9
1977	30.0	14.3[a]	8.6
1981	27.9	13.2	(9.3)[b]
			9.9
1987	(25.4)[b]	11.8	(9.0)[b]
	28.4		10.6

Source: National Center for Education Statistics 1978.

[a]Peak year.
[b]Low alternative projection.

Population migration exerts substantial upward pressure on school expenditures. In particular, population decline, experienced by most large cities, has resulted in sharply declining enrollment. Between 1970 and 1977, about one-half million white families with children migrated from central cities, causing much of the rapid decline in large school systems. In fact, all large city school systems (with the possible exception of Phoenix) lost large numbers of students, as shown in table 5.14. Losses during the 1970s ranged from an incredible 45 percent in St. Louis and almost 40 percent in Cleveland and San Francisco to under 20 percent in Dallas, Houston, and Los Angeles.[6] However, in 1982, enrollment in Los Angeles rose as a result of immigration. Sharp drops in enrollment were not accompanied by similar reductions in expenditures, as outlays per pupil (in constant dollars) soared in many systems. There were exceptions, namely San Antonio, San Diego, and Indianapolis, which were able to control outlays despite enrollment losses. Most school systems, however, had sharp increases, led by Boston, Dallas, Cleveland, and Detroit (see table 5.14).

Table 5.13.   Public School Expenditures, 1964–87 ($billion 1977)

School Year	Elementary and Secondary Operating	Capital	Higher Education Operating	Capital
1964	42.0	7.3	13.0	3.7
1970	64.3	8.3	25.2	5.5
1977	76.5	6.2	30.8	3.9
1981	80.8	5.5	33.7	3.9
1987	93.3	4.5	34.4	3.9
Percent Change				
1968–77	82	−15	14	5
1977–87	22	−27	11	0

Source: See table 5.12.

Table 5.14.   Enrollment and Outlays in Large City Schools, 1970–78

| | Enrollment (in thousands) | | | Outlays per ADA | | | 1980 Enrollment as % of |
City/Region	1970	1980	% Change	ADA 1970	(current $) 1978	% Change	1980 Pop.
North							
Boston	98	70	−28.6	1290	3848	198.3	10.0
Chicago	562	477	−15.1	1633	2594	58.8	13.4
Cleveland	151	91	−39.7	1478	2555	72.9	10.4
Detroit	293	224	−23.5	1213	1948	60.6	13.4
Indianapolis	103	67	−35.0	1477	1584	11.3	9.6
Milwaukee	132	91	−31.1	1579	2352	48.9	14.3
New York	1123	920	−18.1	2184	2707	23.9	13.0
Philadelphia	294	232	−21.1	1922	2377	23.7	13.7
St. Louis	113	62	−45.1	1572	2008	27.7	13.7
South							
Dallas	160	130	−18.8	958	1756	83.3	—[a]
Houston	237	194	−18.1	899	1412	57.1	—[a]
Memphis	147	112	−23.8	1171	1414	20.8	17.3
New Orleans	112	89	−20.5	1136	1647	45.0	16.0
San Antonio	75	62	−17.3	1194	1274	6.7	—[a]
Los Angeles	654	576	−11.9	1268	1949	53.7	19.4
San Francisco	92	56	−39.1	1859	2143	15.4	8.2
San Diego	129	110	−7.8	1542	1743	13.0	12.6
Phoenix	174	184 [b]	5.7	960	1144	18.4	23.3
Washington, D.C.	149	106	−28.9	1545	2368	53.3	16.6
Total Central Cities	13.1	12.0[b]	−8.4	—	—	—	20.1[b]

Source: U.S. Department of Commerce 1981b.

[a]School district not coterminous with municipal boundary.
[b]1978 enrollment and population.

The overall drop in enrollment is explained by the outmigration of white families with children, as well as the reduced birth rate, which would have resulted in reduced enrollment even in cities with modest population gains. Enrollment levels in public schools during the 1970s were also affected by numerous nondemographic factors, including bussing to achieve racial balance, which reduced enrollment in such school districts as Boston, Cleveland, and Memphis.

Current projections are for central city outmigration to continue but at somewhat lower rates. Specifically, both black and white families with children are anticipated to continue leaving cities. Therefore, it is reasonable to assume that large city school systems, with the exception of Los Angeles and one or two others, will have further enrollment reductions.[7] The slight projected increase in the birth rate is not expected to have any measurable impact on large central city enrollment.

Enrollment decline in central cities varies with size. Collectively, central city enrollment did not peak until 1975, but then declined rapidly, by 1.7

million students, in the following three years. Although total enrollment (public and private) in central cities has declined by 8.4 percent since 1970, enrollment by nonwhites has increased. However, this enrollment, too, appears to have peaked during the late 1970s. In large cities, declines have been greater than in smaller cities.

School enrollment in suburban schools peaked in 1975, when over 25 percent of the total suburban population was enrolled in public or private schools. This dropped to 22 percent by 1978, reducing sharply the central city-suburban gap. Indeed, school enrollment on a per capita basis has fallen much more rapidly in suburbs compared to central cities in recent years. Enrollment losses have been substantial even in suburbs gaining population. For example, in Fairfax County, Virginia, the number of residents during the 1970s increased by 31 percent. Nevertheless, school enrollment, which was 133,000 in 1970–71, fell to 127,000 in 1980–81 (Office of Research and Statistics 1982). During the 1980s, older, inner suburbs can be expected to show continuing declines, particularly among the white population. Almost all enrolled growth will be taking place at the urban periphery, that is, in outer suburban areas.

Finally, growth of nonmetropolitan areas paced population increases in suburban areas during the 1970s. After a period of decline, school enrollment actually increased between 1975 and 1978, suggesting inmigration of families with children to these areas. This migration pattern is expected to continue, so school enrollment should stabilize in smaller cities and rural areas. No major increases, however, are expected in these areas unless they are affected by some large new public or private facility.

One factor that will tend to increase education costs, particularly in urban areas of Arizona, California, New York, and Texas, is the immigration of both legal and undocumented aliens. Most of these households come from non-English-speaking regions, such as Mexico and other Central American nations, and reside in large central cities. Further, these households tend to have substantially larger families than the average found in U.S. central cities.[8] Since the cost of providing these foreign-born, non-English-speaking children bilingual education is high, outlays in numerous cities will continue to rise.

In general, the growth of capital outlays has been less than operating costs, so capital outlays as a share of total school outlays have been declining steadily for two decades. This reduction is directly attributable to lower enrollment rate increases in the late 1960s, followed by enrollment reductions in the mid-1970s. Capital outlays are currently concentrated in states with substantial inmigration, such as Arizona, Colorado, and Florida. These states spent $295 in fiscal 1977 per pupil for new facilities. By contrast, the six states with the largest net outmigration in the nation spent only $66 per pupil, or less than 5 percent of total outlays for facilities.

Overall, total outlays per capita—both operating and capital—show no pattern at the regional level. In 1977, for example, among a group of growing and declining states, Pennsylvania and Texas spent the least. Between 1972 and 1977, however, outlays in growing states exceeded those in northern regions. An examination of a group of school districts with sharply falling and growing enrollment indicates that both categories had increases in per pupil outlays substantially more rapid than the rate of inflation.

Higher Education

Outlays for higher education by both state and local government increased substantially in the 1967–77 decade, reflecting higher enrollment as well as an increasing share of enrollment in public institutions. State outlays (both capital and operating) increased from $9.0 billion in 1967 to $21.2 billion in 1977, while local outlays, mostly for junior colleges, increased by a factor of four from $1.2 billion to $4.8 billion.[9] Enrollment rates are the highest, on a per capita basis, in western states. The National Center for Education Statistics (1978) projects outlays to increase to $38.3 billion by 1987, an increase of 9 percent over 1977 (see table 5.13).

Demographic changes do not explain increased expenditures for higher education; increases in enrollment do. The majority of persons attending colleges are between the ages of 18 and 24. As shown in table 5.15, 82 percent of all students in 1970 and 73 percent in 1977 were in this age group. Despite a rise in enrollment among older persons, particularly women 25 to 35 years of age, attendance at private and public institutions will continue to depend primarily on high school graduates. In theory, current enrollment rates could be increased to 40 percent or over, but the proportion of high school graduates attending college, which had increased from 30 percent in 1970 to 33 percent in 1972, declined slightly to 32 percent in 1980. Thus, it appears that current proportions are reflecting the share that colleges are likely to maintain during the mid and late 1980s. In addition, the number of persons in age groups most likely to attend institutions of higher learning will drop during the 1980s.

Putting these trends together, I forecast that college enrollment should remain stable among persons in the 17-to-24 age group to the mid 1980s, and decline thereafter. Enrollment in public colleges, however, should rise, if only slowly, during most of the 1980s, with this growth limited to southern

Table 5.15. Linkage between Demographic Changes and Local/State Revenue

Demographic Characteristic	Revenue Impact
Rapid Household Formation Rate	More residential property and utility taxes, less sales taxes
Increase in Dependent Population	Less income and gasoline taxes
Population Movement	Added revenue in areas of immigration, higher tax burden in areas of outmigration

and western states. Enrollment in both public and private institutions in most northern states should decline slightly after 1985. Additional adult enrollment can be anticipated during the 1980s, but this growth will be offset by fewer persons in the 17-to-24 age group. Further, most adults would attend college on a part-time basis, with public costs per student substantially lower than among full-time enrollees. Decreases in student loans that were offered by the federal government in the late 1970s and were reduced further in the early 1980s could further depress enrollment.

Household Composition

Welfare Assistance.   Aid to Families with Dependent Children (AFDC) is the largest component of welfare outlays. These payments are sensitive to several demographic characteristics, the most important being the type of household being formed. A growth in the number of husband-wife families, for example, reduces the likelihood of AFDC assistance. However, low marriage rates tend to increase the probability of births out of wedlock. High divorce rates mean more AFDC cases; low divorce rates mean fewer cases. A rise in birth rates would presumably be accompanied by a proportionate rise in teenage pregnancies, again leading to more AFDC recipients. An increase in the number of nonwhite births or in the number of female-headed households would have the same impact. Such households, particularly among minorities, are the most likely to have incomes below the poverty level. Current projections are that the number of female households with no husband present will increase from 8.0 million in 1978 to 11.6 million in 1990 (U.S. Bureau of the Census 1979b). This implies a substantial potential increase in AFDC caseloads during the 1980s, since real income is expected to rise only marginally. However, federal as well as state cutbacks in assistance and tighter controls limiting eligibility are countering the caseload rise. Thus, while the number of low income female-headed households continues to rise, welfare payments are not growing as rapidly.

IMPACT OF PROJECTED DEMOGRAPHIC PATTERNS ON REVENUES AND TAX BURDEN

Data from the 1960s and 1970s suggest that demographic factors have less influence on local and state revenue receipts than on service demand. Revenues are more sensitive to economic and political forces. Of course, limits on revenue eventually constrain public sector responses to apparent needs for service. Demographic changes do have some direct or indirect impact on revenues, however, as suggested in table 5.15.

Household Formation Rates

The formation of new households, creating a demand for new housing units, has a significant impact on residential property values, which account for about 60 percent of all real estate subject to the property tax. In contrast, nonresidential property values are more directly linked to the national economy, interest rates, and the level of capital investment than to changing demographic patterns. Thus, projected increases in the housing stock during the 1980s imply a substantial growth in the assessed value of residential property (Muller, Soble, and Dujack 1980; Weicher 1980) In 1979 and 1980, however, property tax collections increased at a rate lower than inflation, a trend continuing into the early 1980s. If the tax limitation movement continues, the 1980s growth in assessed value will not be translated into comparable increases on property taxes. Moreover, increased investment in housing historically has had a negative impact on sales tax collections, which are generally a function of disposable income, savings rate, and the purchases of other (taxable) goods and services.

During the 1980–82 period, a combination of low economic growth and high interest rates reduced the level of new construction, and thus an anticipated source of additional revenue in many localities growing rapidly during the 1970s was not realized. At the same time, residential property values, in constant dollars, also declined for the first time since the early 1930s. Although this trend should reverse by the mid 1980s, it is evident that more "doubling up" is taking place and that household formation rates may be lower than originally projected as a result of housing conditions. This in turn will have a negative impact on local revenue and thus on service levels.

Age Distribution

Changes in the number of persons 16 to 65 years of age (the potential labor force) have some impact on state and local income taxes. New entrants into the labor market include older adults, but the major source of expansion in the work force has been individuals in the 16-to-24 age category. As was shown in the discussion of higher education, the number of persons in this age category will be declining during the 1980s. At the same time, the age dependency ratio (population 65 and over per 100 population 18 to 64) will be rising.

The child dependency ratio (persons under 18 per 100 population to those 18 to 64) will be reduced until the mid-1980s, and then it will rise. To the extent that income tax collections are directly related to the labor force, these collections should be increasing until the mid-1980s. However, the rapid reductions in the dependency ratios during the 1970s will not be observed again, at least not in this century. Therefore, income tax collections, holding political and economic factors constant, will not rise in real terms as it did during the 1970s, when employment grew rapidly.

Migration, Income, and Tax Burden

The ability to pay for public services depends on the level of personal income. Tax burden is typically measured as the percentage of gross income allocated for taxes—local, state, and federal.

Between 1970 and 1978, mean family income in central cities declined by about 4 percent while remaining basically unchanged in suburbs. Most of the real growth was taking place in nonmetropolitan areas, where incomes increased by about 10 percent during the eight-year period.

At the regional level, family income in metropolitan areas increased in growing regions, particularly in the South, but remained practically unchanged in the Northeast. Per capita income growth between 1970 and 1977 was also the lowest in the Northeast—less than 1 percent annually in New York and Connecticut and less than 2 percent annually in the other northeastern states. By contrast, certain states, including Texas, New Mexico, and Mississippi, increased their annual per capita income by 3 to 4 percent in real terms. (Texas and New Mexico had substantial immigration during the 1970s.) In the early 1980s, however, the Northeast's position improved, and income growth in the South and oil-rich states stabilized.

To some extent, differences in income growth reflect the characteristics of outmigrants, who tend to have higher incomes than those remaining behind. The projected continuation of outmigration from central cities to outer areas and from northern states therefore suggests that real income will continue to rise in rural areas as well as in the South and West, although more slowly than during the 1970s. As disposable income at the national level is projected to grow only slowly, this implies that it will drop in the north central states during the 1980s.

Tax collections at the local and state level will probably drop (in real terms) in the industrial northern states. Nevertheless, above-average tax burdens will remain in these states, attributable, in part, to outmigration and more persons 65 years of age and over in northern regions compared to the balance of the nation. The low construction activity, both residential and nonresidential, in most northern industrial states will also contribute to above-average tax burdens.

FINDINGS AND CONCLUSIONS

Demographic factors that are likely to have the most significant influence on the demand for public services during the 1980s include the following:

• Stabilization of birth rates at close to current levels, resulting in only small aggregate public school enrollment growth in the late 1980s, with the exception of school districts with large immigration.

- Fewer persons in the 14-to-24 age group, with resulting lower aggregate crime rates, fewer new owners of motor vehicles, and curtailed college enrollment.

- Growth in the number of 65-and-over households, increasing substantially public sector outlays for health-related services.

- Growth in one-parent, mostly female-headed, households, increasing the demand for AFDC and other public welfare programs.

- Continuing movement of white families with children from central cities and inner suburbs, particularly in northern states, reducing demand for public schools but offset by higher per pupil outlays to meet needs of immigrants.

- Construction of most new housing units in unincorporated areas and in smaller, low density jurisdictions, with rise in the need for roads, sewerage and water treatment facilities, and fire protection in these areas.

- Growth in service demands concentrated in southwestern and western states outside current boundaries of their central cities.

- Higher per capita outlays for public services and municipal wages in the South and West as population and income rise.

Demographic changes during the 1980s most likely to affect local and state revenues and tax burdens include the following:

- Growth in new households leading to 20 million or so additional housing units constructed during the decade. Assuming that current tax rates are maintained, this will result in substantial real rises in outer suburbs, the Southwest, and the West in aggregate residential property values and property taxes.

- Fewer middle-income, central city residents to pay for fixed municipal public service costs, including infrastructure maintenance and debt service.

Given all trends, the size of the local and state sector is expected to remain stable during the 1980s and will contract as a share of the total national economy. This contraction, first noted in the late 1970s, counters the notion of an ever-expanding public sector (see table 5.7). The fundamental causes for the observed shift and projected reversal of earlier trends are political and economic as well as demographic.

The primary demographic cause for the growth of state and local government in the 1970s was the relocation of households from northern industrial states to the South and West, and from the high-density urban core to lower-density areas. In the short run, these movements contributed to increased demand for public services and increased unit costs. Across the nation, more service was provided as growing areas expanded their programs and declining areas maintained services. In addition, per capita costs rose in declining areas and, as jurisdiction size increased, in growing areas as well.

Over time, however, costs should stabilize. Population loss as well as severe fiscal pressures are leading to a decline in the cost of services in central cities. Meanwhile, areas traditionally spending the least for public services, particularly social services—the South and Southwest, as well as non-metropolitan areas—will continue to gain population, so costs should continue to rise. The traditional gap in wages between northern industrial states and the Pacific region in comparison to the South and Southwest will continue to be reduced, if not totally eliminated, during the 1980s.

Since population redistribution is expected to equalize state and local outlays among regions, states, and localities in the long run, then incentives to relocate based on tax differentials will be reduced. However, fiscal incentives to migrate out of the cities may not be totally eliminated since large cities will continue to have above-average costs. A key demographic factor that could increase the demand for public services in large cities is the rising population of Hispanics and other minorities, such as Asians in Pacific states. The effects of increased concentration of minorities and immigrants in cities deserves the attention of researchers.

NOTES

1. Population projections shown in this chapter reflect the assumption that fertility rates will be equal to replacement level. This level corresponds with surveys of young women and is consistent with the small rise in birth rates observed in the early 1980s.

2. Population increases in 1979 and 1980 were the highest in several years, both as a result of more young women in the population, somewhat higher birth rates and a sharp rise in legal civilian immigration, estimated in 1980 and at a post 1920s high of over 650 thousand.

3. As a result of differences in estimating procedures, annual estimates are subject to considerable error. The 1980 census provides the most reliable data on population change during the decade. These data indicated outmigration from cities to be more rapid than projected on an annual basis by the Bureau of the Census. Total population growth was underestimated, probably because of undocumented (illegal) migration.

4. Presumably, the number of illegal immigrants in cities exceeds 1.0 million. This implies a substantial undercount of immigrants in the 1980 census of population.

5. Between 1975 and 1980, the number of city employees per capita in jurisdictions with over 100,000 residents decreased by almost 5%.

6. Houston and Dallas have central school districts, which include only the older parts of each jurisdiction.

7. 1981 enrollment data substantiate this assumption, as enrollment in all large city school districts continues to fall.

8. For example, the typical Mexican family in Los Angeles in 1980 had 1.5 children in public schools, more than twice the number found among non-Mexican families.

9. These statistics, from the Bureau of the Census, differ somewhat from the Department of Education data.

REFERENCES

Manson, Donald M., and Thomas J. Muller. 1981. *The Provision and Cost of Public Services in Appalachian Communities*. Washington, D.C.: Urban Institute (December).

Motor Vehicle Manufacturers Association. 1981. *Motor Vehicle Facts and Figures, 1980*. N.p.: V. P. Polk.

Muller, Thomas J. 1977. Service Costs in the Declining City. In *How Cities Can Grow Old Gracefully*. Committee on Banking, Finance, and Urban Affairs, Subcommittee on the City, 95th Cong., 1st sess. (December).

Muller, Thomas J., Carol Soble, and Susan Dujack. 1980. *The Urban Household in the 1980s*. Washington, D.C.: U.S. Department of Housing and Urban Development (April).

National Center for Education Statistics. 1978. *Projections of Education Statistics*. Washington, D.C.: U.S. Department of Health, Education, and Welfare.

Office of Research and Statistics. 1982. *Fairfax County 1981 Profile*. Fairfax, Va.: Fairfax County Government.

Peterson, George E. and Thomas J. Muller. 1979. *Economic and Fiscal Costs*. Washington, D.C.: Urban Institute.

U.S. Department of Commerce. Bureau of the Census. 1972. *Governmental Finances in Fiscal 1970*. Washington, D.C.: U.S. Government Printing Office.

———. 1975. *Social and Economic Characteristics of the Metropolitan and Nonmetropolitan Population, 1974 and 1970*. P-23, no. 55. September.

———. 1977. *Projections of the Population of the United States, 1974–2050*. P-25, no. 704. July.

———. 1978. *Social and Economic Characteristics of the Metropolitan and Nonmetropolitan Population, 1977 and 1970*. P-23, no. 75. November.

———. 1979a. *Governmental Finances in Fiscal 1977*. Washington, D.C.: U.S. Government Printing Office.

———. 1979b. *Series II Census Projections*. P-25, no. 805. May.

———. 1979c. *1977 Census of Governments, Compendium of Public Employment*. July.

———. 1980. *Boundary and Annexation Survey, 1970–1979*. Washington, D.C.: U.S. Government Printing Office.

———. 1981a. *Current Population Report Series*. P-20, no. 222.

———. 1981b. *Finances of Public School Systems in 1979–1980*.

———. 1981c. *Geographic Mobility*. P-20, no. 368. December.

———. 1982. *Governmental Finances in Fiscal 1980*. Washington, D.C.: U.S. Government Printing Office.

U.S. Federal Bureau of Investigation. 1972. *Uniform Crime Reports for the United States*. Washington, D.C.: U.S. Government Printing Office.

———. 1978. *Uniform Crime Reports for the United States*. Washington, D.C.: U.S. Government Printing Office.

———. 1979. *Uniform Crime Reports for the United States*. Washington, D.C.: U.S. Government Printing Office.

U.S. Department of Health, Education, and Welfare. 1979. *Social Security Bulletin*. DC: U.S. GPO.

Weicher, John. 1980. *National Housing Need and Quality Changes*. Washington, D.C.: Urban Institute.

6

A Political Perspective

John J. Kirlin

The preceding chapters illustrate the strengths, and limits, of empirical analysis. Anton demonstrates how elusive is the control of state and local activity presumed to be desirable by many and pursued by much national policy. The critique of comparative models offered by Larkey, Stolp, and Winer concludes that relatively little is known about why governments grow and decline or about the consequences of such changes. King and Kraemer show the limits inconsistent data definitions impose on scientific approaches to management. Muller's analysis reveals that growth in population and in households is related to growth in governmental revenues and expenditures, but that loss of population does not lead to a commensurate decline in expenditures.

None of the authors provides an explanation for the fiscal limits that arose in the late 1970s, an empirical phenomenon related to each of their topics. They do not attempt to explain this phenomenon, so perhaps their analyses could be extended to do so, but it appears more likely that they would founder on this task. What is missing from these analyses is full exploration of the role of political choice. The authors describe a deterministic world of discoverable and reliable relationships among measurable phenomena. As Miller suggests in her contributions to this volume, this is the perspective dominant in the natural sciences. It is also the perspective of logical positivism, only one approach to "doing" science.

What is needed is a framework that can accommodate such sharp reversals in public policies as occurred in the recent experience with fiscal constraint. Table 6.1 provides aggregate fiscal data that demonstrate the depth of constraint imposed upon state and local governments beginning in 1975. Expressed as a percentage of GNP, measures of state and local fiscal activity increased until 1975, and then uniformly declined. This pattern of increase and subsequent constraint was the consequence of policy choices made in the

Table 6.1. Fiscal Constraint of State and Local Governments, Selected Years
(% of GNP)

Year	Total State and Local Expenditure	Fed. Aid	State Expenditure Own Funds	Local Expenditure Own Funds	State and Local Debt Issuance
1949	7.8	0.9	3.4	3.5	—
1959	9.6	1.4	3.8	4.4	1.9
1969	12.6	2.4	5.3	5.1	2.5
1974	14.3	3.1	6.0	5.2	3.7
1975	15.2	3.6	6.3	5.3	3.7
1976	14.7	3.6	6.1	5.0	3.3
1977	14.3	3.6	5.8	4.9	3.5
1978	14.2	3.6	5.8	4.8	3.2
1979	13.4	3.3	5.6	4.5	2.7
1980	13.4	3.3	5.7	4.4	2.9

Sources: Columns 1–4 from Shannon 1981. Column 5 from Kirlin 1981.

50 states and tens of thousands of local governments. Increases and decreases
in federal grants-in-aid explain only a part of this pattern and lie behind the
policy choices made by state and local governments. In the 1959–76 period
Shannon (1981) counted 627 instances in which states increased taxes or
imposed new taxes. In contrast, in the 1977–80 period, 42 states reduced
taxes, indexed the personal income tax, or adopted one of the types of contemporary fiscal limit (full disclosure laws, property tax levy limits, expenditure lids, or assessment constraints).

When Proposition 13 was adopted by California voters in June 1978, it was
widely regarded as a unique event. Yet table 6.1 reveals that the apogee of
expenditures had come two years earlier; the Jarvis-Gann Initiative may have
dramatized or popularized fiscal constraint, but it was neither the first nor the
typical case. Political choices exercised at many locations, imposing constraints of several forms and in a variety of specific contexts, constitute the
"fiscal limits movement." What is extraordinary, at first reflection, is
achievement of such a sharp reversal *without* central direction.

In a few instances, a contagion or mimicking effect undoubtedly occurred,
especially in the few states that sought (largely unsuccessfully) to imitate
Proposition 13. More persuasive, however, are explanations that find the
causes of fiscal limits in broad social phenomena, stimulating responses that
varied by context (for example, which tax had increased most) and by opportunity (for example, availability of the initiative). Many specific policy
choices combined (with compounding effects as cuts were ultimately made at
all three levels of government) to constitute a stronger political choice than
would have occurred had constraint been mandated from Washington, D.C.

Elsewhere, I have argued that the causes of fiscal constraint are to be found
partially in the declining personal economic situations of citizens and partially

in their rejection of alienating political processes (Kirlin 1982). In the 1965–75 period, policy making and implementation came to be dominated by single-focus interest groups. These groups pursued "vertical" politics, seeking favorable policies at all levels of our federal system. Their successes resulted in the strengthening of functionally specific institutions (departments or extrajurisdictional "regional" bodies, for example). But the traditional political system of this nation, and that to which citizens have access, is "horizontal," based in general-purpose local governments, states, and the national government. In reaction to a shift to interest-group politics, which reduced citizens to clientele, objects of regulation, or taxpayers, fiscal constraint policies provide an opportunity to reassert the primacy of jurisdiction-based politics. The focus of political conflict is shifted from specific programs and policies to general fiscal issues—policy choices for which jurisdictions, with their taxing powers, are the appropriate arena.

The fiscal constraint case suggests that political choice is important. Politically relevant phenomena are not merely observable, they are constructed—the products of human choice and action. Instead of logical positivism, our philosophy of science should be pragmatism (Dewey 1927; Kaplan 1961; Kirlin 1982). Instead of passive social science, our style should be that of design (Ostrom 1980; Miller 1984).

The previous chapters include opportunity for elements of political choice, but none goes so far as this chapter argues is necessary. One way of interpreting Anton's analysis is that localities retain substantial capacity for choice despite attempts by national policy-makers to constrain and direct their activities. Similarly, choice can be seen in the behavior of jurisdictions described in Muller's analysis: some jurisdictions allow growth to occur, others maintain expenditures at levels higher than their demographics would appear to justify. King and Kraemer find that local officials use so-called scientific models to justify, rather than to guide, decisions that are selected for other reasons. After critiquing the formal models of governmental growth, Larkey, Stolp, and Winer turn to organizational process models. These models emphasize bounded rationality and the temporal interrelatedness of choices, an important antidote to the teleological biases of the formal choice models. From this perspective, governmental policies (or at least the budget choices commonly analyzed) are evolutionary. Choice is exercised within the constraints imposed by previous choices.

Even when they are used to address political choice, however, these analyses are only partially satisfying. One reason for their limited utility has already been identified. The biases of logical positivism orient analysis toward discovery of "facts," not the opportunities for choice, thus encouraging a deterministic perspective. A second common limitation of these analyses—widely shared in the literature of political science, public administration, and public policy—is a focus upon the delivery of public services.

For example, contemporary discussions of "governmental" performance focus upon performance in the delivery of public services such as police, fire, or refuse collection at the local government level or antirecession manpower grants at the federal level. This formulation of the issue of governmental performance is of recent origin. Effective and efficient service delivery is important, but service delivery is not the critical role of government. Government is the institution of society with singular obligations to facilitate societal choice-making and action. Its ability to make decisions and to act are the dominant dimensions by which governmental performance should be judged. Choices often revolve around service delivery, and so too does action, but capacity for choice making and action is not synonymous with service delivery. The capacity standard has deep roots in western political philosophy, was the overriding concern of the framers of the U.S. Constitution, and finds modern expression in several important critiques of the functioning of the U.S. political system (e.g., Schattschneider 1960; Wolin 1968; Schon 1971; Janowitz 1976; Ladd 1978; Presthus 1978).

How a political-choice orientation to political systems may guide action and analysis is the concern of this chapter. The effort is normative, both in the sense that values guide the analysis and in the sense that the goal is a fuller specification of the values relevant to future policy-making and evaluations of political systems. A critical initial premise is that definitions of the political system must go beyond jurisdictional boundaries to encompass the intergovernmental system of this nation, the structural fragmentation and complexity of which are among its most distinguishing features. A heuristic model of an intergovernmental system with sustained capacity for making and implementing effective policies is developed. Lindblom's (1977) concept of strategic rationality is central to this task, serving as the keystone in integration of available literature relevant to the model. Finally, an assessment of literature on policy implementation and federalism illustrates how changing the focus of analysis to political functions and values can alter our understanding of public sector performance.

CHANGING THE FOCUS OF ANALYSIS

Equating governmental performance with service delivery performance has at least four roots. The first is the cluster of values and idealized institutions advocated by progressives and traditional American public administration, ultimately based upon presumption of a common public interest, which allows choices concerning societal activities to be reduced to a calculation of the best way to achieve shared goals (Mosher 1975). The second is the expansion of the public sector since World War II, commonly designated as the arrival of the welfare state, one consequence of which has been that the legitimacy of government as a social institution rests increasingly upon its ability to deliver the expanded menu of services (Lowi and Stone 1978). The third is an artifact of the particular state of social scientists' conceptual frameworks and mea-surement technologies, which, as currently used to analyze governmental performance, commonly limit analysis to achievement of particular program objectives. In part, this is merely the specification of the values inherent in the Progressive legacy. For example, the seminal article on measuring municipal performance by Ridley and Simon (1938) has this focus.

Finally, history focuses our attention on administration. Waldo (1980, 64) argues that our conceptions of the political system are the legacy of Greek political philosophy, whereas public administration owes more to Roman practices of governing, which relied heavily upon the administration of laws. Only in the last two centuries, he concludes, have European nations been "first, nationalized; second, democratized; and, third, to some extent, so-cialized." Prior to this period, ownership and sovereignty were closely inter-twined with administration of the personal estates of rulers. Waldo concludes that the values of democracy and of socialism are not easily accommodated in current administrative practice or theory. "It is in the area in which poli-tics/policy and administration/management mingle that the crucial problems of the large modern polity are to be found" (69–70). Several recent evalua-tions of the American political system parallel Waldo's about conflicts be-tween politics and administration, including Janowitz's (1978) application of a social control model, Lowi's (1979) analysis of the consequences of govern-mental accommodation to strong interest groups, Lindberg et al.'s (1975) assessment of the political stresses caused by modern capitalism, and Lindblom's (1977) explorations of the possible trade-offs between markets and political systems as organizing institutions in society.

These analysts (and others) conclude that the political system of the United States, while exhibiting many desirable characteristics, is seriously deficient in its ability to cope with popular demands. Some judge it overly biased toward business (Lindblom 1977) and strong interest groups (Lowi 1979). A more telling critique is that it is unable to develop policies to implement established objectives. Although the potential of the nation is great, the capac-ity of its political system is characterized variously as "weak" (Katzenstein 1977), as often choosing inappropriate policies (Lindblom 1977), and as increasingly "paralyzed" as a consequence of the success of larger numbers of interests organizing effectively (Olson 1977).

The proper focus for an evaluation of the political system of the United States is on the performance of the governmental institutions of the nation *as a set*. This recognizes that services and policies are supposed to reflect a demo-cratic choice process. Also, it acknowledges the federal character of our political institutions and the perception that relationships among jurisdictions have changed dramatically in the last two decades. Overall, the shift in focus toward political functions allows us to articulate beliefs of citizens and schol-ars that the preoccupation with service delivery, which has characterized twentieth-century public administration, has been injurious to the polity (Kirlin 1982).

REQUIREMENTS FOR AN EFFECTIVE
FEDERAL POLITICAL SYSTEM

Judgments concerning governmental performance must be broader than evaluations of service delivery and of single jurisdictions. The issue is the performance of the federal political system. How should such evaluations be made?

One possibility would be to evaluate the performance of functionally specific policy systems. The current intergovernmental system resembles a picket fence (Wright 1978), with greater integration across jurisdictional levels in similar policy arenas than within jurisdictions across policy arenas. Public bureaucracies are organized around similar programs at each level of the federal system (e.g., national, state, and local education departments), and funding sources are fragmented (particularly at the national level, where appropriations committees are highly differentiated, but also at the state and local levels, largely as the result of grants-in-aid and revenue streams tied to specified areas of expenditure).

Evaluations of such vertically linked, intergovernmental policy systems are now being made, often under the label of studies of policy implementation (e.g., Murphy 1971; Pressman and Wildavsky 1973; Williams and Elmore 1976; Ripley 1977). One of the most important inferences to be drawn from these studies is that implementation processes, and, consequently, interrelationships among national, state, and local agencies, vary widely in different policy arenas. Elementary and secondary education differs from community development block grants, and both differ from water quality control programs, and so on. Variety is appropriate, although it should not be concluded that the appropriate interrelationships are developed in all policy arenas. At least three typologies of these patterns exist. Robert Levine (1972) differentiates among four strategies: nonadministered economic systems, administered systems, systems involving comprehensive planning, and bargaining systems. Kirlin (1979) distinguishes three: administrative strategies, organizational environment strategies, and learning system strategies. And the ACIR typology of grants-in-aid (categorical, block, etc.) also provides a partial theoretical framework.

But evaluation of the performance of intergovernmental policy implementation within functions does not yield an appropriate evaluation of the political *system*. An appreciation of the potential difficulties is seen in the contrasts between the metaphor of the intergovernmental system as a picket fence and the description of the American political system in terms of interest-group pluralism. The latter terminology evokes much more complex, mixed, and fluid images. Political scientists argue that interest-group pluralism contributes to the effective functioning of a polyarchy (Dahl 1956), while also suspecting that it encourages exclusion of some individuals and interests (Bachrach 1967) and can contribute to the ultimate paralysis of the political system (Olson 1977; Lowi 1979).

A fuller evaluation of the political system is required. To structure the task, a heuristic model of the desirable attributes of a federal political system can be developed. This model then serves to orient a review of relevant research both as a normative standard against which the functioning of the existing system may be evaluated and as a guide to future research.

The development of a normative model of political performance rests, in turn, on empirical expectations about the rationality and the predictability of social systems. This is the familiar choice between synoptic and strategic views of rationality (Lindblom 1977, 314–29) or between center-periphery and learning system models of innovation (Schon 1971). If one believes that our capacity for rationality is high, that social systems are predictable, and that we can effectively translate policy initiatives into achievements, the ideal political system would be a picket fence composed of hierarchical bureaucracies. More inclusive bureaucracies would relate to less inclusive bureaucracies as central headquarters to field offices. Governmental performance would be improved through more informed, centralized choice-making and more controlled implementation. Conformity to centralized decision-making would be sought, only "planned variations" would be legitimate, and even those variations would be viewed as demonstrations that might become the basis for future national policies. The national government would urge "capacity building" for local governments, seeking to make them more perfect administrative instruments of central policy and more easily audited.

Although presented here so starkly as to be a caricature, this synoptic orientation dominates policy-making processes in the United States, and it is the foundation upon which most policy analysis is based. The urge to pursue synoptic rationality has impact even if the implicit model is never achieved. Language, policy and organizational design, and expectations of officials and citizens reflect the bias.

Alternatively, the ideal political system may be based on a heuristic model that conceptualizes decision-making and action capability to be widely dispersed. This perspective includes doubts about organizational capacity for extensive a priori rationality, the predictability of social systems, and the ability to achieve intentions by changing behaviors. Schon (1971) is a well-known advocate of this perspective, but his work is weakened by its apolitical character, which results in idealization of functionally specific networks dominated by professionals and not held accountable through any political processes. In several publications, Lindblom has explored alternatives to synoptic rationality, expanding conceptualization from a fairly simple incremental model (Braybrooke and Lindblom 1963), through mechanisms of mutual adjustment (1965), to his present formulation of "strategic" rationality (1977), encompassing a family of approaches premised upon recognition of limitations to humans' intellectual capacities "and the consequent need for an intellectual strategy to guide an inevitably incomplete analysis" (314). Although Lindblom does not provide an explicit rationale for the variety of models developed, they reflect differing scopes of inquiry from the individual through successively more aggregate, and complex, societal processes. His classic *Politics, Economics, and Welfare* (Dahl and Lindblom 1953) initiated concern with the broader issues, with much the same orientation seen in his current work, more than a quarter of a century ago.

The contrast between Lindblom's position and that of Simon (1947) and his followers (e.g., Cyert and March 1963; March and Simon 1958; Crecine 1969), who also begin with the assumption that human intellectual capacity is limited, is important. These scholars contend that organizations, though still never perfectly rational and often susceptible to pathologies, provide great advances over individual capabilities. They do not deal explicitly with the issue, but the authors do seem to assume that organizational rationality is sufficient for an effective society (but see March 1978). Also, when dealing with "organized social complexity," they often decompose the total system to more easily analyzed organizational subunits, whose behavior and interrelationships, rather than the functioning of the whole, become the object of inquiry (for a review and an example, see Crecine 1977).

The important point is not that attempts to improve the performance of organizational subcomponents are erroneous or even misplaced, but that what is judged rational at the component level need not be so at the level of an intergovernmental system or of society. Levels of analysis are nested. Just as it is theoretically important to distinguish organizations from individuals, so too is it important to distinguish political systems from departments and state and local jurisdictions. The felicitous joining of individual self-interest and societal wealth perceived by Adam Smith may have only imperfect analogues for organizations and society. For example, Ramos (1976) expresses concerns about the impacts of organizations upon individuals. Lindblom (1977), Janowitz (1976), and Schon (1971) argue that organizations' pursuit of rationality can be dysfunctional to society by resulting in inefficient use of resources or inadequate capacity to adapt to changing conditions.

The two contrasting approaches to rationality—synoptic or strategic—differ on several dimensions of central importance to the intergovernmental system, fundamentally in methods of problem definition and in expectations concerning human intellectual capacity, and consequently in institutional design, policy strategies, and evaluation activities. Table 6.2 contrasts the two approaches to these five dimensions. The basic empirical assumptions that undergird the two approaches to rationality yield very different approaches to institutional design, policy strategies, and evaluation activities. If one believes that problems are clear and permanent, and that individual intellectual capabilities are great or that the capacity of organizations and institutions for rational action is high, then these values carry through into one's approach to action, encouraging institutions, policies, and evaluations premised upon being able to correctly diagnose the problem, develop appropriate policies and institutions, implement policies effectively, evaluate the consequences of these actions, and, if necessary, change policies and institutions in response to

Table 6.2. Synoptic and Strategic Approaches to Policy Making

Approach	Method of Problem Definition	Expectations of Human Intellectual Capacity	Approaches to Institutional Design	Preferred Policy Strategies	Approach to Evaluation Activities
Synoptic	expects clarity, permanence	great, individually, organizationally, and institutionally	"once and for all," hard to change, dominated by professionals, bureaucratic, statist, interventionist, vertical	directive, controlling, permanent, top-down, hierarchical, monopolistic, narrow	seeks definitive universals, evaluation intended for use by central administers, directed from the center, secrecy
Strategic	expects ill-definition, change	limited, individually, organizationally, and institutionally	temporary, malleable, open to influence, market, entrepreneurial, conservative, horizontal	facilitative, variation desirable, policy initiatives fragmented, reversible, broad	seeks partial insight, attentive to context and nuance, evaluation intended for wide use, evaluations originate at many locations, sharing

the evaluations. The alternative starting point similarly influences action, with almost diametrically opposed orientations as to what should be done.

Rule (1978) takes a somewhat different tack but similarly challenges the possibility of synoptic rationality contributing to "social betterment." He starts with a discussion of social problems, arguing that as policy debate moves beyond the most general issues (e.g., environmental degradation is undesirable) into specifics, such as whether any responsive public policy is desired or what such a policy might be, consensus dissolves. Political, that is to say, value, differences quickly emerge. Rule argues that, in practice, "rational" analyses usually serve one specific set of interests in society (e.g., government officialdom, the proletariat); instead of serving any "public interest," they serve segments of society. He does not conclude that rationality and analysis are irrelevant or impossible, but that they are limited to the elaboration of prognoses concerning the state of the world and the likely results of various alternative actions as well as to the estimation of the effects of these alternative actions. The congruence with Lindblom's position emerges here: if there is no public interest upon which to base social actions, and the best that inquiry can do is to develop prognoses and estimate effects, then modesty in aspiration and caution in action are recommended.

What heuristic model of the political system would be appropriate, given a presumption that synoptic rationality is impossible to achieve and that, indeed, action based upon its premises is likely to be not only ineffectual but actually dysfunctional? Several authors provide clues in this effort. Landau (1974) emphasizes redundancy, with overlapping and duplicative jurisdictions providing capacity for error sensing and action, exalting the virtues of "a truly messy system" (188). La Porte (1975) advocates recognition of policy implementation as error making, suggesting that planning be redefined as learning. As to the specific values that should guide institutional design and policy making, he argues for reversibility and functional redundancy (347–51). Evaluation should encourage "error exploring rather than error camouflaging, error embracing rather than error punishing" (352). Wildavsky (1979, 212–36) trenchantly observes that these exhortations directly contravene the central value of organizations: to be stable, predictable, and controlling. Organization and evaluation are said to be incompatible.

Wildavsky's own prescriptions relevant to the political system are not clearly stated but must be teased from his discussion of policy analysis. He not only advocates variety and reversibility but adds another dimension in his discussions of objectives and values (392–406). Values are relevant, first, as the basis of citizenship, which requires that individuals trust the political system sufficiently to participate supportively; second, as conventions, holding that not all is up for possible change and constraining means; and third, as the basis for objectives. Wildavsky argues that objectives change and that a critical requirement of an effective political system is that it allow objectives to change. Opportunity for wide learning and behaviorial change must be provided (pricing petroleum products at the world price so that citizens could comprehend and act, for example, rather than subsidizing oil consumption, "protecting" citizens from the possibility of understanding and individual accommodation). So too must opportunities for leadership be created, in which visions of the future may be defined and, possibly, achieved. What is needed is a political system that allows change in "terminal" public values while maintaining constancy in "instrumental" public values (Rokeach 1973).

Learning and change require the ability to modify or terminate existing institutions and policies, a requirement already suggested to be difficult to meet. Biller (1976) has developed design considerations intended to make policy and organizational termination easier. His most general recommendation is to recognize that whereas organizations are premised upon permanence, markets are exactly the opposite, premised upon impermanent, temporary exchanges. Encouraging the creation of markets and intervention in their workings may often achieve public purposes with less risk of permanence and irreversibility. Another suggestion is to institutionalize the procedures of choice making and change rather than particular organizations and policies. Within organizations, matrix designs may be used, wherein the larger organization achieves permanence while project task forces are routinely created, acted upon, and terminated. Biller's proposed mechanisms routinize the termination of existing policies and organizations, a precondition for learning and adapting, especially in situations characterized by change and uncertainty.

Levine (1972) also urges the use of the market as a social institution for choice making and action, but cautions that many social values are unlikely to be realized through market exchanges. He suggests as alternatives bureaucratic competition (breaking up the monopoly power frequently given public bureaucracies; for an example, see Savas 1977a) and the development of explicit politico-bureaucratic bargaining arenas. Schultze (1970) has advanced similar proposals, urging the introduction of market competition into decisions about production of public goods, fuller imitations of the market in public programs, and partially "regionalizing" the national budget.

A major concern of public choice theorists is the consequence of alternative institutional designs, which are analyzed both formally, through axiomatic theory-building (for a review, see Mueller 1976), and empirically (for an example, see Ostrom, Parks, and Whittaker 1978). Vincent Ostrom has written explicitly about the design of a "compound republic" (1971) and more broadly about the tension between a political system structured to serve hierarchical administrative agencies and a "democratic" administration of concurrent jurisdictions much like that envisaged by Madison in *The Federalist Papers* (1973). Among the suggestions relevant to the design of political systems coming from this perspective are the value of fragmentation and overlap in reducing participation costs and increasing the likelihood of service provision attuned to the desires of citizens; the distinction among different types of goods (most importantly, between "public" and "private" goods), which provides a basis for choosing among alternative decision-rules; and the observation that public services should appropriately be provided by organizations of differing size, the issue of much research. Indeed, the research on alternative arrangements for service delivery (not all emanating from a public choice perspective) suggests that these decisions are among the most important made in shaping the public sector, affecting the kinds of services provided, their costs, and how citizens relate to the jurisdiction (Savas 1977b; Sonenblum, Kirlin, and Ries 1977; Ostrom 1979).

In another context, I have discussed both the forces that are causing change in the political system of the United States and suggested an approach to developing an effective federal political system (Kirlin 1979). New policies based upon the desire for increased equality and in response to the demands of managing an advanced economy have dramatically altered intergovernmental relationships in the last 15 years. One constant theme in this transformation has been the elevation of functional system (e.g., health services delivery, environmental protection) requirements over the needs of the political system. Administrative hegemony has not yet occurred, however, and some counterimpulses exist (e.g., General Revenue Sharing, fiscal limits). Moreover, as a consequence of the different strategies used among specific program areas, the present system is characterized by exceptional variety, not by uniform relationships among jurisdictions, as the simple, geographically oriented, federalism framework suggests. Table 6.3 presents the typology of strategies.

The three classes of strategies progress from those with intentions of achieving a high degree of centralized control and nationwide equivalence of

Table 6.3. A Typology of Policy Strategies for National Policies in a Federal Political System

---

I. Administrative Strategy:
   (a) Support entitlement programs, e.g., Medicaid, AFDC
   (b) Include categorical programs, e.g., Urban Mass Transportation Grants
   (c) Follow universalistic, specific regulations, e.g., Federal Management Circular 74-7, "Uniform Administrative Requirements for Grants-in-Aid to State and Local Governments"
II. Organizational Environment Strategy:
   (a) Include market intervention, e.g., housing subsidies
   (b) Create bureaucratic markets, e.g., directly funded Community Action Programs
   (c) Change the system of legal rights, e.g., Clean Air Act, 1977 Amendments; Civil Rights Acts
III. Learning System Strategy:
   (a) Include block grant programs, e.g., Community Development Block Grants
   (b) Create bargaining arenas under constraints, e.g., A-95 review, Section 208 Water Quality Planning
   (c) Enhance local government fiscal capacity through general revenue sharing programs
   (d) Facilitate local choice, e.g., state statutes which allow for development of alternative structures for delivery of local government services, such as contracting.

Source: Kirlin 1979, 87.

activity to those with exactly the opposite intentions of maximizing a variety of activity while minimizing central control. "Administrative strategies" are based upon synoptic rationality, requiring belief that objectives are clearly chosen, that causal links between desired objectives and policies are known, and that adopted policies may be implemented. The prototypical model for the administrative strategy is the hierarchical organization. "Organizational environment strategies" share certainty concerning objective and causality between policy and effect with the administrative strategy, but differ from that approach in method of achieving the desired objective. Instead of directly controlling organizational behaviors, factors in organizational environments are changed in the expectation of eliciting desired behaviors from the target organizations. Interventions in market dynamics, intended to change organizational behavior through changing "price" signals, is the prototype here. In the third, "learning systems strategy," uncertainty exists concerning both objectives and means. In some cases, a policy objective may exist (e.g., environmental quality) with uncertainty as to the specification of what this objective means in various instances and locales. In other cases, the objective is enhanced capacity of the political system itself, with diffuse expectations that this will somehow improve policy achievement. The best prototype of this strategy may well be our federal system itself. This suggests the potential instability of our 200-year-old institutions in an era of pressures for national policy-making. Centralized administrative strategies seem to be inimical to a federal system. Organizational environment strategies are largely indifferent, and only learning system strategies are congruent with sustaining such a political system.

Two normative arguments concerning design of an effective political system may be drawn from the typology presented in table 6.3. First, a "mixed" intergovernmental system is desirable because it allows appropriate variety in intergovernmental relationships, enhancing the likelihood of successful action in various policy arenas. Second, the functioning of political jurisdictions (especially local governments) should be given greater importance than the achievement of any particular policy objective, because the destruction of viable jurisdictions both disenfranchises citizens and reduces the range of possible policy strategies available to society.

Perhaps the most important observation to emerge from this review of the political system from a perspective sympathetic to strategic rationality is that the visions presented are significant departures from both dominant intellectual habit and present practice. Each of the authors reviewed is critical of the performance of the present political system, and the groping for new conceptualizations and theories is evident. No fully elaborated model of the preferred political system is provided, even by loose usage of that term. What is available are suggestions for the structure of a federal political system that these authors believe would be more effective.

The following common themes emerge concerning the creation of an effective federal political system.

- Maintain a widely dispersed capacity for societal choice-making and action, while also maintaining capacity for focused joint action in critical areas.

- Encourage variation in institutional design, policy strategies, and methods of evaluation.

- Choose policy strategies and institutional designs that are reversible, comprehensive, and nonmonopolistic.

- Where appropriate, use markets, which possess advantages over administrative systems (and also disadvantages).

- Where possible, create "decision situations" where individuals, organizations, and jurisdictions confront the consequences of alternative choices.

- Encourage the use of matrix organizational structures, of competition among bureaucracies, and of bargaining arenas.

- Ensure that value issues are clarified, allowed to change, and developed through leadership.

- In evaluations, emphasize the "context" of the policy as much as its result, as the former factors are critical to others' abilities to innovate and probably to the results obtained.

- Seek to make evaluations error exploring and embracing.

- Maintain the capacity of the political system to make choices and to act, even at the cost of imperfections in achieving particular policy objectives.

Of course, not all will agree with this list of exhortations or with the values upon which it is based. Lowi, for example, advocates the abolition of cities as jurisdictions (1979, 261–63) and the development of juridical democracy characterized by strong congressional rule-making, which would, in his estimate, reduce administrative discretion, cooptation of power by private interests, and ineffectual policy (295–313). But Lowi is primarily judging the American political system by its ability to achieve racial equality. His indictment of its performance on that criterion is telling, though damning the performance of tens of thousands of local jurisdictions on the basis of a single case study (238–58) is presumptuous. The counsel of Schattschneider (1960) is relevant here: Democracy is a system that must work for people as they are; to attack the competence of the citizens, judging them unfit for democracy, is to build the premises of authoritarian regimes. Bertram Gross (1965) has expressed similar concerns, fearing that development of the full potential for social control possible through modern public bureaucracies would result in "friendly fascism." Scott and Hart (1979) conclude that American society has been so restructured to meet the imperatives of both public and private organizations as to warrant the label "organizational America."

Lowi's position, at least, provides effective counterpoint to the values embedded in this analysis. They may be briefly stated: political systems are most importantly institutions of choice making and action; jurisdictions are the critical building blocks of a democratic political system (corporatism, the supression of horizontal, jurisdictional political activity in favor of vertical, interest-oriented, or policy-arena-oriented political activity, is ultimately technocratic, authoritarian, and paralyzing; Schmitter and Lehmbruch 1979); and many jurisdictions are preferable to few, as they encourage participation, increase flexibility, and lower costs of both governance and service provision.

Further insight into what is implied by this strategic perspective on how the political system should be structured may be derived from a review of two familiar and contrasting bodies of literature: the literature on public policy implementation and the literature on federalism. As we shall see, the policy analysis literature is largely based on the synoptic or administered state perspective, whereas the federalism literature focuses on issues concerning the construction of a viable, geographically based, flexible political system.

PUBLIC POLICY IMPLEMENTATION

As a self-conscious field of inquiry, public policy implementation is a phenomenon of the 1970s, with its initiation often marked with the publication of Pressman and Wildavsky's engaging *Implementation* (1973). They stated that only a very few analyses preceded theirs (e.g., Derthick 1972), but this is largely a consequence of their implicit limitation of interest to implementation of national programs through local jurisdictions. A modestly broader net would have revealed more predecessors, including Selznick (1949), Banfield (1961), Anderson (1964), and Kaufman (1967), all with analyses relevant to the local implementation of national programs, plus a few studies of the implementation of public policy changes caused by changes in local government structures (e.g., Sofen 1963; Kaplan 1967) and a good number of studies of urban political systems with policy implementation overtones (e.g., Sayre and Kaufman 1960; Wilson 1970). As will be more fully examined below, the point of this observation is substantive, not mere nit-picking; implementation of a particular kind of policy has received the overwhelming attention of these analysts.

Without a doubt, however, the Pressman and Wildavsky book struck a responsive chord, and studies of public policy implementation have flourished since it appeared. Among the reasons for this surge of interest are (1) the expansion of national domestic programs from the mid-1960s onward, (2) growing perceptions that they were often not realizing the aspirations of their proponents, often because carrying out the good intentions of the policies proved unexpectedly difficult (for representative analyses, see Ginzberg and Solow 1974), and (3) a dissatisfaction with existing theory of possible relevance to these issues. The faults found with existing theory, or at least inferred by the approaches taken to the study of public policy implementation, are varied. Traditional public administration was judged to be too wedded to social action through public bureaucracies and too narrowly focused upon organizational processes (Beam 1977, 1–6). Studies of "federalism" were not rich enough in detail of intergovernmental processes (Kirlin 1978, 1–4). Most analyses of local governments treated them as closed systems and did not encompass the interrelationships among local jurisdictions or with state and national governments (Kirlin and Erie 1972, 182).

An overview of the policy implementation literature may be obtained by dividing it into three subsets: case studies, implementation estimates, and theoretical treatments. Each is considered in turn.

Case Studies

Pressman and Wildavsky's (1973) book was a case study of programs of the Economic Development Administration in Oakland. Derthick's (1972) analysis focused upon a single program, "new towns in town." Murphy (1971) analyzed implementation of Title I of the Elementary and Secondary Education Act. Among the other federal policies whose implementation was analyzed are CETA (Van Horn 1978) and General Revenue Sharing (Nathan et al. 1975), both of which illustrate that implementation "problems" arrive even with formula allocation programs.

Analysts discovered wide variation in the implementation processes of separate programs within the same federal department, as illustrated by Tropman's (1977) study of Social Security. Marshall (1975) reviewed the history of implementing federal poverty and welfare policy, while Frieden and Kaplan (1975) undertook much the same task for "urban" policy. Relatively few studies of the implementation of "social regulation" policies (Lilley and Miller 1977) have been reported, although the American Enterprise Institute has issued some and launched a journal, *Regulation,* which focuses upon this area. Radin (1977) studied HEW implementation of school desegregation policy.

Among the conclusions that emerge from these studies, two have already been mentioned. No matter what the program or the implementation strategy, implementation always turns out to be a much more complex and frustrating process than imagined when the policy was initiated. Second, the patterns of intergovernmental relationships developed in the implementation process vary considerably by policy arena. Additional insights include the amount of "policy making'' that occurs throughout the implementation process; policies are often initially vague, and even where they are relatively clearly specified, the differing interests of the parties whose joint action is required for implementation often result in modifications of original intentions. Some researchers conclude that more flexibility or variation is needed in national policy to better match local variations (e.g., Struyk 1977) or suggest that national government ''bargaining'' with state and local officials is needed (Radin 1977).

Implementation Estimates

Given the action orientation of many analysts of public policy implementation, it is not surprising that they would soon attempt to distill knowledge obtained into a form useful to persons involved in the policy process. Interestingly, and reflecting the centrist orientation of most of this literature, the problem has come to be defined as ''estimating'' the implementation process at the time of policy formulation. Moore (1978) identifies four steps for completing policy ''feasibility'' estimates: (1) identifying major activities required for implementation; (2) gauging sensitivity of policy outcome to the manner in which these major activities are carried out; (3) locating relevant political and bureaucratic actors; and (4) making predictions as to how each actor will behave in implementing the policy. In discussing the writing of guidelines, which are often a critical step in translating broad legislative language into administrative specifics, Rabinovitz, Pressman, and Rein (1976) argue that the ''arena'' in which policies are to be implemented must be assessed, especially with regard to whether an already established pattern of interaction exists appropriate to the desired policy, and that the nature of the policy itself must also be analyzed, especially in terms of its clarity, likely continuity, and measurability of effects. Bardach (1977) urges ''scenario writing'' but also cautions users of its limits.

Theoretical Treatments

Another approach to understanding public policy implementation has been to place it in the context of the whole policy process. Brewer (1978) provides an example, dividing the ''life'' of a policy into six phases: initiation and invention, estimation, selection, implementation, evaluation, and termination. May and Wildavsky (1978) distinguish among agenda setting, issue analysis, service delivery systems, implementation, evaluation, and termination.

The ''phases'' approach suggests that the policy process is neatly rational (although the authors just cited do not do so). Rein and Rabinovitz (1977) have explicitly considered the problem. They identify three stages in the implementation process itself (guideline development and promulgation, resource distribution, and enforcement or monitoring), but argue that the process is not linear but, rather, is characterized by circularity. Moreover, the process is dominated by the interplay among three "imperatives": legal requirements of legislation, requirements for functioning of implementing bureaucracies, and interest groups. Rein and Rabinovitz suggest that the resolution of tension among these three will depend upon the purposes of the policy being implemented (clarity, saliency, and consistency), resources (kind, level, and timing thereof) and the complexity of the administrative processes required.

Smith (1973) also discusses tensions generated in the policy implementation process, conceptualizing them as arising between and within the idealized policy, the implementing organization target group, and environmental factors. Hargrove's (1975) review of the implementation of social policy provides examples of the tensions that arise in implementation processes. Ripley (1972) analyzes the variety of political patterns that arise in federal development programs.

Van Meter and Van Horn (1975) also believe that Pressman and Wildavsky have too quickly concluded that little analytic work relevant to implementation existed prior to their volume, pointing to well-developed literatures on organizational change and control, the impact of public policies (especially judicial decisions), and some studies of intergovernmental relations. They develop a model of the policy implementation process, including attributes of the policy itself (standards and objectives, resources); interorganizational communication and enforcement activities; characteristics of implementing agencies; economic, social, and political conditions; and, finally, the dispositions of implementors. After offering hypothesized relationships among these elements, they conclude that the greatest barriers to effective public policy implementation are inadequate communications, insufficient capability, and opposition of implementors to the policy.

A group of analysts has explored the relevance of organization theory to public policy implementation. Elmore (1978) distinguishes among four distinct models within organization theory that have relevance to the field of implementation: systems management, bureaucratic process, organizational development, and conflict and bargaining. He does not suggest that any single model provides greater success in understanding implementation, only that the models illuminate differing dimensions and are more or less useful in different contexts. Weick (1976) and Crozier and Thoenig (1976) develop still another branch of organization theory, that dealing with interorganizational relations. They advocate a more or less organized (e.g., loosely coupled) system, beyond specific task-related interorganizational networks, to regulate interorganizational relations.

Finally, several analysts whose starting point is public policy implementation have expanded the scope of their concern in interesting ways. Pressman (1975) offers an insightful analysis of the impact that federal programs had on the politics of the city of Oakland and of how the stakes in local politics affected implementation of national programs. Berman (1978) finds it useful to approach implementation as a two-tiered problem: macrolevel implementation problems nationally and microlevel problems locally. The incentives, opportunities, and constraints facing the two levels are very different. He emphasizes the dependency of national policy-makers upon local implementors and despairs of resolving uncertainties in the implementation process unless local governments lose flexibility, which would make policy implementation equally problematic, although for different reasons.

Weaknesses

From the perspective being advanced here, of how a federal political system appropriate to strategic rationality can be developed, the research on public policy implementation in general exhibits two major weaknesses.

First, the research is characterized by centrist and functional biases. Stated starkly, the implicit model is most frequently (imperfect) federal policy-making in narrow functional areas, implemented through (imperfect) local governments. Pressman and Wildavsky's seminal volume had this bias, and it is widely shared. Only a few studies of the implementation of state and local policies are available (e.g., Bardach 1972; Cameron 1978; Mechling 1978; Pesso 1978) in the mainstream of implementation research. One consequence of this bias is a limited user community—most importantly, federal mission agencies and those interested in their programs. This does not mean that the implementation research is erroneous or irrelevant but that it does have greatest meaning for only certain types of implementation problems.

The second weakness emerges from the first. These studies have not come to terms with the political system of the nation, an amazing assertion given the frequency with which attention to political factors is urged. But theirs is a disembodied exhortation, a statement that "politics matters." Certainly it does, but so too do political institutions and constitutions. And the two are not the same. The vision of politics prevalent in this research is of untrammeled interests of individual politicians or organizations.

Much of the public policy literature shares this definition of politics with the policy implementation literature. A typical definition of the field emphasizes "how to make public decisions rigorously and analytically on the basis of systematic quantitative evidence" (Yates 1977, 364). This definition of the role of policy analysis encourages viewing "politics" as a barrier to rationality. In this fundamental regard, policy analysis shares much with traditional public administration, an irony given the considerable effort to distinguish itself from that field. The same ambivalence toward democratic political systems in public administration is convincingly demonstrated by Ostrom (1973), Karl (1976), and Waldo (1980). Fesler (1975) provides an intriguing analysis of how a brief period of explicit attention to political system issues, following World War II, was quickly displaced by the styles of inquiry appropriate to pluralism and behaviorism. The parallels between public administration and policy analysis extend beyond ambivalence regarding politics to the manner in which they resolve the dilemma of pursuing rationality in a society espousing a democratic political system. Public administration embraces professionalism (Karl 1976); policy analysis exalts having a "client" (Yates 1977); and proposals to professionalize the field are advanced (Meltsner 1980). And whereas Beam (1977) discerns a distinguishing feature between the two fields to be a distrust of bureaucracy in policy analysis, Coleman (1980) argues that much policy analysis is supportive of bureaucracy. He especially criticizes policy analysis that

> conceives of information fed back to a single central authority. Its compatibility with bureaucratic theory means also compatability with a monolithic authority structure. It has no place for a conception of differing interests, of democratic political systems in which policy decisions come not from above but from a balance of pressures from conflicting interests. (346)

Ingram and Mann (1980, 16) share this concern, attributing the weakness to presumptions of synoptic rationality. They argue that policies must be judged not only on their impact upon stated objectives, but also upon political institutions. Among analysts of policy implementation, Pressman (1975) and Berman (1978) are rare in their concern with the effects of policies upon political institutions. Berman fears that perfecting implementation processes may destroy local government flexibility, reducing future ability to implement policy. Elsewhere, I (1979) have advanced a similar argument for the protection and nurturing of real capacity to act at the local government level as essential to the ability to implement any but the most narrowly circumscribed and hierarchically controlled policies. Berman (1980) has returned to these issues, distinguishing between "programmed" versus "adaptive" implementation, arguing that implementation strategies must match the context to be effective. His enumeration of five "situational parameters," each with a structured and unstructured type, yields suggestions congruent with Lindblom's (1977) concept of strategic rationality.

Ultimately, however, as was suggested in the first part of this essay, we must not only judge implementation of public policies by the extent to which they achieve intended objectives but be certain that they also strengthen the capacity of our governments as part of a political system. This is a different standard from that currently central to studies of public policy implementation. Wildavsky has recently begun to discuss this issue, arguing that preferences and objectives change and that the political system must be capable of nurturing and crystallizing the changes into action (1979, 43–61). Perhaps these concerns will be as seminal as his earlier work on implementation. McRae (1980) has also recently grappled with this issue. He begins with a conventional definition of the elements of policy analysis (definition of the problem, criteria for choice) but continues to recognize the impact of policies upon politics and to discuss "meta-policy," choices affecting the making of subsequent policies, including many of the issues concerning capacity of the total political system that have long been studied by political scientists.

The argument advanced here, however, goes beyond those offered in the policy analysis literature. We argue that the "capacity of the political system" (for domestic policies) has very little meaning in jurisdictional terms and should be approached from the perspective of developing capacity in the federal system. This political system is federal, at least in its history, and concepts of federalism frame much current analysis of public sector problems, where they are sometimes invoked in policy making. What does the available literature on federalism suggest concerning the performance of the political system?

FEDERALISM

In contrast to the literature on public policy implementation, which emphasizes organizational processes, the literature on federalism commonly focuses on politics. However, as analysts seek understanding of contemporary intergovernmental relations, they sometimes turn to analysis of organizational processes. Elezar defines federalism as first a "form" of government for the United States, using that term to signify "principles, structure, institutions, processes, and techniques all wrapped into one" (1974, 2). He emphasizes that federalism is more than just a political principle in this nation, considering it also to influence civil society. In this argument, Elezar is emphasizing the meaning of federalism as a compact "linking free men in common tasks without violating their respective integrities as partners in the common enterprise" (3).

Federalism is also defined in terms of a division of political power, as does Leach (1970). Landau (1974, 174) states that division of power between the national and state governments is the enduring core concept of definitions of federalism, and this division of powers is the implicit definition recently used by Beam (1980) in exploring the future of federalism. A narrow conception of federalism, as solely a geographical division of powers, may facilitate classification of political regimes, but it misses normative and predictive elements of the model. A reading of Madison's *Federalist Paper* No. 10 yields initial appreciation of both dimensions: preventing domination by factions is desirable and a system of divided powers serves this goal. Diamond argues that federalism is intelligible only by the ends it seeks to serve.

> The distinguishing characteristic of federalism is the peculiar ambivalence of the ends men seek to make it serve. . . . Any given federal structure is always the institutional expression of the contradiction or tension between the particular reasons the member units have for remaining small and autonomous but not wholly, and large and consolidated but not quite. (1974, 130)

In an analysis to which more attention is given below, Diamond continues to argue, following Tocqueville, that the decentralization that exists in the American political system as a result of federalism is critically important to eliciting political involvement by citizens.

The usefulness of the concept of federalism to analysis of the contemporary American political system has been challenged. Beer recognizes that federalism has influenced the development of the current pattern of intergovernmental relations but looks "to modernization as the principal source of the changing division of power between levels of government" (1974, 51). He analyzes phases of modernity, finding that the overall trend is toward centralization of political authority in response to the emergence of large, complex networks of social interaction. Development of the political system is traced through the "pork-barrel," distribution politics of the Jacksonian era, the "spillover coalition," regulatory politics of the Republican period from the end of the Civil War to the New Deal, the "class coalition," redistributive politics of the New Deal era, to the "technocratic," instrumental politics of the postwar period (57). Beer's most interesting analysis concerns the present period of technocratic politics, a primary feature of which is the shift to government itself (from the economic and social environment) of the initiative in policy making. Moreover, much of the policy making in this system entails development of new governmental initiatives to remedy/offset negative spillovers of earlier public policies.

Beer expects technocratic politics to be "pure bureaucratic politics . . . concerned with means rather than ends" (1974, 77). Professional-bureaucratic complexes will coalesce around functional areas, and the central core of professionals will have close integration down through all three levels of government. Analysis will play a large part in policy development and, by the generality of scientific knowledge, will encourage centralization of power and of innovation processes (79–80). The role of subordinate governments becomes "planning and control," defined largely as integrating functionally specific federal policies, and "mobilization of consent," intended variously to "educate the clientele, win their cooperation and endow them with some real power of influencing outputs" (85). Beer's apparent acceptance of the inevitability of this scenario is striking. He laments the prospect of uncontrollable public bureaucracies "mastering man," but he concludes that this is "merely . . . the fortune of all highly developed modern societies" (91). Beer accepts the equation of modern government with service delivery and sees no alternative to an elite technocracy of policy analysts pursuing synoptic rationality.

Beer's deterministic prognoses may prove correct, but Laudau (1974), Ostrom (1973, 1974), Wildavsky (1980), and Diamond (1974) are less sanguine than he about such a future and see more attraction in maintaining "federal" politics. Landau finds it useful to abandon the multiple definitions of federalism in favor of concepts from organization, systems, and information theories (1974, 178–82). A primary problem in all three fields is that of achieving stability, and all three turn to some concept of feedback and self-correction to achieve that end. Landau argues that capacity for feedback and self-correction in a political system requires multiple *independent* channels for information and action, hence his advocacy of redundancy, overlap, and duplication. Landau does not believe that this "multiplexing" need solely be governmental, and certainly need not be limited to the national and state governments as envisaged in the Constitution. Indeed, he echoes much of Beer's analysis of the impacts of the modernizing of society upon political institutions, ultimately concluding that "lateral" redundancy, such as that provided by geographically distinct jurisdictions, must give way to "vertical" integration accompanied by a redundancy of technical authority (194–95). Landau expects stability of this system and also predicts low rigidity. How citizens, individually or collectively, access this system is left unsaid, but presumably this would occur in channels following their functional interests. But what are those channels? Interest groups is the likely response, but such access may be chimerical. And a political system organized around interest groups may have low capacity for making trade-offs (Godwin and Ingram 1980) and may even become paralyzed (Olson 1977).

Vincent Ostrom has explored on several occasions what he perceives to be the virtues of a federal system (e.g., 1971, 1973, 1974). His consistent starting point is the individual, and his criteria for evaluating political systems emphasize satisfaction of individual citizen/consumer preferences (1974, 229–30, 1977, 1511). Ostrom argues that federal structures offer promise of overcoming the "tragedy of the commons," which can result from unrestrained individualistic exploitation of common-property resources and public goods and also provide opportunity to avoid the weaknesses of large bureaucracies (1974, 210–16). He advocates multiorganizational arrangements, varying according to the technology, demand, and other attributes of "public-service industries," with the result that differing arrangements will exist for water provision than for police services, etc. Overlap, duplication, and fragmentation of authority allow "agencies at one level of government . . . [to] take advantage of the capabilities afforded by agencies operating at other levels."

Ostrom believes that, unless restrained, public agencies will progressively impose their organizational definitions of appropriate public policy and services upon the citizenry, and he advances two strategies to control this dynamic. The first is competition among agencies: consumer/citizen sovereignty will hold agencies accountable. The second is adherence to a "positive" constitution, allocating decision-making capabilities and prerogatives among individuals and governmental offices, which can be changed only through constitutional revision processes rather than whimsically.

Wildavsky (1980) argues that even these strategies will not be sufficient to keep government agencies attentive to the citizens they presumably serve. In addition to competition among agencies he advocates "decongestion" of the intergovernmental system, arguing that spending limits upon governmental growth are required to halt the "intergovernmentalization" of everything, wherein clientele seeking new governmental activities spur complementary responses one from another.

> I have been recommending an interactive approach designed not only to implement but to discover what works best. The greater the number and variety of organizations for providing goods and services from government, which constitutes a competitive, citizen-centered approach, the better able the system will be to go one way in regard to this and another to that. The people do not have to postulate either the optimal size of producing units or the optimal pattern of spatial structure. Rather these would be seen as the outcome of citizens, states, and localities getting the best they can, correcting errors as they go along, provided there is an effective financial constraint. (18)

While not so stated, this approach relies upon strategic rationality and is close to the position advocated here. The variety of institutions advocated by Ostrom and Wildavsky is a welcome antidote to the presumption of closure concerning design prevalent in much of political science, public administration, and policy analysis. Exactly *what* is to remain open for choice is not well specified, however. Although sensible in terms of his analysis, Ostrom's emphasis upon "agencies," reinforced by his approach to the analysis of public service industries, could obscure the critical importance of geographically bounded political jurisdictions. These are the arenas in which citizens exercise choice concerning structures for service delivery, and a greater emphasis upon the (jurisdictional) structures for choice, as opposed to the service orientation, would be welcome. Moreover, jurisdictions are especially important to the argument formulated by Wildavsky. Choice processes within jurisdictions not only determine service provision; it is within jurisdiction that any limitations upon governmental spending must arise.

Diamond seeks understanding of the political system of the United States by distinguishing it from previous federal systems (e.g., Greek "polis-federalism" or Montesquieu's "republic-federalism").

> American federalism, is not, strictly speaking, a federal system, but rather a *national system* that is profoundly (and valuably) tilted toward decentralization by its unique admixture of elements of *authentic federalism*. If then it is to be considered a federal system at all, we may term it decentralist-federalism, a pallid successor to polis-federalism and small republic-federalism. It is federalism the end, and hence the nature, of which is no longer properly federal, but rather the end of which is to generate new modes of decentralization. (1974, 135–36)

The distinction between decentralization and federalism entails presumption of legitimate governmental authority, with decentralization recognizing a whole that has primacy over the parts, whereas federalism does not, strictly speaking, recognize primacy of the larger unit. "Decentralization presupposes a nation and rests upon arguments merely as to how the nation ought to be organized so as to achieve liberty or other desired qualities" (136). The distinctive feature of the American political system, according to Diamond, is that decentralization has been "constitutionalized" through division of power between the national government and the states and by certain "federal" characteristics of the national government (e.g., equality of the states in the Senate).

Diamond values this decentralization beyond any value adduced to efficiency or system survival. Following Tocqueville, he intends to turn the "palpable self-interest" of individuals in local affairs (e.g., land use, educational curriculum, traffic patterns) into positive results for society: "nothing less than to make solitaries social men, subjects into citizens, grubby comfort seekers into bearers of rights and hence of virtue in the only form amenable to modern politics, and, finally, the unleashing of the natural store of human energy" (145).

This review of the literature on federalism has revealed fundamental differences concerning the definition of the phenomenon, disagreements as to how it applies to the contemporary situation in this nation, and competing scenarios for future evolution. In terms of the concerns of this essay, this body of literature addresses the design of an effective political system directly, whereas the public policy implementation literature has less direct relevance. Strikingly, some of these analysts anticipate the possibility of a centrally dominated, elite, technocratic political system if not warmly, at least with resignation. More frequently, however, a "federal" system is positively valued. Moreover, these authors are even more prescriptive than are those writing on public policy implementation. In part, this undoubtedly reflects weaker attachment to presumed norms of logical positivism as a method of inquiry. But a good bit of the explanation is a result of the focus upon the whole political system; analysis at that level encourages definition of the values sought through design of political institutions. While the literature on public policy implementation is rarely self-consciously prescriptive regarding the design of the political system, though it commonly implies centralization, the literature on federalism is more self-consciously prescriptive regarding design of the political system.

REPRISE

Removing politics from the study of government is a comfortable habit for researchers. While there may be only a tenuous theoretical or methodological lineage from traditional public administration through evaluators of governmental performance to those who seek to understand public policy implementation, there is commonality in seeking to submerge the value questions central to politics. Government is perceived as a service provider, a dramatically limiting image. Even some students of federalism, an explicitly political approach historically, shift their inquiry to the analysis of service providing agencies. Moreover, the most common unit of analysis is the jurisdiction or the agency within a jurisdiction.

In this chapter I argue that these definitions of governmental performance should be replaced, or at least complemented, by analyses focusing on the capacity of the political system and that a federal definition of our political system is required. The consequences of limiting analysis to service provision within jurisdictions are limited relevance and ineffective (sometimes even dysfunctional) counsel to policy makers.

How analysis should be formulated, given this orientation, is not settled. The proposals advanced here—for shifting analysis to the capacity of the political system, using the concept of strategic rationality as an organizing principle—are plausible but not offered as definitive. Alternatives exist. For example, the frameworks developed by Diamond, Ostrom, and Wildavsky provide entry to similar theoretical concerns. Another possibility would be to employ "systems" language and concepts, a position Landau explores, though not as fully as possible, with his discussion of the advantages of a "multiplexed" political system in reducing the likelihood of system failure. The organizational process model that ties together analyses of innovation and public policy implementation is currently too limited by its attachment to organizations as the unit of analysis to provide much theoretical insight into these issues, but the dimensions of that research emphasizing organization-environment interactions and how an "environment" populated by organizations may be analyzed are promising avenues for development.

Beyond development of general frameworks for analysis, the study of the capacity of the political system would benefit from availability of data that are now very elusive. Two examples will illustrate. There are presently no data series to describe adequately the intergovernmental system. A census of governments exists, but that is only the first, modest, step toward a full description of the intergovernmental system. Absent are at least the following: quasi-governmental bodies, intergovernmental service provision agreements, and mandates and regulations. By and large, what is missing are data about how the interstices among governments are filled. Our understanding of the political system is as partial, unfortunately, as would be an understanding of the human body with knowledge only of the skeleton and circulatory system. The data needed are undeniably difficult and expensive to obtain (and the mental barriers to recognizing their relevance strong), but sampling and focused data collection would be well worth the expenditure of resources.

The second example of needed data requires as large a mental adjustment as does reconceptualization of the political system. Despite the biases inherent in everyday speech and most research literature, relatively few public services are "produced" exclusively by that sector. Coproduction, with individuals, firms, neighborhoods, and nongovernmental groups is the norm, not the exception. Schools do not "produce" education; they coproduce it with the students enrolled, their families, and other contributors (ranging from peers through the Brownies to science clubs), as any parent knows. Yet virtually no analyses of government incorporate coproducers as relevant (see Ostrom 1979 for a brief discussion), and discussions of encouraging coproducers as a conscious public policy remain at the level of interesting exhortations (Berger and Neuhaus 1977). Conceptualization of the range of coproduction relationships possible and development of conscious public policies to enhance these relationships are more likely to advance as data are collected on coproduction. Again, a census is impossible, but much would be gained from sampling and studies focused on particular locales, types of coproduction relationships, or particular public functions.

In terms of action, the perspective advanced here suggests that whatever can be done to strengthen and make more visible the choice-making role of the political system, as opposed to that of service provision, is desirable. Wildavsky supports spending limits as a strategy to achieve this end, others suggest somehow reinvigorating political parties. At a minimum, whatever can be done to slow the march toward a system locked down by the accretion of policies, programs, and bureaucracies that are the products of present dynamics is imperative. One important value to maximize in this, it appears to me, is the vitality of territorially defined political jurisdictions. These units are the common building blocks of many policies and programs and their demise would severely limit the policy strategies available to society. More importantly, they offer the hope, if only the infrequent occurrence, of policy choices that make trade-offs among functionally specific policies and programs. Finally, they are still the vehicles by which the ''humanizing'' political interaction described by Diamond following Tocqueville can occur. If our primary links to the political system become (continue) as clients, regulatees, and spectators, we shall lose (have lost) a valued element of our existence.

REFERENCES

Allison, Graham T. 1975. Implementation Analysis: ''The Missing Chapter'' in Conventional Analysis: A Teaching Exercise. In *Benefit-Cost and Policy Analysis, 1974*, ed. J. Zeckhauser et al., 369–91. Chicago: Aldine.

Anderson, Martin. 1964. *The Federal Bulldozer*. Cambridge, Mass.: MIT Press.

Bachrach, Peter. 1967. *The Theory of Democratic Elitism*. Boston: Little, Brown.

Banfield, Edward. 1961. *Political Influence*. New York: Free Press.

Bardach, Eugene. 1972. *The Skill Factor in Politics*. Berkeley and Los Angeles: University of California Press.

———. 1977. *The Implementation Game: What Happens after a Bill Becomes a Law*. Cambridge, Mass.: MIT Press.

Beam, David. 1977. Policy Analysis versus Public Administration: Perspectives from Implementation, Bureaucratic Politics, Evaluation, and Public Choice. Paper presented at the national conference of the American Society for Public Administration, Atlanta, March 30–April 2.
———. 1980. Forecasting the Future of Federalism. *Intergovernmental Perspective* 6(3): 6–9.
Beer, Samuel H. 1974. The Modernization of American Federalism. In *The Federal Polity,* ed. Daniel J. Elezar, 49–95. New Brunswick, N.J.: Transaction Books.
Berger, Peter L., and Richard L. Neuhaus. 1977. *To Empower People: The Role of Mediating Structures in Public Policy.* Washington, D.C.: American Enterprise Institute.
Berman, Paul. 1978. The Study of Macro- and Microimplementation. *Public Policy* 26(2): 156–84.
———. 1980. Thinking about Programmed and Adaptive Innovation: Matching Strategies to Situations. In *Why Policies Succeed or Fail,* ed. Helen M. Ingram and Dean E. Mann, 205–30. Beverly Hills: Sage.
Biller, Robert P. 1976. On Tolerating Policy and Organizational Termination: Some Design Considerations. *Policy Sciences* 7(2): 133–49.
Braybrooke, David, and Charles E. Lindblom. 1963. *A Strategy of Decision.* New York: Free Press.
Brewer, Garry. 1978. The Scope of the Policy Sciences. New Haven, Conn.: Mimeo Course Syllabus.

Cameron, James. 1978. Ideology and Policy Termination: Restructuring California's Mental Health System. *Public Policy* 26(4): 533–70.
Coleman, James S. 1980. The Structure of Society and the Nature of Social Research. *Knowledge* 1(3): 333–50.
Crecine, John P. 1969. *Governmental Problem-Solving.* Chicago: Rand McNally.
———. 1977. Coordination of Federal Fiscal and Budgetary Policy Processes: Research Strategies for Complex Decision Systems. Paper presented at the annual meeting of the American Political Science Association, Washington, D.C., September 1–4.
Crozier, Michel, and Jean-Claude Thoenig. 1976. The Regulation of Complex Organized Systems. *Administrative Sciences Quarterly* 21(4): 547–70.
Cyert, Richard M., and James G. March. 1963. *A Behavioral Theory of the Firm.* Englewood Cliffs, N.J.: Prentice-Hall.

Dahl, Robert A. 1956. *A Preface to Democratic Theory.* Chicago: University of Chicago Press.
Dahl, Robert A., and Charles E. Lindblom. 1953. *Politics, Economics, and Welfare: Planning and Politico-Economic Systems Resolved into Basic Social Processes.* New York: Harper & Row.
Derthick, Martha. 1972. *New Towns in Town.* Washington, D.C.: Urban Institute.
Dewey, John. 1927. *The Public and Its Problems.* Chicago: Swallow.
Diamond, Martin. 1974. The Ends of Federalism. In *The Federal Polity,* ed. Daniel J. Elezar, 129–52. New Brunswick, N.J.: Transaction Books.
Downs, Anthony. 1967. *Inside Bureaucracy.* Boston: Little, Brown.

Elmore, Richard F. 1978. Organizational Models of Social Program Implementation. *Public Policy* 26(2): 185–228.
Elezar, Daniel J. 1974. First Principles. In *The Federal Polity,* ed. Daniel J. Elezar, 1–10. New Brunswick, N.J.: Transaction Books.

Fesler, James W. 1975. Public Administration and the Social Sciences, 1946–1960. In *American Public Administration: Past, Present, Future,* ed. Fredrick C. Mosher, 97–141. University: University of Alabama Press.
Frieden, Bernard, and Marshall Kaplan. 1975. *The Politics of Neglect: Urban Aid from Model Cities to Revenue Sharing.* Cambridge, Mass.: MIT Press.

Ginzberg, Eli, and Robert M. Solow, guest eds. 1974. The Great Society: Lessons for the Future. *Public Interest* 34(Winter): 4–220 (special issue).

Godwin, R. Kenneth, and Helen M. Ingram. 1980. Single Issues: Their Impacts on Politics. In *Why Policies Succeed or Fail*, ed. Helen M. Ingram and Dean E. Mann, 279–99. Beverly Hills: Sage.

Gross, Bertram. 1965. Friendly Fascism. *Social Policy*.

Hargrove, Erwin C. 1975. *The Missing Link: The Study of Implementation of Social Policy*. Washington, D.C.: Urban Institute.

Ingram, Helen M., and Dean E. Mann. 1980. Policy Failure: An Issue Deserving Analysis. In *Why Policies Succeed or Fail*, ed. Helen M. Ingram and Dean E. Mann, 11–34. Beverly Hills: Sage.

Janowitz, Morris. 1976. *Social Control of the Welfare State*. Chicago: University of Chicago Press.
————. 1978. *The Last Half-Century*. Chicago: University of Chicago Press.

Kaplan, Abraham. 1961. *The New World of Philosophy*. New York: Vintage.

Kaplan, Harold. 1967. *Urban Political Systems: A Functional Analysis of Metro Toronto*. New York: Columbia University Press.

Karl, Barry D. 1976. Public Administration and American History: A Century of Professionalism. *Public Administration Review* 36(5): 489–503.

Katzenstein, Peter. 1977. Between Power and Plenty. *International Organization* 31(4): 587–606.

Kaufman, Herbert. 1967. *The Forest Ranger*. Baltimore: Johns Hopkins Press.

Kirlin, John J. 1978. Structuring the Intergovernmental System: An Appraisal of Conceptual Models and Public Policies. Paper presented at the annual meeting of the American Political Science Association, New York, August 31–September 3.
————. 1979. Adapting the Intergovernmental Fiscal System to the Demands of an Advanced Economy. In *The Changing Structure of the City: What Happened to the Urban Crisis*. Vol. 16 of *Urban Affairs Annual Reviews*, ed. Gary Tobin, 7–103. Beverly Hills: Sage.
————. 1981. An Analysis of the Demand for Debt Issuance by State and Local Governments. Napa, Calif.: Multinational Strategies.
————. 1982. *The Political Economy of Fiscal Limits*. Lexington, Mass.: Lexington Books.

Kirlin, John J., and Steven P. Erie. 1972. The Study of City Governance and Public Policy-Making: A Critical Appraisal. *Public Administration Review* 32(2): 173–84.

Ladd, Everett Carl, Jr. 1978. *Where Have All the Voters Gone?* New York: Norton.

Landau, Martin. 1974. Federalism, Redundancy, and System Reliability. In *The Federal Polity*, ed. Daniel J. Elezar, 173–96. New Brunswick, N.J.: Transaction Books.

La Porte, Todd R. 1975. Complexity and Uncertainty: Challenge to Action. In *Organized Social Complexity*, ed. Todd R. La Porte. Princeton, N.J.: Princeton University Press.

Leach, Richard A. 1970. *American Federalism*. New York: Norton.

Levine, Robert A. 1972. *Public Planning: Failure and Redirection*. New York: Basic Books.

Lilley, William, III, and James C. Miller III. 1977. The New Social Regulation. *Public Interest* (47): 49–61.

Lindberg, Leon, et al., eds. 1975. *Stress and Contradiction in Modern Capitalism*. Lexington, Mass.: Lexington Books.

Lindblom, Charles E. 1965. *The Intelligence of Democracy*. New York: Free Press.
————. 1977. *Politics and Markets: The World's Political-Economic Systems*. New York: Basic Books.

Lowi, Theodore J. 1979. *The End of Liberalism: The Second Republic of the United States.* 2d ed. New York: Norton.

Lowi, Theodore J., and Alan Stone, eds. 1978. *Nationalizing Government: Public Policies in America.* Beverly Hills: Sage.

McRae, Duncan, Jr. 1980. Policy Analysis Methods and Governmental Functions. In *Improving Policy Analysis,* ed. Stuart S. Nagel, 129–52. Beverly Hills: Sage.

March, James G. 1978. Bounded Rationality, Ambiguity, and the Engineering of Choice. *Bell Journal of Economics.* 9(2): 587–608.

March, James G., and Herbert A. Simon. 1958. *Organizations.* New York: Wiley.

Marshall, Dale Rogers. 1975. Implementation of Federal Poverty and Welfare Policy: A Review. In *Analyzing Poverty Policy,* ed. Dorothy James, 3–20. Lexington, Mass.: Lexington Books.

May, Judith V., and Aaron B. Wildavsky, eds. 1978. *The Policy Cycle.* Vol. 5 of *Sage Yearbooks in Politics and Public Policy.* Beverly Hills: Sage.

Mechling, Jerry. 1978. Analysis and Implementation: Sanitation Policies in New York City. *Public Policy* 26(2): 263–84.

Meltsner, Arnold. 1980. Creating a Policy Analysis Profession. In *Improving Policy Analysis,* ed. Stuart S. Nagel, 235–50. Beverly Hills: Sage.

Miller, Trudi. 1984. Conclusion: A Design Science Perspective. In *Public Sector Performance: A Conceptual Turning Point,* ed. Trudi Miller. Baltimore: Johns Hopkins University Press.

Moore, Mark H. 1978. A "Feasibility Estimate" of a Policy Decision to Expand Methadone Maintenance. *Public Policy* 26(2): 285–304.

Mosher, Frederick C., ed. 1975. *American Public Administration: Past, Present, Future.* University: University of Alabama Press.

Mueller, Dennis C. 1976. "Public Choice"; A Survey. *Journal of Economic Literature* (June): 395–433.

Murphy, Jerome T. 1971. Title I of ESEA: The Politics of Implementing Federal Education Reform. *Harvard Educational Review* 41(February): 35–63.

Nathan, Richard P., et al. 1975. *Monitoring Revenue Sharing.* Washington, D.C.: Brookings Institution.

Olson, Mancur. 1977. The Causes and Quality of Southern Growth. In *The Economics of Southern Growth,* ed. E. G. Liner and L. K. Lynch. Research Triangle Park, N.C.: Southern Growth Policies Board.

Ostrom, Elinor. 1979. Productivity in the Urban Public Sector. Paper presented at the Conference on Comparative Urban Policy Research, University of Chicago, April 26–27.

Ostrom, Elinor, Roger Parks, and Gordon Whittaker. 1978. *Patterns of Metropolitan Policing.* Cambridge, Mass. Ballinger.

Ostrom, Vincent. 1971. *The Political Theory of a Compound Republic: A Reconstruction of the Logical Foundations of American Democracy as Presented in "The Federalist."* Blacksburg: Center for Public Choice, Virginia Polytechnic Institute.

———. 1974. Can Federalism Make a Difference? In *The Federal Polity,* ed. Daniel J. Elezar, 197–237. New Brunswick, N.J.: Transaction Books.

———. 1974. *The Intellectual Crisis in American Public Administration.* Rev. ed. University: University of Alabama Press.

———. 1977. Some Problems in Doing Political Theory: A Response to Golembiewski's Critique. *American Political Science Review* 71(4): 1508–25.

———. 1980. Artisanship and Artifact. *Public Administration Review* 40:309–16.

Pressman, Jeffrey. 1975. *Federal Programs and City Politics: The Dynamics of the Aid Process in Oakland.* Berkeley and Los Angeles: University of California Press.

Pressman, Jeffrey L., and Aaron Wildavsky. 1973. *Implementation*. Berkeley and Los Angeles: University of California Press.
Presso, Tana. 1978. Local Welfare Offices: Managing the Intake Process. *Public Policy* 26(2): 305–30.
Presthus, Robert. 1978. *The Organizational Society*. New York: St. Martin's.

Rabinovitz, Francine, Jeffrey Pressman, and Martin Rein. 1976. Guidelines: A Plethora of Forms, Authors, and Functions. *Policy Sciences* 7(4): 399–416.
Radin, Beryl A. 1977. *Implementation, Change, and the Federal Bureaucracy: School Desegregation Policy in H.E.W., 1964–1968*. New York: Teachers College Press, Columbia University.
Ramos, Alberto Guerreiro. 1976. Theory of Social Systems Delimitation: A Preliminary Statement. *Administration and Society* 8 (August): 249–72.
Rein, Martin, and Francine F. Rabinovitz. 1977. Implementation: A Theoretical Perspective. In *Handbook for Organizational Design*, ed. William Starbuck. New York: Elsevier.
Ridley, C. E., and H. A. Simon. 1938. *Measuring Municipal Activities*. Chicago: International City Managers' Association.
Ripley, Randall. 1972. Political Patterns in Federal Development Programs. In *People and Politics in Urban Society*, ed. Harlan Hahn. Beverly Hills: Sage.
Ripley, Randall. 1977. *The Implementation of CETA in Ohio*. Washington, D.C.: U.S. Government Printing Office.
Rokeach, Milton. 1973. *The Nature of Human Values*. New York: Free Press.
Rule, James B. 1978. *Insight and Social Betterment: A Preface to Applied Social Science*. New York: Oxford University Press.

Savas, E. S. 1977a. An Empirical Study of Competition in Municipal Service Delivery. *Public Administration Review* 37(6): 714–24.
———. 1977b. Policy Analysis for Local Government: Public versus Private Refuse Collection. *Policy Analysis* 3(1): 2–26.
Sayre, Wallace, and Herbert Kaufman. 1960. *Governing New York City*. New York: Russell Sage Foundation.
Schattschneider, E. E. 1960. *The Semisovereign People*. New York: Holt, Rinehart & Winston.
Schmitter, Philippe C., and Gerhard Lehmbruch, eds. 1979. *Trends toward Corporatist Intermediation*. Beverly Hills: Sage.
Schon, Donald. 1971. *Beyond the Stable State*. New York: Random House.
Schultze, Charles L. 1970. The Role of Incentives, Penalties, and Rewards in Attaining Effective Policy. In *Public Expenditures and Policy Analysis*, ed. Robert Haveman and Julius Margolis. Chicago: Markham Press.
Scott, William G., and David K. Hart. 1979. *Organizational America*. Boston: Houghton Mifflin.
Selznick, Philip. 1949. *TVA and the Grass Roots*. Berkeley and Los Angeles: University of California Press.
Shannon, John. 1981. The Great Slowdown in State and Local Government Spending in the United States, 1976–1984. Washington, D.C.: Advisory Commission on Intergovernmental Relations.
Simon, Herbert A. 1947. *Administrative Behavior*. Reprint. New York: Free Press, 1976.
Smith, Thomas B. 1973. The Policy Implementation Process. *Policy Sciences* 4:197–209.
Sofen, Edward. 1963. *The Miami Metropolitan Experiment*. Bloomington: Indiana University Press.
Sonenblum, Sidney, John J. Kirlin, and John C. Ries. 1977. *How Cities Provide Services: An Evaluation of Alternative Delivery Structures*. Cambridge, Mass.: Ballinger.
Struyk, Raymond J. 1977. The Need for Local Flexibility in U.S. Housing Policy. *Policy Analysis* 3(4): 471–84.

Tropman, John E. 1977. American Welfare Strategies: Three Programs under the Social Security Act. *Policy Sciences* 8(1): 33–48.

Van Horn, Carl E. 1978. Implementing CETA: The Federal Role. *Policy Analysis* 4(2): 159–83.
Van Horn, Carl E., and Donald S. Van Meter. 1976. The Implementation of Intergovernmental Policy. In *Public Policy-Making in a Federal System.* Beverly Hills: Sage.
Van Meter, Donald S., and Carl E. Van Horn. 1975. The Policy Implementation Process: A Conceptual Framework. *Administration and Society* 6(4): 445–88.

Waldo, Dwight. 1980. Public Management Research: Perspectives of History, Political Science, and Public Administration. In *Setting Public Management Research Agendas: Integrating the Sponsor, Producer, and User,* Office of Personnel Management, 63–70. Washington, D.C.: U.S. Government Printing Office.
Weick, Karl. 1976. Educational Organizations as Loosely Coupled Systems. *Administrative Sciences Quarterly* 21:1–18.
Wildavsky, Aaron. 1979. *Speaking Truth to Power: The Art and Craft of Policy Analysis.* New York: Little, Brown.
————. 1980. The 1980s: Monopoly or Competition? *Intergovernmental Perspective* 6(3): 15–18.
Williams, Walter, and Richard F. Elmore, eds. 1976. *Social Program Implementation.* New York: Academic Press.
Wilson, James Q. 1970. *Varieties of Police Behavior: The Management of Law and Order in Eight Communities.* New York: Atheneum.
Wolin, Sheldon. 1968. *Politics and Vision.* Boston: Little, Brown.
Wright, Deil. 1978. *Understanding Intergovernmental Relations.* North Scituate, Mass.: Duxburg Press.

Yates, Douglas T., Jr. 1977. The Mission of Public Policy Programs: A Report on Recent Experience. *Policy Sciences* 8(3): 363–74.

7

A Public Finance Perspective

J. Richard Aronson
Eli Schwartz

P ublic finance is a well-established, broad field that offers an array of theories and empirical research about the design of government institutions. At its core, it focuses on the conflict between two values that have dominated twentieth-century political competition between the parties—equity (Democratic) and efficiency (Republican). In addition to theory, public finance literature contains empirical tests of how well theories predict real-world outcomes. Normative values and empirical research are often combined in policy analyses to help identify ways to increase equity and efficiency in real-world settings. The following sections contain illustrations of the different types of research in these three areas: theory, empirical research, and policy analyses.

THEORY

Whereas many social scientists have tried to employ only positive or value-free theories, scholars in the field of public finance have developed and applied normative values to the design of political institutions. The two basic values that guide the analysis are equity (or public welfare) and efficiency. Unfortunately, these two values are often assumed to be complete trade-offs.

Major policy variables that presumably influence equity and efficiency include the size of the governmental unit and the degree of centralization/decentralization. Given the underlying conflict in values (crudely stated, Democrats favor equity; Republicans, efficiency), it is not surprising that some public finance theories have been used to justify political positions favoring the growth and centralization of government, whereas others have been used to support the limitation and decentralization of government.

Theories Favoring Government Growth and Centralization

As we have seen in previous chapters, most of the actual growth of government during the 1950s, 1960s, and much of the 1970s took place at the state and local levels. However, the federal government was certainly supportive—indeed stimulative—of this growth. The vehicle for federal stimulation of local government activity was, primarily, various grants-in-aid programs. The justifications for federal (and state) grants-in-aid and other forms of involvement (for example, tax relief and environmental regulation) were drawn from various constructs in public finance theory. Since most of the arguments for centralization have been discussed in the previous chapters, we highlight only major points here.

There are two overriding economic arguments for federal grants-in-aid to state and local governments. The first is the need to take account of geographic externalities that are associated with certain public goods and services. In a country of high mobility and complex social and economic interrelations, such social goods as general education may yield benefits to people who live well outside the jurisdiction providing and financing this function. Since local jurisdictions may not be able to take external benefits into account, economic analysis tells us they may provide less than a socially optimum amount of such goods. Grants-in-aid from larger geographic units (e.g., from the federal to the state government or from the state to the locality) can be used to induce the local units into providing a larger, more desirable amount. It would seem logical that such grants be conditional in design. That is, they are given to the local jurisdiction for the specific purposes that yield the external benefits. As shown in table 7.1, during the heyday of grants-in-aid in the 1970s, over three-quarters of all federal grant-in-aid outlays were specific purpose, or "categorical," grants.

A second economic rationale for grants-in-aid comes from the desire to achieve a type of horizontal equity among governmental units. States or other local units of government do not possess equal fiscal capacity. Essentially, this means that two states that tax their residents at the same rate may not be able to provide equivalent per capita public services. The richer state or jurisdiction can raise more revenue and spend more on public services per person per percentage point of tax than can a poorer one (Buchanan 1950). The alleviation of this problem calls for unconditional grants to the poorer jurisdictions. In this case, what the money is being spent for is not the issue. The objective is to improve the revenue situation of the poorer unit.

Thus, conditional matching grants have been used to take account of geographical benefit externalities, whereas unconditional equalizing grants offset horizontal inequities caused by the unequal distribution of fiscal capacity among local units of government. However, the actual grant-in-aid system that has developed is much more complicated than that which would arise

Table 7.1.   Administrative Breakdown of Federal Grants-in-Aid

Type of Grant	1972	1979	1981[a]
		Outlays ($ billion)	
General-purpose	0.5	8.3	9.6
Broad-based	2.9	11.7	10.0
Categorical	31.0	62.8	76.7
Total	34.4	82.9	96.3
		% Total	
General-purpose	1.5	10.1	9.9
Broad-based	8.3	14.1	10.4
Categorical	90.2	75.8	79.7
Total	100.0	100.0	100.0

Source: Office of Management and Budget 1982, 257.

[a]Estimated.

from pure economic considerations. To quote Break, "The evolution of federal grants-in-aid, which are the life blood of fiscal federalism, has been, like all undertakings in a democracy, a complex mixture of pragmatism, politics, and principle" (1980, 249). Pinpointing some of the other roles of grants-in-aid may therefore be of help in understanding why the system has developed in such a complex fashion.

1. It has long been recognized that the tax system of the federal government is more productive than those of state and local governments. Grants can therefore be viewed in part as a tax-sharing system.

2. There may be constitutional and philosophical obstacles to the national government directly providing certain goods or services. The grant technique avoids a legal confrontation. Without getting directly involved, the national government induces the states to provide the service.

3. Grants may reflect an attitude of skepticism and distrust at the federal level regarding the administrative capacity and political decision-making ability of state-local officials.

4. Grants may simply be a technique of substituting the preferences of federal legislators for that of their local counterparts. (ACIR 1978a, 49–59)

State grants to localities predate the federal programs. (Hovey [1978] provides a good descriptive analysis of the major programs and interrelationships.) Although the states may give considerable funds for such programs as recreation (e.g., open space) and the maintenance of state roads passing through a municipality, the truly vast program is the state financing of local school districts.

The rationale for state aid to education parallels two of the three themes of the federal grant programs. One is equity, the relative subsidization of the poorer districts, and the second is the pragmatic fact that the state broad-based revenue sources (sales and income taxes) have proven more productive over time than the local revenue sources (mainly the property tax). The equity problem arises from the disproportionate property endowment of various school districts relative to the population of school children. This means a child in a relatively poorer district may not receive as well financed an education as one in a richer district. Still, as long as some local autonomy in the administration of the schools and in the tax effort for their funding is allowed, the achievement of absolute equalization is likely to prove impossible. (A detailed analysis of this problem can be found below in the section on policy analysis.)

Theories Favoring Federal Government Limitation and the Decentralization of Functions

In contrast to the movement toward centralization and the federal support of various functions, there are models that support the shift toward decentralization and limited central government. These include the various "public choice" theories about the superior productivity of private sector organizations which have been reviewed in the previous chapter by Larkey, Chandler, and Stolp. Among the major theories to be discussed that analyze alternative measures for providing public and merit goods are Oates's decentralization theorem, Tiebout's migration model, and the theory of clubs.

In many countries, the local governments are for the most part merely administrative units of the central government. The goods and services they provide and the revenue sources at their disposal are determined by acts of the legislature of the central government. Such a system, in which the fiscal responsibility is mainly at the national level of government, is called "unitary." The nations using this system are generally characterized by geographical uniformity in the services they provide and in the means of financing the services.

In the federal system of the United States, however, considerable autonomy is left to state and local government units to vary the mix and quantity of public goods they provide. State and local governments are also free (within constitutional bounds) to design their own tax systems. They determine both the mix of tax sources and the level of taxation. What is the rationale for this autonomy? What sort of function does this decentralization of the provision of certain public goods perform in the overall allocation of economic resources? The case for decentralization is really straightforward. It is believed to be the institutional arrangement which may allow us to come closer to matching the preferences of people for public goods with the amount and mix of public goods they are to receive.

Certain public goods, such as defense, provide benefits that accrue to all the citizens of the nation. Although it is true that not everyone places the same value on such public goods, the benefits are still nationwide, and it makes sense that the responsibility for providing such goods should rest with the national government. However, there are many public goods the benefits of which are confined to a smaller geographic area. The hospitals, school houses, and streets of Bethlehem, Pennsylvania, are not of much benefit to those living in Palo Alto, California.[1] These services do not have to be supplied uniformly across the nation. One city can have a big hospital and another city a small hospital. Decentralization makes it possible for each community to provide a set of public goods and services most in harmony with the likes and dislikes of the citizens of that community. To provide all people with the same set of local public goods is both inefficient and unnecessary. Wallace Oates has put this efficiency aspect of local public decision-making in more formal terms and calls it the "decentralization theorem."

> For a public good—the consumption of which is defined over geographical subsets of the total population, and for which the costs of providing each level of output of the good in each jurisdiction are the same for the central or the respective local government—it will always be more efficient (or at least as efficient) for local governments to provide the Pareto-efficient levels of output for their respective jurisdictions than for the central government to provide any specified and uniform level of output across all jurisdictions. (1972, 35)

Public finance theories that link decentralized or local decision-making to efficiency vary in the degree of realism in their assumptions about the rationality of individuals and organizations. On the unrealistic end of the continuum is the ideal world of unanimous consent. Knut Wicksell, a Swedish economist writing at the turn of the century, pointed out that the mutual preferences of all citizens could be satisfied simultaneously if public decisions were made on the basis of unanimous consent (1967, 72–118).

Assume that all citizens can estimate the benefits to be received from proposed public projects and also know the share of taxes they will have to pay to finance the projects. Suppose, now, that all citizens are presented with a list of projects, each accompanied by a proposed financing scheme. If only those projects with unanimous support were accepted, we could be sure that all citizens would have their welfare improved.

For national public goods, which must be supplied uniformly to all, unanimous-consent voting would result in a system of tax shares that reflected the intensity of each individual's preferences for the good. For local public goods, unanimous-consent voting could be expected to result in menus of public goods that could differ from one governmental unit to another. Unanimous-consent voting is, of course, not very practical. First, there are likely to be some people who either hold extreme views or are perhaps antisocial enough to use their veto power to stop any public activity. More important, perhaps, may be the problem of concealed preferences. Some people may simply pretend to oppose an outcome hoping that they may succeed in getting others to pay for the public goods they would like to consume.

In his famous article, "A Pure Theory of Local Expenditure" (1956), Charles Tiebout offers a more plausible argument for diversified, decentralized government. In general terms, Tiebout envisions (1) a number of localities, each offering a different menu of public goods and (2) a population of perfectly mobile individuals each choosing to take up residence in that community coming closest to matching his preferred mix of public goods and services. If it were possible to charge each individual on the basis of his consumption of public goods, individual preferences for local goods (and taxes) would be perfectly satisfied, and the intranational population distribution would move to an equilibrium.

Tiebout's assumption of perfect individual mobility in choosing between localities creates a substitute for the market process in reconciling differing individual preferences for local public goods. In essence, the Tiebout model is worked out in a travel-costless metropolitan area composed of many political subdivisions or communities. The citizens of the area "vote with their feet"; they sort themselves out by moving to those political subdivisions whose supply of public services and accompanying tax prices fit their preferences. In theory, if mobility is easy and frictions minimal and there are a sufficient number of varying local governments, each community will be settled by a group of people who are quite homogeneous as to their demand for public goods and the tax price they are willing to pay. In this sense, the Tiebout model provides a reasonable approximation to the Wicksellian unanimous vote criteria in the theory of public choice.

The Tiebout model has become the basis of an extensive range of empirical research, which we discuss in the next section. From an empirical perspective, a major problem with the theory is its static quality; it does not anticipate the reaction of one set of actors to the moves of others. One result of such interactions, as we shall see, is to create jurisdictions that are mixed rather than homogeneous in the income and preferences of their constituents.

Another problem with theories that assume consumer mobility is that of congestion costs. When these are counted in, the incremental cost of allowing an additional person to consume a local public good is not zero, as is the case of pure public goods on the national level. The problem of the optimal size of the sharing group for certain mixed goods has been analyzed under the general heading of the "theory of clubs" (Buchanan 1965).

Suppose we have a club providing its members with a common good—for example, a swimming pool. As more members are enticed into joining the club, the per capita costs of maintaining the pool are decreased. After a certain point, however, "congestion costs" rise to offset the decrease in financial costs; the pool is too crowded and the net utility of individual members declines. When this point is reached, it behooves the club to raise dues or otherwise act to restrict the growth in membership. The analogy to the provision of certain publicly provided goods is clear. For example, the per capita cost of a local road system is reduced with an increase in the number of inhabitants; past a certain point, however, population growth brings about traffic congestion, delays, and an increase in the rate of accidents.

The public policy implications of the theory of clubs are interesting. On the one hand, by recognizing the importance of congestion costs, we are led to see that to obtain an optimal size, the sharing group may require some means of restricting its membership. Perhaps the local government can restrict use by charging a price for the good. Nonresidents can be prohibited from the use of the town parks; this recognizes congestion costs on one level, but it does not solve the question of finding the optimum number of residents. When there is a large degree of publicness (or interrelated utilities or neighborhood effects) contained in the good, the application of the theory of clubs becomes difficult. Thus, when the general benefits of a certain level of education or preventive health care flow beyond the individual, the problem becomes more complex. It may be possible to find the optimum number of children for a given school or school district, but the problem of finding a place and financing an agreed-upon level of education for every school child remains. In the end, it is this class of problem that proves the most difficult for the policy makers and administrators to adjudicate. (See, for example, Ng 1973; Berglas 1976; Adams and Rogers 1977; Helpman and Hillman 1977.)

Conclusion

The arguments in favor of more centralized government functions focus on equity (the redistribution of some income and the welfare of all citizens) to the neglect of other objectives, whereas the arguments for decentralization and the limitation of governmental functions focus on efficiency and free choice. Results imply that citizens who favor equity must be for centralization, whereas the citizens who value efficiency must be for local democracy. Apparently, we cannot have combinations of equity and local democracy or efficiency and centralization.

But the simplifying assumptions required to equate equity with centralization, and efficiency with decentralization, are clearly problematic, as we will see in more detail in the next section. When we take into account the interdependence of the decisions that citizens (and their governments) make over time, connections between political objectives and government structure blur. In the real, complex world it may be possible for local governments and the national government to pursue both equity and efficiency. We explore this thought in the last section of this chapter.

EMPIRICAL RESEARCH

The results of empirical research on grants-in-aid and other initiatives from the national level have been reviewed in preceding chapters of this book. Clearly, theories that extol the virtues of centralization and ignore the problems of efficiency are incomplete. There are inefficiencies associated with centralizing decision making at the national level. Having discovered these inefficiencies, researchers and readers may conclude that theories that advocate decentralization in the name of efficiency are empirically sound and are good guides to policy. But the association of centralization with inefficiency does not prove that decentralization, under current conditions, will improve efficiency. Indeed, what little empirical research there is on formal theories about decentralization suggests that their predictions are as problematic as predictions made by formal theories favoring centralization. Since other authors in this book have dealt with empirical research about centralization, we focus our review on the Tiebout hypothesis, the most popular of the theories that equate efficiency with decentralization and local government diversity.

Many analysts have attempted empirical tests of the Tiebout hypothesis. The search for confirmation of the theory has proceeded in two directions. In one thrust, attention has focused on real estate values. The idea is that people pay an entry fee, that is, buy housing, to take up residence in their preferred community and that people will be willing to bid up housing prices in those jurisdictions that can provide a given level of services at a relatively low tax rate. In the most often quoted work of this type, Wallace Oates provides statistical support for this presumed behavior (1969, 1973).[2]

The concept of an entry fee casts some light on the seeming paradox of high property values coexisting with high tax rates. The generalized theory of tax capitalization considers taxes as a deduction from income. The annual tax burden on a given piece of property can be capitalized at the going interest rate and subtracted from the value of the property. This would lower the price that people are willing to pay for property located in a relatively high tax locality. (The tax capitalization phenomena would hold true even if the tax were not a property tax but a local income tax. A potential resident would pay relatively less for an equivalent parcel of property located in a high income tax area.) Of course, the theory of tax capitalization is one-sided because it leaves out the value of the public services that may be supported by the taxes. The capitalized value of these public goods can attach to property values as easily as the taxes. Presumably, for a given sorting of population across towns there would exist an optimum level of services and matching taxes which would maximize the values of each community.

In a second series of studies, the main concern is with actual migration patterns. To what extent do people actually move from place to place on the basis of fiscal differences between communities? The bulk of the empirical analysis has concentrated on the migration effects of geographically different welfare benefits. Richard Cebula has reviewed many of these studies and comes to the following conclusions.

> The literature . . . seems to indicate that interarea welfare level differentials may well exercise a perceptible positive impact on various groups of migrants, particularly the poor (both whites and nonwhites). . . .
>
> Certain of the studies examined . . . find migration patterns sensitive to interarea differentials in property tax levels (and/or other fiscal variables). In particular, it has been found that the economically "advantaged" tend (on average) to prefer low property tax areas, whereas the economically "disadvantaged" are apparently insensitive to property tax levels. (1979, 75)

Aronson and Schwartz (1973), in their study based on the Tiebout hypothesis, do not look at any one expenditure category. Instead, they attempt to predict migration patterns based on the hypothesis that people will move to the town with the highest difference between benefits received by the individual from public services and taxes paid by the individual. They explain fiscally induced migration as follows: The mix and volume of local expenditures are determined through nonmarket political processes, and the benefits of these expenditures presumably accrue equally to each resident of the community. However, the taxes to pay for the public goods are usually based on property values, on sales, or on income. Therefore, roughly speaking, real income is redistributed from rich to poor within each locality. Thus, an individual who is relatively rich in his locality may find it advantageous to migrate to another locality where, given his existing income and wealth, he will be relatively poor. It is also apparent that a relatively poor person might find it advantageous to move to a richer town in order to secure an even larger real income transfer. The pattern of migration would follow a cycle. There is an economic motivation for the relatively rich to leave a locality to escape the burden of financing poorer people. The poorer people, however, might be expected to follow closely behind, thus creating the conditions for a repetition of the cycle.

The result, unanticipated in the Tiebout model, would be a continuous disequilibrium as the poor chase after the rich and the rich move out to found new towns or communities. The movement would be slowed, of course, by various personal inertias and immobilities, by the costs of moving, by increasing commuting costs, and by the conveniences and benefits involved in developing an economic structure that would provide a mix or variety of private goods in a proximate area. An external method of stemming a disequilibrium population flow is through the use of such devices as minimal lot size or other zoning regulations. However, these devices are not likely to be permanent. They may not be quite lawful; moreover, they run contrary to the interests of developers, builders, and those older residents with large blocks of vacant land that they may be ready to sell.

The findings of this research indicate the importance of "perverse migration,'' which takes place not as a move motivated by market sector factors (e.g., to obtain a better job) but as a move motivated simply by a desire to obtain a better fiscal surplus. Such movements can be socially costly. Most often, they do not improve output, and they lead to no final equilibrium.

What possible changes in the tax expenditure structure would reduce fiscally induced migration? They would consist of such measures as (1) equalizing welfare payments over the nation and supporting such programs through the federal fisc, (2) supporting public schools through a statewide levy and giving each district approximately the same support per school child, and (3) financing purely local services with user charges. In effect, we return to square one, a largely unitary system of public finance. In order to reduce the inefficiencies of the marketplace, we are encouraged to tolerate the supposed inefficiencies of centralized government.

The findings of empirical tests of the Tiebout hypothesis and their possible implications are typical. The theory identifies rational behavior for a given set of actors under given conditions, and by and large people behave as predicted. However, their actions change conditions for others, who react in ways that alter the initial conditions and, therefore, the dictates of self-interest. This results in behavior that alternatively confirms and discredits theories that relate centralization and decentralization to equity and efficiency. Sometimes central action promotes efficiency; sometimes decentralization promotes equity. As we will see in the next section, policy analyses are increasingly oriented toward taking advantage of these variables to simultaneously increase equity and efficiency.

POLICY ANALYSIS

The policy literature suggests the complexity of the intergovernmental system. In the real world, action by the central government often compensates for problems at the local level, and vice versa. The intergovernmental system is neither centralized or decentralized, and its structure is in flux. Moreover, implicit definitions of equity and efficiency vary and are sometimes contradictory. Although equity is generally associated with centralization and efficiency is generally associated with decentralization, the correspondence is by no means perfect.

The policy literature is characteristically normative. It focuses on explicit, desired objectives and uses empirical research or logical deduction to assess alternative strategies to reach these objectives. This reflects the closeness of applications to classic theories about government performance.

The Property Tax

In spite of continuing strong criticism, the property tax is still a major source of local government finance. In 1977, property tax revenues amounted to over $60 billion, which represented more than 20 percent of all state-local general revenues, more than 33 percent of all state-local tax revenues, and more than 80 percent of all local tax revenues (ACIR 1979). Nevertheless, the property tax has been criticized for many reasons, including the disputed charge that it has a highly regressive final incidence.

The general conclusion that the property tax is regressive follows from budget studies showing that, as incomes rise, housing expenditures (rentals or the imputed costs of owner-occupied houses) decline as a percentage of income. (That is, poor people spend a larger percentage of their income on housing than do rich people.) If the property tax is considered mainly a tax on housing, the property tax burden as part of the outlay for housing represents a larger proportion of a poor person's income than of a rich person's income. Similarly, since poorer people tend to use a larger portion of their income for consumption than do richer people, that part of the property tax thought to be passed forward through higher prices of goods is also shown to be regressive. On the other hand, as an offset, that part of the tax that falls on land remains with the landowner. It can generally be surmised that rich people own proportionately more land relative to their income than do poorer people.

The possible regressive incidence of the property tax is best described by the measurements made by Pechman and Okner in *Who Bears the Tax Burden?* (1974). One can see in table 7.2 that if we assume that the tax on land is borne by landowners and the tax on improvements is shifted in the form of higher prices of shelter and consumption, the incidence of the property tax does not appear much different from that of sales and excise taxes.

However, recent studies by Aaron (1975) and by Browning and Johnson (1979) have tended to cast doubt on the presumed regressivity of the property tax. The authors suggest an alternative view of property tax incidence in which all owners of capital may be considered as sharing the property tax. The argument proceeds in the following fashion: If all capital is taxed and the supply of capital is unaffected by the tax, the tax burden falls on property income rather than being shifted forward to consumers in the form of higher prices for goods. If only some capital is taxed, the economic reaction will be that assets move to more lightly taxed areas or uses. The reaction will continue until the rate of return on capital, net of taxes, is the same in all uses. The result of the adjustment process is that the burden of tax is felt by all owners of capital and not simply by those whose property is subject to direct taxation (Maxwell and Aronson 1977). (Of course, the reduction of the returns from capital could have the long-term effect of reducing the total supply of capital.)

The distribution of the tax burden according to these alternative incidence assumptions is shown in the last two columns of table 7.2. The estimates indicate that the burden of the property tax may be more progressive than is generally believed. (For a detailed description and analysis of the various views of property tax incidence, see Break 1974.)

Table 7.2.   Estimated Effective Rates of Property and Sales Taxes under Two Sets of Incidence Assumptions, by Income Class, 1966

Adjusted Family Income ($ thousand)	Orthodox Incidence Assumption[a]				Alternative Incidence Assumption[b]	
	Tax Rate (%)		Rate Relative[c]		Property Tax Rate (%)	Property Tax Rate, Relative
	Property Tax	Sales and Excise Taxes	Property Tax	Sales and Excise Taxes		
0–3	6.5	9.2	191	184	2.5	83
3–5	4.8	7.1	141	142	2.7	90
5–10	3.6	6.4	106	128	2.0	67
10–15	3.2	5.6	94	112	1.7	57
15–20	3.2	5.1	94	102	2.0	67
20–25	3.1	4.6	91	92	2.6	87
25–30	3.1	4.0	91	80	3.7	123
30–50	3.0	3.5	88	70	4.5	150
50–100	2.8	2.4	82	48	6.2	207
100–500	2.4	1.7	71	34	8.2	273
500–1,000	1.7	1.4	50	28	9.6	320
1,000+	0.8	1.3	24	26	10.1	337
Total	3.4	5.0	100	100	3.0	100

Source: Pechman and Okner 1974, 59; Maxwell and Aronson 1977, 139.

[a]The tax on land is borne by landowners, and the tax on improvements is shifted in the form of higher prices of shelter and consumption.
[b]The burden of property taxes on both land and improvements is apportioned according to property income.
[c]The average tax rate is assigned a value of 100; the rate relative for each income-class group is a percentage of the average.

Circuit Breakers.   An inherent problem of the property tax is its effect on people who have stable or declining incomes. Many older people may hold property whose value is disproportionately high relative to their income. This is not an economic miscalculation; in an inflationary environment, it can result from a perfectly well thought out lifetime income plan. For example, a family at an earlier point bought a house, so one part of the family savings consists in amortizing the mortgage; the expection is that at retirement, the heads of the household may supplement their lower explicit income by living in their own housing. For such people, the inflationary rise in the value of their property can result in a disastrous change in their economic situation. The taxes based on family income and consumption may actually decline; nevertheless, the tax on housing continually rises. It should be noted that although most attention has been given to the tax impact on the elderly, the same problem will affect anyone who has purchased housing on the basis of an expected income flow and who finds property taxes rising at a faster rate than his income.

The social dislocation caused by the steep rises in property value has not escaped the observation of students of taxation or the attention of state legislatures. The observed difficulties have led to the design of a set of fiscal devices known as "circuit breakers" (ACIR 1967, 1975; Cook and Quindry 1969; Cook 1973; Lochner and Kim 1973; Quindry 1973; Shannon 1973; Bendick 1974; Aaron 1975). ACIR describes circuit breakers as "tax relief programs designed to protect family income from property tax overload the same way an electrical circuit breaker protects the family home from current overload" (1975, 2). That is, when the property tax burden on an individual exceeds a predetermined percentage of personal income, the circuit breaker goes into effect to relieve excess financial pressure.

Circuit breakers may be built on formulas using either the threshold approach or sliding scale approach. Under the threshold approach an acceptable level of taxation is defined as some fixed percentage of household income. The amount by which the actual property tax exceeds this level qualifies for relief. On the other hand, when a sliding scale is used, a fixed percentage of property tax is rebated to taxpayers within each income class; the percentage of property tax rebatable is lower the higher the income class (ACIR 1975; Maxwell and Aronson 1977). The circuit breaker technique is usually built into a state's income tax system. Either rebates are credited against an individual's state income tax liability or the taxpayer receives a refund check.

Circuit breakers are not without their critics. First of all, it is obvious that the loss in revenues due to the exemption of part of the tax base is made up by the other taxpayers. Second, it is argued that the special reduction in tax rates may lead to a misallocation of housing resources; older people may be encouraged to hold on to housing that would better be relinquished to the market to be purchased and used by younger or larger families. (For a good discussion of these problems, see Aaron 1975.)

Reverse Mortgage.   One substitute proposal for circuit breakers is the reverse mortgage, whereby the value of the house could be drawn down over the life of the older resident-occupiers in the form of a life annuity (Guttentag 1979). A variant of this plan would at least defer the tax payments and allow them to accrue with interest against the value of the house. The taxing authority would ultimately recover the accumulated taxes by selling the house at the time of the settlement of the estate. A difficulty of this scheme is that the house might become neglected and deteriorate through the neglect of maintenance when the amount of accrued taxes began to approach the value of the property.

Property Tax Classification.   Another recent "reform" of the property tax concerns the farm and open-land classification laws, which are designed to blunt the impact of the rise in values of open lands or farms adjacent to quickly spreading urban areas. When such lands are assessed at the same ratio to market value as other properties in the jurisdiction, the rise in the property levy may be so large as to make the continued use of the land for farming quite unprofitable. Farmers of long standing are forced to give up their operations and sell their land to commercial or housing developers; this outcome does not necessarily please the farmers or the adjacent property owners, who had originally thought they were moving into a rural environment. The special classification laws passed by many states in recognition of the urban-fringe problem lowers the assessment ratios on woodland and grazing or farm properties as long as the owners keep them in their original use. Although these laws may slow the displacement of farmers reluctant to leave their lands, there is a counterargument that this type of legislation increases the price of the remaining available land; it thus reduces the available housing opportunities for those remaining in the city. (There are even some who argue that racist motives underlie the property classification laws.) In any case, it might be noted that the classification legislation does increase *the* net capital gains the farmer will obtain over his holding period whenever he finally does decide to sell (see Coughlin et al. 1978). (For a general review of various property tax relief mechanisms, see Gold 1979.)

Formula Research, School Finance, and State Aid Formulas

Historically, the local property tax was the main source of support of local education. For some time now, however, the property tax revenues have been surpassed by various grants out of the general revenues of the states, and more recently there has been a considerable supplement of support from federal funds granted to various local educational programs and projects. Nevertheless, the property tax continues to be by far the largest portion of local educational units' own-revenues. (For an excellent set of descriptive data on school financing, see ACIR 1977.)

Recent court cases have challenged the inherent equity and the constitutionality of a system in which intrastate differences in the quality of education was a reflection of differences not in the preferences of citizens making up the local school district but rather in the level of wealth and income of these districts. It has been argued that because children in richer school districts would attend better-funded schools than children in poorer districts, the child in the poorer district was of necessity denied "equal protection of the law" under the various interpretations of the state constitutions. (For a detailed discussion of problems involved in reforming school finances, see Coons, Clune, and Sugarman 1970; ACIR 1973; Reischauer and Hartman 1973.) The results of these cases have impelled the various state legislatures to try to devise formulas that would eliminate, or at least reduce, school-expenditure discrepancies (per school child) across the various districts. Such formulas are more difficult to devise than one would imagine; it is not easy to prevent a district from raising differentially more money and spending it on educational supplements if its citizens so desire. In any case, most of the formulations for reducing the inequities in local school finance have perforce stopped short of the radical solution of turning the state into a unitary school district. Most administrators would be content with an equity goal that was definitively stated and set within boundaries. Such a goal, for example, would state that the difference between the lowest-expenditure district per school child and the highest-expenditure district should not vary by more than 50 percent.

One state-funding scheme designed to elicit a response toward more equal educational spending is district power equalization (DPE). In this plan, the grant per student that the state awards a district is given by the following equation:[3]

$$G_i = t_i(W_k - W_i)$$

where

$$
\begin{aligned}
G_i &= \text{the DPE grant per student to the } i^{\text{th}} \text{ district} \\
t_i &= \text{the tax rate of the } i^{\text{th}} \text{ district} \\
W_k &= \text{the wealth per student of the key district} \\
W_i &= \text{the wealth per student of the } i^{\text{th}} \text{ district}
\end{aligned}
\tag{1}
$$

To implement the plan a key district, which receives no state subsidy, is designated. Districts poorer than the key district receive state subsidies, whereas those that are wealthier have a portion of their locally raised revenues recaptured.[4] Under this plan, the size of the state grant is inversely related to a district's wealth.

The portion of local expenditures financed by the state is given by the state-aid ratio (SAR) when

$$SAR = 1 - \frac{W_i}{W_k} \tag{2}$$

DPE affects the price of education as seen by a given school district. To the district that receives no aid, one dollar of education costs one dollar. However, a district half as rich as the key district has half of its budget paid by the state and thus faces a price of fifty cents for each dollar's worth of educational expenditure. The price (P) of education can be expressed as follows:

$$P = 1 - SAR \tag{3}$$

and substituting equation (2) into equation (3), it follows that

$$P = \frac{W_i}{W_k} \tag{4}$$

Thus, under DPE a district that is 1 percent poorer than the key district will face a 1 percent lower price for educational expenditures. Will a DPE state-funding system have the effect of equalizing the level of expenditures per student among districts of similar educational preferences?

Martin Feldstein has pointed out that the answer depends on two behavioral parameters; the district's price elasticity of educational expenditures $\left(\dfrac{\Delta E}{E}\right/$ $\dfrac{\Delta P}{P} = \beta,\ \beta < 0\Big)$ and the district's wealth elasticity of educational expenditure $\left(\dfrac{\Delta E}{E}\middle/\dfrac{\Delta W}{W} = \alpha,\ \alpha > 0\right)$. Feldstein's analysis shows that DPE will achieve its goal only when $|\alpha| = |\beta|$. When $|\alpha| > |\beta|$, grants based on a DPE formula will fall short of inducing the poorer districts to spend at the level achieved by the more wealthy districts. On the other hand, if $|\beta| > |\alpha|$, then a DPE formula will actually induce the poorer districts to spend more per student than the richer districts. Feldstein offers a grant formula that takes account of the values of α and β and therefore achieves expenditure equalization. Several studies have aimed at measuring the value of these elasticities: Denzau 1975; Coughlin, Berry, and Plant 1978; Black, Lewis, and Link 1979; Gilmen and Morgan 1979; Aronson and Hilley 1981.

The attempt to achieve expenditure equity (i.e., equalizing expenditures per student among school districts in a state) has been pursued because of society's concern for the well-being of its children. There is, however, another problem of equal concern; the equitable treatment of taxpayers. In a system of local governments, relatively poor districts can match the level of services provided in relatively rich districts only by taxing themselves at higher rates than those in effect in the richer districts. DPE programs would induce poorer districts to spend more than they would otherwise. Aronson and Hilley (1981) show the trade-off between expenditure equity and taxpayer equity. That is, inducing poorer districts to increase their spending on education may create a system in which local tax rates are forced much higher in poor districts relative to rich districts.

Concern with problems of school finance has also stimulated further interest in the area of measuring fiscal capacity. There have been attempts to build indexes that take account of personal income as well as the district property tax base (Ladd 1975; Thornton 1981).

Tax Restrictions: Proposition 13

Citizen perception of the inequity of some taxes and the ineffectiveness of many programs in reaching their goals has led to a growing movement to pass into law restrictions on the growth of local taxes. The types of restrictions that have been used are not the same across the states. In a number of states, limits have been placed on revenues alone. In other states, however, limits have also been placed on expenditures. Sometimes the limits have been in the form of amendments to state constitutions; at other times, the limits are simply acts of the legislature. The modern movement to limit governmental activity began in California with an attack on the property tax. Spearheaded by Harold Jarvis, the California experience culminated in voter passage of the famous Proposition 13.

The rationale for the successful attack on the property tax may perhaps be understood in the light of some of the factors discussed in the section on the property tax. The revolt against the property tax stems from the combination of the proportionately greater growth of property values relative to incomes and perhaps also from the increasing use of such sophisticated devices as the computer in keeping assessments up to date. The success of the assessor in pushing assessment values right behind rising property values means that (especially in boom areas such as California) the property tax escalates faster than income and, of course, various governmental units find themselves riding a wave of rising revenues.

The essential features of Proposition 13 have been neatly summarized by Oakland (1979):

> The Jarvis-Gann Amendment, or Proposition 13 as it has come to be known: (1) restricts the property tax rate to no more than one percent of assessed value, (2) sets assessed value for a property which has not been transferred since 1975–76 equal to its fair market value in that year plus two percent per year (compounded); in the event that the property has been transferred since 1975–76, the market value at the time of sale is used (plus the two percent growth factor); and (3) requires that new taxes or increases in existing taxes (except property taxes) receive a two-thirds approval of the legislature in the case of state taxes, or of the electorate, in the case of local taxes. (387)

Although the initial voter approval of the initiative that placed Proposition 13 into the California constitution caused considerable trepidation among local state officials, in the actual event the belt-tightening and the cutting of programs was less than anticipated because the state government had a considerable surplus to parcel out to the local governments. However, the initial passage of Proposition 13 has been followed by the passage of Proposition 4, which in essence is an attempt to further restrict increases in governmental activity. Proposition 4 limits increases in governmental spending to increases in population and to either the consumer price index or state per capita personal income, whichever is lower. Thus, we have to recognize that although the Jarvis movement and Proposition 13 were most heavily directed against the property tax, there is some implication that the voters have also been registering a more general protest against the size of the public sector.

The underlying forces leading up to Proposition 13 and the potential economic and financial impact of tax limitation legislation were the topics studied at a conference held at the University of California, Santa Barbara, in December 1978. The proceedings of the conference, subsequently published in the *National Tax Journal* (supplement) (1979), contain some important insights into the tax limitation phenomenon.

Shapiro, Puryear, and Ross, for example, suggest that Proposition 13 may best be explained not as a simple reaction against a Leviathan government but rather as "an expression, by the property owner–voter, of dissatisfaction with bearing a growing share of the public financial responsibility" (1979, 4). They observe that between 1965 and 1979 the assessed values of single-family housing in California increased at a much faster rate than did the assessed values of commercial and industrial property in that state. They also point to public opinion findings that implied that Californians were generally satisfied with the level of public services they received (Citrin 1979; Shapiro, Puryear, and Ross 1979).

A logical reaction to tax restriction legislation is the increased reliance on user charges. This enables the distribution of the tax burden in a different manner without necessarily reducing the delivery of public services (Shapiro, Puryear, and Ross 1979; White 1979). California local governments have responded to Proposition 13 by increasing a variety of fees and imposing new ones. According to the California Building Industry Association, median construction-related fees and service charges across the state rose 26 percent between the spring of 1978 and the spring of 1979. Business and license fees have also been raised. Many museums now charge for entrance, fees have been raised at beaches, campgrounds, and parks, and fines for overdue library books have increased (Rodgers 1981). Shapiro et al. also point out that legislation that changes the mix of taxes in favor of sales and income taxes may, by favoring these even more elastic revenue sources, actually promote a larger, rather than smaller, public sector.

In another interesting contribution, Brennan and Buchanan (1979) suggest that the taxpayer revolution can be satisfactorily understood only in a public choice setting they call the nonbenevolent despot model. In such a system, constitutional rather than electoral constraints may be needed to express citizen preferences.

Is the current wave of tax and spending limitation movements a transitory phenomenon? Michael Boskin feels "that nothing could be further from the truth" (1979, 37). "The concern over government spending and taxes is primarily a concern over the total tax burden and the aggregate amount of spending at all levels of government" (38). Taxpayer unrest has developed because "all growth in income in the United States since 1973 has been either eaten away by inflation or gone into government spending" (38). Antitax legislation is bound to have serious effects. Not all states have sufficient surplus to serve as a fiscal cushion against the new limits. And since the federal government is itself in a belt-tightening mood, it is not likely that the tax limitation pressure will be mitigated by increased federal aid to the state and local governments. State and local governments will be forced, therefore, to increase their productivity, make greater use of fees and charges, and shift some services to the private sector. In her analysis of the tax and expenditure limitation movement, Deborah Matz (1981) recognizes these forces and concludes: "It seems more likely than not that even if the limitation movement per se has lost some of its momentum, fiscal austerity at all levels of government will prevail. The biggest losers stand to be the poor and lower income families who may not be able to afford new or increased user fees or private service contracts.'' On the other hand, it must be recognized that many programs to aid the poor have been badly designed, so that the indigent are encouraged over the working poor, and poverty and administering to poverty seem to be permanently institutionalized.

Efficient Allocation of Public Goods—User Charges

The developing voter resentment of the growth of broad-based taxes has brought about the tax limitation movement; it has also increased interest in user charges. User charges are fees or prices charged for the use of public services; as such, they fall on the direct user of the service (according to his use) and not on the general citizenry. Supposedly, charges can gauge the public desire for the service and may give a better signal of the intensity of demand than that provided by a government official, who may be trying to translate the social utility function of his constituency into a demand for public goods. Moreover, user charges may conserve resources because there is a tendency toward waste in the use of "free goods."

On a more pragmatic level, the great advantage of user charges from the view of the administrator is that they take some of the burden off the broad-based levies. Thus, according to table 7.3, from fiscal year 1973 to 1977, the increase in all local charges was 57.0 percent. The increase in local taxes (own sources) was considerably less, 41.1 percent. Of course, a large portion of the increase in user revenues is represented by the utility revenues, which were no doubt largely offset by higher operating costs over this period.

*Table 7.3.*ı Selected City Government Revenues, 1972–73 to 1976–77 ($ million)

Source of Revenue	Fiscal Year					% Change 1972–73 to 1976–77	
	1976–77	1975–76	1974–75	1973–74	1972–73	Current $ (%)	Constant $ (1972) (%)
Charge (total)	17,766	15,869	13,852	12,167	11,316	57.0	19.7
Current	6,872	6,161	5,443	4,927	4,533	51.6	15.6
Utility revenue	19,682	9,504	8,217	7,067	6,619	61.4	23.0
Liquor store revenue	212	204	192	173	164	29.3	−1.4
Tax (total from own sources)	26,067	23,336	21,135	19,434	18,477	41.1	7.6
Property	15,653	14,165	13,046	12,244	11,879	31.8	0.5
Sales and gross receipts	5,805	5,109	4,555	3,931	3,567	62.7	24.1

Source: U.S. Department of Commerce 1979, table 1.

Some of the potential for further increases in revenues from charges can be seen in table 7.4. It is clear that at present, charge revenues do not cover full costs for many activities. This may be partly due to the inherent merit-good or public-good aspect of at least part of the service. Nevertheless, it should be possible, for example, to cover all of the sewerage collection and treatment costs by an increase in charges. Garbage and refuse collection is probably another "underpriced" area. Many cities make no charge for collecting garbage and cover the costs out of general revenues. Of course, a charge system might run into difficulties if it encouraged people to dispose of their refuse in the city streets or vacant lots. Yet, many jurisdictions do operate successfully with privately owned and regulated fee-charging collectors, and other cities use municipal fee systems.

Highway charges cover only about 17.5 percent of total costs. In general, tolls are collected only on bridges, tunnels, and the like; most of the city streets are free. However, the growing pollution and automobile congestion costs of many cities may lead to some experimentation in the implementation of charges for the use of city streets (Mushkin 1972; Downing 1977).

The practical implementation of user charges involves two somewhat interdependent decisions: (1) whether the charges should cover full cost, and (2) how the rates should be structured to obtain efficient use of public facilities. It would seem at first that, once having decided to employ a fee system, the government should set the fees to cover full costs. Not so fast. Given a private market system for most goods, we can assume that a good provided by the government is a merit good or service, otherwise it would have been left in the private sector. A merit good is one that the populace should be encouraged to use because it has spillover utility or value to the rest of society. This implies that user charges should not cover full cost. They should be carefully constructed so that the fees pay for strictly individual benefits but general revenues cover perceived social benefits. This is a matter of both equity and efficiency.

The problem of the careful design of user charges may be illustrated by the problem of education. Surely, one could establish a fee system for elementary

Table 7.4.   Charge Revenue as a Percentage of Expenditures, 1976–77 (%)

Service	% Expenditure
Parking	128.8
Water supply	127.5
Airports	96.9
Sewerage	37.7
Hospitals	34.0
Highways	17.6
Parks and recreation	15.6
Sanitation	10.3

Source: U.S. Department of Commerce 1979, table 8.

education. However, because one desideratum of a democratic society is that every child should obtain at the minimum an elementary education so as to establish a fundamental level of civilized discourse, the largest part of elementary education will be "free" to the parents of the participant. On the other hand, higher education may have a lesser degree of common utility and thus could be financed in alternate ways. Tuition might be charged and set somewhat below full cost to allow for the social utility; scholarships and loans could be used to cover tuition costs for those unable to meet the tuition charges currently.

Refining User Charge Systems

Marginal Cost Pricing.   Many public goods (or enterprises) for which rates are charged fall into that area of economic activity classified as natural monopoly. This is the sector of the economy in which competition would involve a wasteful duplication of capital. Essentially, over a given geographical area, some services have decreasing costs that can be captured only by a single enterprise, and thus it becomes inefficient to duplicate the facility. A monopoly or franchise is the most efficient way to service the area. Natural monopolies are either privately owned or directly owned governmental enterprises that are franchised and regulated by the government. (It should be noted that the public utility commissions may be brought in to rule on rates and charges even for a government-owned facility. This is especially true if the service is used by adjacent jurisdictions.)

Any discussion of optimal rate structure for declining cost facilities (i.e., those in which the average cost decreases with the volume of use) involves the theory of marginal cost pricing. (A classic article in this area is, of course, Hotelling 1938.) Marginal cost pricing deals with the question of obtaining not the maximum *revenue* but the maximum *social utility* from the existence of a public facility. In the case of a decreasing cost facility, the implementation of marginal cost pricing may necessitate the incurring of a deficit. Thus, suppose a facility requires a large capital investment but its operating costs are negligible—that is, the marginal cost of an additional user is quite low. Theory dictates that it is wasteful to have idle capacity and that sunk costs do not count; therefore, the proper price is the marginal cost of serving the next user. In this case, however, a price equal to marginal cost does not cover average cost; the facility operates with a deficit, which will have to be covered out of general revenues. Nevertheless, this may be the most efficient and equitable way of using the facility.

Two-Part Tariff.   A number of alternatives of marginal cost pricing or of user charges have been suggested that may eliminate the problem of the deficit. One of these is the two-part tariff. The two-part tariff consists of a fixed charge or capacity charge covering the capital costs, which is placed on every user entitled to use the facility, and a user charge for each unit used based on the variable or marginal costs of production. There has been much discussion, especially on the equity aspects, of the optimum formulation of two-part tariff systems (Baumol and Bradford 1970; Mohring 1970; Feldstein 1972; Oi 1972; Ng and Weisser 1974).

Presumably, the logic behind the two-part tariff assumes that running costs are constant (or change only minimally) throughout the range of operations and that *there is open capacity* at all times. Therefore, there is no particular reason to ration the use of the facility once it is installed. A two-part tariff can be designed to cover total costs; it also encourages full use of the existing facility since the individual's average cost declines with greater use. However, the two-part tariff does not give the public authority any good demand or revenue guidelines as to how large a facility should be installed initially or the subsequent rate of expansion. It does nothing to encourage consumer saving of capital; nor does it encourage deferral of use when the system is congested or capacity is strained.

Peak-Load Pricing.   A closer examination of the question of marginal cost pricing reveals that it often can be resolved into a peak-load problem. That is, if the facility is designed to accommodate a certain peak demand (e.g., rush hour on the transportation system and late-afternoon use for the electric utility system), at the off-peak period, there will be idle capacity and low costs of service. A theoretical solution to the problem is obtained when peak users (which might include almost everyone) pay a peak-load price, one that covers the full costs, including the total-capacity costs that their demand has called forth. The off-peak users pay a price that covers only incremental marginal or operating costs and that may be quite low depending on the level of operating costs at the time they enter the system.[5] (See, for example, Vickrey 1971; Bailey 1972; Panzar 1976.)

A properly designed peak-load pricing system would have many advantages. The purpose of peak-load pricing tariffs is not simply to provide equity in the charges to peak and off-peak customers. Peak-load pricing can perform an allocative or efficiency function. It would entice some use from the peak period to the off-peak period. This means more service could be derived from existing facilities without straining capacity. Moreover, the shift in demand would have the effect of reducing total costs; it would have the eventual effect of reducing the total amount of planned capacity required at peak, thus saving society scarce capital. By indicating to the planners the total amount of service that would actually be demanded at the peak price, it becomes possible to make decisions as to the optimum size of the plant or facility. Lastly, a peak-load pricing scheme may cover total costs, thus obviating the need to subsidize the facility with monies from other revenues. (For the classic debate on the two-part tariff vs. peak-load pricing, see Lewis 1941a, 1941b; Rowson 1941.)

In some cases, such as toll bridges or roads, a peak-load user price would not be difficult to initiate. It simply involves charging a minimum toll off-peak and collecting a significantly higher toll at the periods of high congestion. In many other cases, however, such as water or electricity supply, the implementation of an on-peak–off-peak pricing system faces considerable practical and operational difficulties. In electricity supply, it involves the installation of complex and expensive meters to register use by peak and off-peak periods. It requires the calculation of a demand charge for a user who has a large but random demand, which forces the facility to acquire additional stand-by capacity to accommodate his uncertain entrance onto the system. Moreover, if the facility was originally designed to accommodate demand under an average-cost charge system, the initiation of an on-peak–off-peak charge scheme might result in an uncovered peak—that is, excess capacity at peak. The cost of this idle facility would have to be covered until the system size could be adjusted to the new demand.

Another difficulty arises in a dynamic growth situation, in which economies of scale (i.e., a larger facility initially costs less per unit of capacity) make it desirable to build ahead of demand. That is, it is economically desirable to install a larger initial capacity than existing use requires. In this case, current actual demand will be below capacity even at peak. It would seem that the rules of marginal cost pricing would require that the charge be set at the out-of-pocket operating cost; the facility might then incur a relatively large deficit. In such a case, however, some version of a shadow pricing system should prevail. The extra installed capacity must be looked upon as an inventory to be used at some future date. The pricing system in this case should be designed along the lines of long-run marginal cost analysis (Bailey 1972). The charge system should be designed as if the extra capacity did not exist and as if the peak demand fully utilized the size structure which would have been built if current demand had been predicted to remain stable. In this situation, the peak users would pay for capital costs even if at that point open capacity existed.

When to Employ User Charge Systems. In contrast to the ability-to-pay or equity justification underlying most broad-based taxes, user charge systems find their justification in the benefit/cost or efficiency theories of taxation. These theories hold that those who receive the benefits of a public good are the ones who should pay the costs. This has the advantage of making sure that the good is not wasted. However, the user charge system contains a paradox at its very center; public goods by definition provide interrelated or common utilities so that the value of the benefits accruing to any single individual is difficult to measure. According to Abba Lerner's classical notation, public or merit goods are those whose the marginal social utility (MSU) exceeds the marginal private utility (MPU). Society finds it desirable that such public or merit goods as basic education, recreation, or preventive health services be consumed at a higher level than would be the case if every user were charged his full costs.

The situation in which the employment of user charges is most applicable is in the "public provision of private goods." In an essentially private economy, those private goods that might be provided by a public authority are items, such as water or electricity, that are uneconomic to produce in a competitive manner because it would involve a costly duplication of facilities. (Of course, it should be noted that an alternate form to public ownership for producing these goods is a franchised, regulated public utility.) In any case, since the benefits of these goods are comparatively easy to trace, a properly designed user-charge system to allocate costs and conserve resources seems eminently appropriate.

To return to the more difficult situation, when user charges or fees are to finance public or merit goods, one must decide how much of the cost is to be covered. It is generally held that one of the functions of the public sector is the provision of equity. The public sector provides for some redistribution of income (or goods) so that a given level of "social necessities" is available to everyone, including the poor. Many user charges fail to perform this last function because they attempt to cover the full cost of merit goods.

Nevertheless, in the case of the natural monopoly, it is doubtful that the user charge should be used as a redistributive device. There are cogent arguments to the effect that poor people should be given direct money grants (either through a reformed welfare system or a negative income tax) and that thereafter they should pay the same prices as anyone else for private-type goods whether delivered through the market or distributed via the public sector. This no doubt makes pricing efficient. A problem arises, however, in instances when the poor prove incompetent and deprive themselves of necessary and desirable services.

DESIGNING MULTIDIMENSIONAL MODELS:
A SUMMARY

A new generation of public administrators, who are better trained in the use of technical tools and better able to assimilate the information and methods imbedded in the field of public finance, is appearing. They are being pushed by the constraints of the present situation toward the use of more fiscal information and more precise theories and models in order to design efficient, viable methods of delivering services within the limits of the resources available.

The pressures of resource limitation have moved some emphasis on programs away from equity considerations and toward efficiency. Nevertheless, it is doubtful that the value of equity will be totally abandoned. Clearer statements of goals are required as well as the creation of systems, methods, and models that can come close to reaching these goals with a minimum of waste and economic disruption.

Public finance, which has a long intellectual history, contains many models that are being refurbished and implemented in the world of practical policies. Many years ago, it would have been rare to find an administrator who understood the subtleties of marginal cost or the logic of peak-load pricing. Today, the concept is clearly on the wing. Under the pressure of the rising scarcity of energy, water, and transportation facilities, the use of peak-load pricing is being contemplated in such areas as the pricing of electricity, water, and access to bridges.

In a similar vein, the theoretical distinction between private utility and social utility is leading to a rethinking of the pricing or charging mechanisms that might be applied in such a field as education. Here the task is to design tax and charge systems so that while the general welfare aspects of the activity are subsidized, the personal utilities are financed by the recipients.

Lastly, studies of the assumptions of the Tiebout model, revealing its inherent flaw in being unable to predict a stable or equilibrium distribution of population, cast a new light on the debate between centralization (presumably, equity) and decentralization (presumably, efficiency) in the provision of services. The Aronson-Schwartz study (1973) indicates that where the imputed fiscal transfer (value of services minus taxes) differs, poor people will move to richer areas, creating a continuously disequilibrating cycle. This being so, the centralization-decentralization debate couched in the usual terms is in large part irrelevant. Here the problem is designing public goods delivery systems such that the variety and amount and the financing of localized amenities and personalized services could be decided and controlled at the local level while broad-based programs could be federalized or centralized in order to prevent regional or state differences from inducing perverse migration patterns.

In short, given the data that have become increasingly available and the greater sophistication of the analyses, it may be possible to design and administer systems that better account for dynamic variables. Having established normative value goals, such systems will be designed to accommodate behavioral variables so that the polity moves toward the designated goals. Given due care in design and administration, the goals might be multidimensional, and properly designed systems may provide some net gain both in increased equity and in efficiency.

NOTES

1. Local services may affect people other than residents, such as visitors to the city, and people also move from one city to another. This means that even local public goods can provide some benefits that may be described as national in scope.

2. The empirical techniques used by Oates have been examined in detail. (Pollakowski 1973; Gustely 1976) There has also been a strand of thought which suggests that in a Tiebout equilibrium, property taxes may be considered pure benefit levies—that is, they are the prices of public services and property values are therefore unaffected by the tax level. (Edel 1974; Hamilton 1976) For a formal analysis of alternative hypothesis of the Tiebout model, see Epple (1972).

3. The formulas actually used by states are more complicated than that shown in equation (1). In Pennsylvania the state subsidy given to a district depends on the number of students, local wealth, per student cost of education, population density, and various poverty factors.

4. Recapture features have not appeared in actual state subsidy plans. This prevents the plan from having a full, equalizing effect.

5. In certain industries, for example, electrical utilities, the system is so designed that the variable operating or output costs are higher at peak than off peak. A distortion of demand arises when all users are charged the same "average costs" both off and on peak.

REFERENCES

Aaron, Henry, J. 1973. What Do Circuit Breaker Laws Accomplish? In *Property Tax Reform,* ed. George E. Peterson. Washington, D.C.: Urban Institute.

————. 1975. *Who Pays the Property Tax?* Washington, D.C.: Brookings Institution.

ACIR. 1967. *Fiscal Balance in the American Federal System.* A-31, 1. Washington, D.C.: U.S. Government Printing Office.

————. 1973a. *City Financial Emergencies: The Intergovernmental Dimension.* A-42. Washington, D.C.: U.S. Government Printing Office.

————. 1973b. *Financing Schools and Property Tax Relief: A State Responsibility.* Washington, D.C.: U.S. Government Printing Office.

————. 1974. *General Revenue Sharing. An ACIR Re-evaluation.* A-48. Washington, D.C.: U.S. Government Printing Office.

————. 1975. *Property Tax Circuit Breakers: Current Status and Policy Issues.* Washington, D.C.: U.S. Government Printing Office.

————. 1977a. *Block Grants: A Comparative Analysis.* A-60. Washington, D.C.: U.S. Government Printing Office.

————. 1977b. *Measuring the Fiscal "Blood Pressure" of the States, 1964–1975.* M-111. Washington, D.C.: U.S. Government Printing Office.

————. 1977c. *Significant Features of Fiscal Federalism, 1976–1977.* Washington, D.C.: U.S. Government Printing Office.

————. 1977d. *Significant Features of Fiscal Federalism, 1976–1977.* Vol. 3, *Expenditures.* Washington, D.C.: U.S. Government Printing Office.

————. 1977e. *Understanding State and Local Cash Management.* M-112. Washington, D.C.: U.S. Government Printing Office.

————. 1978a. *Categorical Grants: Their Role and Design.* A-52. Washington, D.C.: U.S. Government Printing Office.

————. 1978b. *Countercyclical Aid and Economic Stabilization.* A-69. Washington, D.C.: U.S. Government Printing Office.

————. 1979a. *Significant Features of Fiscal Federalism, 1978–1979.* M-115. Washington, D.C.: U.S. Government Printing Office.

————. 1979b. *State-Local Finances in Recession and Inflation: An Economic Analysis.* A-70. Washington, D.C.: U.S. Government Printing Office.

Adams, Ray D., and Jeffrey S. Rodgers. 1977. Income and Price Effects in the Economic Theory of Clubs. *Public Finance* (2).

Aronson, J. Richard. 1975. Projections of State and Local Trust Fund Financing. In *State-Local Finances in the Last Half of the 1970s,* ed. Attiat Ott et al. Washington, D.C.: American Enterprise Institute.

―――. 1979. *Municipal Fiscal Indicators.* Washington, D.C.: Urban Consortium, for U.S. Department of Housing and Urban Development.

Aronson, J. Richard, and John L. Hilley. 1981. Taxpayer Equity on the Financing of Public Schools. *Selected Papers in Educational Finance,* ed. Esther Tron. Washington, D.C.: U.S. Department of Education, National Institute of Education, School Finance Project.

Aronson, J. Richard, and Arthur E. King. 1978. Is There a Fiscal Crisis Outside of New York? *National Tax Journal* 31(June).

Aronson, J. Richard, and James R. Marsden. 1980. Duplicating Moody's Municipal Credit Ratings. *Public Finance Quarterly* (January).

Aronson, J. Richard, and Eli Schwartz. 1973. Financing Public Goods and the Distribution of Population in a System of Local Government. *National Tax Journal* 26(June).

―――. 1976. Determining Debts' Danger Signals. Management Information Service Report. Washington, D.C.: ICMA.

Bacon, Robert and Walter Eltis. 1978. *Britain's Economic Problem: Too Few Producers.* 2d ed. London: Macmillan.

Bahl, Roy. 1978. *The Fiscal Outlook for Cities.* Syracuse, N.Y.: Syracuse University Press.

Bailey, Elizabeth E. 1972. Peak-Load Pricing under Regulatory Constraint. *Journal of Political Economy* (August).

Baumol, William J., and David F. Bradford. 1970. Optimal Departures from Marginal Cost Pricing. *American Economic Review* (June).

Bendick, Marc. 1974. Designing Circuit Breaker Property Tax Relief. *National Tax Journal* 27(March).

Berglas, Eytan. 1976. On the Theory of Clubs. *American Economic Review* (May).

Black, David, Kenneth Lewis, and Charles Link. 1979. Wealth Neutrality and the Demand for Education. *National Tax Journal* 32(June).

Boskin, Michael. 1979. Some Neglected Economic Factors behind Recent Tax and Spending Limitation Movements. *National Tax Journal* 32(June).

Break, George, F. 1974. The Incidence and Economic Effects of Taxation. In *The Economics of Public Finance,* ed. Alan S. Blinder et al. Washington, D.C.: Brookings Institution.

―――. 1980. Intergovernmental Fiscal Relations. In *Setting National Priorities: Agenda for the 1980s,* ed. Joseph Pechman. Washington, D.C.: Brookings Institution.

Brennan, Geoffrey, and James Buchanan. 1979. The Logic of Tax Limits: Alternative Constitutional Constraints of the Power to Tax. *National Tax Journal* 32(June).

Browning, Edgar, and Johnson, William. 1979. *The Distribution of the Tax Burden.* Washington, D.C.: American Enterprise Institute.

Buchanan, James. 1950. Federalism and Fiscal Equity. *American Economic Review* (September).

―――. 1965. An Economic Theory of Clubs. *Economica* (February).

Cebula, Richard J. 1979. A Survey of the Literature on the Migration Impact of State and Local Government Policies. *Public Finance* (1).

Citrin, Jack. 1979. Do People Want Something for Nothing?: Public Opinion on Taxes and Government Spending. *National Tax Journal* 32(June).

Clark, Terry. 1977. Fiscal Management of American Cities: Funds Flow Indicators. *Journal of Accounting Research* (supplement).

Cook, Bill D. 1973. The Circuit Breaker Approach for Granting Property Tax Relief, with Special Emphasis on Wisconsin and Minnesota. Pt. I, app. E. In *Financing Schools and*

Property Tax Relief: A State Responsibility, ed. ACIR. A-40. Washington, D.C.: U.S. Government Printing Office.

Cook, Bill D., and Kenneth E. Quindry. 1969. Humanization of the Property Tax for Low-Income Households. *National Tax Journal* 22(September).

Coons, John E., William H. Clune, and Stephen D. Sugarman. 1970. *Private Wealth and Public Expenditure.* Cambridge: Cambridge University Press.

Coughlin, Robert, David Berry, and Thomas Plaut. 1978. Differential Assessment of Real Property as an Incentive to Open-Space Preservation and Farmland Retention. *National Tax Journal* 31(June).

Dearborn, Philip M. 1977. Elements of Municipal Financial Analysis. New York: First Boston Corporation.

Denzau, Arthur. 1975. An Empirical Survey of Studies on Public School Spending. *National Tax Journal* 28(June).

Dommel, Paul R., and Richard P. Nathan. 1978. Measuring Community Distress in the United States. Paper presented at seminar on Measuring Local Government Expenditure Needs, Denmark, December.

Downing, Paul, ed. 1977. *Local Service Prices and Their Effect on Urban Spatial Structures.* Vancouver: University of British Columbia Press.

Edel, Matthew, and Elliott Sclar. 1974. Taxes, Spending, and Property Values: Supply Adjustment in a Tiebout-Oates Model. *Journal of Political Economy* 82(5): 941–54.

Epple, Dennis, Allen Zelenitz, and Michael Visscher. 1978. A Search for Testable Implications of the Tiebout Hypothesis. *Journal of Political Economy* (June).

Feldstein, Martin. 1972. Equity and Efficiency in Public Pricing: The Optimal Two-Part Tariff. *Quarterly Journal of Economics* (May).

———. 1975. Wealth Neutrality and Local Choice in Public Education. *American Economic Review* (March).

GAO. 1979. *Funding of State and Local Pension Plans: A National Problem.* Washington, D.C.: U.S. Government Printing Office.

Gatte, James F., and Leonard Tashman. 1976. Equalizing Matching Grants and the Allocative and Distributive Objectives of Public School Financing. *National Tax Journal* 29(December).

———. 1978. Reply. *National Tax Journal* 31(June).

———. The Wealth Neutrality of District Power Equalizing Grants in Public School Financing: Additional Evidence. Business Research and Services Center Working Paper, series no. 78-2.

Gilmen, Robert, and Daniel Morgan, Jr. 1979. Wealth-Neutral Grants for Public Education. *Public Finance Quarterly* (June).

Gold, Steven D. 1979. *Property Tax Relief.* Lexington, Mass.: D. C. Heath.

Greenough, William, and Francis King. 1976. *Pension Plans and Public Policy.* New York: Columbia University Press.

Gustely, Richard D. 1976. Local Taxes, Expenditures, and Urban Housing: A Reassessment of the Evidence. *Southern Economic Journal* 42(April): 659–65.

Guttentag, Jack. 1979. New Life in the Old Family Mortgage. *Wharton Magazine* (Summer).

Hamilton, Bruce. 1976. The Effect of Property Taxes and Local Public Spending on Property Values: A Theoretical Comment. *Journal of Political Economy* 82(3): 647–50.

Helpman, Ethanam, and Arye L. Hillman. 1977. Two Remarks on Optimal Club Size. *Economica* (August).

Hotelling, Harold. 1938. The General Welfare in Relation to Problems of Taxation and Railway and Utility Rates. *Econometrica* (July).

Hovey, Harold. 1978. State-Local Intergovernmental Finance. In *State and Local Government Finance and Financial Management: A Compendium of Current Research*, ed. John E. Petersen, Catharine L. Spain, and Martharose Laffey, 95. Washington, D.C.: Municipal Finance Officers Association, Government Finance Research Center.

Johnson, Marvin, and Judith Collins. 1978. Equalizing Matching Grants and the Allocative and Distributive Objectives of Public School Financing: A Comment. *National Tax Journal* 31(June).

Ladd, Helen F. 1975. Local Education Expenditures, Fiscal Capacity, and Composition of the Property Base. *National Tax Journal* 28(June).

Lewis, Arthur W. 1941a. The Two-Part Tariff. *Economica* (August).

Lewis, Arthur W. 1941b. The Two-Part Tariff: A Reply. *Economica* (November).

Lochner, Allyn O., and Kim, Han J. 1973. Circuit Breakers on Farm Property Tax Overload: A Case Study. *National Tax Journal* 26(June).

Margolis, Julius. Forthcoming. Fiscal Problems of Political Boundaries: The Central and Suburban Cities. In *Management Policies in Local Government Finance*. Washington, D.C.: ICMA.

Matz, Deborah. Forthcoming. The Tax and Expenditure Limitation Movement. In *Urban Government Finances in the 1980s*, ed. Roy Bahl. Beverly Hills: Sage.

Maxwell, James A., and J. Richard Aronson. 1977. *Financing State and Local Government*. Washington, D.C.: Brookings Institution.

Moohring, Herbert. 1970. The Peak-Load Problem with Increasing Returns and Pricing Constraints. *American Economic Review* (September).

Moody's. 1977. *Moody's Analytical Overview of 25 Leading U.S. Cities*. N.p.: Moody's Investors Service.

Mushkin, Selma J. 1972. *Public Prices for Public Products*. Washington, D.C.: Urban Press.

Myers, Will, and John Shannon. 1979. Revenue Sharing for States: An Endangered Species. *Intergovernmental Perspective* (Summer).

Nathan, Richard P., Allen D. Manvel, and Susannah E. Calkins. 1975. *Monitoring Revenue Sharing*. Washington, D.C.: Brookings Institution.

National Tax Journal 32(supplement). 1979. Proceedings of a conference on Tax and Expenditure Limitations, University of California, Santa Barbara, June.

Ng, Y. 1973. The Economic Theory of Clubs: Optimal Tax Subsidy. *Economica* (August).

Ng, Y., and M. Weisser. 1974. Optimal Pricing with a Budget Constraint: The Case of the Two-Part Tariff. *Review of Economic Studies* (July).

Oakland, William. 1979. Proposition 13: Genesis and Consequences. *National Tax Journal* 32(June).

Oates, Wallace E. 1969. The Effects of Property Taxes and Local Public Spending on Property Values: An Empirical Study of Tax Capitalization and the Tiebout Hypothesis. *Journal of Political Economy*. 77(6): 957–71.

————. 1972. *Fiscal Federalism*. New York: Harcourt Brace Jovanovich.

————. 1973. The Effects of Property Taxes and Local Public Spending on Property Values: A Reply and Yet Further Results. *Journal of Political Economy* 81(4): 1004–8.

————, ed. 1975. *Financing the New Federalism*. Baltimore: Johns Hopkins University Press, for Resources for the Future.

Office of Management and Budget. 1982. *Special Analysis: Budget of the U.S. Government, FY 1981*. Washington, D.C.: U.S. Government Printing Office.

Oi, Walter Y. 1972. A Disneyland Dilemma: Two-Part Tariffs for a Mickey Mouse Monopoly. *Quarterly Journal of Economics* (May).

Ott, Attiat, and Jang Yoo. 1975. *New York City's Financial Crisis: Can the Trend Be Reversed?* Washington, D.C.: American Enterprise Institute.

Panzar, John C. 1976. A Neoclassical Approach to Peak-Load Pricing. *Bell Journal of Economics* (Autumn).

Peat, Marwick, and Mitchell & Co. 1978. *Financial Warning Indicators Handbook.* Washington, D.C.: ICMA.

Pechman, Joseph, and Benjamin Okner. 1974. *Who Bears the Tax Burden?* Washington, D.C.: Brookings Institution.

Petersen, John E. 1974. *The Rating Game.* New York: Twentieth-Century Fund.

———. 1981. Pension Fund Management. In *Management Policies in Local Government Finance,* ed. J. R. Aronson and E. Schwartz. Washington, D.C.: ICMA.

Petersen, John E., Catherine L. Spain, and Martharose Laffey, eds. 1978. *State and Local Government Finance and Financial Management: A Compendium of Current Research.* Washington, D.C.: Municipal Finance Officers Association, Government Finance Research Center.

Pollakowski, Henry O. 1973. The Effects of Property Taxes and Local Public Spending on Property Values: A Comment and Further Results. *Journal of Political Economy* 81(4): 994–1003.

Quindry, Kenneth E. 1973. Residential Property Tax Relief for Senior Citizens in Maine and Vermont. Pt. II, app. E. In *Financing Schools and Property Tax Relief: A State Responsibility,* ed. ACIR. A-40. Washington, D.C.: U.S. Government Printing Office.

Reischauer, Robert D., and Robert W. Hartman. 1973. *Reforming School Finance.* Washington, D.C.: Brookings Institution.

Rodgers, James D. 1981. Local Sales and Income Taxes and Miscellaneous Revenues. In *Management Policies in Local Government Finance,* ed. J. R. Aronson and E. Schwartz. Washington, D.C.: ICMA.

Rowson, R. B. 1941. The Two-Part Tariff. *Economica* (November).

Shannon, John. 1973. The Property Tax: Reform or Relief? In *Property Tax Reform,* ed. George E. Peterson. Washington, D.C.: Urban Institute.

Shannon, John, and Frank Tippett. 1978. An Analysis of State Personal Income Taxes and Property Tax Circuit Breakers. Paper presented at the 46th meeting of the National Association of Tax Administrators, June.

Shapiro, Perry, David Puryear, and John Ross. 1979. Tax and Expenditure Limitation in Retrospect and in Prospect. *National Tax Journal* 32(June).

Summers, Anita. 1979. Proposition 13 and Its Aftermath. *Business Review* (March/April).

Thornton, Robert J. 1981. Towards the Development of More Comprehensive Measures of School-District Wealth. *Selected Papers in School Finance,* ed. Esther Tron. Washington, D.C.: U.S. Department of Education, National Institute of Education, School Finance Project.

Tiebout, Charles. 1956. A Pure Theory of Local Expenditure. *Journal of Political Economy* (October).

Tilove, Robert. 1974. *Study of Public Employee Retirement Systems.* New York: Twentieth Century Fund.

Touche Ross & Co. and First National Bank of Boston. 1979. *Urban Fiscal Crisis: A Comparative Analysis of 66 U.S. Cities.* New York.

U.S. Congress. Joint Economic Committee. 1980. *Trends in the Fiscal Condition of Cities, 1978–1980.* April.

U.S. Congress. House of Representatives. 1978. *Task Force Report on Public Employee Retirement Systems.* Washington, D.C.

U.S. Department of Commerce. Bureau of the Census. 1979. *City Government Finances in 1976–77*. Washington, D.C.: U.S. Government Printing Office.

Vickrey, William. 1971. Responsive Pricing of Public Utility Services. *Bell Journal of Economics* (Spring).

Wicksell, Knut. 1967. A New Principle of Just Taxation. Reprinted in *Classics in the Theory of Public Finance*, ed. R. A. Musgrave and A. Peacock.
White, Michelle. 1979. Government Response to Spending Limitations. *National Tax Journal* 32(June).

8

Management and Accountability Models of Public Sector Performance

Ronald W. Johnson
Arie Y. Lewin

The problem of measuring the performance of private or public sector organizations is fundamental to any society concerned with the accountability and performance of its institutions. In the private sector it has been assumed that, in the long run, the discipline of the marketplace motivates corporations to strive for cost efficiency and maximization of profit, facilitated by a feedback system that informs managers about the quality of their decisions. Even though it is apparent that private firms pursue multiple goals, the market system, though imperfect, still provides for economic (as distinct from social) indicators of performance with such measures as profits, rates of return on investments, and market shares.

In contrast with the private sector, the public sector lacks both an analogue for profit-seeking behavior and an adequate feedback system to learn about the quality of decisions. As a result, evaluating the performance of government organizations and guiding performance improvement is difficult. This has not kept the public from judging governmental institutions and finding them wanting. Popular movements for tax limitation and responses to opinion surveys provide sufficient evidence that the performance of the public sector is deficient in the view of many citizens (ACIR 1980; Wright 1981). These opinions, however, are formed around general impressions rather than around well-defined performance measures. In this chapter, we examine several rigorous models and methods for evaluating public sector performance.

As we have seen in prior chapters, the public's critique of government can in part be represented by normative models of *political performance*. These models deal with questions of equity and collective choice, and can be used to make design choices about political institutions. Normative models of public *service delivery*, the subject of this chapter, are used to improve service delivery efficiency and effectiveness. Some of the models we review are internally oriented; that is, they aim to enhance managers' abilities to improve performance. Others are more externally oriented; that is, they aim to provide citizens with more precise indicators of performance as a means of enhancing feedback to public managers. We conclude with models that bridge internal and external orientations and link performance indicators with information about actions to improve performance.

Two basic conceptions of performance underlie much of the literature. The *engineering* approach defines performance as a ratio of resources consumed (inputs) to standard units of work produced (e.g., horsepower, kilowatt hour). For a given mechanical design, a theoretical absolute level of performance is defined, and the performance of every machine is measured against that standard. The *economic marketplace* approach associates levels of production with resources consumed, but the theoretical limit of performance is not specified. Public sector analysts have borrowed parts of the engineering and marketplace concepts of performance, although not always with explicit discussion of underlying assumptions.

To evaluate public sector performance models, we assume a basic organizational model that treats the public sector as a production system that transforms inputs into outputs (see figure 8.1). Outputs reflect the goals of the general public, of narrow elites, of public managers, or of some combination. Models for improving public sector performance then relate to some aspect of the goal measurement process, the production process, or both. Thus, an organization with a program planning and budgeting system and an intervening performance measurement system has the capability to determine whether it is achieving its goals. To the extent that these measures are made public, the public also has the means to determine whether public institutions are meeting their expectations. This production model is fundamental to various approaches to improving or measuring effectiveness through program planning and budgeting and performance indicators.

Measuring the efficiency of an organization is the critical focus of performance assessment. To accomplish this task it is necessary to relate the utilization of resources to the production of outputs. Ideally, efficiency measures utilize knowledge about both the production process and its performance potential. For example, the theoretical performance of an internal combustion engine is calculated from its engineering design data, and its actual efficiency is then related to its potential efficiency. In the case of public sector organizations, such efficiency calculations are not feasible at present because it is not possible to specify the organizational production system or to compute its theoretical output capacity. Furthermore, we lack single output measures that

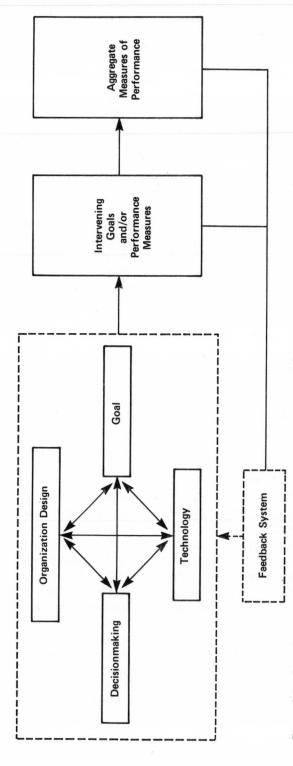

Figure 8.1 Organizational Model of the Public Sector as a Production System

satisfactorily capture the full range of public sector goals. The basic problem of transforming multiple, noncommensurate output measures into a single aggregate performance indicator remains, though some methods hold promise of producing an assessment of overall productivity.

Although measurement is more difficult for the public sector, approaches taken to increasing effectiveness and efficiency are largely the same as for private sector organizations. These efforts center on organization design/redesign strategies, application of the management sciences to improve decision making and information processing, technological innovation to increase productivity, and new public disclosure mechanisms to enhance the effectiveness of feedback systems. Implicit in all of these approaches is the assumption that improvement on any of the above dimensions will lead to better organizational performance.

For private sector organizations, the existence of such aggregate measures of performance as profits and rates of return on investments makes it possible (at least, in theory) to test cause and effect relationships, track performance over time, and derive aggregate relative performance measures. In contrast, citizens, whose investment in governmental organizations through taxes is both considerable and largely involuntary have no ready means of evaluating their "return on investment." Tiebout's classic market analogy of citizens "voting with their feet" depends on the availability of some level of information about the relative performance of local governments (1956). However imperfect the available information about the relative performance of private organizations may be, it far surpasses the information about public organizations.

Despite such limitations, there is a considerable body of research on public sector production functions and performance indicators. Optimization models have been used to good effect for public services whose outputs are easily quantified. These models define theoretical frontiers consisting of levels of output at which, subject to constraints (e.g., a budget limit), an organization cannot further improve its performance. Other models offer market-type comparisons by estimating output levels for similar "producers" of the same public service. These comparisons reveal performance differences, making it possible for efficiency to be rewarded. Promising models are examined in three sections: (1) internal management approaches, (2) external accounting approaches, and (3) external performance measurement approaches.

MANAGEMENT APPROACHES TO IMPROVED PUBLIC SECTOR PERFORMANCE

The performance models evaluated in this section are focused primarily on the production function. That is, the key variables are those that describe the production process itself. Four relatively distinct models are discussed. The first has been labeled by most of the literature as the "goal model." Major emphasis on this model is given to the goal specification process. Offshoots of the model build general approaches to improving performance around the act of goal definition itself (e.g., improved instructional performance is hypothesized to be a function of defining behavioral objectives). A second general model virtually ignores goals, objectives, or associated measures, focusing on the characteristics of the production system itself. This "systems model" hypothesizes that improved performance results from effective organizational design. The third approach shares many of the characteristics of the goal model, especially its focus on output and outcome measures. We have labeled this approach the "decision systems design model." It is distinguished from the goal model, which generally relates to single organizations, by its concern with large-scale decision systems in identifiable interorganizational relations. The fourth category actually consists of a collection of models, primarily drawn from operations research, oriented to very specific problem-solving situations.

Goal Models

Much of the literature presenting goal models has focused on private sector organizations. Generally, organizational performance is equated with effectiveness, which is measured as goal attainment or productivity. The goal model of effectiveness relies on a formal specification of a hierarchy of goals, objectives, and measures of effect. However, it does not necessarily adopt official goals; in fact, most of that literature argues that official policies are only one part of the set of goals that an organization pursues.

> In summary, . . . measurement for management decision proceeds from the assumptions that the organization pursues goals and objectives and has measures of performance; the organization serves a client; it is comprised of sub-units which themselves pursue goals and objectives and have measures of performance; it operates in the context of a series of constraints and demands which constitute its environment; it has a managerial function which makes decisions on the allocation of resources; it has a designer who conceptualizes the organization and its measurement system; the designer's intent is to maximize the value rendered to the client and, there is a guarantor for the organization, its performance and its measurement system. (Mason and Swanson 1977, 13)

Similar statements of the goal model approach emphasize that effective organizations are those that organize around a set of objectives, determine the activities necessary to achieve those objectives, and allocate resources to those activities. Effectiveness is thus seen either as an undefined by-product of a goal-focused decision-making structure or as a set of discrete measures of the effects of specified organizational activities. As applied to governmental organizations, the goal model of effectiveness has stressed the analysis of program costs in relation to program effects. Military systems were among the early programs thus analyzed (Hitch and McKean 1960; Hitch 1965; Knorr 1967), but extensions of the model have also been made to diverse functions such as health and welfare (Rivlin 1961; Goldman 1968; Grosse 1970).

In a narrower version of the goal model approach, measurement attention is directed to the internal organizational goals of different subunits. Simon et al. (1954) focused on the use of accounting data within a firm to serve three purposes:

1. Scorecard questions related to performance in relation to preset standards.

2. Attention-directing questions related to problem detection.

3. Problem-solving questions related to alternative methods of task performance.

Recent analyses of the use of accounting-based information for organizational performance assessment go beyond the strictly internal data sources suggested by Simon et al. and suggest the need for external evidence of the outcomes of organizational activities (Anthony 1978).

Systems Models

Goal models are generally used to equate performance with effectiveness and to focus on measures of goal attainment. In contrast, systems models often do not measure effectiveness at all. Barnard's vague definitions of efficiency and effectiveness are typical. His classic work described effectiveness as the attainment of desired ends, and his unique, nonquantitative definition of efficiency provides a basic clue to contemporary analysis of effectiveness (1938, 19). To Barnard, efficiency is satisfaction of individual motivations. Thus, an efficient organization is one that provides the minimum number and types of incentives necessary to obtain maximum productive behavior from employees. Barnard's sense of efficiency has become almost the basic concept of effectiveness in a large body of contemporary literature (not necessarily with attribution to Barnard as the source). In its contemporary form, this Barnard-like approach is variously labeled a systems approach, a systems model, or a natural systems theory of organization effectiveness (Georgopaoulos and Tanenbaum 1957; Etzioni 1960; Enthoven and Smith 1971). That is, organizational effectiveness is considered such a difficult concept to operationalize that the systems model appears to posit effectiveness as an unmeasured resultant of a variety of system characteristics. Campbell describes the position in this way:

> The natural systems view makes the assumption that if an organization is of any size at all, the demands placed on it are so dynamic and complex that it is not possible to define a finite number of organizational goals in any meaningful way. . . . Since ultimate criteria of organizational functioning are so hard to conceptualize and measure, the next best thing is to measure variables representing the state of the system. (1977, 20)

The search for an operational concept of effectiveness, in this view, is abandoned in favor of a search for the set of variables hypothesized to lead to effectiveness. One of the most often cited representatives of this approach is the paper by Seashore and Likert in *Harvard Business Review,* which argued that managerial style, participation by lower-level personnel in organizational decision-making processes, and consultative communication patterns will lead to increased effectiveness (1969).

> The highest producing managers, on the average, do not achieve their high-productivity, low-cost operations by putting direct, hierarchical pressure on their subordinates. They obtain high productivity levels by building cooperative organizations that have high motivation, high performance goals, efficient communication, and good teamwork, and that seek in every way to achieve the organization's objectives in the most economical and most efficient manner.

Literally thousands of pages of print have been devoted to identifying additional variables linked to a still largely unmeasured concept of effectiveness. Among these sets of variables are:

- Environmental characteristics
  Input set
  Output set
  Task environment

- Individual characteristics
  Motivation
  Incentive

- Structural characteristics
  Centralization/decentralization
  Hierarchy
  Leadership style

In that general body of literature, preference is given to specifying the sets of variables and interrelationships that are theorized to lead to effectiveness (Pennings 1976; Van De Ven and Ferry 1980). In the smaller subset of empirical literature, which attempts to test some of the hypothesized relationships, effectiveness is measured either as net profit or as reputation for productivity in private sector organizations, or as multiple indicators of goal attainment in public and private sector organizations.

Decision Systems Design Models

The specific body of literature concerned with governmental efficiency is a twentieth-century phenomenon. In the nineteenth century, customs duties and excise taxes provided sufficient revenue for federal expenditures, and little concern was voiced for either the budget size or the results of budget expenditures. The earliest concerns for measuring efficiency in government and devising mechanisms for its achievement appeared around the beginning of this century (Taft 1912; Lee and Johnson 1982).

The more recent literature on achieving efficiency and effectiveness through planning and decision-making structures, however, draws heavily from post–World War II developments in operations research and systems analysis (Knorr 1967). The classic application of this tradition to governmental organizations is McKean's *Efficiency in Government through Systems Analysis, with Emphasis on Water Resource Development* (1958). Relying on an economic concept of efficiency, adherents to this tradition have emphasized the application of systems-analytic techniques to maximize outputs in relation to inputs or minimize inputs to achieve a given level of output. Where possible, they have also argued that price imputations, shadow prices, or estimated dollar values should be attributed to the outputs of governmental projects to permit application of the cost-benefit analytic model (Lee and Johnson 1982). Prest and Turvey's survey article defines this approach as aiming to "maximize the present value of all benefits less that of all costs, subject to specified constraints. . . . Further, it implies the enumeration and evaluation of all the relevant costs and benefits" (1965, 3).

The measure of efficiency implied in this approach is a welfare economics concept of total-system efficiency. That is, a system (e.g., economy, government, organization) is efficient "when every reorganization that augments the value of one variable necessarily reduces the value of another" (Ferguson 1972, 491). The application of this concept of efficiency led in the 1960s to systems design efforts to create a decision-making context within which governmental expenditures could be compared for their relative "rates of return." In other words, governmental programs could be made more efficient by paying explicit attention to measures of both program inputs and program outputs and making resource allocation decisions on a comparative basis (that is, comparisons among program alternatives).

The first major application of the structured comparison approach to a large governmental program was to defense systems. Building on earlier attempts to improve defense budgetary practices, the Defense Department in the early 1960s under Robert McNamara attempted to link systematic planning with budgetary decisions. For a while, the appeal of planning, programming, budgeting system (PPBS) seemed universal. President Johnson ordered its application to all civilian agencies in 1965, and numerous state and local governments joined in by redesigning their budgetary decision systems. In part because of overselling by proponents and overreaction of opponents, the grand systems design features of PPBS have gradually disappeared, taken on new names, or otherwise disguised any link with the legacies of the sixties.

The distinctive character of the decision system-design approach, as far as the concepts of efficiency and effectiveness are concerned, has not disappeared, however. Federal, state, and local governments routinely collect large amounts of data on program inputs and outputs. And they just as regularly attempt to describe program success and failure in terms of input/output comparisons. Zero-based budgeting attempts to structure the resource allocation decision around program accomplishments, requiring that an agency or program defend not only its recommended budget changes but its budget base as well. Sunset legislation takes perhaps the most conservative theoretical stance. That is, after a period of time, an agency is required to demonstrate the harm that would occur if it were abolished, and if it cannot demonstrate substantial consequences, there is presumably no rationale for its continuation.

Despite its dedication to the measurement of output and input, the planning, programming, decision systems approach has a significant limitation: outputs are not measured for the organization as a whole. Thus, after all the manipulation of program data, overall performance is defined in terms of internal processes, as it is in the systems model. That is, if the decision-making system is structured according to the PPBS model, then the result is assumed to be overall system efficiency (or effectiveness or both). Efficiency and effectiveness are thus implicitly defined as products of decision structures rather than as operational concepts in and of themselves.

Specifically, output-oriented decision structures collect volumes of measures of program inputs and outputs for individual activities, and measures are rigorously defined with respect to program objectives (e.g., miles of highway paved, number of clients serviced, number of jury trials). Although useful to the specific activity that produced the output, these activity-focused measures do not aggregate very well into a sense of the efficiency of the organization or governmental unit. For example, the time, materials, and equipment used in relation to a number of miles of highway paved may say something about the efficiency of highway paving. However, since the department also may be responsible for hole patching, marking safety crossings, erecting crash barriers, and so forth, the separate efficiencies of each activity are difficult to interpret as some aggregate indicator of departmental efficiency. In the next subsection, we look at an almost entirely distinct body of literature, which focuses on the specific application of optimizing and nonoptimizing techniques to particular governmental activities.

Management Sciences Models

The systematic application of the management sciences to improve decision making and information processing in organizations originated, as noted above, in World War II, when applied mathematics and simulation techniques were used in the Defense Department. Since then, the fields of operations research and management sciences have developed as separate disciplinary fields with theoretical and applied orientations. As we saw in the previous section, the more general systematic approach involved in systems analysis techniques led to general strategies for decision-making systems designs such as various PPBS models. More specific management science applications in industry and government involve optimizing and nonoptimizing techniques. Thus, depending on the characteristics of the decision—scope, location in the organization, unique or recurring nature, substance, and ultimate application—different types of analytical methods have been applied. These methods include descriptive, physical, simulation, mathematical, prediction and optimization, deterministic and probabilistic, dynamic and recursive, econometric, and input/output models, as well as mathematical programming formulations and decision-tree analyses. The application of such methodologies also involves choice of analytical approach, determination of data requirements and data availability, and implementation.

The decision-making problem situations to which these methodologies have been applied include planning, policy analysis and policy making, project management, manpower planning, environmental analysis and resource management (e.g., air pollution, solid waste, water resources), urban development (land use, zoning decisions), urban management, transportation planning, law enforcement and criminal justice, fire suppression, educational planning and operations and health care planning and delivery (Davis and Weidenbaum 1969; Cooper 1970, 1972; Gass and Sisson 1974; Lewin and Shakuu 1976). The uses to which specific management science technologies have been applied are primarily in those governmental services whose characteristics most closely resemble private sector organizations. Issues are cast often in terms of solving "what if" types of policy questions, scheduling problems (queuing models), location of service over a geographic area (warehousing and transportation models), and planning and control problems (PERT, CPM, GANTT).

Although there have been some successes in solving specific governmental service delivery problems, these applications of specific techniques do not really address the overall governmental performance problem. This latter point is best illustrated by the NYC-RAND studies in the early 1970s involving resource allocations and increased productivity of the New York City fire and police departments (RAND 1979). The NYC-RAND fire project is probably best known for the impact that the studies had on fire service deployment in New York City between 1972 and 1976. In 1972, for example, the RAND team and its models played an important role in providing the analyses that resulted in the decisions to disband six fire companies and permanently relocate seven others. It must be noted, however, that those decisions were made in the course of a long political process and that the preferred solution of the RAND team did not include disbandment of companies.

Overall, between 1972 and 1976, 26 companies were disbanded in New York City, representing about a 7 percent reduction in force or a commensurate increase in productivity. In addition, the RAND studies resulted in better work-load balancing and the use of part-time companies, adaptive response strategies, computerized dispatching, and other innovations. Yet to this day controversy abounds regarding the effectiveness and efficiency of the outcome of these studies and how the implementation of NYC-RAND studies related to the overall performance of New York City (Chaiken et al. 1980; Wallace and Wallace 1980).

AUDIT-BASED ACCOUNTING MODELS

The more internally oriented, management-improvement-type models discussed in the previous section tend to focus on the organizational production function rather than on the measurement of organizational performance. Although the scope of these models ranges from narrowly focused management tools, like scheduling, to very broad decision systems designs, like PPBS, the emphasis is on the design or redesign of the processes by which public sector outputs are produced. The models discussed in this section, though also exhibiting a wide range, are more oriented toward the measurement of outputs. They have a common link to accounting-based approaches in that accounting methods and auditing are emphasized. These models also are transitional, in that the more broad-based, full-scale management audits with which this section concludes consider both the level of outputs and the organizational production process. Included in this section are discussions of the public sector counterpart to the corporate annual report and the broad-scale management audits of federal agencies conducted by the General Accounting Office (GAO).

Urban Annual Reports

Several authors have focused explicit attention on the use of the citizen/government feedback loop as a means to improving governmental performance. For example, Lewin and Blanning (1974) have proposed that municipal governments be required to publish an annual report to their residents similar to the annual report published by corporations for their stockholders. They argue that the various constituents of a local jurisdiction have a legitimate need for information about the activities of a city government not unlike those of investors in a corporation. Traditionally, the investors in a municipality were considered to be its bondholders, and the disclosure of municipal financial information was tailored to meet their needs. Following the corporate example, there is a need to define the group of direct and indirect investors in a municipality. Such a definition reaches beyond the traditional view of bondholders as the sole investors in a municipality. The rationale for requiring municipalities to publish an annual report is based on the need to provide municipal investors with information equivalent to that received by their corporate counterparts and on the need to achieve greater accountability of municipal governments to their publics.

A successful development of a formalized municipal reporting requirement must answer several intervening questions:

1. Who are the users of municipal performance information?

2. What are their information needs?

3. What should be the structure and content of the report?

4. How and by whom should a report be certified, and what are the issues involved in implementation?

There is a substantial body of literature dealing with the first question. In a public report on the financial disclosure practices of the American cities (a joint project of Coopers & Lybrand and the University of Michigan), two groups, municipal taxpayers and investors in securities, are cited as important users (1976). The Council on Municipal Performance (1974), in its concluding volume on *Municipal Securities Regulation,* identified the primary and secondary users of financial disclosure documents, and a similar classification was made by Anthony (1978). However, to date, municipal reporting has not developed an accepted list of users or potential users whose information needs should be met. Corporate reporting, on the other hand, has developed such a list. This list, included in *Basic Concepts and Accounting Practices underlying Financial Statements of Business Enterprise* (Accounting Principles Board 1975), is divided into two user types—those with a direct interest and those with an indirect interest. The direct users—owners, creditors, suppliers, management, taxing authorities, employees, and customers—have or may have a direct economic interest. For a corporation, indirect users—financial analysts, stock exchanges, lawyers, registration authorities, financial press, labor unions, trade associations, and special interest groups—are those whose function is to assist or protect those who have or may have a direct interest (Lewin and Scheiner 1978).

In the municipal reporting context, the concept of users must also be expanded beyond the traditional definition of equity owners and debt holders. A more comprehensive definition should include citizens who reside in or are potential residents of a municipality and any individual, group of individuals, or business firms investing in land, buildings (including homes), or leasehold improvements within a municipality. A significant percentage of these actors are making what are, for them, substantial investments. Individuals who purchase homes are typically making the largest investment of their lives. Business firms also make substantial investments in municipalities, which require careful examination of alternatives. Furthermore, all of these investors can be viewed as purchasing through their payment of taxes a portfolio of services whose costs and benefits must be assessed by them. Volkswagen's decision on the location of its first U.S. factory is an excellent example of the relationship between a potential investor in a locality and that locality, and of the information needed by the investor to choose the location of the investment. All these investments and purchases of municipal services are typically made by individuals and corporations without access to the same type of information disclosed to investors in corporate securities.

Although there is some consensus on who are the potential users of an urban annual report, there is less agreement on the contents of such a report. Much of the research has focused on fiscal and financial reporting (Anthony 1978; Williams 1978; Drebin 1979). Lewin and Cahill have developed a more detailed general model for municipal financial and performance statements (1976). It is clear, however, that any application of the concept of an urban annual report will require a consensus on the structure and content of such a report. Although such a consensus is still far off, some municipalities have experimented with annual reports of the type proposed by Lewin and Blanning (1974). Notable among them are Sunnyvale, California, and Dallas, Texas.

Technical implementation of the municipal annual report concept does not require or imply a need for a consensus on the *internal* decision-making structure or on the *internal* information processing of a local government. Such a consensus does not exist in the case of business firms either, yet comparisons of performance go on routinely among shareholders, financial analysts, lenders, and so forth. However, further research is needed on how an urban annual report could be used in situations where one or more services are provided on an interjurisdictional basis by different jurisdictions (e.g., water and mass transportation districts). In principle, it is feasible to make the necessary adjustments, on an ad hoc basis, to enable comparisons of performance. At this time, however, the problem of achieving comparability in the case where some services are provided interjurisdictionally remains.

The political feasibility of implementing the concept of an annual report is yet another problem. A priori there is no reason to expect any political bureaucracy to opt voluntarily for opening itself to public scrutiny. Public bureaucracies have been described as motivated to secure independence from outside control (Rogers 1968; Hawley and Rogers 1974). Further, most state and local governments can be described as a collection of loosely coupled, quasi-independent agencies motivated to maintain their independence by securing support for their programs directly from the relevant legislative bodies, often bypassing the governor, cabinet secretary, or mayor (Crecine 1967; Gerwin 1969, 1973; Davis and Reuter 1972). In addition, the resistance of bureaucracies to change, the stability of municipal resource allocation decisions, the incrementalism of the budget process, and the limited control of mayors over budget requests and appropriations have been reported (Lewin and Shakuu 1976).

Finally, it is important to recognize the episodic nature of public interest in the problem of public sector performance at the national, state, or local level. Without public interest and participation in the performance evaluation of local government, the likelihood of such an idea being implemented decreases. Clearly, the issues involved with the political feasibility of the concept are not well understood and merit further study.

Broad-Scope Management Audits

The independent audit of governmental performance offers another strategy based on the public disclosure mechanism to achieve accountability, efficiency, and effectiveness on the part of governmental systems. Traditionally (and to date, in most states and city governments), the role of the comptroller was limited to legislative compliance audits—verification of the legality of the expenditures by state and local governments. Within the federal government, a few of the states, and Canada, a gradual shift has occurred in the role and function of the independent comptroller. In this section we focus on the broad-scope or comprehensive audit as it has been applied by the GAO.

The Budget and Accounting Act of 1921 resulted in two new agencies: the Bureau of the Budget (now the OMB), as part of the executive branch, and the GAO, as part of the legislative branch. The GAO is by statute directly and solely responsible to the Congress under the direction of the comptroller general, who serves for a single term of 15 years. The comptroller general has the discretion to initiate audits but must also undertake audits requested by chairpersons of congressional committees.

Starting from a narrow legislative compliance view of its function, the GAO, under the direction of former Comptroller General Elmer B. Staats, gradually broadened the definition of its function toward an emphasis on performance audits and program evaluation. Evaluating program results and attaining program goals are among GAO mandates as a result of the Legislative Reorganization Act of 1970 and the Congressional Budget Reform Act of 1974 (Staats 1976).

These audits are designed to examine all phases of management activities with respect to financial compliance, economy and efficiency, effectiveness of results, and propriety of goals and means to achieve these goals. Financial compliance involves a determination of (a) whether financial operations are properly conducted, (b) whether the financial reports of the audited entity are presented fairly, and (c) whether the entity has complied with applicable laws and regulations. *Economy and efficiency* concern the utilization of resources and the causes of any inefficiencies or uneconomical practices. *Effectiveness* involves a determination of management's objectives and the extent to which these objectives have been attained. *Propriety* refers to a determination of the appropriateness or acceptability of objectives as well as of the methods, processes, and procedures employed to achieve these objectives with respect to legislative intent.

Under the comprehensive audit the GAO determines the scope of the audit. Furthermore, the audit report is submitted to Congress with a response from the agency or program that has been audited. It then is up to Congress to initiate or mandate corrective action. Through its comprehensive audit procedures (which are still evolving), the GAO motivates accountability and concern with efficiency and effectiveness. These goals are attained because agencies adjust their own behavior in anticipation of the audit and through disclosure, which may prompt, and often results in, focusing legislative oversight (Churchill and Cyert 1966; Churchill et al. 1976).

It is important to note that research on the effectiveness of the comprehensive audit approach remains to be carried out. Rigorous case studies are needed, because the comprehensive audit is generally an in-depth study of a single program (e.g., the armed forces' recruitment practices) or an agency (e.g., the FBI) and is not at all amenable to comparative analyses.

PUBLIC SECTOR PERFORMANCE MEASUREMENT

The final set of models that have been applied to the problems of measuring and improving public sector performance treat performance measurement explicitly. Performance measurement models range from approaches that focus almost exclusively on the output side to more integrative models that include analysis of the production function.

Performance Indicators

Considerable credit for the early application of applying efficiency and effectiveness concepts to governmental organizations goes to the local government service delivery effectiveness projects of the Urban Institute (UI). The UI approach resembles the planning, programming, decision system approach in linking performance measurement with analysis and thence to resource allocation decisions. It differs substantially from PPBS, however, in that it recommends elaborate, hierarchical program structures. The focus is on specific services, regardless of which governmental unit produces the service. A summary paragraph from one UI report characterizes the approach.

> The measures and data collection methods in this report focus on those procedures appropriate for periodic measurement in order to permit tracking of problems, progress, and trends. These procedures were not developed to identify *why* conditions are as they are, nor *what should be done* about them. Accurate information about the outcomes of a service is, however, likely to be of significant help to local decision makers. Such information should aid in identifying priorities for necessary in-depth program analyses or evaluations. (Hatry et al. 1977, 4)

The above excerpt places the UI approach squarely in the program analysis tradition and is, as we said, reminiscent of the program budgeting literature. Whereas the PPBS-type approach is aimed at developing a comprehensive decision-making system, however, the UI approach focuses more narrowly on the potential outputs of governmental activities and the development of indicator lists for the periodic assessment of these activities.

The UI approach begins with a statement of objectives for each service to be assessed. These general statements of objectives are then the base from which measures are derived. For example, one UI document defines the objective for effective solid waste collection as one that will "promote the aesthetics of the community and the health and safety of the citizens by providing an environment free from the hazards and unpleasantness of uncollected refuse with the least possible citizen inconvenience" (Hatry et al. 1977, 4). The statement describes both the ends sought (promotion of aesthetics, health and safety) and the general means for accomplishment (keeping the environment free of the hazards of uncollected refuse). Performance (in this case defined as effectiveness) measures are then derived from the key terms in the statement of objectives—aesthetics, health and safety, citizen convenience and satisfaction. Fifteen measures are derived, such as appearance ratings, rodent bites, and citizen complaints. None of the measures includes amount of garbage picked up, frequency of collection, or other measures of volume often associated with a service. Since these latter measures are not logically deducible from the statement of objectives, they are therefore excluded.

One might argue that other measures are easily added to the UI set and that no one can be assured that all relevant measures are included; indeed, Hatry has stated that potential users are warned that the UI objectives may not match those of a particular community, and other measures should be considered (personal communication 1980). Although this is true, the crux of the issue is not the number of measures but the methodology employed. Ultimately, the methodology is self-limiting, either in the attempt to achieve a consensus definition of objectives across communities (or even within a single community) or in relying on the objectives as an a priori basis for defining measures.

Finally, as is true of other major performance measurement efforts, the UI approach does not include a data reduction technology for aggregating its multiple performance indicators. Thus, both managers and citizens may find it difficult to draw conclusions about overall performance on the basis of mixed results on individual measures.

Comparative Performance Analysis

Methods that compare actual performance measures across governmental jurisdictions to provide citizens with reference points solve some of the difficulties noted above. However, examples of this approach are not numerous, with "probably the most extensive effort . . . by the Research Triangle Institute" (National Productivity Council 1979). The logic behind this approach stresses the idea that governments do different things.

> Local governments vary in the kinds of services provided, data collection/accounting procedures, and level of professional competence, all of which complicate making broad generalizations about the kinds of performance measures to collect. In addition, performance can differ in different service areas in relation to area, topography, climate, population, citizen desires, etc. (Johnson 1978a, 6)

Thus, each local government about which performance data are collected is encouraged to assess its own standing vis-à-vis other jurisdictions in light of its own goals and objectives and its own knowledge of the local circumstances reflected in the comparative data. The five service areas included in the RTI study were fire protection, police services, solid waste collection, street maintenance, and the court system.

This study was an extension of the comparative logic developed in a multiphase analysis of fire service delivery systems, also conducted by RTI. Working initially with the Urban Institute's list of effectiveness measures and the theoretical structure of Schaenman and Schwartz for fire service productivity measurement, the RTI study developed a system for combining concepts of efficiency *and* effectiveness within a single comparative framework. In the first stage, the comparative performance of over 1,500 communities in the delivery of fire prevention and suppression services was measured, focusing on alternative service delivery patterns. Based on this first-stage analysis, 5 communities were selected for a continuing second-stage, intensive analysis of the underlying structural and process causes of performance variations (Johnson 1978a, 1978b).

The essence of the comparative approach is its definition of performance as a relative concept. Highly structured decision systems, such as those described above, compare programs within an organization and over time, but they do not compare performance across jurisdictions. The approach taken by the Urban Institute provides for comparison over time against a priori defined standards and includes some citizen involvement and feedback. The RTI comparative program includes a more highly developed citizen feedback component; comparison across jurisdictions focuses the attention of both citizens and decision makers on the *relative* performance of their own jurisdiction vis-à-vis other jurisdictions they feel are similar. Although there may be sound reasons for different levels of performance across jurisdictions, the interjurisdictional comparative framework provides the medium for a citizen/official feedback dialogue.

The concept of relative performance evaluation through the use of appropriate comparison, or "reference," groups is not new or unique. The concept of a reference group was introduced by Hyman (1942), developed by Merton (1957), and applied to goal formulation and goal attainment by March and Simon (1958) and Cyert and March (1963). In general, organizations utilize (social) reference groups in goal setting and performance evaluation when the criteria of desirability are ambiguous or when cause and effect relationships cannot be specified with precision.

The comparative approach embodied in the RTI research and other projects supported by the National Center for Productivity (and later by the Office of Personnel Management) differs philosophically from other, more measurement-oriented approaches. The measurement-oriented approach argues for major improvements in measurement techniques and data collection systems, which must then be applied uniformly across jurisdictions before comparisons are meaningful. Lack of uniformity in data collection procedures, inadequate or noncompatible record-keeping systems, and differences in service delivery patterns, according to this skeptical point of view, render comparisons across jurisdictions worthless (Hatry 1980). The contrasting point of view is supported by representatives of cities that participated in comparative studies. The RTI demonstration project included follow-up interviews with the city managers, police and fire chiefs, and public works directors in the 87 participating cities and 20 control group cities (for whom no comparative data were collected/reported). Officials were overwhelmingly (90 percent) favorable to the notion of cross-city comparisons, even those based on different data systems and measurement assumptions (Johnson 1978a). Other research in the realm of individual behavior and organization theory supports the utilization of relative comparisons even in situations that are not strictly comparable.

The issue needs to be faced squarely, although the current emphasis on individual public employee productivity does not provide a favorable climate for enlarging the scope of demonstration activities, as discussed below. Skeptics argue against interjurisdictional comparisons on the grounds that realizing the necessry standardization of measures is not financially feasible. Advocates of interjurisdictional comparison argue that, even with less than ideal data bases, jurisdictions want to see how they compare with others and are quite capable of providing their own controls or caveats for different service delivery objectives or different data systems. The contrast in these points of view also may stem from the skeptics' greater reliance on measurement techniques and the advocates' greater emphasis on citizen/government feedback mechanisms.

Measuring and Reporting Relative Efficiency of Units Performing Similar Tasks

In prior sections we noted the difficulties associated with both goal measures of effectiveness (goal attainment) and systems measures of performance (listings of performance indicators). Further, we have noted the lack of any acceptable aggregate measures for municipal performance and the problems associated with combining multiple performance measures and relating them to the utilization of multiple inputs. In brief, the aggregation problem arises from the multidimensionality of measures, the multiplicity of possible evaluations (e.g., of fire services, of parks and recreation departments), and from the multiplicity of system constituencies (e.g., neighborhoods, property owners, businesses, lenders, regulatory agencies). Furthermore, in the case of public sector organizations (e.g., municipalities, criminal justice systems, school districts) the multiple inputs and outputs, in addition to being noncommensurable, often cannot be valued through market prices. It therefore would be desirable to have an aggregation procedure capable of

- Deriving a single summary measure of the relative efficiencies of a set of decision-making units in their utilization of input factors to produce outputs.

- Handling noncommensurate multiple outputs and multiple input factors.

- Not being dependent on a set of a priori weights or prices.

- Handling qualitative factors, such as "sensitivity to public needs," in addition to quantitative factors.

- Being theoretically based, transparent, and reproducible.

Although Connolly and Deutsch (1980) argue that the search for such a measure is misguided and that "the performance measure designer can justifiably abandon such a search," it seems that at least one newly developed analytical technique has all the desirable features mentioned above. The Data Envelopment Analysis (DEA) technique was developed by Charnes, Cooper, and Rhodes (1978), based on a concept of efficiency originally proposed by Farrell (1957). The DEA procedure is designed to evaluate the relative efficiency of public sector decision-making units performing similar missions for which actual measures of input factors and outputs (e.g., performance indicators) are available. The procedure is most appropriate for evaluations by program managers (e.g., city managers) who cannot redirect resources to other programs (because they are more "profitable") but need to maximize the level of output from the resources (budgets) assigned to them, given the noncontrollable factors affecting the performance of their unit. The DEA technique is based on the economic concept of Pareto optimality, which states that a given decision-making unit (DMU) is not efficient if some other DMU, or some combination of other DMUs, can produce the same amount of output using less of some resources and not more of any other resource. Conversely, a DMU is said to be Pareto efficient if the above is not possible.

The output of the DEA procedure is a relative efficiency score, which can be used to rank the performance of each DMU, and information about potential increases in outputs, or conservation of resources, that inefficient DMUs can render efficient. Thus, the DEA methodology is a direct extension of the work on comparative performance measures discussed earlier. In addition, using historical data, an individual DMU can assess the impact of organizational redesign, changes in systems and procedures, and the introduction of new technology. The DEA technique can also be applied within jurisdictions, for example, to assess the efficiency of schools within and between school boards districts.

It must be recognized that the DEA method is still in its developmental phase. Since their original publication, Cooper, Rhodes, and Charnes (1982) have demonstrated the application of the DEA technique by evaluating results from the program Follow-Through experiment in U.S. Education. Bessent et al. (1980) have applied the DEA to assess productivity of the schools in the Houston independent school district. Lewin, Morey, and Cook (1982) have demonstrated the applicability of the DEA to measuring the administrative efficiency of courts. Charnes et al. (1982) have developed an axiomatic proof of the conditions for a DMU to be Pareto efficient and a method for analyzing the robustness of the efficiency scores. Lewin and Morey (1982) have recently completed a comparative validation study of the DEA methodology as well as a review of the DEA in public sector applications (1981). Schinaar has also utilized the technique in HUD-sponsored research on Community Development Block Grant Cities (1980).

It is beyond the scope of this paper to undertake a comprehensive review or an analytical assessment of the DEA technique. Our purpose in describing the methodology is to note a new and rapidly evolving state-of-the-art application from the management sciences, which may make a significant contribution to the problem of relative performance evaluation. The approach is of particular interest because it could make the concept of relative performance evaluation feasible.

Assuming that the technique proves to be transparent and reproducible, it could have a major impact on facilitating relative performance evaluation of municipal governments and of specific programs within and across jurisdictions (e.g., police departments between cities, within a state, or across states). The DEA approach would also facilitate the relative comparison of performance from the perspective of different constituencies (Lewin, Morey, and Cook 1982). Furthermore, the rankings obtained from the application of the DEA technique could serve as a diagnostic to identify outstanding cases for further study to determine the sources of efficiencies and inefficiencies through the application of comprehensive audits.

CONCLUSION

From a measurement point of view, there is much more to be said about the refinement of concepts, operationalization of indicators, and improvements in data collection procedures, all of which would contribute to advancing the state-of-the art in public sector performance measurement. We have not attempted to review these aspects of measurement theory. Such improvements in measurement per se are linked inextricably to further advances in the theory of public sector organizational behavior. Although much effort has been and continues to be directed at improving microlevel aspects of public sector organizations, the existing state of development in the field precludes describing any bureaucracy in terms of its overall organizational production function. Thus, obtaining a single performance measure for a public organization is at present beyond the state of the art.

Given these stubborn methodological problems, we have focused on models that could result in immediate improvements in local government responsiveness and efficiency. These include various public disclosure approaches—municipal annual reports, independent, broad-scope management audits, comparative performance indicators, and relative efficiency scores. This emphasis does not imply an argument against continued research on microlevel processes and measurement improvements. Our perspective, rather, is that improvements in public sector performance due to developments in the theory of public organizations must be coupled with better methods of public disclosure and feedback to public officials. Public sector performance is inherently a policy process; it is not limited to economic allocation issues, and citizen feedback processes are currently the best-understood mechanisms for making decisions about the adequacy of government performance.

In our view, further insights into the effectiveness and usefulness of accountability and performance models will be achieved only as a result of intermediate and longitudinal field studies. An in-depth, multiyear study of the Sunnyvale, California, experiment, with its annual report, might have resulted in some important insights. Similarly, much could be gained from a before-and-after study of agencies and programs subjected to a broad-scope management audit by the GAO. Such studies may indeed have been done, but we have found no references to them. The interjurisdictional comparative project conducted by the Research Triangle Institute did assess the disclosure aspects of comparative performance measures and found self-report evidence of decision behavior in response to relative rankings.

The DEA methodology clearly has much potential. It is attractive because its application results in relative efficiency scores based on ratios of inputs to outputs. Furthermore, it provides a means for estimating the maximum potential productivity increases for an organization considering only the variables under the control of management. Its computational feasibility in various settings (e.g., court systems, public safety departments, water works, municipalities, school systems) has been demonstrated. Further research is needed to assess its impact (as a result of public disclosure of rankings and of productivity improvement potential) on actual improvements of the affected bureaucracies.

But no real progress can be achieved with any approach involving disclosure and comparative measures of performance unless consensus can be reached on what is essential information about public sector performance and on standards for reporting this information. As long as local governments ignore generally accepted, minimal standards for accounting and each jurisdiction is free to report on its performance as it sees fit, no meaningful input/output comparisons are feasible.

The growing public concern with the accountability and performance of public institutions has clearly placed this issue on the public agenda. It will ultimately be resolved through the public policy process. It is our hope, however, that these political decisions will be based on better knowledge about performance than we have today. Major breakthroughs in practice and methods are occurring. Information about their effects and prospects for broader application would contribute to serious efforts to improve public sector accountability and performance.

REFERENCES

ACIR. 1980. *1980: Changing Public Attitudes on Governments and Taxes.* Washington, D.C.: U.S. Government Printing Office.

Accounting Principles Board. 1975. *Basic Concepts and Accounting Practices underlying Financial Statements of Business Enterprise.* Accounting Principles Board Statement No. 4. Reprinted in *American Institute of Certified Public Accountants, Professional Standards Accounting.*

Aldrich, H. E. 1971. Organizational Boundaries and Interorganizational Conflict. *Human Relations* 24:279–87.

Aldrich, H. E., and J. Pfeffer. 1976. Environments of Organizations. *Annual Review of Sociology* 2:79–105.

Anthony, Robert N. 1978. *Financial Accounting in Nonbusiness Organizations: An Exploratory Study of Conceptual Issues.* Stamford, Conn.: Financial Accounting Standards Board.

Argyris, Chris. 1964. *Integrating the Individual and the Organization.* New York: Wiley.

————. 1968. Some Unintended Consequences of Rigorous Research. *Psychological Bulletin* 70:185–97.

————. 1973. Personality and Organization Revisited. *Administrative Science Quarterly* 18:141–67.

Barnard, Chester I. 1938. *The Functions of the Executive.* Cambridge, Mass.: Harvard University Press.

Bennis, Warren G. 1969. *Organization Development: Its Nature, Origins, and Prospects.* Reading, Mass.: Addison-Wesley.

Bessent, A., W. Bessent, J. Kennington, and B. Regan. 1980. An Application of Mathematical Programming to Assess Productivity in the Houston Independent School District. Technical Report OR 8011, Dallas: Southern Methodist University Press.

Black, Guy. 1967. Systems Analysis in Government Operations. *Management Science* 14(3): B-41–B-58.

————. 1968. *The Application of Systems Analysis to Government Operations.* New York: Praeger.

Blake, R. R., and J. S. Mouton. 1969. *Building a Dynamic Corporation through Grid Organization Development.* Reading, Mass.: Addison-Wesley.

Campbell, John P. 1977. On the Nature of Organizational Effectiveness. In *New Perspectives on Organizational Effectiveness*, ed. Paul S. Goodman and Johannes M. Pennings. San Francisco: Jossey-Bass.

Chaiken, J., E. Egnall, P. Kolesar, and W. Walker. 1980. Response to Communication on RAND-HUD Fire Models. *Management Science* 26(4): 422–32.

Charnes, A., William W. Cooper, and Edward Rhodes. 1978. Measuring the Efficiency of Decision-Making Units. *European Journal of Operations Research* 28:429–44.

Charnes, A., W. W. Cooper, A. Y. Lewin, R. C. Morey, and J. Rousseau. 1982. Data Envelopment Analysis: A Non-Archimedean Proof and Robustness Calculations. Durham, N.C.: Fuqua School of Business, Duke University.

Chase, Samuel B., Jr., ed. 1968. *Problems in Public Expenditure Analysis*. Washington, D.C.: Brookings Institution.

Child, J. 1974. Managerial and Organizational Factors Associated with Company Performance, pt. 1. *Journal of Management Studies* 11:175–89.

———. 1975. Managerial and Organizational Factors Associated with Company Performance, pt. 2. *Journal of Management Studies* 12:12–27.

Churchill, N. C., W. W. Cooper, V. Govindarajan, J. D. Pond, and S. G. San Miguel. 1976. Developments in Comprehensive Auditing and Suggestions for Research. Paper presented at the 2d Symposium on Auditing Research, University of Illinois.

Churchill, N. C., and R. M. Cyert. 1966. An Experiment in Management Auditing. *Journal of Accountancy* 14:39–43.

Connolly, Terry, and Stuart J. Deutsch. 1980. Performance Measurement in a Multinodal System. Atlanta: Georgia Institute of Technology.

Cooper, William W., ed. 1970. Urban Issues I. *Management Science* 16.

———. 1972. Urban Issues II. *Management Science* 18.

Cooper, William W., Edward Rhodes, and Abraham Charnes. 1982. A Data Envelopment Analysis Approach to Evaluation of the Program Follow-Through Experiment in U.S. Public School Education. *Management Science* 28.

Coopers & Lybrand and the University of Michigan. 1976. *Financial Disclosure Practices of America Cities: A Public Report*. New York: Coopers & Lybrand.

Council on Municipal Performance. 1974. *Municipal Securities Regulation*. 10 vols. Vol. 10. New York: Council on Municipal Performance.

Crecine, John P. 1962. *Governmental Problem-Solving: A Computer Simulation*. Englewood Cliffs, N.J.: Prentice-Hall.

———. A Computer Simulation Model of Municipal Budgeting. *Management Science* 12(11): 786–815.

Cyert, Richard M., and James G. March. 1963. *A Behavioral Theory of the Firm*. Englewood Cliffs, N.J.: Prentice-Hall.

David, W. Taylor. 1979. The Assessment of Public Agency Responsiveness: A Pilot Study in an Urban Context. *Urban Systems* 4(3/4): 243–54.

Davis, M., and M. Weidenbaum. 1969. *Metropolitan Decision Processes: An Analysis of Case Studies*. Chicago: Rand McNally.

Davis, Otto A., and Frederick H. Reuter. 1972. A Simulation of Municipal Zoning Decisions, pt. 2. *Management Science* 19(4): 39–77.

Dorfman, Robert, ed. 1965. *Measuring Benefits of Government Investments*. Washington, D.C.: Brookings Institution.

Drebin, Allan R. 1979. Governmental versus Commercial Accounting: The Issues. *Governmental Finance* 3:3–8.

Enthoven, Alain C. 1967. *The Systems Analysis Approach: Planning-Programming-Budgeting*. Washington, D.C.: U.S. Government Printing Office.

Enthoven, Alain C., and K. Wayne Smith. 1971. *How Much Is Enough? Shaping the Defense Program, 1961–1969.* New York: Harper & Row.

Etzioni, Amitai. 1960. Two Approaches to Organizational Analysis: A Critique and a Suggestion. *Administrative Science Quarterly* 5:257–78.

————. 1964. *Modern Organizations.* Englewood Cliffs, N.J.: Prentice-Hall.

Farrell, M. J. 1957. The Measurement of Productive Efficiency. *Journal of the Royal Statistical Society* 120, pt. 3, series A.

Ferguson, C. E. 1972. *Microeconomic Theory.* 3d ed. Homewood, Ill.: Richard D. Irwin.

Financial Accounting Standards Board. 1980. *Objectives of Financial Reporting by Nonbusiness Organizations.* Stamford, Conn.: FASB.

Førsund, F. R., C. A. Knox Lovell, and Peter Schmidt. Forthcoming. A Survey of Frontier Production Functions and of Their Relationship to Efficiency Measurement. *Journal of Econometrics.*

Friedlander, F., and H. Pickle. 1968. Components of Effectiveness in Small Organizations. *Administrative Science Quarterly* 13:289–304.

Gass, Saul I., and Roger L. Sisson. 1974. *A Guide to Models in Governmental Planning and Operations.* Washington, D.C.: U.S. Environmental Protection Agency.

General Accounting Office. 1974. Suggested State Auditing and Acts and Constitutional Amendments. Report to the Congress by the Comptroller General of the United States, Washington, D.C.

————. 1976. Revenue Sharing Act Audit Requirements Should Be Changed. Report to the Congress by the Comptroller General of the United States, Washington, D.C.

Georgopaoulos, B. S., and A. S. Tanenbaum. 1957. A Study of Organizational Effectiveness. *American Sociological Review* 22:534–40.

Gerwin, Donald. 1969. *Budgeting Public Funds: The Decision Process in an Urban School District.* Madison: University of Wisconsin Press.

————. 1973. An Information-Processing Model of Salary Determination in a Contour of Suburban School Districts. *American Educational Research Journal* 10(1): 5–20.

Goldman, Thomas A., ed. 1968. *Cost-Effectiveness Analysis: New Approaches in Decision Making.* New York: Praeger.

Grosse, Robern N. 1970. PPBS: A Support for Decision Making in the Health Field.

Hatry, Harry P., L. Blair, D. Fisk, J. Greiner, J. Hill, Jr., and P. Schaenman. 1977. *How Effective Are Your Community Services? Procedures for Monitoring the Effectiveness of Municipal Services.* Washington, D.C.: Urban Institute and the International City Management Association.

Hawley, Willis D., and David Rogers, eds. 1974. *Improving the Quality of Urban Management.* Beverly Hills: Sage.

Hirsch, P. M. 1975. Organizational Effectiveness and the Institutional Environment. *Administrative Science Quarterly* 20:327–44.

Hitch, Charles J. 1965. *Decision Making for Defense.* Berkeley and Los Angeles: University of California Press.

Hitch, Charles J., and Roland N. McKean. 1960. *Economics of Defense in the Nuclear Age.* Cambridge, Mass.: Harvard University Press.

Hyman, Herbert H. 1942. The Psychology of Status. *Archives of Psychology* (269).

Johnson, Sally S. 1978a. *Comparative Performance Measures for Municipal Services.* Research Triangle Park, N.C.: Research Triangle Institute, for the U.S. Civil Service Commission, Bureau of Intergovernmental Personnel Programs.

————. 1978b. *Municipal Fire Service Workbook*. Research Triangle Park, N.C.: Research Triangle Institute.

King, John L., and Kenneth L. Kraemer. 1980. Information and Reporting for Local Government Fiscal Management. Working paper. Irvine: Public Policy Research Organization, University of California.

Kirlin, John J. 1979. Toward a Perspective on (Inter) Governmental Performance in the 1980s. Mimeo.

Knorr, Klaus. 1967. On the Cost-Effectiveness Approach to Military Research in *Planning-Programming-Budgeting*. Subcommittee on National Security and International Operations. Washington, D.C.: U.S. Government Printing Office.

Lee, Robert D., Jr., and Ronald W. Johnson. 1977. *Public Budgeting Systems*. 2d. ed. Baltimore: University Park Press.

Lewin, Arie Y., and Robert W. Blanning. 1974. Urban Government Annual Report. In *Improving the Quality of Urban Management*, ed. D. Rogers and W. D. Hawley. Beverly Hills: Sage.

Lewin, Arie Y., and Gerald A. Cahill. 1976. Annual Reporting by Municipal Governments: An Extension of the Corporate Report. In *Policy Sciences: Methodologies and Cases*, ed. Arie Y. Lewin and Melvin F. Shakuu. Elmsford, N.Y.: Pergamon.

Lewin, Arie Y., and Richard C. Morey. 1982. Comparative Empirical Studies of the Data Envelopment Analysis and Its Extensions. Working paper. Durham, N.C.: Fuqua School of Business, Duke University.

————. 1981. Measuring the Relative Efficiency and Output Potential of Public Sector Organizations: An Application of Data Envelopment Analysis. Durham, N.C.: Fuqua School of Business, Duke University. Reprint forthcoming in *International Journal of Policy Analysis and Information Systems*.

Lewin, Arie Y., Richard C. Morey, and Thomas J. Cook. 1982. Evaluating the Administrative Efficiency of Courts. Durham, N.C.: Fuqua School of Business, Duke University. *Omega* 6:468–80.

Lewin, Arie Y., and James Scheiner. 1978. Requiring Municipal Performance Reporting: An Analysis Based upon Users' Information Needs. Working paper no. 207. Durham, N.C.: Fuqua School of Business, Duke University.

Lewin, Arie Y., and Melvin F. Shakuu. 1976. *Policy Sciences: Methodologies and Cases*. Elmsford, N.Y.: Pergamon.

Likert, Renesis. *New Patterns In Management*. New York: McGraw-Hill.

Litchfield, Nathaniel, and Julius Margolis. 1963. Benefit-Cost Analysis as a Tool in Urban Government Decision-Making. In *Public Expenditure Decisions in the Urban Community*, ed. Irwin Schaller. Washington, D.C.: Resources for the Future.

Maas, A. 1966. Benefit-Cost Analysis: Its Relevance to Public Investment Decisions. *Quarterly Journal of Economics* 64.

March, James G., and Herbert A. Simon. 1958. *Organizations*. New York: Wiley.

Mason, Richard O., and Burton E. Swanson. 1977. Measurement for Management Decision: A Perspective. Los Angeles: Graduate School of Management, University of California. Mimeo.

McCullough, J. D. 1966. *Cost Analysis for Planning-Programming-Budgeting Cost-Benefit Studies*. Santa Monica: RAND Corporation.

McKean, Roland N. 1958. *Efficiency in Government through Systems Analysis, with Emphasis on Water Resource Developments*. New York: Wiley.

Merton, Robert K. 1957. The Role-Set: Problems in Sociological Theory. *British Journal of Sociology* 8:74–89.

Mohr, Lawrence B. 1971. Organizational Technology and Organizational Structure. *Administrative Science Quarterly* 16:444–59.

National Center for Productivity and Quality of Working Life. 1978. *Total Performance Measurement: Some Pointers for Action.* Washington, D.C.: National Center for Productivity and Quality of Working Life.
National Productivity Council. 1979. *Federal Actions to Support State and Local Government Productivity Improvement: Report to the National Productivity Council.* Washington, D.C.: U.S. Government Printing Office.

Ostrom, Elinor, Roger B. Parks, and Gordon P. Whitaker. 1979. Purposes, Performance Measurement, and Policing. Bloomington: Indiana University Workshop in Theory and Policy Analysis. Mimeo.

Pennings, Johannes M. 1976. Dimensions of Organizational Influence and Their Effectiveness Correlates. *Administrative Science Quarterly* 21:688–99.
Prest, A. R., and R. Turvey. 1965. Cost-Benefit Analysis: A Survey. *Economic Journal* 75:683.

Quade, E. S. 1966. *Systems Analysis Techniques for Planning-Programming-Budgeting.* Santa Monica: RAND Corporation.

RAND Fire Department Project. 1979. *Fire Department Deployment Analysis.* New York: Elsevier-North Holland.
Rivlin, Alice. 1961. *Systematic Thinking for Social Action.* Washington, D.C.: Brookings Institution.
Rogers, David. 1968. *110 Livingston Street.* Random House.
Rousmaniere, Peter F. 1979. Municipal Securities Regulations: A Public Perspective—The Way Back toward Accountability in America's Cities. New York: Council on Municipal Performance.

Schinaar, A. P. 1980. An Algorithm for Measuring Relative Efficiency. Fels Discussion Paper no. 144. Philadelphia: University of Pennsylvania.
Seashore, Stanley E., and Renesis Likert. 1969. Assessment of Organizational Performance. *Harvard Business Review.*
Simon, Herbert, George Kozmetsky, Harold Guetzkow, and Gordon Tyndall. 1954. *Centralization versus Decentralization in Organizing the Controller's Department.* New York: Controllership Foundation.
Staats, Elmer B. 1976. The Role of Public Administrators in a New Era. Address presented at the Nova University Commencement Exercises, Fort Lauderdale, Fla.

Taft, William Howard. 1912. Economy and Efficiency in the Government Service. H. Doc. no. 458.
Thompson, James D. *Organizations in Action.* 1967. New York: McGraw-Hill.
Tiebout, Charles M. 1956. A Pure Theory of Local Expenditures. *Journal of Political Economy* 64:49–60.

Van De Ven, Andrew H., and Diane L. Ferry. 1980. *Measuring and Assessing Organizations.* New York: Wiley.

Wallace, R., and D. Wallace. Communications on HUD Fire Models. *Management Science* 26(4): 418–22.
Weidenbaum, Murray L. 1966. Program Budgeting: Applying Economic Analysis to Government Expenditure Decisions. *Business and Government Review* 7:22–31.
Wildavsky, Aaron. 1975. *Budgeting: A Comparative Theory of Budgetary Processes.* Boston: Little, Brown.

Williams, James M. 1978. Accounting Auditing and Financial Reporting. In *State and Local Government Finance and Financial Management: A Compendium of Current Research,* ed. John E. Petersen, Catherine Lavigue Spain, and Martharose F. Laffey, 86–94. Washington, D.C.: Government Finance Research Center.

Woodward, Joan. Industrial Organization: Theory and Practice. London: Oxford University Press.

Wright, J. Ward. 1981. *Tax and Expenditure Limitation: A Policy Perspective.* Lexington, Ky.: Council of State Governments.

9

Conclusion: A Design Science Perspective

Trudi C. Miller

The authors of the previous chapters have noted problematic and promising aspects of the literature on public sector performance. In this concluding chapter I highlight what we have learned and partially develop and apply a design science approach to political science that is consistent with these lessons.

WHAT HAVE WE LEARNED?

Governments Are Diverse. Years of research, premised on implicit assumptions that political systems and their components are similar, lead us to reject such assumptions. The accumulated evidence shows that most empirically established relations among variables such as political preference, citizen participation, political party, institutional function and implementation do not hold up over space (across jurisdictions or nations) or over time (across historical stages).

Government Behavior Is Stable, If Idiosyncratic. In general, future organizational behavior is predictable from past behavior. New ideas and goals may be incorporated in practice, but progress is usually slow. Thus, longitudinal theories and models that project events as a function of past decisions are remarkably accurate, at least in the short run. The stability of organizational behavior and its adaptability to diverse environments, values, and options explains why generalizing about variables and functions across cases is difficult.

Qualitative Changes Do Occur. Historically significant changes are infrequent. However, the laws and conventions that describe and enforce regularities in social behavior do change, sometimes dramatically, as a result of political action. From a quantitative perspective, this means that the forms and parameters of equations and the boundaries between exogenous and endogenous variables are altered. Political science needs models that represent, explain, and forecast structural changes that are popularly thought of as historically significant events.

Strict Empiricism Is Inadequate.   Because they do not take account of the ideological determinants of future qualitative changes, models that are restricted to currently observable behavior are incomplete; models should also include normative views and their probable consequences. This requires translating political perspectives into quantitative empirical measures and equations that predict (or target) future behavior.

Social Scientists Know How to Quantify Normative Theories.   The fields of public finance and management science are replete with examples of quantitative normative models. Most of these "rationalistic" theories, however, are static. As a result, they frequently generate inaccurate predictions of behavior over time. A science that is capable of explaining, forecasting, and shaping organizational performance will rely on dynamic models.

Data Are Critical.   Assumptions about the validity and reliability of data must reflect the diversity of units of government. For example, the U.S. federal system contains over 80,000 subunits that are called "governments." For these units, even apparently comparable data on personnel, functions, accounts, and so on are likely to be based on different underlying definitions. Moreover, these definitions evolve over time as a result of political actions and other factors.

MODERN SCIENCE

As Anton observed, the current problem with public sector performance is largely an intellectual one. The chapters of this volume document prevailing criticisms of what once were the accepted theories and methods of social science, public administration, and policy making. They also advocate alternative research approaches. The remaining challenge is to develop a framework for thinking about politics, management, and science that embraces the criticisms and the new approaches. The objective of this conclusion is to sketch out such a perspective.

At the heart of the intellectual problem of political science and scientific management is an inappropriate definition of "science." I call this outdated definition the "natural science" perspective and recommend that it be replaced by a more modern and appropriate "design science" perspective.

"Natural science" represents the approach to public administration and political science that has prevailed for most of the twentieth century. It is drawn primarily from analogies with Newtonian physics and biology.[1] The implicit assumptions of this nature-focused approach are that (1) the laws that govern human behavior exist independent of human control, and (2) the units of analysis in social systems are highly similar over time and space.

The conventional quantitative methods of social science reflect these implicit empirical assumptions. Research designs are intended to avoid threats to validity that could be introduced by the scientist. Although experiments are intrusive and change behavior, their purpose is passive—to discover underlying laws of social behavior. Statistics are crafted to identify central tendencies, and comparative research has, until recently, been the ideal.

Common sense as well as the findings of empirical research indicate that we should explore alternatives to quantitative methods that assume a stable, autonomous world composed of similar cases that behave according to nature-given laws. Social science textbooks are filled with chapters acknowledging that social institutions are not like physical objects or biological species (Nagel 1961; Campbell and Stanley 1963). To cope with this divergence, most social scientists use elaborate control methods and statistical adjustments to find true comparison groups, and many conditions are specified on "generalizations." Such refinements are insufficient; findings are almost always disputed when they move beyond bland description. If, as the literature reviews indicate, cases are diverse and social reality is to a large degree constructed by free-thinking humans, then no amount of methodological fussiness can make the old-fashioned natural science approach reflect social reality.

What I call the design science approach to political science replaces the implicit assumptions of natural science with explicit assumptions that are more consistent with the accumulated results of empirical research on social systems. Like natural science, design science borrows heavily from the hard sciences. Specifically, fields that to some degree create the objects that they study are called design sciences. Computer science, which deals with an entirely manmade subject, is a clear example. Herbert A. Simon introduced design science in *The Sciences of the Artificial* (1969). My adaptation of Simon's formulation for political science borrows heavily from C. West Churchman (1971) and his colleagues.[2]

As I define it, design science quantifies relationships between human controls and the forces of nature. The dominance of the humanistic element over the natural element (or vice versa) depends on the object of science—specifically, the degree to which it is subject to qualitative change at the direction of humans. In some sciences (for example, astronomy) human control is negligible, and the assumptions and methods of natural science hold. But many experimental sciences have a design element to them, because the experiments (for example, in nuclear physics or genetics) change what we call nature.

Reflecting the advance of knowledge, the design aspect of science is growing in importance relative to the natural component. Owing to science and technology, less of what we observe is controlled by natural law and more is controlled by human law and manipulation of nature. The growing importance of the design component of science (and reality) is reflected, for example, in the elevation of engineering to the status of a directorate in the National Science Foundation and in the rapid growth of computer science in the NSF budget. Moreover, scientific work is increasingly driven by performance objectives (Knorr 1981). Biologists create hybrids to meet human goals, chemists create new materials, engineers and computer scientists develop technologies. *Creation* is a better word than *observation* for much of what is now called "one science" by the National Science Board.[3]

To put it another way, much of modern science is highly experimental. Manipulations of the objects of science are no longer minor, all things held constant; they are major, involving basic structures. For example, through experiments scientists have created several generations of computers, and unique scientific breakthroughs (e.g., computer chips) are often the best basis for generalizing about what the average computer will look like in the future. It follows that the hypotheses of design science are not generalizations or predictions about current behavior but are assertions that new levels of performance can be attained and diffused under the right conditions. Such propositions cannot definitively be rejected using existing data, because scientists work to remove barriers to the achievement of what are thought to be attainable ends, and they are sometimes successful. The hypotheses of design science are empirical, but they can be supported only in the future.

Because the methods of the "hard sciences" embrace the growing power of humans over nature, they are beginning to resemble what social science would be like if it were to let down its "natural science" defenses. Indeed, as the creation of key instruments, potentialities, and forecasts involves more humanistic and social variables, interest in social science grows among physicists, engineers, mathematicians, and other hard scientists, many of whom work on what are essentially social science questions in the fields of operations research, systems analysis, and decision and management science.[4]

The recent influx of hard science methodology into social science should improve the latter's external validity. The modern hard sciences offer an array of methods and measures that can quantify the various dynamic aspects of social reality, which are poorly represented by conventional methods. For example, from physics come indicators of disorder that may help to measure prospects for qualitative changes in social systems.[5] Disorder is maximized when the probability (P_j) that a system could exist in states ($j = 1, 2, \ldots N$) is $P_j = 1/N$ for all j; or, all states are equally likely. Disorder = 0 (order prevails) when a single $P_j = 1$; or, only one state is possible. Using this measure we might show how political behavior in the 1980s differs from political behavior in the 1950s. In the 1950s social institutions were strong, behavior was predictable, and politics were unimportant (Campbell et al. 1960). In contrast, the 1980s are characterized by discontent and unpredictable behavior, and students of elections and public opinion discuss the possibility of a "critical election" that will transform the system to a qualitatively different, new steady state (Ladd 1980; Scammon and Wattenberg 1980).

Quantitative models of order and disorder have already been used to simulate qualitative change in urban areas over time. The urban area is carved up into sectors containing actors with preferences about location (Allen 1981). In its early stages, urban development tends to be predictable because the rational choices for industries and private citizens are obvious (e.g., the industry locates near the railroad, individuals locate close to work). At later stages, however, when congestion and decay set in, everyone is likely to be discontented (the probability of movement from a sector is high), but the relocations that individuals and businesses can make to improve their situation are not obvious, in part because they are interrelated. Thus, in early stages of urban development around well-defined transportation facilities, the assumptions of natural science are likely to hold; behavioral patterns are relatively well determined and predictable and political actions are not very important. In the disorderly phase, however, governmental action and intellectual leadership may be necessary to develop consensus about land use and to enforce the ensuing decisions. Following this new political construction of social reality, citizens and businesses can once again make independent, self-serving decisions with predictable consequences.

More familiar to students of public sector performance are quantitative models of organizational hierarchy that draw heavily from the fields of computer science and biology (see Simon 1969, 1977). Many of these mathematical representations are compatible with modern theories of management discussed in Kirlin's chapter. For example, analogies to alternative computer architectures (parallel processing) have been used to illustrate the theoretical perspective that organizational performance in modern societies will be enhanced if opportunities for participation and learning replace detailed management controls (Cohen 1982).

In sum, design science brings social science closer to the modern hard sciences, drawing new quantitative models from them. In addition to conventional social science methods that assume a well-determined, well-ordered world (e.g., fixed, independent laws and similar cases), the modern sciences offer methods to represent qualitative change and diverse cases. Armed with quantitative models drawn from all the disciplines of science, social scientists can articulate alternative political perspectives on social diversity and change, using rigorous methods. Political science is status quo oriented not because it is scientific but because it employs an old-fashioned view of science that focuses on the standardized and static aspects of political systems.[6]

THINKING ABOUT PUBLIC SECTOR PERFORMANCE

Political perspectives imply normative/empirical theories about social structures and dynamics. They make assumptions about the diversity of cases, the rates of social change, and the control that humans have over nature. For example, Socialists tend to assume that governmental departments and subnational units are or should be similar in their parts and functions. Conservatives and humanists celebrate diversity and call for a reduction of governmental red tape. Liberals argue that increased socioeconomic equity is required to maximize productivity in an advanced economy. Populists—the bulk of American citizens—marry the conservative perspective on red tape with the liberal perspective on equity.[7]

It follows that the simplifying assumptions undergirding social science methods overlap with the assumptions undergirding political perspectives. For example, the natural science perspective assumes similarity and autonomy, so its applications encourage standardization and insulation from alternative value perspectives. The difference between the design approach and the natural science approach is that design science is pluralistic—any model of a viable political system can be used to illuminate actual behavior. Nevertheless, design science is also political (normative) in its implications because the simplifying assumptions of any formal model will generate pressures to make reality conform. For that matter, "pluralism" is a political perspective.

In table 9.1, the natural science and the design science perspectives are contrasted. The underlying assumptions of design science are consistent with the research findings about political systems highlighted at the beginning of this chapter. However, these assumptions do not apply to all aspects of political systems. Some aspects (e.g., those that reflect absolute limitations in the ability of humans to process information) are better explored by the natural science approach. Also, design science uses natural science–style methods to address aspects of social systems that have been designed according to the natural science model. For example, standardization and autonomy characterize many aspects of financial management systems and, in this area, methods based on the assumptions of natural science work fairly well. Similarly, experimental natural science methods are used to analyze and debug complex computer systems. The natural science model is often useful, but its underlying assumptions about the similarity and autonomy of the structure of cases limit its ability to address true innovations, such as a shift in computer architecture to parallel processing.

In contrast, the specialty of design science is to quantify the creative processes that drive qualitative change in systems such as the universe of microcomputers, or the U.S. federal government. The components of these systems are diverse and subject to manmade incremental and qualitative change; these generalizations undergird the research approaches of design science in table 9.1.

Given the detail of table 9.1, we can explore the implications of simplifying assumptions for research methods and politics. From the natural science perspective, laws of social behavior are autonomous and external to scientific inquiries, and types of governments and their components are similar and consistent over time and space. As suggested above, this view of reality is pregnant with political implications. It implies the existence of a qualitatively unchanging, knowable, and orderly world in which central authorities can design laws that are consistent with the findings of science and applicable across the nation and over the decades (see especially Anton and Kirlin).

The empirical assumptions underlying design science are quite different. Most regularities in political attitudes and behavior are assumed to be the products of deliberate moral, intellectual, and political activities. Being partly manmade, they change over time, and given variations in conditions and values, they are different from place to place.

The empirical assumptions of our version of design science are also pregnant with political implications. If governmental structures and laws are largely manmade, then no caste of priests, noblemen, or scientists can claim that they are dictates of God or nature. Moreover, if institutions are diverse, then few laws are likely to fit most cases. At the same time, because social and political institutions are partly manmade, reform is possible. Observed behavior, such as the dominance of some classes over others or even the existence of classes, might be changed by political action. Indeed, the most important political implication of design science is that social choice is not only possible, but is also the factor that creates social structures and drives social dynamics. Social reality is constructed partly by intellectual, social, and political activity, of which social science is a part. Design science focuses on this central feature of social system dynamics; natural science (as it is conventionally applied) denies its existence.

Moving from the "empirical assumptions" to the "methodological approaches" column of table 9.1, we can explore the differences between how the natural and design approaches "think." Among the contrasts, two stand out. First, design science deals with a broader range of options than does natural science. Second, design science, for the most part, focuses on extreme cases of good and bad performance, whereas natural science deals with all cases, focusing on the general or average case.

Table 9.1. Natural and Design Science

Science Paradigm	Empirical Assumptions		Methodological Approaches			
	System	Cases and Laws	Purpose	Goals and Risks	Typical Methods	Focus
Natural Science	natural, autonomous	consistent over time & space	estimate central tendency	not considered	unobtrusive, inductive, comparative, & static	general case
Design Science	manmade, or partly manmade	diverse, subject to incremental & qualitative change	optimize—maximize performance subject to constraints	quantified & linked to constraints & resources	obtrusive, deductive, open-ended, experimental, & dynamic	extreme cases from the perspective of desired outcomes

Note: The distinction between natural and design science is borrowed from Simon (1969). However, my definitions draw heavily on Churchman (1971) and related publications. Overall, this is an idealized version of applied research approaches that are found in the fields of decision and management science and related fields (see footnote 2).

An Extended Array of Tools for Reform

Natural science is limited to objective variables and relationships that exist "out there," largely beyond human control. Thus, most methods call for identifying the effects of a single policy change, all other things held constant. Standard statistical packages do this automatically, identifying as most important those variables that by themselves, without reinforcement, have the greatest influence on the average. In effect, the standard policy analysis simulates a reform in which policy makers preserve existing institutions and existing allocations of most resources. This model simulates the behavior of the average decision maker, who is not especially committed to a specific goal. The estimated effects of reforms that result from this style of research are minimal (see Miller 1981a, 1981b).

In contrast, design science encourages policy makers to consider a broader array of tools for reform. The science concerns maximizing performance, so experiments are not intended to explain behavior in general, and every factor that is not constrained for an explicit reason is used to realize the performance objective. Thus, experiments simulate reforms in which motivation is perfect and totally focused on stated objectives, except for specified constraints that reflect prior commitments and resource limits. For most cases, estimates of feasible performance levels ("frontiers") will be too high, but these optimistic forecasts do show managers and employees what they might accomplish if they were to mobilize their resources.

As implied by the discussion above, another factor or resource emphasized in the design science model—and largely overlooked in conventional social science—is the importance of clarifying ideals. Analysis is focused by objectives that are precisely and quantitatively defined. Constraints—other obligations and resource limitations that cannot be sacrificed—are also specified. This rigorous translation of values into expectations for behavior brings the force of logic and salience to bear on performance; it captures patterns of thought that are used in the social construction of reality. Thus, even though design science is largely quantitative, it is compatible with humanistic perspectives that emphasize moral leadership and motivation (Burck 1981; Harmon 1981).

Finally, the idealized version of design science presented in table 9.1 exploits feedback; its models evolve as knowledge is added over time. By contrast, in the classic natural science experimental design (or policy analysis using a single regression equation), increments to knowledge and new opportunities over time are neglected. Instead, a measured "intervention" is launched at the beginning (t_1) and held constant, along with everything else, until the end of the experiment, when the effects of the intervention can be recorded (or predicted). Design science uses a different methodology. Because generalizations about the effectiveness of specific procedures are not expected to hold up over time or space, the design scientist changes strategies in light of additional information and reactions to the intervention. In a design science experiment, the "intervention" is constantly being perfected in light of early results and contextual changes.

Because of its methodological characteristics, the design science experiment produces knowledge that differs in kind from knowledge produced by the classic experiment. The classic experiment yields estimates of the effect of an isolated intervention in general. In contrast, a design science experiment estimates a frontier of performance that can be attained given prior commitments and resource limits. For example, a design science experiment might show that despite constraints (carefully measured) typical of the average school, exceptional teaching (poorly defined) can allow an average class of black students to perform way above expected levels (carefully documented). Knowledge about performance possibilities contributes as much to theory and practice as does knowledge about the effects of well-defined interventions. For example, the results of the experiment above would challenge theories that explain the lower average achievement levels of blacks in terms of genetic or socioeconomic limits on learning ability.

In summary, then, design science embraces at least three factors to improve performance that natural science eschews: (1) commitment (utilizing all resources and changes that are not constrained for specified reasons), (2) ideas (spelling out the implications of goals for behavior), and (3) follow-through (using feedback and open-ended, dynamic models).

Contrasts in knowledge produced by the two sciences were also noted. Natural science produces precise information about the average effects of changing specific inputs, all other things held constant. To the degree that structures and processes are similar and consistent over time, such knowledge about general laws of behavior is useful. Imagine, for example, the benefit from an experiment that produced reliable information about isolated changes that result in marginal improvements in the performance of the human heart. Design science, on the other hand, produces information about performance levels which can be realized despite typical constraints. Successful experiments challenge theories (often espoused by producers) that low performance is dictated by conditions beyond human control, and they document that heretofore unrealized heights of achievement can be realized. Moreover, assuming that cases are diverse, the attendant loss of specific "how-to" information is not of great importance.

A Focus on Extremes

The second major difference between natural and design science involves the focus of the former on all cases and the latter on extreme cases. From the natural science perspective, the best research is comparative, involving a large sample of the universe of cases over time. This approach yields estimates of central tendencies that reflect durable, common patterns of behavior.

Ideally, generalizations apply to all cases. If they do not, researchers attempt to generalize about conditions that predict different patterns of behavior (Nagel 1961). A major disappointment for natural science–oriented social scientists is the variance in research results about allegedly comparable phenomena (see the chapter by Larkey, Stolp, and Winer). For example, "meta-analysis" on relatively clean data (the academic achievement of public school students) in one country (the U.S.) within one historical period (roughly 20 years) leaves 80 percent of the variance in the error term (Glass 1979).

In contrast, design science usually focuses on one case at a time and its performance frontiers (high or low). The performance frontier is an empirical statement of what the world would look like if an objective were maximized under specified conditions that reflect current trends and other commitments. The result is an estimate of the highest level of performance consistent with available resources and policy constraints, and the relevant comparison is between actual performance and this estimated frontier.

The focus of design science on outlying behavior reflects underlying assumptions (see table 9.1) about the importance of human control. Performance depends on human determination to excel (or to avoid risks) as well as on material conditions. In an organization that is committed to reform, performance frontiers—targets for behavior—may be better predictors of future behavior than are extrapolations from existing practices. Similarly, because the dedication of leaders to a given objective varies, statistics describing performance across cases are generally avoided. Rather, highly motivated leaders and organizations that perform close to the frontier are identified, and their achievements are studied to learn about prospects for achieving that objective. Resistant leaders, who perform way below the average, are also identified; failures are studied to determine the degree to which they reflect constraints or willful (punishable) disregard for the law. Reflecting the diversity of values and procedures among organizations, most cases do middling jobs of achieving a given objective. These cases do not teach the scientist much about maximizing performance, but rough knowledge about typical behavior is used to define outstanding performance.

Finally, the achievement of a performance frontier in a single case may be the key to predicting future performance levels in the average case. Breakthroughs that may be achieved at high cost by dedicated innovators are diffused over time, and the price of improvement often decreases with replication (Radner, Feller, and Rogers 1978). Therefore, in a rapidly evolving area of knowledge, future average behavior is likely to reflect current best practice. Similarly, knowledge about the probability and severity of bad performance is significant in predicting and shaping the future. In areas where performance breakthroughs are less dramatic and appealing, however, forecasts of the future are based on existing trends (see, for example, Muller).

A shift in focus from the general to the extreme case has profound implications for management. According to the working assumptions underlying the natural science approach, cases are similar and structure is stable. Thus, empirical research on typical cases can identify superior procedures, and managers should require that these procedures be followed exactly by all cases to raise system performance. Moreover, according to the static assumptions of natural science, procedures can be mandated for an indefinite period.[8]

In contrast, the design approach assumes that it takes unusual dedication and insight to achieve a performance breakthrough. Also, cases adapt to diverse conditions, so there are few "best practices" to apply across jurisdictions, and detailed regulations are avoided. Thus, the design science view is consistent with popular political perspectives that favor decentralization.

More important, the focus on extremes opens up options for governing complex political systems that are not reflected in classic formal theories. According to classic theories, such as those discussed by Aronson and Schwartz, centralization and decentralization are opposite ends of a continuum; so if policy making is decentralized to allow for the diversity of local governments, then the achievement of national goals, such as equity, must suffer. The idea that decision making must be either centralized or decentralized in turn leads to political conflict. For advocates of equity and reform, the loss of efficiency that results from national efforts to standardize procedures is a necessary cost of social progress. For advocates of efficiency, the abandonment of national reform is an acceptable price for freedom, community control, and productivity. Working within the existing paradigm, advocates of equity and efficiency think they are playing a zero-sum game.

Unlike the prevailing approach, the design science approach does not generate conflicts between central and local goals. First, diversity is assumed, so there are few attempts to specify detailed procedures for all cases. This allows for decentralized decision-making and, according to theory, efficiency. At the same time, national reforms are pursued by emphasizing factors that raise performance—commitment, ideas, follow-through—and extreme cases that illustrate desired and punishable behavior. (This design science perspective is compatible with traditional and modern theories of federalism; see Kirlin.)

More specifically, to pursue unity and decentralization simultaneously in the contemporary federal system, longstanding and basically popular policy objectives (e.g., equal opportunity, environmental protection, independence for the elderly and handicapped, basic welfare, and educational opportunity) should be defined precisely and, to the degree feasible, quantitatively in order to specify what the world would look like if these ideals were to be realized. For most ideals, this requires decomposing and defining various interpretations and dimensions of the objective; for example, "equal opportunity" can mean equal facilities, equal outcomes, equal treatment of equals, minimum standards, or a reduction in the variance of attainment.[9] Once a range of legitimate interpretations is identified for each policy, local governments can choose among acceptable sets of interpretations and pursue national goals with strategies that are consistent with local resource limits and policy priorities.

In addition, rewards and punishments could be used to create incentives for improvement. Measures of performance would emphasize simultaneous achievement of several interpretations of the objective and resource and policy constraints. Jurisdictions that achieved high levels of performance on several dimensions of the reform at reasonable cost without serious sacrifice of other legitimate goals would be monitored to provide evidence to others that reform is feasible and desirable. Jurisdictions that refused to mobilize slack resources to conform to national priorities would also be identified, and the worst cases would be punished with certainty. Complaint data, newspaper reports, and superficial inspections would probably suffice to identify cases at the high and low ends of the performance dimension. Such cases would then be investigated in detail to determine the appropriateness of praise or prosecution.

In addition to avoiding conflicts between national unity and local control, this focus on the performance of extreme cases is consistent with a realistic view of measurement and data possibilities. First, most modern policy goals do not seem to be measurable for average or normal behavior. As illustrated above, concepts such as "discrimination," "clean air," and "opportunity" are composed of multiple indicators. As a consequence, they are defined only for extremely bad or extremely good cases where scores are consistently low or high. Thus, descriptions of extreme cases provide holistic illustrations of reform objectives, while descriptions of normal cases (which reveal mixed results on diverse indicators) have little meaning. Second, the focus on extreme cases is a realistic adaptation to diversity. Given diversity, it is rarely feasible to develop comparable performance data for each of the universe of cases. Even basic accounting concepts and definitions of functions, goals, structures, and personnel categories vary from government to government, and data are often missing.

Owing to conceptual and comparability difficulties, performance measurement and incentive systems that are aimed at all cases are usually doomed from the beginning (see King and Kraemer for a discussion of data limits). These problems do not, however, affect measurement systems aimed at extreme cases. Even given bad measures and incomplete data, a large deviation from the average across a set of indicators attracts attention, so extreme cases can be identified by poor information systems. Indeed, consensus among observers about very good and very bad behavior can often be achieved without reference to quantitative data on all cases, because rough ideas about average performance are sufficient to establish a base line. Thus, nonquantitative search procedures, such as monitoring the press and reviewing complaint data, can be effective in identifying cases that would be several standard deviations out on a good measure.

Overall, by focusing on extremes, the design science approach eliminates many apparent trade-offs between red tape and reform, paper work and information, centralization and decentralization, equity and efficiency, and reform and continuity. Debates about these issues that still dominate twentieth-century politics belong to an earlier era when national goals were basic (e.g., literacy, voting) and meant to be applied as minimum standards across all cases. In contrast, to achieve today's more ambitious, condition-dependent objectives (e.g., environmental protection, human development), and to mobilize today's more ample material and human resources, we need to modernize our thinking. The design science approach substitutes moral appeals, good examples, and incentives for most detailed rules and regulations. This encourages creativity in achieving national objectives through methods that are consistent with local priorities and conditions.

We should clarify, finally, that not all national or political reform objectives are best pursued by focusing on extremes. Some basic rights, such as voting and free speech, are never completely secure and continue to require the imposition of procedural standards. Also, standardization can be equated with "good government" in the control of many operational processes, such as financial management. In general, however, rigorous analyses of political goals according to the degree to which they require standardizing the structures of cases (e.g., local governments, businesses) should encourage a shift to the design science approach.

SUMMARY

The accumulated findings of empirical studies reported in the preceding chapters provide the basis for developing a new approach to research, management, and law enforcement. In fact, state and local governments are diverse, and their slow adaptive behavior is usually constrained by varied prior commitments, resource levels, and conditions.

On the other hand, even during the short period that governmental performance has been monitored rigorously and quantitatively, sharp departures from apparently stable patterns of behavior have occurred. For example, mathematical expressions relating various variables to governmental expenditures have been altered as a result of the tax limitation movement. Such historical examples of qualitative change provide theoretical grounds for developing dynamic models that combine operational definitions of "ideal" social institutions with descriptions of current institutions.

As chapters 7 and 8 indicate, the methods of public finance and management science can be used to create normative models. A major problem with existing methods, however, is that they are basically static. Also, inaccurate assumptions about data and the similarity of cases are common. Better models will be dynamic (taking account of reactions and qualitative changes over time), and their treatment of diversity and data will be more realistic (see Miller 1981b, 1983).

Overall, chapters 1 through 8 indicate that the prevailing natural science perspective is based on empirical assumptions that are not congruent with research findings. Key aspects of social behavior are not similar over space and time, and social dynamics are not independent of ideas (scientific or otherwise) about them.

Chapter 9 introduces an idealized design science approach to political science that also borrows from the hard sciences, especially from so-called applied fields, such as engineering, computer science, and operations research. These "sciences of the artificial" provide rigorous models for dealing with many humanistic aspects of social systems, including the ways that institutions evolve under the partial control of humans (as do computers, rockets, and hybrids).

Using design science models, social scientists can quantify diversity as well as central tendency, disequilibrium as well as equilibrium, disorder as well as order, and human laws as well as natural laws. This, in turn, allows for the rigorous articulation of alternative political perspectives, which are based on contrasting assumptions about social structures and dynamics.

Applications of design science to the political and management problems that characterize the late twentieth century are especially appealing. The switch from natural to design science encourages more complete use of current (ample) levels of intellectual and material resources. Alternatives for improving performance that can be quantified include: (1) altering all resource levels and procedures that are not constrained owing to other commitments, (2) exercising moral and intellectual leadership, and (3) exploiting feedback about interactions between policies and the environment over time. Another empowering feature of design science is its focus on extreme cases. This makes it possible to monitor and influence collective behavior without standardizing data or imposing common laws on all cases. In many policy areas, holistic knowledge and unified action can be realized in the absence of uniformity and coercion.

The promise of design science is to remove apparent conflicts between getting things done and being scientific. Practice is improved because practitioners are allowed (indeed, encouraged) to use the full range of available human and material resources. At the same time, research on social systems becomes more scientific because accurate assumptions about social systems—especially the role that ideas play in determining social structures and dynamics—undergird quantitative models (see table 9.1).

There is no design science of public sector performance yet, but the components do exist—empirical findings of past social scientific research, methods for quantifying normative political theories, dynamic models from the modern hard sciences, and knowledge about measurement and data. It seems feasible to construct a political science that builds on realistic assumptions about social structures and dynamics (see Miller 1983).

Moreover, developing design science could eliminate the portion of our national performance problem that is intellectual. Conventional ideas about science and management are old-fashioned; they do not reflect the nation's growing store of mental and material resources. But this bad news embodies good news: given an intellectual framework that encourages mobilization of existing assets, rapid improvements in productivity and performance can be expected.

NOTES

1. See Daniels (1971) for a history and analysis of the origins of American ideas about science and their influence on public administration and other applied fields.

2. Design science as it is described in this conclusion does not exist as a coherent paradigm. Rather, my definition combines promising features of social science methods (especially decision and management science) with empirical findings about political systems. The resulting approach bears little resemblance to conventional research in the fields of policy and management science, where most models continue to be built around fixed values and relationships. However, research priorities and approaches are shifting toward interactive technique, dynamic models, feedback, and graphical displays of information. While these developments are driven by the needs of practice and the growing capabilities of computers, they are also consistent with the dictates of theory.

3. In its 1981 report on science, the National Science Board broke from tradition and told stories of scientific progress, which included the history of the development of computers and the semiconductor. The board argued that there is now "one science" that includes what used to be called "applied fields," such as computer science and engineering, on an equal status with the older disciplines (National Science Board 1981).

4. These observations are drawn from my experiences directing the Decision and Management Science Program at the National Science Foundation, which was established in February 1982. Emphasis in the first years has been to define the intellectual focus of the field. Representatives of disciplines that range from physics to psychology are involved.

5. See Montroll (1981) for several applications.

6. See Lindblom (1982) on the conservative implications of conventional political science. For quantitative arguments see Miller (1981a, 1981b).

7. In general, the American Enterprise Institute's *Public Opinion* (1978–82) is an excellent source of information on the thinking of the public and its implications for politics; see especially October/November 1980. See also Nie and Anderson, (1974).

8. This natural science or scientific management approach has been implemented in the U.S. federal system. For an empirical study of the growth and effects of detailed mandates in the federal system, see Lovell and Tobin (1981).

9. See Miller (1977, 1981a) for a quantitative decomposition of the verbal goal of equal opportunity.

REFERENCES

Allen, Peter M. 1981. Self-Organization in Human Systems. In *Essays in Societal Systems Dynamics and Transportation,* ed. David Kahn. Cambridge, Mass.: U.S. Department of Transportation, Transportation Systems Center.

American Enterprise Institute. 1980. *Public Opinion* 3 (October/November).

Burck, Charles G. 1981. Working Smarter. *Fortune* (June 15).

Campbell, Angus, et al. 1960. *The American Voter.* New York: Wiley.

Campbell, Donald T., Julian C. Stanley. 1963. *Experimental and Quasi-Experimental Designs for Research.* Chicago: Rand McNally.

Cohen, Michael D. 1982. The Power of Parallel Thinking. *Journal of Economic Behavior and Organization* 2.

Churchman, C. West. 1971. *The Design of Inquiring Systems: Basic Concepts of Systems and Organizations.* New York: Basic Books.

Daniels, George H. 1971. *Science in American Society: A Social History.* New York: Knopf.

Glass, Glen V. 1979. Policy Research for the Unpredictable. *Educational Researcher* 8 (October).

Harmon, Michael M. 1981. *Action Theory for Public Administration.* New York: Longman.

Knorr, Karin D. 1981. *The Manufacture of Knowledge: An Essay on the Contextual and Constructive Nature of Science.* Oxford: Pergamon.

Ladd, Everett C., Jr. 1980. Realignment? No. Dealignment? Yes. *Public Opinion* 3 (October/November): 13–15.

Lindblom, Charles E. 1982. Another State of Mind. *American Political Science Review* 76 (March): 9–21.

Lovell, Catherine, and Charles Tobin. 1981. The Mandate Issue. *Public Administration Review* 41 (May/June): 318–30.

Miller, Trudi C. 1977. Conceptualizing Inequality. In *Evaluation Studies Review Annual,* ed. Marcia Guttentag, 2: 334–50. Beverly Hills: Sage.

———. 1981a. Articulate Statistics and Educational Equity. *Policy Sciences* 13: 205–26.

———. 1981b. Political and Mathematical Perspectives on Educational Equity. *American Political Science Review* 75: 319–33.

———. 1983. Science That Fits. Theme paper presented at the annual meeting of the American Political Science Association, Chicago, September 1–4.

Montroll, Elliott W. 1981. On the Dynamics of Technological Evolution: Phase Transitions. In *Self-Organizing and Dissipative Structures,* ed. W. C. Schive. Austin: University of Texas Press.

Nagel, Ernest. 1961. *The Structure of Science: Problems in the Logic of Scientific Explanation.* New York: Harcourt Brace & World.

National Science Board. 1981. *Only One Science: Twelfth Annual Report of the National Science Board.* Washington, D.C.: U.S. Government Printing Office.

Nie, Norman H., and Kristi Anderson. 1974. Mass Belief Systems Revisited: Political Change and Attitude Structure. *Journal of Politics* 36 (August): 540–91.

Radner, Michael, Irwin Feller, and Everett Rogers. 1978. *The Diffusion of Innovations: An Assessment.* Evanston, Ill.: Northwestern University Press.

Scammon, Richard M., and Ben J. Wattenberg. 1980. Is It the End of an Era? *Public Opinion* 3 (October/November): 2–12.

Simon, Herbert A. 1969. *The Sciences of the Artificial.* Cambridge, Mass.: MIT Press.

———. 1977. *Models of Discovery.* Boston: D. Reidel.

Contributors

THOMAS J. ANTON is the A. A. Taubman Professor of American Institutions in the Department of Political Science at Brown University. Recently he left the University of Michigan, Ann Arbor, where he directed the Intergovernmental Fiscal Analysis Project and the doctoral program in urban and regional planning. His latest book, *Moving Money*, analyzes changes in federal expenditures, including grants and loans, over time and across geographic areas.

J. RICHARD ARONSON is a professor of economics and director of the Fairchild-Martindale Center for the Study of Private Enterprise at Lehigh University. A specialist in public finance, he has authored or coauthored *Financing State and Local Governments, Management Policies in Local Government Finance, State and Local Finances in the Last Half of the 1970s*, and *The Scorecard*. He is currently working on a new text on public finance for McGraw-Hill.

RONALD JOHNSON is a senior political scientist and director of the Center for Population and Urban-Rural Studies with the Research Triangle Institute in North Carolina. His research has focused on performance measurement for local governments, emphasizing the relationship between performance and resource allocation decisions. His popular text, *Public Budgeting Systems*, addresses the role of information in financial decision-making and is the standard reference work for graduate courses in public budgeting.

JOHN LESLIE KING is an assistant professor in the Department of Information and Computer Science and in the Graduate School of Management at the University of California, Irvine. His research evaluates computing uses and the management of computers. His books include *Computers and Local Government, Computers, Power, and Urban Management*, and the forthcoming *Dynamics of Computing*.

JOHN J. KIRLIN is a professor of public administration at the University of Southern California. His recent research has assessed the impacts of tax and expenditure limitations, resulting in several articles, chapters, monographs,

269

and a book, *The Political Economy of Fiscal Limits*. He is the senior editor of *California Policy Choices*, a new annual volume analyzing policy choices available to state and local governments in California.

KENNETH L. KRAEMER is a professor in the Graduate School of Management and in the Information and Computer Science Department as well as the director of the Public Policy Research Organization at the University of California, Irvine. He is the author of many books on the role of information systems in local government in the United States and other countries. His three most recent books are *The Management of Information Systems, Computers and Politics,* and *Public Management*.

PATRICK D. LARKEY is the head of the Department of Social Sciences at Carnegie-Mellon University. Some of his research centers on how governments do and should make financial decisions. His numerous publications include *Evaluating Public Programs* and *Increasing Government Efficiency and Effectiveness*.

ARIE Y. LEWIN is a professor of business at the Fuqua School of Business Administration at Duke University. He is the author of three books and many research articles that have appeared in various journals, including *Academy of Management Journal, Accounting Review, Decision Sciences, Science, Personnel Psychology,* and *Journal of Mathematical Sociology*. He has also published columns in *Business Week, Dunn's Review* and *Planning Review,* and is departmental editor for organizational analysis, performance, and design for *Management Science*.

TRUDI C. MILLER is a political scientist and 1980 winner of the Franklin L. Burdette Pi Sigma Alpha Award for the best paper at the annual meeting of the American Political Science Association. Her recent publications in the *American Political Science Review* and *Policy Sciences* advocate the use of "articulate statistics" to close the gap between policy questions and research methods in research on education. She is currently program director for Decision and Management Science at the National Science Foundation.

THOMAS MULLER has been an operations analyst and economist at the Urban Institute since 1971, specializing in research on urban development and the impact of federal policies. He has conducted many studies of the causes and effects of urban growth and decline, and has published extensively and testified regularly before Congress on these and related subjects.

ELI SCHWARTZ holds the Charles MacFarlane Chair Professorship of Economics at Lehigh University. He is a recognized authority on public and private finance and has written extensively on investment decision-making, the cost of capital, discount rates, and present value theory. He is coeditor of *Management Policies in Local Government Finance*. His latest book, *Trouble in Eden: A Comparison of the British and Swedish Economies*, deals with the economic problems of high-income transfer economies.

CHANDLER STOLP is an assistant professor of public policy and economics at the Lyndon B. Johnson School of Public Affairs at the University of Texas, Austin. His research has focused on approaches to specifying and evaluating models of public sector resource allocation processes.

MARK WINER is an assistant professor of policy analysis at the University of Maryland. He has published papers in the areas of committee decision-making and public choice.

Index

Equity: and grants-in-aid, 194–96, 206–8; and revenue structure, 202–11; tradeoffs, 199–202, 208. *See also* Time

Federal grants-in-aid: growth/decline of, 25–30, 132, 162, 195; inadequacy of information about, 42–43, 122–23; multiple goals and complexity of, 31, 40, 42, 194–96; as stimulus for state and local growth, 41–50, 194–96; success of, in controlling state and local behavior, 35, 42–52. *See also* Grants-in-aid
Federalism, 17, 181–85; changes in, 51–52; data and, 42–43, 115–23; designs for alternative systems, 166–75, 194–200, 262–64; in Europe, 49–50. *See also* Federal grants-in-aid; Intergovernmental changes
Formulas for grants-in-aid, 42, 206–8
Friedman's flop, 21–23
Functions vs. jurisdictions, 172–75, 179–82

Government, definitions of, 161–65; and measuring government growth, 66–69, 88–89. *See also* Baseline data; Normative standards in empirical research
Government contraction, explained by: declining birth rate, 132, 135–36, 150, 157–58; declining federal grants-in-aid, 132, 150, 155, 162; decreased population redistribution, 135–36; economic stagnation, 136, 141, 157, 162; equalizing costs of services across jurisdictions, 135, 141–49, 157, 159; political choice, 161–64; tax-limitation movement, 132, 136, 141, 156, 161–64. *See also* Government growth, theories and explanations for
Government growth, theories and explanations for: assorted and conflicting, 29–30, 65–66, 89–90; Baumol's Disease, 80–81; bracket creep, 70–71; bureaucratic behavior, 27–29, 78–79, 84–87; conservative views, 31, 81; displacement-effect hypothesis, 70, 90; executive leadership, 79; insurance programs, 30; intergovernmental lobby, 28–29; interest groups, 79–80; Keynesian fiscal policy, 82–84; legislative procedures, 76–79; Marxist arguments, 81–82; national government behavior, 23–27; openness of the economy, 71–72; past decisions, 84–87; population migration within the United States, 135–36, 158–59; socioeconomic

determinism, 18–21; state and local expansion, 35, 51–52; tax systems, 73, 84–85; voters, 73–76; Wagner's Law, 69–70, 71–72, 90; welfare expenditures, 30–31. *See also* Baseline data
Grants-in-aid: formulas for, 42, 207–8; justifications for, 194–96

Inductive theory: adequacy for predicting significant changes, 8–9, 88–94, 161–64, 252
Information systems: and accounting, 13–14, 116–19, 244–45; for intergovernmental management, 42–43, 115–23, 263–64; in local government, 105–14; for operations, 105–8, 113–14, 120–22; for planning and management, 106–14, 232; political aspects of, 111–13; uses of, 103–4. *See also* Standardization
Intergovernmental changes, 51–52; balance of power, 23–27, 181–82; evaluating the success of federal programs, 46–48, 175–81; freedom and, 21–23; global vs. empirical perspectives, 17–18, 32–33; growth primarily at state and local levels, 35, 41–42; information systems and, 122–23; intergovernmental lobby, 27–29; Kirlin's design to accommodate, 164, 166–75, 185–87; mutual dependence among levels, 48–50; reduction of number of state and local governments, 37–40; state and local independence, 42–46. *See also* Demographic changes; Federal grants-in-aid; Federalism
Intergovernmental lobby, 27–29

Legislative decision-making, 76–79
Longitudinal analysis: recommendations for, 16, 93, 244; for rigor in tests of predictions, 91–94. *See also* Change, quantitative representations of; Stability of government behavior; Time

Management science: applications in the public sector, 110–11, 224–50; history of, 230–34; political aspects and uses, 111–13; success of, in operations, 6–7, 106–8, 113–14, 120–22. *See also* Information systems; Standardization
Measurement. *See* Baseline data; Information systems; Normative standards in empirical research; Performance measurement
Migration: impact of, on public sector